DATE DUE

THE CHICAGO PUBLIC LIBRARY

FEB 1 7 1998	APR 1 2 2000
AUG 0 1 1998	MAY 2 3 2000
AUG 0 5 1998	MAY 3 0 2000
AUG 1 2 1998	JUL 2 0 2000
	AUG 2 6 2000
AUG 2 0 1998	SEP 1 0 2000

Liberalism and Affirmative Obligation

Liberalism and Affirmative Obligation

Patricia Smith

New York   Oxford
Oxford University Press
1998

Oxford University Press

Oxford   New York
Athens   Auckland   Bangkok   Bogotá   Buenos Aires   Calcutta
Cape Town   Chennai   Dar es Salaam   Delhi   Florence   Hong Kong   Istanbul
Karachi   Kuala Lumpur   Madrid   Melbourne   Mexico City   Mumbai
Nairobi   Paris   São Paulo   Singapore   Taipei   Tokyo   Toronto   Warsaw

and associated companies in
Berlin   Ibadan

Published by Oxford University Press, Inc.
198 Madison Avenue, New York, New York 10016

Library of Congress Cataloging-in-Publication Data

Smith, Patricia G.
Liberalism and affirmative obligation / Patricia Smith.
p. cm.
Includes bibliographical references and index.
ISBN 0-19-511528-7
1. Political obligation. 2. Liberalism. I. Title.
JC329.5.S64 1998
320'.01'1—dc21   97-30465

1 3 5 7 9 8 6 4 2

Printed in the United States of America
on acid-free paper

For my mother and father
Russell and Evah Smith
With much love and gratitude

Preface

[L]iberty without equality is a name of noble sound and squalid result.

Hobhouse, 1912.

The liberal theory of moral and legal responsibility has always rested heavily on the distinction between positive and negative duty. But the general doctrine that rests on this distinction has not been carefully treated. If we examine this doctrine carefully and adjust it slightly to reflect longstanding moral and legal practices that have always been embedded in and central to liberal societies, as well as presupposed in liberal theory, it becomes apparent that the traditional framework supports a moderate liberal view of social responsibility better than a so-called atomistic individualist perspective. Thus, with slight adjustment, the liberal tradition, including the doctrine of positive and negative duty which is usually taken as a limit on obligation, instead supports more extensive positive duties than libertarian individualists tend to admit. Such is the thesis of this book. Pursuing this thesis, I develop a liberal theory of affirmative obligation which I call cooperative individualism. Its purpose is to support the middle ground taken by thinkers such as John Stuart Mill, L. T. Hobhouse, John Dewey, and John Rawls. Its motive and perspective thus fall in the line of thought that Hobhouse in 1912 called "the new liberalism," a theory committed to reconciling social justice with individual freedom on liberal grounds.

I have received a great deal of help on this project as it developed over the years, most of which I can no longer acknowledge individually. Pieces of it were read in colloquia at the University of Kentucky, at Harvard University, and at the University of Konstanz in Germany, as well as at meetings of the American Philosophical Association and the International Association for Philosophy of Law and Social Philosophy. I want to thank the participants for their many helpful comments, although they are unfortunately too numerous to list. Some special thanks are in order, however. Carol Gould and Larry May helped me clarify my ideas on reciprocity and on the function of individuals within groups, both ideas that are critical to the concept of membership I develop in this book. But I no longer know whether this clarification came from conversations with them or from reading their work. Ken Kipnis and Joan Callahan helped me think through issues of professional responsibility in the same dual way. More generally, I would like to acknowledge a debt of gratitude to Joel Feinberg and Virginia Held, who have influenced my substantive views, my method, and my intellectual development by their work and their example. I would also like to thank my colleagues at the University of Kentucky for years of support, friendship, and collegial conversation. Many people gave me specific comments on parts of the book. I want to thank James Rachels for his helpful and supportive comments on chapters 2 and 3. Joan Callahan, with her usual generosity and rigor, provided me with detailed comments on chapters 5 and 7. Larry May and Rex Martin gave me invaluable comments on chapters 8 and 9. Ann Cudd read the entire manuscript, offering extensive and thoughtful comments overall and especially on chapter 4. Despite fairly substantial revisions, I doubt that I have satisfied all their penetrating questions. Yet the attempt has certainly made this a better book. Finally I would like to thank my husband, Yuri Breitbart, for un-characteristic patience, very characteristic support, and always stimulating and challenging conversation. His contribution can never be measured.

Contents

Liberalism and Affirmative Obligation

Positive and Negative Duty in the Liberal Tradition

An Overview

1. Minimal Morality and the Dark Side of Human Nature

> Whatsoever, therefore, is consequent to a time of war where every man is enemy to every man, the same is consequent to the time wherein men live without other security than what their own strength and their own invention shall furnish them withal. In such condition there is no place for industry, because the fruit thereof is uncertain: and consequently no culture of the earth; no navigation nor use of the commodities that may be imported by sea; no commodious building; no instruments of moving and removing such things as require much force; no knowledge of the face of the earth; no account of time; no arts; no letters; no society; and, which is worst of all, continual fear and danger of violent death; and the life of man solitary, poor, nasty, brutish, and short.[1]

This is what Thomas Hobbes thought life would be like without a civil society to bring order and morality into the world: a war of all against all. Anarchy. Almost the worst situation imaginable. Almost. Organized aggression (such as Hitler's death camps) is arguably worse, but if so, anarchy runs a very close second. Anarchy is the antithesis of peace.

Hobbes argued that peace is the fundamental value. And what did he mean by peace? What is required for peace? Hobbes was not concerned about foreign war — which is bad enough. Hobbes's concern was civil unrest — war in your own yard, on your own street, in your own home. Hobbes's concern was fundamental, personal insecurity, such as that caused by terrorism, social upheaval, or a prevalence of violent crime; freedom from that kind of insecurity is what Hobbes meant by peace.

We may not agree that peace is worth any price, but the value of security looms large when it is lost. Peace is one of those quiet values that tend to be overlooked when present but become painfully significant once gone. There is much insight in Hobbes's observations on humanity and war. As he noted, human beings have the capacity to degenerate quickly into brutes. We are capable of doing each other great harm and injustice. We are capable of regarding one another as somehow less than human, as enemies, beasts of burden, obstacles, or stepping stones. In doing so we affect the kind of life it is possible to lead. And these problems have never really diminished.

The value of security is no less significant now than it was at the time Hobbes made his observations on human nature and civil society. Moral development proceeds in tiny steps. There are many ways in which little progress has been made since the days of civil war in England. Hobbes's observations on the human capacity for collective self-destruction are as apt today as they were in 1651. Both individually and collectively human beings often treat each other badly. We need not dream up hypothetical cases to make this point clear. Just read the newspapers.

The effects of such aggression and lawlessness ripple through communities, causing changes in the way of life. For example, just a few years ago in a quiet university town in the United States, a woman was brutally murdered as she worked in her office one night. People became afraid to work in their offices at night. Security was tightened at the university. Guards were placed on the doors. Identification cards were required to enter the buildings after hours. Thus, the lifestyle was changed. And this is indicative of similar changes that have occurred all across the United States and in many other countries as well. Is all this any cause for alarm? Yes and no. It certainly does not amount to anarchy in most of the world. Nor is it, however, peace. Hatred is alive and well, and may live next door to you. If hatred is in good standing, violence is not dead, and security is tenuous.

In one sense we have progressed since the time of Hobbes. We have progressed in science and technology. Unfortunately, this very progress has enabled greater violence with greater ease and efficiency. It is now possible for the smallest country to threaten the greatest, and the weakest person to threaten the strongest. It is now possible for one man in a pickup truck to blow up a large building full of people or poison a water supply that endangers an entire city. We are all now truly vulnerable to one another. Science and technology may have progressed with great strides, but morally speaking we human beings still have a long way to go. And the progress of science now makes our moral failing disastrous.

The idea behind this parade of horrors is simply to illustrate Hobbes's point of 350 years ago, that human beings are prone to harm one another. There is a dark side to human nature, a side where selfishness and greed, hatred and envy grow. Ambition may cause disregard for others. Character may be corrupted by power or deprivation or any number of other factors, even bad luck. The end result is the unfortunate picture just painted. All too many people are more than ready to disregard the rights and freedom, and even the life and safety, of others in pursuit of their own interests. The result is a world full of problems, hardship, and suffering directly caused by human beings. So Hobbes was right that when security is gone it impairs all other values. In that sense it is fundamental. It is a necessary condition for a decent human life. It is fundamental in the sense that it is minimal. We cannot manage well on less.

Hobbes's insight, and the beginning of the liberal tradition, is that rational individuals, for their own self-interest, must agree to a collective force that will protect them from one another. The foundation of the liberal state is the common acceptance of that authority, and to provide that basic protection of individuals from one another (as well as from foreign invasion), insuring the minimal requirements for personal security, is the most basic obligation of the state. All liberals seem to agree with that purpose as a central premise of constitutional democracy. Thus, the foundation of the liberal tradition is negative. Following Hobbes, it presumes the worst about human nature, and asks how to forestall its likely effects, and thus promote peace.

What Hobbes did not acknowledge, but all liberals from Locke onward have done, is that peace is not enough. It is not enough to protect individuals from one another. Hitler's death camps were not organized by private citizens but by the authority of the state. The "killing fields" of the Khmer Rouge or the Bosnian Serbs were not the result of anarchy but organization. The slaughter of Tiananmen Square was an act of government. American slavery and South African apartheid were enforced by the power of the state. So not only may individuals harm one another, the state may harm us all. The negative liberal presumption must be applied to state power as well as to individual inclination. Thus, it is clear that while state power is necessary, it must also be constitutionally limited to respect the freedom and rights of all individuals as a requirement of justice.

Like peace, justice is fundamental in the sense that it is a minimal requirement. We cannot manage on less. We cannot afford to dilute commitment to these values. The worst things human beings do to one another are prohibited specifically by justice. All the terrors just enumerated are precisely what are opposed by the basic requirements of justice and the priority of negative duty, the prohibition against harm. The value of justice in the liberal tradition requires that every individual must be regarded as an end in himself, every human life is intrinsically valuable, and therefore harming any innocent human being is seriously immoral. There are basic rights to life, liberty, and security that no one—no individual, no state—is entitled to overstep.

The important achievement of liberal individualism is precisely that it makes individuals ultimately important—as compared with terrorists, Stalinists, Fascists, and other fanatic believers, who may view individuals as disposable to a cause. I have been told that in Soviet Russia there was a saying, "When chopping wood, splinters fly." For a liberal individualist, a human being can never be merely a splinter. But the idea that humans can be still thrives. It is the basic presumption of all terrorism. In fact, such feelings never disappear entirely. They lurk, always available, especially in hard times. This fact can be verified easily by reading the newspapers of any given month of any given year.

We cannot delude ourselves into thinking that the dark side of human nature can ever be destroyed altogether. It is always there, and will always be there. It grows in the best of people in the worst of times, and remains in the worst people even in the best of times. It must always be combatted, and the recognition of this fact—of the eternal dark side of human nature—explains why negative duty must be regarded as presumptively overriding. It is a way of thinking that must always be promoted, fostered, taught. Individuals are sacred. They cannot be disposed of, terrorized, walked over, or used even for a good cause. Individuals must be respected as such. Without that respect we are susceptible to all the terrors just enumerated.

Thus, the requirements of justice and negative duty provide the bottom line, the moral minimum, without which we cannot live decent lives. As with justice, negative duty is fundamental: we cannot live well on less. Such is the founding presumption of the liberal tradition.

The most significant contribution of liberal individualism was the recognition and promotion of this moral minimum as having universal application through the development of the concept of basic human rights and civil rights. The great human rights movements of the eighteenth and nineteenth centuries stood for a profound change in perspective that we often take for granted today, although many countries have not yet recognized it and many individuals are already willing to forget it. It stood for the idea that basic moral prohibitions against the harmful treatment of others are universal. This minimum should not depend on special connections, characteristics, social position, or family name. All human beings are entitled to be secure from unjust interference and harmful acts. In this respect, all human beings count as equals, morally speaking, without regard to their personal circumstances or characteristics. According to this view, there is no one so lowly that he or she just doesn't count, morally speaking.[2] Thus, the most fundamental premise of liberal thought is that every individual is morally significant. Important implications follow from this premise.

First, liberalism stands for the limitation of privilege. Admittedly, it does not eliminate privilege, but it does set moral limits on it. No one is so privileged that assault, murder, robbery, or fraud are not moral infractions. Justice prohibits such acts for rich and poor alike, and for terrorists and dictators as well, no matter how great their objective. On this view, no one is disposable to a cause.

Second, liberalism stands for individual freedom, and requires justification for its restriction. It stands against slavery in any form. No one is entitled to own someone else.[3] All are entitled to equal freedom to conduct their own lives without interference.

Third, liberalism began the fight against intolerance and discrimination. Everyone is entitled to the basic respect and consideration that is due each human being as a human being. No one can be legitimately dismissed or eliminated from moral consideration on irrelevant grounds. No one would claim that these principles are yet universally held, let alone universally obeyed. Yet, these are the basic commitments of liberal individualism.

The commitment to minimally decent treatment for all human beings embodied in the liberal individualist tradition provides the essential foundations for universal human rights. While we have been slow to learn the real meaning of these commitments, and even slower to live by them, the foundations of current understandings of the moral worth of every individual are rooted in the liberal commitment to universal justice and human rights against aggression. All these are very significant but fragile accomplishments that require continuous support.

It is important to remember, however, that the human rights (and even the civil rights) of the classical liberal tradition have always been *viewed* as negative. They are rights against aggression and interference, rights to be left alone to pursue one's own projects and plans. They correlate with negative duties: duties not to perform harmful acts. It is this negative character that allows such duties to be coherently universalized and that provides the moral minimum that I have described as a significant achievement.

But, of course, this does not account for all moral responsibilities, since many responsibilities are less than universal and more than minimal. Many are affirmative rather than negative. The liberal tradition has not handled these positive duties as well as negative duties. Yet positive duties are of crucial importance within liberal societies today, and always have been. They are the building blocks of social life; but liberal theory provides a very sketchy account of them. So, having here made my case for the traditional liberal view of negative duty, I will devote the rest of this book to developing a fuller account of positive duty that is compatible with that view.

2. The Traditional Doctrine of Positive and Negative Duty

Traditionally the liberal view of positive duty is contained in the abstract doctrine of positive and negative duty. At this point it will be useful to lay out that philosophical doctrine as it is typically represented.[4] It provides a clear, coherent, but very abstract rationale for the rather vague intuitions of the historical tradition associated with liberal individualism and the priority of justice.

Briefly, the philosophical doctrine is as follows. All people, being moral agents, have moral duties of various sorts, and these duties differ from one another in various ways: both conceptually and morally, for example. There is a morally relevant distinction between positive and negative duties in particular.[5]

Negative duties are prohibitions; they restrict actions. They set out what we may not do to others without violating their rights (often referred to as negative rights—rights not to be interfered with or harmed). For example, we cannot attack, rob, kill, lie to, manipulate, or defraud our fellow human beings because we all have rights not to be treated in such ways. Justice requires that these rights be respected. Negative duties are based on the value of justice and respect for individual dignity, autonomy, freedom, and rights.[6]

According to this view, negative duties are very strict: universal, fundamental, and—according to some (Kant, for example)—absolute. Although there is debate about the absoluteness of negative duties, it is clear (among those who accept this theory) that even if they are not strictly speaking absolute, they are very strong and presumptively overriding moral considerations.[7] This is one part of the individualist tradition that is clear. Negative rights are protected by law or moral standards virtually everywhere. They form the core of any criminal code. They are the clear cases. Negative duties prohibiting one individual from harming or interfering with another are universally recognized in legal or moral codes or both. That is to say, all societies recognize negative duties of some sort, and some negative duties (for example, prohibitions against murder and incest) are recognized by virtually all societies.

Contrasted with negative duties are positive duties. Positive duties are based on the value of human charity or benevolence (as opposed to justice). They are duties requiring positive action, duties to help others (as opposed to prohibitions against harming others); and they hold generally (as opposed to universally).[8] The difference in application, then, is that we all have negative duties not to harm others that hold universally, that is, against everyone at all times. We all have a positive duty to help others in general but exactly how and when we fulfill that duty is left up to each of us.

Another way to put the point is to note that negative duties are specified. They are owed to every person. It is not left up to me to decide when to fulfill the duty (for example, it is not left up to me to determine when I may not murder or defraud someone; I never may do so). Positive duties, on the other hand, are unspecified. Positive duties are owed to someone or other but to no one in particular. According to the traditional view, I am wrong (that is, immoral) if I never help anyone, but I do not wrong anyone in particular (that is, I do not violate anyone's rights). It is up to me to decide whether I should volunteer my services at the local soup kitchen, work for famine relief, or be a Boy Scout leader. Whatever I choose, the others have no ground to complain (to me, at least). Immanuel Kant (and other philosophers) called this contrast the distinction between duties of perfect obligation (specified ones) and duties of imperfect obligation (unspecified ones).[9]

What this view reflects is the traditional idea that negative duties correspond to negative rights and are universal. But there are no universal positive rights or duties. Although I have a duty to help someone or other, no one has a right to my help. (Unless, that is, I assume a special obligation to some particular person. Positive duties may correspond to positive rights only in cases of special obligations due to special relationships, such as contractual or parental ones. These are called special positive duties.) The usual contrast is that negative duties (duties of justice) are strict, are universal, and correspond to universal negative rights (rights against harmful actions). Positive duties (duties of charity) are unspecified, are general, and do not have correlative positive rights (rights to positive assistance).

Finally, positive duties are considered to be fairly weak moral requirements, at least in a certain sense. Exactly how weak (or for that matter, how variable) they are is not at all clear, but certainly as compared to negative duties they are rather weak. If they are not always overridden by negative duties (as is held by some), at least they are almost always overridden.[10]

All these ideas are not without controversy, of course. I will have much more to say about them and other features of the doctrine of positive and negative duty as I lay out my own position in subsequent chapters. For the present I am just reviewing the basic outline of the doctrine as it is usually described. I am not here evaluating it.

Now, given that negative duties are prohibitions against wrongful actions, and that positive duties are injunctions for good actions, it has been quite natural to view these contrasts in terms of acts and omissions. The violation of a negative duty is a wrongful action. The failure to meet a positive duty is a wrongful omission. Thus, the traditional view has grown up that bad or harmful acts are worse than bad or harmful omissions, even when the consequences are the same. And it is thought that if a conflict (or dilemma) should arise in which the only choice is a harmful act or a harmful omission, the harmful act should always be avoided.[11]

By means of this doctrine, obligations are provided with both foundations and limits. Negative duties are prohibitions founded on justice, are universal, and are

very stringent. Yet, negative duties are limited in the sense that they require no action. You and I can meet all our negative duties to the entire world in one fell
swoop, so to speak, by simply refraining from doing all those things (murder, assault, robbery, fraud, etc.) that we ought not to do, and could not do without violating someone's rights. We can meet all these prohibitions without doing anything
at all.

Positive duties are affirmative obligations based on benevolence. Special positive duties may be exacting and strict, but they are limited in scope. That is, they are
owed only to a few people in virtue of some special relationship or transaction.
General positive duties are unlimited in scope (that is, they are owed to anyone in
need) but are (somewhat paradoxically for a duty) "optional" in application because all particular cases are left unspecified, are left to the discretion of the agent.
In this sense general positive duties are not considered as strict as other duties. In
fact, in terms of any particular case, general positive duties are not duties at all, that
is, not obligatory. The duty is general. The application in any particular case is
supererogatory. So all duties are supplied with both foundations and limits, the limits in the case of general positive duties being supplied by each individual person
who is confronted by the needs or demands of some other person, organization, or
cause.

I believe this description is a reasonable representation of the traditional liberal
individualist view of moral responsibility as it relates to the doctrine of positive and
negative duty. This view is generally associated with philosophical theories that take
individual justice, rights, autonomy, and freedom as fundamental and overriding
values. It tends to be featured in libertarian positions.[12] Generally, it is found in
Kantian views,[13] but it is also central to natural rights theories, whether descended
from John Locke or from Thomas Aquinas.[14] All these make a sharp distinction between positive and negative duties. Furthermore, the distinction is found in many
utilitarian views (that of Mill, for example) as well as in some social contract and in-
tuitionist theories, although it is not central to them.[15]

It is also worth noting that the doctrine of positive and negative duty has long
been significant, if not predominant, both in popular thinking and in philosophical
discussion, although in popular thought the rationale for the behavioral rules may
not be considered. Nevertheless, the doctrine is very influential, and is reflected in
many moral traditions and formal institutions of law, government, and religion,
among others. Wrongful actions are strictly prohibited by law or morality. These
duties are strong and clear. Helpful action and positive aid are encouraged, but not
strongly and clearly, and not as obligations. Certainly they are not required, in
popular thought. They are hardly duties — more like ideals. And even as ideals the
priority or centrality of positive duties are not terribly clear in everyday thinking.

In philosophical discussion the doctrine of positive and negative duty has always been controversial, and in the last twenty-five years or so it has been seriously
called into question. Issues of social policy regarding foreign aid, public assistance,
corporate responsibility, medical care, and good Samaritan legislation (to name just
a few examples) all seem to suggest that the traditional individualist doctrine as just
described provides an impoverished view of affirmative obligation. That is not to
say that it is wrong (or right) but that it simply does not explain enough. People with

more utilitarian or communitarian or socialistic inclinations argue that traditional individualistic views cannot provide answers for pressing twentieth-century problems like those just mentioned.[16] Furthermore, issues of euthanasia and withdrawing medical treatment have raised difficult problems for the traditional distinction between acts and omissions, which is thought to be crucial to the doctrine of positive and negative duty. In some cases the label 'act' or 'omission' may look very arbitrary. Is turning off a resuscitator, for example, an act or an omission, and should it make a moral difference which we call it?[17]

Even the foundations of the doctrine of positive and negative duty have been challenged as deficient in several regards. For example, utilitarians and others who are concerned about society as a group argue that freedom and justice are very important but not more important than other values, such as economic security and general well-being. Individuals are very important but not more important than the common good, the welfare of all. It is clear that what I am calling the traditional individualist doctrine of positive and negative duty has many problems.

Nevertheless, given that there are flaws, it is worth investigating whether these flaws are correctable. There are at least strong intuitive grounds that support the distinction: most people (if they think about it) do think acts are different from omissions. Most people think doing something is different from not doing something. Most people do think causing something is different (even morally different) from not preventing it. And certainly most people think harming someone is worse than not helping, at least in most circumstances. Rather than deny such distinctions altogether, a more fruitful approach may be to ask what they amount to. How do they relate to one another? Of what moral significance are they, if any?

Furthermore, there is one obvious source of mistake and inadequacy regarding the doctrine of positive and negative duty that is clearly correctable. It is the extreme lack of attention to the nature and extent of positive duty. To say simply, as the traditional view does, that you have a general duty to help out on occasion and how you fulfill it is up to you hardly amounts to a theory. A moral theory should provide guidance for making decisions in particular cases. To remedy that lack the theory needs to be explicated and perhaps expanded. Once that lack is remedied, the doctrine will look rather different, or so it seems likely. Indeed, with careful formulation, I think, the doctrine of positive and negative duty may have considerable explanatory power, which is, after all, just what a distinction is for. With that in mind, this book is dedicated to the exploration of the doctrine of positive and negative duty and to the examination of special positive duty in particular.

3. Four Contemporary Challenges

As just noted, affirmative obligation is not the strong point of liberal individualism. Libertarians construe it as strictly contractual (or narrowly biological), leaving our social welfare in the hands of volunteers, clinging tenaciously to the "invisible hand," or turning themselves into economic egoists who deny social responsibility altogether.[18] Moderate liberals (like me) try to come up with arguments that explain how rational individuals would adopt affirmative policies for social responsibility if they thought about it, and then conclude that everyone should accept such policies whether they think about it or not.[19] Yet the tension between competing values in balancing theories is strained, and the question is how one arrives at social cohesion or moral integrity by beginning with unrelated individuals. Utilitarians really have the most sensible and integrated explanation of social responsibility in terms of the common good. Unfortunately and ironically, in adopting an individualistic foundation, the utilitarian theory has no natural limits to the obligations it could impose, and indeed some theorists have followed its natural implications to oppressive universal duties.[20] All these fall within the general purview of the Western liberal tradition which, like Noah, has produced many descendants who differ enormously from one another. Overall, then, it should be noted that there is no single, unitary liberal view on affirmative obligation. The issue is highly controversial *within* liberalism, and this is possibly not a correctable situation. Still, examining the controversy over affirmative obligation lays bare the conflict over the nature of individualism itself, and the foundations of liberal commitment. This examination can be viewed in terms of four basic challenges to contemporary liberals.

The first of these is the question of how to construe the nature of individuals, especially in relation to other individuals or communities. Communitarians have long criticized individualists for relying on social institutions and traditions, the value of which they ignore or deny. This criticism should be taken seriously and addressed explicitly. Liberal individualism does not clearly account for the need for social cooperation, for interpersonal reliance and trust. Without these values, selfishness and indifference may undermine compliance with the negative duties established by justice. It may have been a mistake of the liberal tradition, with its emphasis on the significance of the individual, and under the influence of its libertarian wing, to construe the individual as radically self-sufficient. This is seriously inaccurate. No human being is self-sufficient in fact. We are the most social of all creatures. Even someone who eventually becomes a hermit in the wilderness is first raised and socialized by a family for many years.[21] No one else has any real claim to self-sufficiency at all. Human beings are not only radically free, we are radically social. We die alone. Thus, the atomistic vision of human nature is not a description of human beings at all.

Yet, it should be acknowledged that liberals are not in agreement on this view of human nature. While some (libertarians, in particular, but not all of them) adopt an atomistic or abstract perspective for purposes of argumentation, I would suggest that most liberals are not atomistic individualists at all. Individualism is a moral position about the significance of individuals, not a metaphysical thesis intended to explain human nature. Still, the challenge for those of us who reject atomistic individualism but support liberalism is to provide a more adequate account of human nature, or the function of individualism, within liberalism that preserves the integrity of the individual without alienating her from human relations or social institutions.[22] I believe that providing a fuller account of affirmative obligation will be a step in that direction.

The second challenge to contemporary liberals is provoked by the limited view of justice developed within the individualist tradition, namely, by focusing on the idea of noninterference. Justice as noninterference is basic, and I have already urged as strongly as I know how that this crucial value must be preserved. It does not follow that justice stands for nothing else, however. Historically and currently, it includes a broader range of considerations than noninterference alone. The oldest idea of justice is thought to be reciprocity, which is undoubtedly the basis of retribution as a theory of punishment.[23] It has been suggested that ideas of reciprocity are prehistoric and even instinctive in human beings and some other social animals. Reciprocity, along with concern for kin, may provide the starting point for the evolution of an ethical point of view.[24] Human beings have always been social beings, and justice is a social value. Early ideas of justice have to do with the proper distribution of burdens and benefits, obligations and privileges—ideas that develop into rather sophisticated notions of fairness, desert, and distributive justice over time.[25] None of these elements of justice are adequately covered by the idea of noninterference, although the simplest conceptions of noninterference in terms of refraining from harm, or respecting the bodily integrity and property of others within one's own group, are equally old. Plato represented justice as fittingness or harmony—a place for everyone and everyone in his place. Aristotle described it as the virtue that comprehends all other virtues and applies them to one's neighbor. Included in his account of justice are notions of distribution and reciprocity. Thus, for the Greeks, justice was the socializing virtue.[26]

The problem with current liberal conceptions of justice is that too often they *emphasize* justice as noninterference to the virtual exclusion of all other aspects traditionally associated with the fuller concept: reciprocity, fairness, and fittingness.[27] This tendency is far from uniform, however. In perhaps the major work of political philosophy in this century, John Rawls was concerned with a more comprehensive interpretation of justice, and specifically with justice as fairness.[28] Yet, despite the power of the theory, the Rawlsian flank is engaged in an uphill fight for the high ground. I think it is fair to say that the predominant tendency in liberalism is still to view the concept of justice narrowly as noninterference.[29]

To account for positive duty adequately, however, the broader concept is necessary. To account for positive duties well, we must have a fuller notion of justice that includes traditional elements of fairness, reciprocity, and trustworthiness. Like many liberals, however, I see no reason to suppose that this broader conception of justice is incompatible with liberalism, despite the furor caused in some quarters by Rawls's books. Justice has always been a balancing act. It is not for nothing that its primary symbol is the scale. It has always comprised more than one component, the weighing of which is what the enterprise of practical judgment is about. To restrict that process by assuming that the bounds of justice are defined exclusively by negative duty is an oversight that needs attention. Thus, the work begun by Rawls to articulate an adequate concept of justice that includes more than restrictions on interference needs to be continued.[30] Explaining special positive duty adequately contributes to that project.

The third challenge to contemporary liberals is to reformulate what it means to say that the state should remain neutral as to competing visions of the good. This has been interpreted as "value neutrality," which in turn has sometimes been interpreted roughly as relativism. But that is simply an incorrect interpretation. Liberalism is not committed to relativism. In fact, liberalism is not even compatible with relativism, since it stands for certain basic values such as freedom and justice. Yet if that is the case, then what exactly does it mean for the state to remain neutral as to competing visions of the good? Liberals have not yet supplied a clear account, although some are beginning to address this issue.[31]

It is apparently unduly optimistic to suppose as a principle of social organization that each individual pursuing her own values and interests alone will produce a fair and moral community. The moral sentiments apparently must be cultivated. And they are not cultivated by a culture of individualistic egoists. Liberalism, however, is not egoism. Liberals adopted a stance of value neutrality, thinking it necessary for tolerance. This may have been the wrong way to articulate the point. And this mistake may have allowed egoism to flourish; yet liberalism is not egoism.

If we consider, for example, the ideas of Adam Smith, which were surely a powerful influence toward the development of egoistic individualism within the liberal tradition, we find not egoism but great concern for the common good. Indeed, Smith dedicated an entire book to formulating his *Theory of the Moral Sentiments* and considering the importance of their cultivation for the common good as well as for personal excellence.[32] Too bad that book is so overshadowed by his other work. Even if we consider *The Wealth of Nations*,[33] the bible of laissez faire economics that everyone reads, the idea behind that work clearly was not egoism, or relativism, or value neutrality, but rather a commitment to the common good and to individual freedom, coupled with the premise that the former could be obtained by the protection of the latter.[34] On reflection it appears that this approach was unduly optimistic, and should at this point be viewed as a thought experiment that failed.

It does not follow from this failure, however, that the individual is not significant, or that freedom is not fundamentally valuable, or that liberalism necessarily deteriorates into relativism or egoism. It does suggest that social cooperation must be cultivated, and that trust must be earned. These crucial social values will not simply emerge by magic out of protected self-interest in the form of free markets as Smith envisioned them. The invisible hand apparently will not accomplish that. We need more direct tactics for promoting basic moral values as well as the social virtues of cooperation, trustworthiness, and responsibility, at least at present. An educational goal of this sort was one with which Smith, at least, had considerable sympathy. He was, after all, one of the earliest reformers to urge the education of the lower classes as a public investment.[35] Exactly how a common commitment to these values is still compatible with tolerance is a project worth working out, although not in this book.

Cultivating virtues of cooperation and responsibility, I think, would not undermine the liberal commitment to justice and negative duty, but instead would only reinforce that commitment. Furthermore, liberal societies have always recognized these social virtues indirectly in doctrines of law and morality (as I shall indicate) because no society can survive without them at some level. The interesting quirk of the liberal tradition is that it relies on the social virtues without providing an account of their place within a liberal state. I think it is time not only to recognize them but to acknowledge that liberal societies rely on them and therefore must reinforce them to oppose their deterioration. Admittedly, this position might easily be confused with a conservative view. As applied to certain values, however, it happens to be right, and is not, I think, incompatible with liberalism. Indeed, some philosophers have recently been working to articulate what liberal values would be, and, not surprisingly, these accounts include values of responsibility and cooperation.[36]

Interestingly, conservatives seem to find themselves in a contradiction that is rather a mirror image of the problem of the liberal individualist who relies on values for which she cannot account. Conservatives regularly extol the virtue and significance of tradition and urge the necessity of its protection. But they also regularly argue that central planning is what we cannot do, or at least not well. Tradition must evolve naturally, even organically. That is why we should not interfere with the market: we do not know the effects of our interference, and our chances are better in relying on the accumulated wisdom of practicing participants over time than on the shining brilliance of a single bright light (or small group of them) who happen to be in a position to invent public policy. The thing is, if you cannot interfere with tradition, then it is not exactly clear how you would go about protecting it either. Blocking its evolution (whether decline or progress) is presumably as great an interference as promoting it.

Apparently, we must commit to certain values one way or another. Whether we commit to old values or to new ones, we are still just committing to a set of values. For this commitment we should be able to provide reasons. The traditionalist supposes that a new set of values may be worse than the old set, whereas the reformer supposes that a new set can't be worse than the current one. Karl Marx looked at common workers in 1848 and said, What could be worse than this? About seventy years later Joseph Stalin showed us what could be worse. Revolutions do not often help the common man, much less the common woman, who are the first to be oppressed and assaulted. Of course, Stalin never outdid Hitler, and Hitler was in many ways a traditionalist. Any view can produce its monsters if the significance of each individual is forgotten.

Commitment to this significance is the good side—the indispensable side—of individualism, and why I would rather try to build on a liberal tradition than another one. I think acknowledging basic moral values or social virtues is not contradictory to the framework of liberal theory. In fact, the needed theoretical framework is there, in the form of the doctrine of positive and negative duty, once a more adequate theory of positive duty is developed. Such a theory will not answer the major questions posed here regarding value neutrality. It will not explain what it means for the state to remain neutral as to competing visions of the good yet not be neutral with regard to all values. That is, it will not explain the extent of tolerance. Yet it can show, I think, how the debate over values can continue *within* liberalism, rather than constitute an objection to the liberal or individualist approach to political theory.

The fourth challenge to contemporary liberals that is intrinsic to understanding positive duties is the challenge of understanding their scope and priority. This challenge arises because the distinctive feature of positive duties is that, unlike negative duties, meeting them requires resources. Whereas universal negative duties are totally dischargeable, positive duties must be allocated.[37] Thus without a coherent theory of scope and priority, positive duties lead to what James Fishkin in *The Limits of Obligation* has called the problem of moral overload.[38] There he observed that the moral principles of liberal individualism that work well on a small scale break down when applied to large-scale problems. Positive duties cannot be coherently universalized, since universal positive duties are impossible for individuals alone to meet.[39] In fact, as distressing as Fishkin's observations may seem, they are actually more optimistic than is warranted. Not only on the large scale but even on the small scale, positive duties, if taken seriously, cause special problems for traditional liberalism. Given human limits, positive duties must be ordered and limited. Thus a theory of scope and priority is absolutely necessary to make sense of affirmative obligations.

This is basically an allocation of resources problem. It has often been construed as a conflict of duty problem, but it does not (necessarily or typically) involve a conflict of positive with negative duty. In fact, positive duties (or at least competing claims to one's time and resources) conflict with one another far more than they conflict with negative duties. How often must we decide between saving someone's life and telling a lie? Conflicts between positive and negative duties pose fascinating conceptual puzzles but they are phenomenologically uncommon.

Yet philosophers seldom get past these theoretically interesting but factually infrequent issues to the mundane daily problems of moral responsibility that people run into all the time. In daily life do we have trouble *figuring out* our negative duties, by and large? By and large we do not. It may be inconvenient to meet these requirements, but it is not often hard to figure them out. Do you want to be a moral person? If you do, then you cannot lie, cheat, steal, rape, murder, pillage, or generally do in your fellow human beings. Most people who care about being moral do not have a lot of trouble with this, conceptually speaking. Negative duties may be inconvenient, or even terribly difficult to meet on occasion, but morally speaking, they are not difficult to figure out.[40]

Positive duties are hard to figure out. Furthermore, they pose problems every day, all the time—or whenever we let ourselves think about them. These are problems people struggle with constantly. How should I conduct my life? What do I owe? Should I be spending more time with my children, or should I be spending more time on my work? Do I owe more to my clients, patients, fellow employees? Should I be more serious about my civic duty—am I being a responsible citizen? Should I donate more to charity? Should I be more actively supportive of my church, my synagogue, the causes I say I believe in? If I am responsible about meeting my obligations, is any of my time or money my own? Am I mistaken to think that I am entitled to any freedom or comfort as long as there are others who need help?

The most significant difference between positive and negative duties is that positive duties require time and resources to meet, and negative duties do not. (See chapter 3.) There is a constant clamor of claims that compete for our time, energy, attention, resources. It is an enormous task to order these competing claims or to decide which should be recognized at all. Justice, as traditionally construed in terms of noninterference, and the priority of negative duty, even if accepted as absolute, tell us virtually nothing about how to do this.

Recently, some philosophers have begun to work through the problem of allocating resources as such,[41] and of formulating priorities by analyzing moral responsibility in terms of roles and other institutional divisions of labor.[42] I believe that this is a step in the right direction. It is one of the most prominent issues of our time, and certainly one of the most pressing challenges facing moral philosophers and policymakers today. This book is dedicated to contributing to its solution. One approach, I contend, lies in a better understanding of the doctrine of positive and negative duty.

4. General Positive Duty: The Scope of Charity

The most common comparison made between positive and negative duty is between universal negative and general positive duty. As explained earlier, this distinction provides a clear and convenient contrast and thus serves a certain useful function. But general positive duty has also been the focus of most of the controversy over the doctrine of positive and negative duty. A great deal of this debate is centered on the conceptual and moral claims of the act/omission distinction: What is the moral difference between an act and an omission? What is the moral difference between initiating a causal sequence and failing to intervene in one? What is the difference between causing harm and failing to prevent it? and so forth. These issues are significant ones that must be largely deferred to another occasion.[43] But they are not the only issues at stake; there are also issues of duty, especially the relative strictness of positive and negative duty.

I find it convenient to think of these issues of general positive duty as falling into roughly two sets of problems. The first I call the problem of absolutism; I will deal with it in chapter 2, focusing mainly on the context of bad Samaritan legislation. The second I call the problem of validity; it is raised here primarily within the context of world hunger, and will be considered in chapter 3.

Bad Samaritan legislation would legally enforce a general positive duty to provide easy rescue to imperiled strangers. This proposal has caused a major controversy within Anglo-American legal scholarship that is in some ways rather surprising.[44] Looked at objectively and from a cool distance, it concerns a minor exception to the discretionary aspect of the general doctrine of positive and negative duty in certain narrowly confined special circumstances, namely emergencies. Is there a duty to assist a severely endangered victim if the aid can be provided without risk or serious inconvenience to the rescuer? It is very widely agreed that there is such a moral duty; the controversy is over the nature of the duty (is this a perfect or imperfect duty, how stringent is it, etc.) and over whether it is appropriate for legal enforcement. This debate has raised all the fascinating issues of causation and agency associated with the act/omission distinction, as well as the question of the relative strictness of the duties involved and the practical puzzles of delineating the scope of the duty. All these are very challenging intellectual issues and so, in that respect, it is not surprising to find them much discussed. On the other hand, considering the relatively minor consequences such a statute would have (they have long been in force in many countries of the world—all of continental Europe, for example—without any particular special consequence following from them), the level of controversy over them within the United States in particular, and Anglo-American legal systems more generally, is intriguing.[45] This controversy is obviously over a matter of principle—but what principle? What is at stake here? One perspective on the point is that it is an issue of theoretical purity: Can there be a universal positive right?[46] Should an exception be allowed to the general doctrine of positive and negative duty, or is it absolute? A different perspective might construe the issue in terms of the meaning of individualism itself.[47] When can the government legitimately tell me what to do? Just what does individualism stand for? What does moral autonomy mean? The two perspectives are not unrelated, and exploring their interaction will figure prominently in my considerations in chapter 2. The question is, What does it do to the doctrine of positive and negative duty to allow a narrow exception? Thus the problem of absolutism.

The issues associated with what I have called the problem of validity are much broader and more thoroughgoing. Some critics have challenged the validity of the doctrine of positive and negative duty altogether, especially in the form of the distinction between killing and letting people die or between causing and failing to prevent harm.[48] These, of course, are the same issues raised regarding duties of good Samaritans within the narrow context of emergencies. The good Samaritan context—which always involves one (or a few) determinate victims with a clear, specifiable need, and a possible right to a particular act of assistance against a specifiable individual (or small group of them)—is thus on the fringe between general positive duties and claim rights. But the broader debate over validity often takes place within the context of world hunger or disaster relief—involving vast numbers of people, indeterminate claims of ongoing or chronic, even if severe, need, most generally for material goods (food, medicine, shelter), and addressable in the form of monetary contribution that could as appropriately be given by one donor as another—and thus forms the paradigm or core case of general positive duty. If there is any such thing as a duty of charity, here, one would think, is where it would apply. It is not usually suggested that any rights are involved here, nor does anyone urge legal enforcement of the duty.[49] Rather, the debate is about how seriously the duty should be taken, what it commits us to as moral beings, and whether traditional distinctions, including the act/omission distinction and the doctrine of positive and negative duty, are really excuses we make to let ourselves off the moral hook, so to speak, so that we can live affluent lives with little attention to and no serious moral pangs over those who are starving.

At issue is the scope of responsibility, affirmative responsibility in particular, and the question is whether the traditional doctrine of general positive duty can explain it well enough. That question is crystallized in the interface of the two sets of issues. Most people think that it would be reprehensible to watch a swimmer drown without bothering to throw him a line. But if we are justified in requiring a random bystander to throw a line to a drowning swimmer, then why aren't we justified in requiring other charitable acts that save lives as well? Why not require donation to famine relief, for example, or disaster assistance, or aid to war refugees, and so on? On the other hand, if we are not justified in requiring contribution to all charities that save lives, then why isn't saving the drowning swimmer just a matter of personal conscience as well? What exactly explains the difference? What are the basic principles that define the scope of responsibility for us? Are there any such principles? Could there be, or are we fundamentally inconsistent on such matters? If there could be such principles, will they refine the traditional doctrine of general positive duty, or refute it? These questions provide the focus of chapters 2 and 3. However they are answered, they should provide a clearer, even if more complex, account of general positive duty.

5. Special Positive Duty: An Ignored Moral Category

Unlike general positive duty, special positive duty is not often discussed as a moral category on its own terms, especially not as a very significant one. It is usually just mentioned as a sort of specialized subset of the broader class of general positive duties, approximately as I laid it out in section 2. At least, what I tried to do there was to set out the description as it is usually made. I am responding here to the fact that most commonly the significant distinction is taken to be the distinction between positive and negative duty, whereas the distinction between special and general positive duty is noted in passing but otherwise largely ignored. I think that this is a mistake. In fact, I believe that special positive duties as a class constitute a hidden bridge within the liberal tradition, between universal negative duties and general positive duties, that may provide a basis for social responsibility, and the development of the social virtues. Explaining why will be the task of the next six chapters—the bulk of this book. Here I would just like to set out briefly why I think that special positive duty should be considered a significant moral category on its own terms, and possibly why it has not been so viewed in the past.

First, it is worth noting that although the distinction between special and general positive duty is not apparently taken to be of theoretical importance, it is nevertheless widely recognized. The most frequently noted point of difference between special and general positive duties is that unlike general positive duties, special positive duties are owed only to a particular person by another particular person in virtue of some special relationship or transaction. Furthermore, unlike general positive duties, special positive duties are not optional, that is, they are not duties of imperfect obligation. On the contrary, they are correlated with special positive rights.[50] These are significant points of difference between general and special positive duties, which have been widely noted, but largely ignored, I suspect, because special positive duty has not been viewed as a theoretically interesting separate moral category.

What has not been sufficiently recognized, I think, is that in addition to the differences just enumerated, there is a foundational difference between general and special positive duty. And what is that foundational difference? At least in some clear cases, it is the difference between a foundation of justice and a foundation of benevolence. That being the case, the difference between them is even greater than is generally supposed. In fact, the differences between special and general positive duties are arguably as great as the difference between general positive and negative duties. Again, this foundational difference has the odd character of having been noted in the past but simply not emphasized—in fact, basically disregarded.

To see the importance of this omission, consider the features of special positive duty a little more carefully. Special positive duties are generated by special relationships such as parental or professional relations, or transactions such as promises or contracts. They are specified by the practices that constitute those relations, or by the purposes implicit in them, or by explicit agreement.[51] For example, my duty to provide for my children is specified by the general practices of parenthood, often expressed as the settled expectations of the community. My duty to teach my classes and hold a reasonable number of office hours is specified partly by my contract and partly by the general practices of the teaching profession, again in terms of the reasonable expectations of the community in view of the purpose of that profession. Of course, the simplest case of special positive duty is one of simple and explicit agreement: say, my duty to wash your car, since I agreed to do it this afternoon for five dollars, which you paid me. (In fact, not many interesting cases are this simple kind, even though we philosophers seem to be inordinately fond of using cases like it as examples.)

And what is the general foundation of these duties? Whatever it might turn out to be, it is not benevolence or charity, which is a clear contrast between special and general positive duties. Special positive duties are not duties of charity. I will suggest, in fact I will argue, that they are duties of justice, as manifested in the values of trust, fairness, and reciprocity; and as an initial consideration in that direction I would point out that in every clear case of special positive duty we are involved with a correlative right. The violation of a right is considered to be a violation of justice. For example, Kant used the violation of a promise as a paradigm of te violation of a perfect duty (i.e., a duty of justice), even though the duties that are most often generated by promises (and contracts, for that matter) are positive, not negative duties. So Kant clearly thought that the significant distinction was not between positive and negative, but between perfect and imperfect duties (as did Mill, just to cite another major thinker who drew the distinction in that way). Obviously, at least some positive duties are duties of justice, and certainly not duties of benevolence. I don't think that claim should be controversial.

A contract, a business agreement, or an impersonal promise need not imply any benevolence at all. If a painter contracts to paint my house, neither party is entitled to benevolence on that ground, nor is the agreement based on or derived from benevolence. If the painter breaks the contract, he or she will be condemned not for a lack of benevolence, but for a breach of contract or, in other words, a breach of trust. I am entitled to rely on the painter to meet the terms of the contract—no more, no less. And I am so entitled as a claim of justice in the form of trust or reliance.

Wouldn't it be nice if it all turned out to be just that simple? It isn't, of course. Naturally, the contract cases are comparatively easy. Remember that special positive duties are specified by the practices that constitute the special relations that generate the duties. Of course, if we pick as our example the practice of promising (or contracting, which is often described as just a special case of mutual promising) then we are going to come out with a confirmation of the analysis that Kant gave of promising as a paradigm of duties of justice. Unfortunately, it does not necessarily follow that all special positive duties are duties of justice, for that will depend on the foundation of the relationship that generates the duty in any particular case. At least that is all one can assume at this point. That is why I want to consider three rather harder cases, namely, natural (or family) obligations, professional obligations, and political obligations, in chapters 4–9. Until I do that, it would be irresponsible to claim here and now that the foundation of all special positive duties is justice. But I do claim, here and now and without further evidence, that whatever the foundation turns out to be, benevolence alone is not adequate to account for special positive duties as a class.

By way of preliminary support for that claim in chapters 4 and 5 I will plunge directly from the easiest case (the simple agreement with my painter) into the hardest (natural relations or family duties). Suppose we consider family relations as the foundation of certain special positive duties and rights (which they certainly are). This foundation one would expect to be the strongest possible candidate for duties of benevolence, yet it seems to me that insofar as rights and duties are implied, this is not the case. I will argue shortly that these duties are justified by the ideas of mutual reliance, reasonable expectation, or shared cost in a common enterprise, and that these ideas are founded on notions of fairness and trust that are derivatives of justice rather than benevolence.

Don't get me wrong. I have nothing against benevolence in general, and I certainly do not mean to suggest that it is out of place in family relations. It is just that I would expect much more to follow from benevolence than mere duties. Duties are minimally enforceable obligations; obligations that it is reasonable to expect anyone who is in a family relationship to meet. Considerations of benevolence would surely take one much further.

But let me expand on this point a bit, for it provides an interesting example of a point raised earlier. While these duties are minimal, as compared to the implications of benevolence, they are much more intrusive (being positive) than duties one ordinarily associates with justice. Here it appears already that the foundations of positive duties (even duties founded on promises) are not really captured well by the traditional notion of justice as noninterference, or respect for autonomy. Some of them can be manipulated to make them fit into that traditional view—they do fit the notion of respect for rights, after all—but it seems to me that it will be more illuminating to examine the nuances of justice as fairness, trust, and mutual reliance or reciprocity than to spend time bending these ideas to fit the narrow view of justice as noninterference.

In any case, the foundation of special positive duty cannot be captured by benevolence alone, as appears to be the case with general positive duty, and this foundational difference is widely overlooked, or its significance disregarded, because special and general positive duties are commonly lumped together as two forms of the same duty, or special positive duty is viewed as a subcategory of the more general class. But if the foundational point made here is correct, then special and general positive duties should not be merged at all, for there is as much difference between them as between positive and negative duties. Foundational distinctions make a rather significant difference indeed.

Thus, it is quite misleading to lump positive duties together as though they constitute a single coherent class and then refer to them as duties of benevolence or charity. They should not be conflated. Once it is clear how different they are, it should be obvious that no useful purpose is served by referring to them together. Furthermore, if positive duties are treated as a single class over all, there is no more reason to refer to them as duties of charity than as duties, say, of trust. General positive duty is no more representative and is possibly less representative of that class than special positive duty. Affirmative obligations, more often than not, are based on special relations or transactions. So it will more often be true that positive duties are founded on trust or reciprocity than on benevolence. Thus, special positive duty should not be conflated with general positive duty or considered a subcategory of general positive duty. Indeed, it would make sense to view them the other way around. More important, positive duties, overall, are not duties of charity or benevolence.

If all this is true, both the formal and the foundational distinctions suggest that the important contrast with regard to duty is not the contrast between positive and negative duty but the contrast between perfect and imperfect duty. But why, then, is the contrast so commonly drawn between general positive and negative duty, as if that were the significant distinction? And why is the importance of special positive duty so widely overlooked or disregarded?

Several considerations may be operative. For one thing, there is an obvious connection between special and general positive duties in that all of them involve positive duties—affirmative obligations hence are all significantly different from negative duties, which are, after all, prohibitions. In terms of rights, however, this is not the important distinction, or so I have suggested. So Why—given the powerful force of the development of rights during the past two or three centuries of the individualist tradition—have special positive rights and their correlative duties been so sorely neglected within liberal theory?

To answer this question most clearly, we need to consider the general focus of the liberal tradition and the background against which it was opposed. First, special positive rights and duties could be viewed as founded in special privilege, and it is precisely the old regime of special privilege that liberalism opposed. Special privileges of birth, nobility, position, and rank were what the moral war of the liberal movement was being waged against. Thus, it was with good reason that liberal theorists were focused on what was wrong with special privilege, since a great deal was wrong with the ancient system of inequality. So they can hardly be faulted if they failed to consider that special relationships might provide a morally defensible foundation for some legitimate obligations. At least until fairly recently, the force of the liberal tradition has been to challenge and limit special obligations (as related to special privilege), not to contemplate their legitimacy. It is not hard to see, however, that such a perspective might easily lead theorists to overlook what needs to be preserved and refined from the old tradition that it is opposing.

Second, the focus of liberal moral theory has been on universal and often unconditional moral considerations, certainly not on narrow, contingent ones. Thus, special positive duties would naturally be considered theoretically uninteresting. If you are looking for what is universal in morality, a study of special positive duty will not give it to you. Indeed, as I pointed out in the first section, the greatest accomplishment of liberal individualism was to establish the moral groundwork for minimal universal moral duties, or human rights. This achievement was the result of a focus on the significance of the individual human being without regard to special connections or position; that is to say, on the universal in morality. Thus, one could say metaphorically that the liberal perspective was facing in the opposite direction from considerations of special positive duty.

For these reasons, the general thrust of the liberal worldview made it convenient to view special positive duty as a small subclass of, or exception to, the general class of positive duties, which is to say, general positive duties of charity or benevolence. But this view badly misrepresents the conceptual and foundational properties of special positive duties. I think it also misrepresents their scope and significance.

Thus, third, given the thrust of modern Western individualism, and despite diverging trends of socialism, Marxism, and communitarianism, it has been convenient to think of society as composed largely of atomistic individuals connected to other individuals only by a few contractual relations, and even fewer natural relations, that generate a few special positive duties. Such duties cannot be the central focus of political or moral philosophy for a strict individualist, since special positive duties impinge greatly on freedom and are founded on special relations. Negative duties are more compatible with the individualistic ideal of freedom. This view would naturally lead to downgrading the significance or prevalence of special positive duty because it is the flip side of upgrading self-sufficiency.

But the facts of the world are that human society and personal human life is structured and formed by an extensive web of natural and contractual relations, often informal ones, which generate extensive special positive duties. We all have them. They are what life is made of: special positive duties to family, to friends, to coworkers, colleagues, employees, customers, fellow worshipers, citizens, party members, team members, or promoters of a common cause. Special positive duties are the result of all our commitments, engagements, agreements, activities, and associations. Much of our lives are spent fulfilling or receiving the benefits of them.

The business of living is more concerned with special positive duty than it is with negative duty, which, although always present and significant, fades into the background precisely because it is negative. How much of the life of an ordinary person (yours or mine) is directly focused on meeting our requirements not to kill, rob, or assault others, for example? And everyday life is very much more concerned with special positive duty than with general positive duty, which turns up only now and then, and is optional in any given case. Special positive duty is the morality of daily life for ordinary people. Yet, until quite recently special positive duty has been discussed so little that, as I pointed out earlier, its foundations have not yet been clearly articulated. This is hardly surprising, given the focus of the liberal tradition on universal prohibitions, individual freedom, and the priority of consent. Such a perspective translates naturally into a theoretical preoccupation with a contractual model of analysis.

Thus, the final factor that leads to the disregard of special positive duty as a morally interesting category is that the liberal tradition considered family relations theoretically uninteresting, since they cannot be universalized, and all other special relations to be covered by the notion of contract. This approach reduces special positive duties to individual agreements and thus makes them compatible with the highly individualistic thrust of traditional liberal theory.

It also provides another connection between special and general positive duty, namely, the idea of voluntariness. That is, it may be that both special and general positive duties are viewed as voluntary in ways that negative duty is not. General positive duty is widely construed as discretionary in any particular case, and thus voluntary. Special positive duty is not voluntary once acquired, but I suspect that it is viewed as voluntary in its acquisition. You only have special positive duties if you agree to be in the relationships that generate them — at least that has been the common view.

The clear paradigm that follows is the contract. The contract model of analysis has provided some important insights, but it has some real deficiencies as well. I consider this issue at some length in chapters 6–7; for now it is sufficient merely to mention it.

Overall, then, despite the significant difference of form and foundation between special and general positive duties that I have just noted, it is quite understandable why special positive duties have been largely ignored by moral philosophers until recently. The potential connection of special obligations with historical privilege, the fact that they are not universalizable, and the mistaken impression that they are narrow (or not extensive) created the general attitude that special positive duties are not an important topic for moral investigation. Furthermore, insofar as they needed to be dealt with as social phenomena, they were thought to be best represented by the idea of contract, which captured so well their essential characteristic: voluntary assumption.

I

CLARIFYING GENERAL POSITIVE DUTY

What then is your duty? What the day demands.

Goethe

The world is quickly bored by the recital of misfortune, and willingly avoids the sight of distress.

W. Somerset Maugham

Special Circumstances and the Bad Samaritan Exception

Jane Austen characterized obligation as a fat friend who breaks his leg on your front walk after tea, obliging you to care for him through months of convalescence. Some obligations are not acquired by consent. In liberal theory, affirmative obligations are almost exclusively focused in terms of individual consent (or contract). Yet, actual obligations in liberal societies appear to derive from many sources: from being a citizen, from owning property, from engaging in certain activities, from living in a particular place, from being related to someone, perhaps even simply from being in the wrong place at the wrong time. Obligations appear to come attached, like price tags, to other things we value. There might be any number of grounds for justifying them apart from or in addition to consent or contract.

In this chapter and the next I will consider the last of these suggestions: the possibility of acquiring an obligation merely by being in the wrong place at the wrong time. This has been debated over the past three decades or so (and discussed for much longer) as the problem of the bad Samaritan.[1] If you just happen to see a stranger incapacitated by an emergency situation that you could easily address, without risk to yourself, are you obligated to help just because you happen to be there? Can you really find yourself under an obligation based on nothing more than coincidence? The prospect of any such possibility rests very uneasily on a liberal foundation, with its strong focus on autonomy and freedom.[2]

The traditional liberal response, of course, has been to subsume such cases within the framework of general positive duties as imperfect duties of charity. General positive duties as duties of charity fit in nicely with the liberal commitment to autonomy, since imperfect duties of charity are determined in particular cases by the agent who takes on the responsibility in question. That eliminates the problem of obligations simply cropping up by coincidence, and it keeps the theory elegant and consistent. There are no exceptions. The duty to aid in an emergency, like all other general positive duties, is an imperfect duty, which means that it is left to the discretion of the agent in any particular case. Thus, it is justified by consent. It is voluntarily assumed. Consequently, it may be a good thing for you to volunteer your assistance, but no one has a right to it, at least in the absence of a special relationship. In short, the distinction between positive and negative duty is morally significant and absolute: negative duties are perfect duties, and positive duties are not. It follows that there are no universal positive rights and that the duty of the good Samaritan is not a perfect duty.[3]

The problem with this approach is that it makes aiding an emergency victim merely a matter of personal conscience no matter what the circumstances might be, and there are cases in which this idea grates badly on our moral intuitions. It doesn't seem quite right to say of the thirty-eight witnesses to the now famous Kitty Genovese murder that it was uncharitable that none of them bothered to call the police, but after all it is a matter of personal conscience whether one contributes anything to a stranger. What else can be said, however, if general positive duties are not perfect duties; absolutely, not ever? The fact is that the traditional liberal approach does not handle such cases well. The result has been considerable debate and consternation that have called into question the entire liberal framework of positive and negative duty, when progress might be better served by focusing instead on the particular issue itself.[4]

I want to suggest that the liberal idea of general positive duty as imperfect duties of charity works well in most cases. The general framework seems to be correct, but it should be viewed as a general framework, not as an absolute doctrine.[5] Although general positive duties are and must be ordinarily imperfect—the exercise of charity that is within the discretion of the agent in any given case—the duty of the good Samaritan is a special exception. First, it is such a serious duty that it functions like a negative duty, in that the failure to meet it generates condemnation in every case. That is to say, it is not within the discretion of the agent in any particular case where it applies. Furthermore, it is a perfect duty that is attached to a correlative right to emergency aid that is held by the victim. Finally, it only arises in special circumstances that make it something like a special positive duty. Because of these special properties, it does not fall neatly within the prearranged categories of special and general duties. It is not exactly a general positive duty, and consequently it need not be imperfect. It may clarify our understanding of general positive duty, I hope, to see that the duty of the good Samaritan does not actually fit in that category. It doesn't eliminate the category either. It is merely an exception.

1. On Clear Cases and Perfect Duties

Many philosophers who are committed to theoretical purity, perhaps, have tried valiantly to confine the duty of the good Samaritan within the framework of imperfect duties of charity, but it just doesn't fit there.[6] Consider the following scenario. Suppose a man has a heart attack in front of my house. He drags himself up my front walk, crushing my prize tulips, and knocks weakly at the base of my front door. As I open the door he whispers hoarsely, "Help me! Please! Call a doctor!" To which I reply, "Oh, I'm sorry. I just helped a fellow at the office last week. Try next door."

If the case involves an imperfect duty of charity, my answer ought to be perfectly adequate. It clearly is an adequate justification for declining to help on many occasions that you have done your part elsewhere. That is a useful classification. However, the fact that the heart attack case cannot be dealt with that way shows that this duty does not fit in that class. (It does not, of course, show that there is no such class.)

Perhaps it would be more plausible if I said to the man, "I'm sorry, I don't believe in gratuitous assistance for heart attack victims. These things are a matter of personal conscience, after all. You have your causes, I have mine." But that really will not do, will it? I think not, as long as a human being is dying on my front porch; and I think that this shows that there are clear cases of positive duties that are not imperfect, that is to say, not optional, not charitable, not matters of individual conscience. They do not have the characteristics traditionally ascribed to imperfect duties. They are duties in the same full-blown sense as negative duties not to cause harm: functionally they are perfect duties. Indeed, in some cases they can be shown to override some negative duties. Thus they are clearly perfect duties, for an imperfect (and therefore discretionary) duty could not rationally override a perfect duty.

Let's change our case a bit. Suppose Frank and his father are hiking in an isolated area near my house when Frank's father has a heart attack. Just to make the issue of duty clear, suppose that Frank in fact hates his father, or at least is greedily awaiting a fat inheritance. He would really rather have the inheritance than his dad's companionship, and the only reason he hangs around is to keep the will in his favor. Nevertheless, he is not a monster. He has never considered killing his father for the money or even wished him dead. Still, now that he is in this precarious situation, he can't help but be a little tempted to do nothing, but he does believe strongly in doing his duty. No one is around for miles, but he can see my house not far away. There are telephone lines running to it and a fence around it bearing a "no trespassing" message. Doesn't he have a duty to violate my private property, to trespass in order to get to a phone?[7] Suppose further that he does enter my private yard and knock on the door, but he gets no answer. Apparently no one is home, but when he tries the door it comes open.

Ordinarily, he has no right to enter my yard, much less my house. In fact he has a perfect negative duty to me (as he would to any homeowner) not to violate my privacy or property rights. He has a perfect negative duty not to intrude on any other people, and that includes me. Furthermore, this is not a trivial duty, but a serious one. Under the circumstances, however, does he not have a positive duty to help his father that overrides his negative duty not to intrude on others? If he decides not to do it (not to intrude), and lets his father die while he hikes fifteen miles to the next public phone, would we accept his excuse that he could not violate his duty to respect the private property of other people? Would we consider it a justification? I believe that most people would not only disagree with his decision, they would condemn him for it. That is, they would not simply say, "Well, if it had been me, I would have done things differently, but then to each his own." I think most people would say he was wrong—unreasonably rigid. If so, what would the basis for that condemnation be? It would have to be, I think, his failure to make a reasonable effort to help his father, even if it meant that he had to infringe the rights of others that he would otherwise be expected to respect. That does not mean that he could justifiably violate *any* negative duties whatsoever. He could not rightfully shoot me, if I refused to let him in to use the phone, for example. But walking on my property, even in my house, seems a small infraction compared to letting his father die, even if the former violates a negative duty and the latter "only" a positive one. If all that is correct, it appears that at least sometimes a positive duty may override a negative one.

It might be objected that the case of Frank's father involves not a general imperfect duty, but a special positive duty, which is much stronger, and itself a perfect duty, which can sometimes cause this kind of conflict with negative duties.

Suppose then, that we change the case yet again. Suppose that the heart attack victim is not Frank's father but just another hiker who happens to clutch his chest and fall down on the trail right in front of Frank near my front gate. Everything else remains the same. Does that one fact change the whole story? Would we now say that Frank is off the hook? Has he no obligation to help as long as the victim is a stranger to whom he owes no special duty? I believe that the moral reaction of most people would be the same as in the other case. If all Frank has to do is walk through my gate and into my house to use my phone (admittedly without my permission and in my absence), I think most people would condemn him for not doing so. I would. But why should we condemn him if the situation now involves merely an imperfect duty of charity? If it is just a matter of personal conscience (and trespassing, remember, is not just a matter of personal conscience, but the violation of a right), why wouldn't Frank be correct to say, "I would have helped but the sign on the gate said 'no trespassing,' so there was nothing I could do." If the traditional doctrine is correct, then that statement should not only be right, but clearly right. So why isn't it?

It isn't clear, I submit, because we are not involved here with an imperfect duty, but rather a perfect duty. This could be due to several factors. It could be that an appeal to the basic value of respect for human life and security turns the imperfect duty to help others into a perfect duty analogous to universal negative duties that are founded on the same value. It could be that the special circumstances pick out the agent and victim in emergencies, turning the imperfect duty into a special positive duty and thus a perfect duty. It could be a hybrid duty that relies on both of the factors just mentioned. Any of these approaches could potentially provide a foundation for regarding the duty to aid in an emergency as a perfect duty. Let me consider these possibilities as I review the objections to moving in this direction.

2. Rights and Duties of Justice

Here it should be acknowledged that perfect duties are ordinarily thought to generate correlative rights, and it is precisely in terms of rights that a major objection to the idea of a perfect duty to aid a stranger is often framed. In a frequently quoted passage, J. G. Murphy has put the objection in its clearest terms:

> I can be highly morally lacking even in cases where I violate no one's rights. For example, I am sitting in a lounge chair next to a swimming pool. A child (not mine) is drowning in the pool a few inches from where I am sitting. I notice him and realize that all I would have to do to save him is put down my drink, reach down,

grab him by the trunks, and pull him out (he is so light I could do it with one hand without even getting out of my seat). If I do not save him I violate no rights (strangers do not have a right to be saved by me) but would still reveal myself as a piece of moral slime properly to be shunned by all decent people.[8]

Does Murphy's position entail that the duty of the good Samaritan is not a perfect duty? Joel Feinberg, while disagreeing with Murphy's position, has noted that two basic characteristics have traditionally been associated with perfect duties as defining conditions: correlative rights and determinate parties.[9] In clear cases involving emergency rescue, such as the heart attack victims I discussed earlier or Murphy's sunbather, there are certainly determinate parties involved.[10] But what about correlative rights? Does it follow from my view that there is a right to such aid? I think it does, but showing it will require separate argument.

Is there a moral right to easy aid in emergencies? Note first that the heart attack cases (or Murphy's case, or any such clear cases) show that there is a duty of easy rescue that is generally recognized (at least the violation of it is widely condemned) and that applies universally in much the same way that negative duties apply. That is to say, it applies in every relevantly similar case, and it does not matter whether one has helped at other times or places. Notice that even as Murphy denies that there is any right to aid in the case he constructs, he severely condemns the heartless sunbather for not helping. Imagine how odd it would have been if Murphy had declared that before we could determine whether the sunbather was a "piece of moral slime" we would first need to know whether he has helped others on other occasions. Obviously, whether he has helped others on other occasions is not relevant in Murphy's case. Unlike moral judgments about imperfect duties, the moral judgment with regard to easy rescue will be condemnation in every clear case in which the duty is not met. The question is, What sort of moral condemnation is involved here? If I leave the heart attack victim to die on my front porch, with what moral infraction will I be charged? Why is Murphy's sunbather a piece of moral slime?

The sunbather and I will certainly have exhibited a character flaw. We have shown ourselves to be extremely insensitive to the suffering and even the life of another human being. Apparently we just don't care whether the emergency victims live or die, people would say. Indeed, insensitivity at that level would ordinarily be described as psychotic. Anyone who literally does not care whether another human being dies in front of him is so seriously abnormal as to put himself outside the scope of moral agency. Suppose that you happened to witness the incident on my front porch. If you called out to me, "Help that man!" and I said, "Why?" and you said, "Because he's dying!" and I replied, "So what?" then you would immediately reassess your situation and adjust the way you dealt with me accordingly, because you would know that you were not dealing with a normal human being. You are faced with an amoral monster (or a philosopher constructing a counterexample). Describing such behavior as constituting a character flaw is not false, but it does seem rather inadequate. What more is needed? Given the judgment that anyone who engages in such conduct or holds such an attitude is an amoral monster, it would seem that some way must be found to capture the idea that my behavior is not just defective, but completely unacceptable. I am not merely showing my insensitivity, but revealing myself as residing beyond the bounds of moral agency.

Many philosophers, lawyers, and judges have tried to capture this idea by using strong language of condemnation, while denying the duty in law or the right of the victim to be saved. (Murphy is doing exactly this in the passage quoted.) Consider a similar approach in a legal opinion from the case of *Buch v Amory*.

> Suppose A., standing close by a railroad, sees a two year old babe on the track, and a car approaching. He can easily rescue the child, with entire safety to himself, and the instincts of humanity require him to do so. If he does not, he may, perhaps, justly be styled a ruthless savage and a moral monster; but he is not liable in damages for the child's injury, or indictable under the statute for its death.[11]

The primary focus of the opinion in *Buch* distinguishes legal obligations from moral ones—but notice that it also uses harsh language to condemn this behavior in the strongest possible terms, while yet denying any legal duty in the particular case. This goal and approach is the same as Murphy's in the moral context. Thus, the view is sometimes expressed in terms of denying rights and sometimes in terms of denying duties. It takes the form of combining a denial of any right or duty with condemnation severe enough to make it clear that the conduct is totally unacceptable without question. What we need to understand is the rationale that justifies such condemnation in the absence of a duty.

It relies in all cases, I think, on a particular conception of justice: justice never requires positive aid outside of a special relationship. Justice generates only negative rights and duties. Consequently, there can be no violation of justice from the mere refusal to help a stranger, no matter how slight the effort or egregious the result. Such cases involve only a lack of sympathy—an outrageous lack of sympathy, perhaps, but no violation of duty.

A number of reasons have been offered for holding such a view, all of which are generally aimed at what I would call theoretical purity or the issue of absolutism. They are all very closely related to one another, so it is hard to say which is the most basic premise, or how a derivation of them should run, but all rest on the distinction between positive and negative duty.

There is no duty to benefit others, it is claimed, but only a duty not to interfere with them. Justice requires only negative duties. The question, of course, is why? This claim is sometimes thought to be supported by the view that there is no right to aid; there is only a right to noninterference. So it could be said that there is no perfect duty to rescue because there is no right to aid. But the question is still why, for claiming no right and claiming no duty are just two ways of saying the same thing. Which statement is more basic depends on whether one supports a rights-based or duty-based moral theory. However the question is put, referring to rights or duties as such is shorthand that assumes an argument that justified the claim that a right or duty exists. Assuming that perfect duties and rights are correlative (which they are by definition), if a duty is established, then a right can be derived from it, or vice versa. But first the duty or the right must be established on some rationally acceptable moral grounds. Thus, merely referring to rights or duties as such, without further argument, is vacuous, and the claim, sometimes made, that there is no perfect duty to aid in an emergency because there is no right to assistance begs the question at issue.

3. Duties of Justice and Duties of Benevolence

The answer, therefore, must be found in the basic value or values on which the rights and duties are premised. Indeed, the argument is often made that positive duties are grounded in the value of benevolence, while negative duties are required by justice; but justice does not require positive aid. Justice involves only what is owed to others, and all that is owed to others in general is nonharm and noninterference.

At least part of this claim is true by definition. It is true by definition that what justice requires is owed. As I noted earlier, justice is fundamental in the sense that it is minimal. The requirements of justice are the bottom line, so to speak, falling below which is unacceptable. Injustice is, then, by definition a violation of one's duty or someone's right. This much is necessarily correct. It is entailed in what justice means.

The claim that there is no duty to aid in an emergency is an additional claim, however, that is not true by definition. It follows instead from a particular substantive view of the nature and scope of justice that requires rational support and justification. So the question remains, Why is there no duty to aid others in any circumstances whatsoever? And one cannot help but wonder why the condemnation is so strong in every case, if there really is no duty. Why is the bad Samaritan characterized as a moral monster or a piece of moral slime if saving the baby was truly a matter of individual conscience? Why can't the bad Samaritan say to his critics, "Look. I just gave to cancer research yesterday and helped two old ladies across the street the day before. I wasn't planning to save any babies today. Do I have to be benevolent even when I don't feel like it? I didn't owe that baby anything, after all, and I had already helped other people." If we are involved with an imperfect duty, why won't that work? It won't work, I want to suggest, because a failure of benevolence is insufficient to account for the infraction.

Is all this about a failure of charity or benevolence at all? In one respect it certainly is, and that might be what misleads us. Such behavior does indeed demonstrate a lack of concern for the well-being of others. Again, however, saying that does not quite capture the magnitude of the fault, or the severity of the criticism in clear cases. Lack of concern at this level demonstrates a total disregard for the value of the victim's life or safety. That being the case, I suggest that it is not only a lapse of sympathy, not merely a lack of concern, but also a violation of justice. Why? To put it in Kantian terms that seem appropriate here, justice requires respect for all persons as ends in themselves, without regard to who they are, who they know, or what station they may hold. To disregard the value of another person's life altogether is to fail to respect that person as a human being who has at least minimal intrinsic moral value.

As Joel Feinberg has argued, the duty to aid may be overdetermined in special emergency situations.[12] The failure to aid may exhibit a lack of concern and also violate a minimal duty of justice to which a correlative right appropriately attaches. Similarly, causing harm will usually demonstrate a lack of concern for the victim, but Kant insisted that causing harm is wrong because it violates a duty to respect others as moral beings. Behavior can be wrong for more than one reason. Immoral conduct can contradict more than one value.

Admittedly, the Kantian point is correctly construed in negative terms ordinarily. Because a person is an end in herself—because a person has intrinsic moral worth—justice requires us not to engage in harmful or coercive acts against her. Furthermore, since we are autonomous beings who are responsible for ourselves, we are not ordinarily required by justice—that is, we have no universal duty—to aid the world at large (at least not one based on individual justice). All this is central to the liberal individualist conception of justice. Perhaps the most important and attractive feature of the classical individualist tradition is that it takes as its foundation the significance of every individual. It stands for individual rights to life and liberty.

These rights have indeed been interpreted negatively. That is, you have the right not to be harmed, coerced, or interfered with, but you have no right to aid in general. Why not? Because you are a free autonomous being, and free autonomous beings are responsible for themselves. It is immoral to interfere with autonomous individuals and inappropriate to require others to take responsibility for them in any ordinary circumstances. That is the moral position on which the doctrine of positive and negative duty relies. It is perfectly sensible and presumably defensible in general.

However, it is overstated insofar as it ignores the fact that human beings are not omnipotent, even if we are autonomous. Perfectly responsible, autonomous, and independent persons can find themselves in circumstances beyond their control. It happens to most of us sooner or later. And it is not necessarily a sign of irresponsibility or fault. It is simply a fact of humanity that we are all at least occasionally vulnerable.

Now my question is, How can it be consistent for a tradition that takes as its cornerstone the significance and moral worth of each and every individual to abandon the commitment to human life precisely when it is seriously threatened beyond the individual's capacity to combat the threat? Are individuals only valuable when they are totally self-sufficient? If so, who would ever qualify as valuable? Is human life only to be protected when one is in control and not if one is overwhelmed by special circumstances? Why? Why should a tradition that takes human worth as basic hold a view like that? How could a tradition founded on the intrinsic worth of all individuals validly arrive at such a conclusion?

It is understandable for the tradition to hold that there is no general duty for human beings to underwrite one another, or depend on one another in general. The presumption of individual freedom and personal responsibility supports that position. But an emergency is by definition an abnormal situation, and one that requires rescue implies that the victim is incapacitated to the extent that rescue is necessary. If the victim could fend for himself, he would not need a rescuer, and the duty would not arise. Thus, the argument from autonomy does not apply here, precisely because it is an abnormal situation in which autonomy is overwhelmed.

There is a further objection as well. The extreme view that no aid is ever a perfect duty leads to the conclusion that there is no prohibition against the willful disregard of human life or safety in emergencies. What is wrong with Murphy's pool lounger, for example, is that he regards the child's life as totally worthless. For him that child's life has no value, no significance whatsoever. It is not worth even enough to put down his drink. Such an attitude must be incompatible with the individualist tradition, which supposedly takes as its very foundation the significance of every person as an end in himself, the intrinsic worth of each and every individual as a moral being. It does not make sense for members of this tradition to be able to or be allowed to regard one another as worthless (at least in their actions). It is inconsistent with our most fundamental value—the value of every individual. So it seems to me that some members of the individualist tradition have taken a wrong turn to adopt an absolutist position on the doctrine of positive and negative duty that leads to a view that there is never a positive duty to aid in an emergency, even when that implies that a victim's life is worthless, and that the willful disregard of that human life is tolerable.

It might be objected here that no such implications can be drawn from the mere failure to aid. Murphy's pool lounger need not feel that the child's life is worthless, it will be argued. He need not disrespect the moral personhood of another individual. All he needs to hold is that it is not his responsibility to do anything about the situation. It is not his child, after all. Nor is he a lifeguard. He has assumed no special duty. He has agreed to no affirmative obligation. He is just sitting in a lounge chair minding his own business. So he is not responsible for a random stranger.

I do not think that this argument can withstand scrutiny, however. Suppose that I demolished a condemned building (of my own) knowing that a crippled, homeless person was always hiding upstairs on the third floor. Could I exonerate myself by (truthfully) saying: "Look, I did not knock the house down in order to kill the old man. I just needed to get rid of the house. I harbor him no disrespect as a moral being. I agree that his life is valuable, but if he couldn't save himself, it's his problem."

No one would accept an argument like that where negative duties are involved, and why not? In the context of the requirements of justice, respect for persons refers to how they must be treated, not to what private feelings one may have about them. To say that justice requires respect for persons is to declare a standard of conduct that must be consistent with a strong commitment to individual freedom and autonomy while still acknowledging the intrinsic moral value of others.

The question is, Can the bad Samaritan meet that standard? Can the bad Samaritan disregard with impunity a dying victim and still respect the intrinsic worth of all persons? What would that mean? One cannot claim to hold a value yet deny that it has any implications whatever for one's conduct. In clear cases, the need for assistance may be so crucial to the continued existence and basic well-being of the victim, and the comparative ease of providing the aid so slight, that withholding it amounts to a denial of the value of the victim's life and safety.

In unclear cases, declining to help is consistent with respect for persons, because unclear and generalized cases of need compete with many other cases of need, all of which cannot be met by any single individual. This is the point of imperfect duties of charity. The individual must be able to choose from among competing claims. If you help some of the time your general duty has been met. No one will blame you for not giving to the heart fund if you gave to cancer research instead, even if additional lives could have been saved with additional donations to the heart fund. Unless a special duty or a clear emergency is involved, claims of need all cluster under the general duty of charity. This is not to disrespect the intrinsic value of those in need, but rather to acknowledge the human limits of potential donors. No one can satisfy all needs, and so the commitment to freedom requires that individuals should be able to choose the recipients of their charity without complaint from others.

But clear cases of emergency, as I have shown, do not work this way. In a clear emergency, it makes no sense to claim to respect the intrinsic worth of a person's life yet leave her to die if you could easily save her. Such behavior is simply inconsistent with respect for the value of human life. So I believe that the objection cannot stand, and I shall retain my conclusion that withholding easy aid in a clear emergency is inconsistent with the most basic and minimal respect for persons. Indeed the view that the matter is one of personal conscience only (that is, an imperfect duty) implies that the victim's life is worthless and that willful disregard for that life is tolerable.

Since these implications are unacceptable, the only reasonable conclusion is that justice does require emergency aid that can easily be offered, because nothing less than that is compatible with a minimal respect for the value of individual human life, which is the foundation of the liberal individualist tradition.

4. Reconsidering Rights and Duties of Justice

The traditional liberal view holds that by definition what justice requires is adherence to duty; and duties of justice are perfect duties. Thus, it follows from the argument of the prior section that there is a perfect duty of justice requiring emergency assistance in clear cases. And if there is such a duty of justice, then there is a correlative right, because duties of justice are perfect duties, and perfect duties have correlative rights. What justice requires, as already noted, is owed. Consequently, the moral infraction of the bad Samaritan is the violation of another's rights.

I suspect that some will find this implication even more uncomfortable than the duty of justice for which I have just argued. Since I am more interested in duties than in rights here, I prefer not to dwell on this point. Nevertheless, it seems to me correct that a victim has a right to emergency assistance if it is available. It accords with the requirements of reason, and with our moral intuitions as well, if we think it through carefully.

However, some philosophers have noted that the phenomenology of emergency interaction does not match the characteristics ordinarily associated with rights and duties. Rights, after all, can be demanded; rights are what we are entitled to. But the behavior of victims in need of help does not correspond to that description at all. Victims typically plead or beg for help, and they usually express gratitude after being saved. Such conduct is ordinarily associated with charity and favor rather than rights and duties. Consequently, some have argued that even though we may criticize the bad Samaritan for a lack of sympathy or concern for others, which is certainly a moral failure, it is not a violation of justice unless the victim is entitled to demand that the aid be provided.[13]

Other philosophers have responded that the special circumstances account for the behavior of victims. A person in fear for her life is hardly in a position to demand her rights, even in cases where no one would deny that she has them. Consider, for example, a clear case of special positive duty: a drowning swimmer has a right to the reasonable efforts of the lifeguard on duty to save her, but it is doubtful that she will think in terms of her rights as she is gasping her last breath and hoping that the lifeguard will see or hear her. She is at the mercy of any rescuer, after all; even if she has a right to aid, she has no way to enforce it on the spot. Thus, it is hardly surprising if she feels relieved and grateful to be saved, even if the lifeguard is only doing his job. We would not conclude, however, that given her behavior she must not have any right to the aid of the lifeguard, who was hired specifically to assist swimmers in just such emergencies.[14]

An even more obvious example is provided by the violation of negative rights. Consider the victim of a violent attacker. The victim may well plead for his life, give away his money in hope of gaining mercy, and even feel grateful for being released unharmed. It certainly would not follow that, given his behavior, he had no right to life or to security from harm, or that the attacker was not violating that right. People are not always in a position to enforce their rights, and when they are not, then different behavior may be more compatible with concern for their survival. Thus, we cannot consider the behavior of victims to be conclusive evidence of the status of their rights.

Furthermore, even if the victim is impaired by the emergency situation, it seems to me that if they could, others would demand the victim's rights for him. Consider the lifeguard case. If you saw the woman drowning, wouldn't you run to the lifeguard and say, "Hey! Look! There is a woman in trouble out there! Hurry up!" Ordinarily the duty of the lifeguard is so obvious that you wouldn't even think of stating it explicitly. But suppose he didn't respond (for some strange reason), and you couldn't swim, and no one else was available? Wouldn't you demand that he do his duty? I would. And we would be right to do it.

Now consider Murphy's case. Suppose that you are up on the balcony of the hotel overlooking the pool. You see the baby floundering in the water, and Murphy's lounger sitting within arm's reach of it. Wouldn't you yell to him to save the baby? Ordinarily, one would not expect to do any more than call attention to the situation, assuming that anyone who saw it would correct it. Furthermore, in most circumstances, if you are close enough to see it, then you might well be in just as good a position to correct it as the pool lounger is. Emergencies require speed; and your duty is the same as his. So your proper response in most circumstances is to act yourself, not demand that someone else do it. Thus, the circumstances where demanding action of the bad Samaritan is appropriate will be rare, but it doesn't follow that he has no duty. If you called from the balcony to the pool lounger, and he just looked at you and said, "I don't want to get involved," wouldn't you be outraged? Wouldn't you demand that he pull that baby out of the water before it was too late? Wouldn't it be appropriate for you to be indignant if he didn't? This is behavior appropriate to the violation of rights and duties.

I think that there are two factors that make all this not obvious. The first is circumstantial. The victim is not in a position to demand her rights (but as I have shown, nothing follows from that). In clear cases there is no other bystander, so there is no one to object to the bad Samaritan's conduct, or even to know about it. If, on the other hand, there is another bystander, then that person has the same duty as the bad Samaritan, so the appropriate response would simply be to act, not to demand that someone else act. Consequently, the circumstances in which it will be appropriate for someone to demand the victim's rights will be restricted to those rare occasions in which someone is in a position to see or somehow know about the situation but not in a position to do anything about it personally. Given the rarity of such circumstances, it is hardly surprising that it has been overlooked. Once it is noted, however, demanding appropriate behavior on the part of the bad Samaritan is not hard to imagine at all. In fact, it would be very odd if the response to the failure to act in such circumstances were not indignation.

The second factor that should be noted is the common slippage between moral and legal rights. In Anglo-American systems there is (almost) no legal right to be rescued, but that does not mean that there is no commonly recognized moral right. So, we must distinguish moral enforcement from legal enforcement of rights or duties. What does it mean to have a moral right and thus be morally entitled to demand that the correlative duty be performed? I have a right that you not lie to me. In what sense is it enforceable? It is enforceable in the sense that I can morally condemn you for violating my right. I can accurately accuse you of wronging me. I have a moral grievance against you that I can convey to anyone else who will listen. I can appropriately criticize you to your friends and associates, and appeal to the community (to those you and I know) for moral censure. Is my right enforceable in any other respect? No. Can I demand that you honor my right in any other way? No. Public censure and individual condemnation are the enforcement mechanisms of morality. That is what moral enforcement means. The fact that I cannot take you to court for lying to me or breaking your promises does not confuse anyone into thinking that I have no moral right that you not treat me that way. The same should be true of the right to minimal assistance in an emergency. Thus, the common behavioral objections do not hold.

Yet, it is often suggested that while the failure to aid is a moral failure, it is not a violation of justice. One wonders, Why? I asked earlier what sort of moral infraction is committed by the bad Samaritan. Why should we construe that infraction as the violation of a duty that has a correlative right (a perfect duty)? Consider this question a little further. What kind of offense occurred? The bad Samaritan has not undermined society at large or defied a communal goal. That construction seems inappropriate. It is not the general welfare that he is impairing (except indirectly and secondarily). Furthermore, he is not merely debasing himself or exhibiting a character flaw. As noted earlier, that construction seems grossly inadequate. He is not primarily hurting himself.

The person who is hurt primarily and directly is the victim. Now, it does not follow automatically that if one is hurt one is thereby wronged. I may be hurt by a rival who bests me in competition for a job, but I am not therefore wronged by her. I am not wronged unless I am denied that to which I am entitled. Thus, a wrong is often defined as the violation of a right. So, the question gets shifted to: Why should we think that the imperiled victim has a right to minimal aid?

As I argued earlier, the foundation for a right to emergency aid is exactly the same as the foundation for negative rights not to be harmed, namely, the minimal requirements of justice to respect the intrinsic worth of all persons. Any argument that applies to negative rights also applies to the right to a reasonable (or at least a minimal) effort to provide critically needed emergency aid. All are based on and derived from the basic commitment to respect the intrinsic moral worth of all individuals that is widely recognized as the core of liberal individualism.

Of course, if the commitment to respect for persons is denied, then my argument will not go through. Denying that commitment, however, dissolves liberal individualism at its heart. It is precisely that central and fundamental commitment to the significance of each individual that makes liberal individualism worth defending. As I have shown, that commitment entails a duty of easy rescue in clear cases. Since that duty is required by justice, it is a perfect duty that implies a correlative right to aid on the part of the victim. Yet, other objections to this position have been made. I will turn to them now.

5. Causing Harm and Failing to Prevent It

It is widely held that causing harm and merely allowing harm to occur are morally distinct. There is a perfect duty not to cause harm, but there is no perfect duty to prevent harm. Thus, refraining from providing affirmative assistance is merely failing to provide a benefit. As one legal scholar put this longstanding Anglo-American view:

> however revolting the conduct of the man who declined to interfere, he was in no way responsible for the perilous situation; . . . he simply failed to confer a benefit upon a stranger. . . . The law does not compel active benevolence between man and man. It is left to one's conscience whether he shall be a good Samaritan or not.[15]

This view has been both widely held and commonly disputed for over a century, and in recent decades the issue has become highly controversial. This view, in fact, is often considered the basis for the objection discussed earlier that Murphy's pool lounger need not disrespect the moral worth of the drowning baby. He merely denies responsibility for helping in such circumstances. I have argued that such disavowals of responsibility are incompatible with the respect for persons that lies at the heart of liberal individualism, but one reaction to my position might be that Murphy's pool lounger "was in no way responsible for the perilous situation." That is to say, he did not cause it. "[H]e simply failed to confer a benefit upon a stranger," and conferring benefits upon strangers is a matter of personal conscience.[16]

Several responses have been made to address this position. It has been argued that causing harm and allowing harm to occur when one could prevent it are morally equivalent, and, more specifically, that killing someone and letting her die are morally equivalent.[17] Since I will discuss this position in the next chapter, I will not pursue it here. If the position is correct, it does not undermine the duty for which I have been arguing. Rather it reinforces and extends it.

Another response is that the "no duty to aid" position, as just construed, employs a flawed conception of 'benefit'. Joel Feinberg has distinguished between benefits that maintain the recipient's interest at the status quo ante, and those that provide a net gain. Providing minimal aid to an imperiled victim, he notes, merely restores the victim to the position held before the onset of the crisis. It does not confer a windfall profit, as suggested by the language of 'benefit'. So it seems misleading to speak of conferring benefits here when the victim receives at most a return to the normal position that merely enables any human being to survive—a position held by the victim just prior to the emergency.[18]

I believe that Feinberg's analysis is basically correct, but I fear that the response of an opponent would be to ask why the good Samaritan has an obligation to restore the victim to his status quo ante anyway. My answer in the previous section was that some interests are so basic to human existence and minimal well-being that ignoring their impairment in easily correctable emergencies is equal to denying the value of human existence and minimal well-being altogether. Although he does not argue for this explicitly, I believe that Feinberg's position assumes this stance as well.

A third response to the "no duty to aid" position is suggested by Douglas Husak's analysis of liability in criminal law in terms of control, rather than traditional notions of causation as such. Husak has argued that in many contexts the idea of "being in control of a situation" provides a more accurate and informative picture of liability (or excuse) than reference to causation has been able to provide.[19] I think this view is clearly right, and it applies in moral contexts at least as well as in legal ones.

Analyzing responsibility in terms of control does not preclude analysis in terms of causation, for causing coincides with being in control in some circumstances. But the idea of being in control often provides a much better explanation of responsibility. Consider, for example, how the notions of cause and control interact in determining liability or blameworthiness. One way of ascribing blame (or credit) is to say, "You did it" or "You caused it": to claim that you brought about the state of affairs at issue. Ordinarily, this implies that you initiated some chain of events that led (rather directly) to the circumstances in question. Now, what can that mean, other than that you exercised control over some state of affairs in a way that brought about certain consequences that could be traced to your act or influence?

Furthermore, it usually (although not always) also implies that you remained in control over that chain of events. If you begin some process (say, steering a boat on a collision course), but John takes over and carries through, it is ordinarily thought that John "caused" the outcome, and is responsible for it, not you (although you may be a contributing factor.) Why should this be, other than the fact that John took control? Both of you are causal factors, on a scientific analysis; that is to say, both of you are part of the causal network. Why should John be picked out as *the* cause, simply because he is the last influence to be factored in? The commonsense answer is that the significant factor in imputing responsibility is the factor of control. John is responsible because when he took the wheel he assumed control.

Furthermore, if it is not accurate (or fully accurate) to say that John took control (suppose that he was just following your orders at gunpoint), then to the extent that you were in control, you will be considered responsible. This illustrates that responsibility is often better explained by reference to control than to cause. It becomes even clearer in special cases involving excuses, omissions, or special positive duties.

Consider excuses. In the same way that "You caused it" is a (prima facie) attribution of responsibility, "I couldn't help it" is an excusing statement. Even if Myrtle destroyed your garden by driving her car through it, she is not blameworthy if it was impossible for her to do otherwise. Suppose, say, that her brakes suddenly failed (through no negligence on her part) as she backed out of your driveway, and there was nowhere she could turn to avoid the garden. She was causally responsible for the destruction of your garden, but she was not morally responsible (not at fault or blameworthy), because she was not in control.

Even in law, such excusing conditions are often recognized as mitigating liability. A charge of homicide or manslaughter can sometimes be excused, for example, if it can be shown that the individual could not help what he did, even though he was not justified in doing it. In one case, a man was excused from the charge of manslaughter in a car accident, because a swarm of bees flew in his window causing him to lose control of his car. Similar excuses have been granted for losing control of one's car in medical emergencies, such as epileptic seizures, if the driver had no good reason to expect such attacks and thus to take precautions for them.[20] In all such cases, if the person who caused the harm could not reasonably have been expected to be in control over such circumstances, that lack of control excuses the actor from responsibility for the harm. Thus, what explains these cases is not the presence or lack of causation, but the presence or lack of control.

Similarly, responsibility for omission is best explained by reference to control, and not causation. Indeed, debate has raged over the causal status of omissions for three decades, without substantial progress of a determinate sort. That is, although a great deal of thoughtful and insightful discussion has clarified the issue, no argument of a determinative sort has been given (or now seems possible) that "scientifically" or "objectively" an omission can be demonstrated to be (or not be) a cause. It just depends on how the notion of a cause is construed.[21]

My own view is that the attribution of responsibility for omissions is better handled by focusing on the element of control in any case. Take any of the bad Samaritan cases that I have already considered. What reason can we give for imputing to me an obligation to help the heart attack victim on my front porch? The commonsense answer is that I am in control of that situation. Obviously, the victim is not in control, and no one else is around. If anyone is obligated to correct the situation, it has to be me. There isn't anyone else. Similarly, the case of Murphy's pool lounger, or the hiker who finds the heart attack victim on the isolated trail. What makes these cases clear is that it is clear who is in control. There is only one person in each case who can act, so if ought implies can, only one person in each case can be obligated.

Of course, it can be argued that no one is obligated in such circumstances, but I have tried to expose the implications of that position as incompatible with the basic liberal commitment to respect individual human worth. If my arguments on that point are persuasive, then the bystander is obligated on a liberal view. Whether this argument is accepted or not, however, it still appears that the idea of being in control provides a better account of responsibility for omissions than an account premised on causation.

Consider next the case of special positive duties. Why, for example, do we attribute responsibility to doctors for the well-being of their patients, or to parents for the well-being of their children? Again, the answer dictated by common sense is that doctors and parents presumably have control over the well-being of their patients or children. Reference to special positive duties illustrates the fact that control over many situations is often prearranged by custom and understanding, by the expectations of the community, or by contractual or informal agreement or consent. How do such arrangements relate to the issue of causation? Arrangements that generate special positive duties make clear that responsibility applies whether an act or an omission is involved, thus mooting that particular debate regarding causation. What explains this is that responsibility in the form of control is designated in advance by custom or agreement by the fact of the special relationship.

In ordinary circumstances, according to the liberal tradition, in the absence of a special relationship or agreement, individuals are responsible for themselves. Why? Because it is reasonable to assume (respecting the autonomy of individuals) that they are in control of their own lives. Again, being in control explains the doctrine.

In special circumstances, where emergency conditions overwhelm the autonomy of the victim, the responsibility for minimal assistance falls to the closest person who is able and available to meet it. By overcoming the ability of the victim to maintain responsibility for her own well-being, the circumstances shift the responsibility to the next available person who can clearly meet it without prejudice to himself. Thus, in emergencies the circumstances as such shift responsibility from the victim, who no longer has control over the threat, to the next available person who does have control or could easily exercise control over it.

It follows that the duty of the good Samaritan is rather like a special positive duty. The circumstances pick out both the victim and the potential rescuer, forming a special relationship between them that would not obtain between other persons in other circumstances. In this respect the duty of the good Samaritan is not like a negative duty, for it is not universal in the same sense. Negative duties apply to all people. But the duty to aid is much more restricted in scope. While founded on the same universal respect for human worth, it simply does not arise—it is not activated, if you will—in any ordinary circumstances, but applies only in the special context of emergencies that overwhelm the autonomy of the victim but are within the control of an available bystander. I would call that a certain form of special relationship, and thus the duty is a form of special duty.

I do not want to press this analogy too far, for after all, there is no preexisting relationship between the parties, as is the hallmark of special positive duties. Yet we can see that in scope the duty to aid does not function quite like a negative duty, either. For this reason, I would suggest that this duty is a hybrid that falls somewhere between negative duties and special positive duties. It may, then, be in something of a class by itself. Wherever it falls between these two, however, it will clearly be a perfect duty, for all these are perfect duties. That explains why it doesn't function like a duty of charity.

6. Commitment to Freedom and the Limits of Individualism

It is sometimes argued that recognizing a right to emergency aid would clash with the basic liberal commitment to freedom;[22] but that simply is not the case in the context of easy rescue. I have already noted that by definition an emergency is an abnormal occurrence. It is not something that happens every day. If it were it would be a chronic condition, and emergency rescue would not apply to it. As a matter of fact, or empirical generalization, a duty of easy emergency rescue is unlikely to affect most people at all. Take my own case, for example. I have lived a rather average life for over fifty years now, and I have never once been confronted with a stranger who needed an emergency rescue by me. I think that is very common. Most people will never be confronted with such a situation at all. Those who are confronted once are very unlikely to be so confronted a second time. This could hardly be described as an overwhelming restriction on freedom. I recognize this duty myself, and I hope that I would do my best to meet it if the relevant circumstances ever arose. But in fact, it has never restricted my freedom one iota to have this duty.

Beyond the statistical infrequency with which this duty is activated, it is defined in very narrow terms. After all, it is not a duty of heroic rescue, nor of enduring sacrifice. It is defined in terms that make it more or less a mild inconvenience. It amounts to a phone call, a short detour, or a temporary rearrangement of one's plans for the day, perhaps. Murphy's sunbather could have met his duty to rescue the baby in thirty seconds without even getting out of his chair, if he had chosen to do so. The duty to the heart attack victim on my front porch could have been discharged with a simple phone call. Clear cases require very little. With such narrow limits built in, they could hardly be described as a serious restriction on liberty, even if it is true that they are minimally intrusive. That is, even if they are random, and one cannot prepare for them, the imposition they create is so small and so infrequent that it cannot sensibly be construed as a serious restriction on liberty. Many other recognized and accepted duties create much greater impositions.

An analogous objection is sometimes formulated in terms of autonomy. It is argued that requiring aid is an enforcement of charity that violates moral autonomy. Since morally autonomous individuals are entitled to decide for themselves how they will distribute their resources, it violates their autonomy for the community (and certainly for the law) to make such decisions for them.[23]

Like the objection based on freedom, this objection cannot withstand scrutiny. Requiring minimal respect for individual worth is no more a violation of autonomy in this case than it would be in the case of negative rights and duties. We do not allow individuals to decide personally on a case by case basis whether they will refrain from killing or assaulting others, for example. I suppose it could be said that this prohibition violates their moral autonomy, since we do not leave it up to them to determine their own moral code.

But it is generally thought that falling below the minimal requirements of justice to respect the personhood of all others is not within the bounds of individual conscience. Minimally decent treatment of others is required. Ordinarily such minimal duties can be met by merely refraining from harmful and offensive acts, but in clear cases of emergency need, failing to respond with minimal decency displays the same unacceptable lack of respect that the violation of negative duty implies. The same arguments that support the enforcement of negative duties also support the insistence on a duty of decent treatment in an emergency. Such minimal social obligations are not thought to be a violation of autonomy in the case of negative duties and there is, by parity of treatment, no reason to consider it so in the case of easy rescue. In clear cases the restriction of freedom is very minimal, and the restriction of autonomy is no greater than it is when applied to negative rights and duties that are almost universally recognized by those who hold theories based on the recognition of significant individual worth and freedom.

Thus, the objection that the duty of easy rescue creates an unreasonable restriction on freedom (or autonomy) simply does not hold up at all in clear cases. Instead, clear cases are rare and relatively small inconveniences. Such obligations cannot be what the objection based on freedom is about, nor the concern over rights. In fact, there is every reason to recognize a perfect duty to provide minimal aid in emergencies, founded on basic principles of liberal thought, and no objection to doing so holds up well at all, as I have just shown.

Accordingly, what I termed the problem of absolutism is addressable. The theoretical purist, who claims that there cannot be a universal positive right or duty, can be answered. The duty of the good Samaritan is not universal in function, since the special circumstances serve to define its scope in a way that makes it analogous in function to a special positive duty. Thus the duty is individually dischargeable, despite the fact that it is based on the same universal foundation as negative rights and duties, namely, the respect for all human beings as having equal moral worth. Furthermore, given that foundation, the individualistic purist who claims that the good Samaritan duty (or any perfect, general, positive duty) exceeds the bounds of the liberal commitment to freedom and autonomy is shown to be mistaken. Not only is this duty not incompatible with liberal individualism, in clear cases it is compelled by the basic liberal commitment to respect for persons.

So, it is not the clear cases, but the unclear cases that provide cause for worry. Thus, the real issue for those concerned about rights is not whether it is reasonable to recognize a right to minimal assistance for the heart attack victim on my front porch, but how to distinguish the victim on my front porch from the starving masses in disaster-stricken lands. If those in need have rights to assistance, how can one afflicted victim be distinguished from the millions of others who are in need as well? Do they all have rights to be saved? If the heart attack victim has a claim against me, do all the others have a claim as well? The real issue for those concerned with freedom is not whether clear cases of emergency rescue restrict freedom unduly, but whether, having accepted such a duty in clear cases, we can define it with sufficient clarity to prevent ourselves from sliding down a slippery slope to oppressive positive duties to help many others in less clear cases. There is good reason to worry about this possibility (although it doesn't undercut the points made here with regard to clear cases). The question is, What does it do to the doctrine of positive and negative duty to admit a narrow exception? Does it undermine the distinction between positive and negative duty altogether? This question leads to what I earlier called the problem of validity: Can the distinction between positive and negative duty in the last analysis be defended, or are positive and negative duty morally equivalent?

3

The Duty of Charity and the Equivalence Thesis

In two widely discussed and important articles, James Rachels and Peter Singer have formulated powerful arguments to the effect that there is no morally relevant difference between positive and negative duties as such (or at least between killing and letting die), and consequently that our general failure to save the lives of many who now die from starvation and malnutrition is more or less equivalent to negligent homicide. Indeed, Singer has argued that morality requires us to give to famine relief and thereby save all those we can from starvation and malnutrition until we would be "sacrificing anything of comparable moral importance." He further notes:

> Since the situation appears to be that very few people are likely to give substantial amounts, it follows that I and everyone else in similar circumstances ought to give as much as possible, that is, at least up to the point at which by giving more one would begin to cause serious suffering for oneself and one's dependents—perhaps even beyond this point to the point of marginal utility, at which by giving more one would cause oneself and one's dependents as much suffering as one would prevent.[1]

Most people find this position alarming and unreasonable or dismiss it out of hand as wildly implausible. As Phillipa Foot has put it, we may consider ourselves less than virtuous if we fail to contribute to famine relief, but we do not consider ourselves murderers for it. Thus, she argues, positive and negative duties are not morally equivalent. If we do not send food to the starving and some of them die, it may be wrong of us, but it is not equivalent to sending them poisoned food. In this context to consider positive and negative duty to be morally equivalent is highly unintuitive.[2]

Yet, intuitions can be wrong, as Singer and Rachels point out. We often believe intuitively what is conventional or convenient. Our intuitions often reflect merely what we are used to, or what people around us think. If the intuitive position articulated by Foot is rational, we should be able to provide rational argument to support it.

Suppose one of those starving children were right here in front of us, in the same room, Rachels suggests. Wouldn't we be immoral—seriously immoral—almost like murderers, if we let her die when we could have easily fed her?[3] My answer, of course, has to be yes. That is precisely the position for which I just argued in chapter 2. But then, Rachels queries, what exactly is the difference between *that* starving child and all the others we so conveniently ignore? It cannot be a difference between positive and negative duty, as Foot claims, because the demise of that distinction is what we just accepted by accepting the perfect duty of the good Samaritan. Is he right? Is that necessarily what we are committed to?

Or is there a principled way to draw a line between the starving child standing in front of you and the masses who are dying from famine in distant lands? Once we take that first step, is there any rational stopping place short of total dedication to a life of public service? Can a good Samaritan be moderate?

Before I go further with this set of questions, it may be worth noting one thing. The (minimal) perfect duty in the clear case has already been established on moral grounds, whether or not it turns out that unclear cases make it impossible to distinguish in principle, to draw a bright line between the heart attack victim on my front porch and the masses dying of famine—that is, between what I have called the perfect duty of the good Samaritan and what we ordinarily consider to be imperfect duties of charity. The moral argument provided in chapter 2 is not undermined by the slippery slope objections considered here, in the following respect. Morally speaking, it cannot follow from a slippery slope argument that we have lesser obligations than the minimal obligation justified in the previous chapter, because the slippery slope argument does not deny any of the arguments made there. It simply points out that given the difficulty of drawing a principled distinction between the duty accepted and other duties that are much more extensive, we might be committing ourselves to much more exacting obligations than we initially acknowledged or intended. That is a pragmatic argument, not a moral one. In no way does it undermine the moral obligation in the clear case. It merely points out that we may be stuck with difficult decisions in unclear cases. Such an argument may be relevant to public policy decisions (which must consider practical consequences). For example, it could be relevant to deciding whether the moral obligation should be legally enforced.[4] But it is not a moral argument, and it does not undermine a moral obligation. Thus, the minimal moral obligation in the clear case has been established (by the arguments in chapter 2). What we must determine now is whether the moral duty might be greater, not whether it can disappear.

I think that the duty to rescue can be distinguished from other positive duties. What we need first, I suggest, is a clarification of the nature of the perfect positive duty: the clear case, the heart attack victim on my front porch. What exactly are its features and limits? I propose to set out here the nature of the duty as already intuitively accepted (by all of us—or anyway almost all of us) regarding the clear case. That may yield some clues about limits. I will also attempt to provide moral justification for defining the duty as I set it out here.

Having once defined the clear case, I will address the criticisms leveled by philosophers such as Rachels and Singer who argue for much broader duties than those ordinarily recognized. In order to assess their claims fairly, it is important first to have a clear understanding of the duty as it is ordinarily accepted. What are the properties of this duty? What properties must it have in order to be the duty I claim is already generally accepted as morally binding in the same way that negative duties are?

1. Preventing Serious Harm with Minimal Cost

One of the most obvious elements of the duty, as generally accepted, is that it is *minimal*. No one is obligated to incur great cost or risk to herself in order to help a random stranger. You are not, presumably, obligated to take the heart attack victim into your home and nurse him back to health, yourself, over a period of weeks or months or years. Your duty is simply to call an ambulance.

In fact, there is a social factor here which is coincidental but significant in most good Samaritan cases. It is a matter of fact that in most cases where a good Samaritan duty is at issue, there are social mechanisms set up to provide great assistance — indeed, life-saving assistance to emergency victims with very little expenditure of individual time or effort. We have socialized the burden of aiding victims. In order for these social mechanisms to work, however, some random individual who just happens to be on the scene has to initiate them. Someone has to activate the process. Someone has to call the ambulance. So, in fact, in a modern society the duty to aid very often amounts to no more than a duty to initiate the social mechanisms that are set up to prevent the harm. You need not prevent the harm yourself. This is simply an interesting social fact. It tells us nothing about the intrinsic properties of the duty, but it does explain why the duty may occur more often, as a perfect obligation, in a modern society than it once did. It is now more often possible than it once was to prevent great harm with minimal individual effort.

Even though initiating social mechanisms is what the duty often amounts to in modern times, we should not define the duty that narrowly. That would be a mistake. It would leave Bentham's famous drunk with his head in a puddle, and no one under a duty to turn his head.[5] It would also leave Murphy's pool lounger under no duty except to call some official (which would clearly be useless in the circumstances described).[6] It would surely be immoral to leave such victims to their fate merely because no social mechanisms are involved in saving them. Some emergencies require personal intervention beyond or other than notifying officials. Yet, they may still involve minimal effort, as both Bentham's and Murphy's cases demonstrate.

There are some subtleties encountered in determining what counts as minimal. What is minimal effort for one person may not be for another. What is risky for one is not for another. Individual limitations or incapacities are certainly relevant as excusing conditions. The interesting question is whether increased capacities generate increased obligation. This is much less clear. The general standard is based on average abilities. Still, a doctor may be held to a higher standard that reflects her special knowledge, while a karate expert is not held to an increased standard despite special abilities. Even though such nuances show that there are complexities to be worked out, they do not undermine the basic point.

The general point is simply that *as accepted* this duty is *very minimal*. It requires virtually no risk, and minimal cost or inconvenience to the agent. Judith Thomson captured this point trenchantly by correctly identifying the subject matter of this discussion as the "minimally decent Samaritan."[7] We are not really talking about goodness here.

That leads to a second property of the duty as generally accepted. The relevant circumstances involve *serious harm* or at least an immanent risk of such harm. Harm is notoriously difficult to define, but it should not cause problems here, since the relevant circumstances involve clear cases of very serious harm.

Suppose you are entering a taxi and someone rushes up to you and declares, "If I can't use this taxi, I will miss my plane!" You are not bound to relinquish your taxi, although it would be gracious of you to do so. Inconvenience to the "victim" is not sufficient to generate this duty. Nor, I think, is property loss or damage, although that is less clear. Part of this unclarity is due to the fact that any emergency that meets the conditions ultimately set out in this chapter will involve personal danger as well as property damage. Having a duty to report a fire is the most obvious example. The general reason for not including property loss or damage, as such, is that harm to property does not in itself incapacitate the victim in a way that necessitates external intervention by a random stranger. This, as I will show shortly, is another crucial condition of the duty. If a victim can act on his or her own behalf, then the intervention of a good Samaritan is not necessary. It does not follow, of course, that there is no imperfect duty of charity to help such victims, but only that it does not fit the description of the perfect duty discussed in the previous chapter. That duty was very minimal, and the harm involved was seriously incapacitating to the victim. So, generally speaking, property loss simply will not meet all the conditions required to generate the duty argued for in chapter 2.[8]

By and large, then, the subtleties of defining harm need not detain us; our subject matter involves no borderline cases. Death and serious bodily injury are uncontroversial (perhaps to the extent of being uninteresting) instances of harm.[9] These two elements—alleviating *serious harm* with *minimal cost or risk*—set the parameters of the duty as ordinarily accepted. Setting these boundaries make it clear that the duty is minimal in the same way that negative duties of justice are minimal: we cannot do less and claim to respect the basic value of persons.

It has been suggested, however, that evaluating the duty in these terms involves us in unprincipled cost/benefit analysis, when what we need is a clear treatment that distinguishes the duty of the good Samaritan in principle from all other positive duties.[10] If all we are doing here is eliminating serious harm at minimal cost, there are many opportunities to do that outside the context of emergency rescues. So why stop there? Why not proceed (as, for example, Singer does) all the way to a point of marginal utility? Cost/benefit analysis provides no particular distinction between the emergency context and any other. It is equally applicable to emergency rescue, economic policy, welfare reform, famine relief, or any number of other issues. Why should one duty be considered a perfect duty analogous to negative duties, while others are considered imperfect duties of charity? Cost/benefit analysis cannot tell us that.

The answer to this concern is that if the only principle involved in our analysis were one that directed us to balance serious harm against minimal cost and do what promoted the best consequences on balance, it would indeed be cost/benefit analysis, and that would not provide any principled distinction between the perfect duty of the good Samaritan and any other situation (such as famine relief) in which cost/benefit analysis could coherently be applied. But, first, the principle at issue here is not a principle of marginal utility. Second, even if it were, it is not the only principle that defines the duty.

Why is it not a principle of marginal utility? We are not directed by it to balance the harm against the cost. What justifies the duty is not the achievement of great benefit at little cost. On the contrary, great harm and minimal cost merely define the boundaries of the duty. The justification for each of these elements is different from cost/benefit analysis. It is not (simply) that acting according to this principle promotes utility (although, presumably, it does). Rather, it is that basic minimal respect for the intrinsic value of human personhood is not compatible with a total disregard for the well-being of others. Consequently, serious harm to others cannot be ignored with impunity.[11]

So, balancing the benefit against the harm is not the basic issue. If it were, I presume that it would require much more than the minimal duty discussed here. Instead, this duty provides the bottom-line, minimal moral requirement that is compatible with a basic respect for human life (which is why, as I have argued, it is appropriate to consider it a duty of justice).

Evaluating the application of the duty in particular circumstances may require contextual judgment and common sense. It is not susceptible to logical demonstration, but neither is it cost/benefit analysis. What these two elements do is provide information about the scope of the duty. They set its limits. They do not provide its justification. The requirements of justice as respect for persons does that.

2. Being Selected by Circumstances

The central and defining feature of the duty to aid is that an individual must be directly confronted by or uniquely positioned to address a clear, immediate need that cannot be addressed in any other way. The potential rescuer is selected by the circumstances, and thrown into a position of control over the emergency by the incapacity of the victim and the absence of any other mechanism or resource to provide relief. This is a default duty, a duty of necessity. It is never activated unless rescue is necessary, and no other means of rescue are available. As accepted, I believe these clearly are the features of the duty. As justified, I have already shown why justice requires nothing less. This is the minimum, but is it the maximum? And if so, why should it be so limited?

For one thing, if the victim is not incapacitated, then the victim is responsible for herself. Respect for autonomy requires it to be so. We are all responsible for our own lives, unless and until special circumstances incapacitate us. Only then is a rescuer required to intervene. Thus, the duty of the good Samaritan does not arise unless the victim is threatened by serious harm that is somehow outside her control but clearly within the control of the potential rescuer. This can include a simple incident such as calling out a warning to someone who does not perceive a clear danger. Whether that failure of perception is due to a particular handicap or to negligence or chance, it would in any case put the victim out of control over her own safety. Thus, intervention—at least in the form of a warning—is appropriate. If the victim were fully aware of the circumstances, and was basically in control of them, it would not be appropriate, much less required, to intervene. Thus, no duty arises unless the victim is incapacitated.

In addition, if any other social or individual arrangement were available to deal with a victim in distress, again, the good Samaritan duty would not arise. Specifically, if anyone were available to help who had a special positive duty to the victim (such as a relative) or a duty to deal with such emergencies (such as a lifeguard), any such special positive duty would eliminate the necessity for the intervention of a stranger. Suppose, for example, that a mother and child were walking near you in the park, and the child suddenly darted away and fell into the fish pond. It is not your duty to save the child, but the mother's, unless some special circumstance makes you uniquely positioned to save the child when the mother could not do so. We (wisely) prearrange most of our responsibilities in the form of special positive duties based on natural or contractual relations. It is both more equitable and more efficient to handle affirmative obligations in that way. So the duty of a random stranger should not arise unless the circumstances are such that arrangements of special positive duty are not possible to handle it.[12]

Similarly, many of our greatest needs have been socialized. We have hospitals and shelters, insurance plans and pensions, fire departments and police to address the needs we would be hard pressed to handle alone. Such pooling arrangements provide greater security, efficiency, and equity of distribution than we could possibly hope for without them. So, again, if social mechanisms are available to address needs and burdens, they create duties that obviate the necessity for duties among strangers. If you drive past an auto accident that is being attended to by police or rescue workers, your duty is to get out of the way, and not to intervene. Insofar as emergencies can be handled by prearranged social mechanisms, they eliminate any duty on the part of random strangers.

Thus, the duty of the good Samaritan is a default duty. It picks up only those emergencies that fall between the cracks of any prearrangement that it is possible to make. This limitation is justified because it accords with the values of equity, efficiency, and freedom, all of which are promoted by prearranging affirmative obligations rather than leaving them to chance.

It follows that the duty to rescue is fundamentally *random* and *individual*. What properties must this random individual have? The general knowledge that people are in trouble somewhere is clearly not sufficient to create an obligation to aid within this framework. One must be directly confronted by an emergency situation. One must be in a unique position to supply a crucial immediate need. But what counts as being directly confronted or uniquely positioned to aid? At a minimum, the agent must be in a position to be aware of the problem, identify it as a problem, and act on it. That would require both knowledge and control over the situation.[13]

The duty may not require physical confrontation. The bystanders who watched from upper-story windows as Kitty Genovese was slowly murdered provoked widespread condemnation in that none of them called the police. The same has been true of crimes witnessed on closed-circuit television, but not reported. It appears that such distancing mechanisms reduce the likelihood that an agent will act, but they do not remove the duty to act. That is, people are still condemned for not acting in such circumstances. Why? All the witnesses in the Genovese case knew that a serious harm beyond the control of the victim was occurring, all had control over calling the police, and none had sufficient reason to think that anyone else would correct the situation. The Genovese case is a clear case in the sense that all the elements are there: knowledge of serious harm, control over addressing the harm, and necessity for individual intervention. A person's life requires at least a phone call. Nothing less is enough.

But what about something more? Suppose a person merely has reason to suspect that there *may* be a problem. Suppose you are on a trip that takes you near a city that you know has recently been flooded. Chances are good that someone may need help, perhaps even desperately need help. But you do not actually see anyone in trouble. Are you obligated to seek it out? Are you obligated to exit the highway and patrol the city streets looking for someone in trouble? Should you check people's homes and yards as well? No such obligation is generally accepted, nor could one be justified. Since checking out every suspicious situation would be an unreasonable restriction on the personal freedom of the agent, and could result in unwanted inquiry in many cases—that is, it could promote serious invasions of privacy—it makes sense that we do not consider it a duty for random individuals to investigate possible problems.

A side effect of this limit, however, is that the unclarity of some situations could result in real emergencies not being corrected, because they are not identified. The moral question is whether a social policy (or moral standard) of minimal or maximal intervention is better, all things considered. The answer should not be hard to formulate. Since it seems reasonable to suppose that social arrangements could handle such problems (if and when they should be handled) much better than random strangers, and given the unacceptable risk of bad side effects (invasion of privacy, restriction of freedom, accidents) coupled with the availability of better social alternatives, no such individual duty could rationally be justified. There is clearly no accepted individual duty for random strangers to correct general social problems, or to seek out possible problems that might exist hidden from public view. The duty of the good Samaritan relates only to problems that confront the agent with a clear, immediate unaddressed need over which he has control. This is what distinguishes the duty from all other positive duties. It is *a duty that arises when and only when circumstances select an agent as uniquely in control of addressing an emergency that cannot be handled by the victim or by prearranged social mechanisms.* These features define the duty.

3. Individual Duties and Multiple Parties

Although the duty of the good Samaritan is now well defined and distinguished from other positive duties, there are features that require further elaboration and defense. The duty is necessarily individual for all the reasons given in the previous section. It is individual in two respects. First, it is individual in the sense that an individual has it. It is not, and cannot be, a social or collective duty. Indeed, it is precisely concerned only with those special circumstances that cannot be handled by prearrangement, whether private or public. (There may be associated social duties, such as duties to provide social mechanisms for correcting emergencies, but that is clearly a separate issue and involves a different sort of duty.) The duty I am concerned with here is essentially individual in that it requires individual rather than social action.

Second, it is basically owed to an individual. Of course, an emergency may involve more than one person. Several people might be injured in an auto accident, for example, all of whom will be helped by the same phone call. This situation still falls within the scope of the individual duty. These two features have been the source of enormous confusion and controversy, so I will deal with each of them at some length. The problems arise in unclear cases that involve multiple parties. I will consider first the problem of multiple witnesses or potential rescuers.

Multiple Witnesses and Defeasibility

I have argued here that the duty to rescue is distinguishable from all other general duties to aid in that the circumstances uniquely specify a particular agent or witness as in a special position to supply aid that is needed immediately and is not addressable by prearrangement. It should also be recognized that the duty is defeasible in the sense that if one person fills the need it rebuts the duty of all others. But then how (if at all) is the duty of one witness affected by the presence of others? Is a person less obligated to rescue when others are equally in a position to help? Is the presence of others a relevant excusing condition?

This question refers to one of the most problematic features of the duty to aid in emergencies. In terms of what is commonly accepted, there is a great deal of confusion about this factor. Two points, however, are clear. First, it is clear that if one person acts it rebuts the duty of everyone else. This is perfectly sensible, since the action of one person eliminates the condition of immediate need as to all others.

Second, if no person acts, all who were present are equally condemned for not acting (as was demonstrated, for example, by the general outcry against the thirty-eight people who did not help Kitty Genovese). This shows that although the duty is defeasible, it is still a full-blown duty that holds against everyone who could have helped, until someone helps, and if no one helps.

But is the duty weakened by the defeasibility condition? Are people considered less blameworthy for not rescuing a victim in clear peril if others could have rescued him just as easily? I believe this issue is quite unsettled, for the most part because people confuse (illegitimate) excuses with (legitimate) excusing conditions. It may be common for people to excuse their own shortcomings by pointing out that others have done as badly, but no one who thinks about it accepts that as a legitimate excuse. "Sure, I stole a few supplies from the office, but everybody does it." "I know I broke my promise to help with the meeting, but people break promises to me all the time." No one really accepts such excuses as legitimate excusing conditions, let alone as justifications for wrongdoing.

But it may be argued that the duty to aid in emergencies is a different case, or at least a special case in which the appeal to "everybody else" makes more sense, hence carries more weight than usual. It is not that one is excused in these cases because everyone else is just as bad (or so the argument goes) but because it is reasonable to think that someone else will be better. That is, if there are many other people around, it is more reasonable to assume that someone else will fulfill the duty. The victim does not necessarily need *me*; he just needs someone or other. So if I leave while others are still on the scene, I have not eliminated the victim's only chance for rescue. Presumably, the last person to leave does that. Thus, in terms of the criteria just laid out, there is not a clear, immediate need for *my* help, but only for someone's help. I am not uniquely needed if others are available, so the uniqueness condition is not fulfilled. Something is wrong with this line of reasoning, but what is it?

Let us consider a hit-and-run case to see if it provides clarification. Bad Sam 1 is sprinting to an appointment, already late, when he sees a pedestrian hit and left lying in an empty side street. He pauses momentarily, looking around. No one is in sight; the injured man does not move. Nevertheless, Bad Sam 1 sprints on, telling himself that someone will surely come along, or perhaps the victim is just stunned, who knows?

What is his infraction? He is not malicious. In fact he is not even (necessarily) indifferent.[14] Although he is a far cry from a "good neighbor," he hopes someone else will help the victim, or that things will turn out all right somehow. But he is not willing to inconvenience himself to correct the situation, so he makes up excuses for himself. That the excuses are illegitimate is obvious in his case.

There is no reason to assume, without investigation, that someone hit by a car and lying still in the street may not be seriously injured after all. The probability of serious injury is too high to allow such an assumption. It is also unreasonable to assume that someone may come along, if no one is in sight. That is simply blind hope based on no evidence. To be realistic, Bad Sam must acknowledge that aid might be needed immediately, and that no one else may provide aid immediately. Given that all the conditions set out earlier are met in this case, Bad Sam is guilty of gross irresponsibility (if not indifference) in disregarding the victim's right to minimal emergency aid and his own duty to provide it under the circumstances. The infraction is rather like recklessness or negligence in that it is taking an unreasonable risk in disregard of serious harm to someone else.[15]

The case of Bad Sam 2 is just like that of Bad Sam 1, except that at least one other person is also present. Is Bad Sam 2 less blameworthy? It would seem that her assumption that someone else may help is not as unreasonable, since at least someone is there who *could* help. But Bad Sam 2 has no way of knowing whether the other stranger *will* help. The other stranger may be hurrying to an appointment just as Sam 2 is. (The other stranger could be Sam 1, who just wasn't observant enough to see Sam 2.) That being the case, the assumption is still unreasonable. Given the seriousness of the stakes, it is unreasonable for Sam 2 to leave without very good evidence that the duty will be fulfilled. So Sam 2 still has insufficient evidence for a decision to leave.

Suppose five people are present. If there is no communication among these people, the same argument applies. Suppose there are twenty-five people. The same argument still applies, although admittedly it now seems grossly unintuitive. Yet, without communication no individual has any way of knowing whether any other individual will act. It may be natural to assume that the more people there are present, the more likely it is that someone will help the victim. That is what the thirty-eight people who watched Kitty Genovese be murdered all assumed. Some statistical and psychological studies have indicated that the more people are present in an emergency, the higher the probability is that the assumption will be made that someone else will act. That assumption counteracts the probability that someone *will* act, leaving the probability of aid roughly the same or worse as the number of witnesses increases.[16] The results cited in these studies may seem counterintuitive, but that fact itself supports rather than undermines the statistical evidence. In any case, I believe that it makes one point clear.

If it was unreasonable for Sam 1 to leave the scene of the crisis because he had insufficient evidence that someone else would come along to correct it, then the same is true even if there are other people around. This point is supported by the fact that our common intuitions about what would be reasonable to assume as evidence are proven wrong by statistical studies. Given the seriousness of the stakes — life itself or severe injury — it is not reasonable to assume someone else will take responsibility unless you see someone do it. Short of that, you still have insufficient evidence for a decision not to aid, and more particularly for a decision to leave before aid is provided. There are both pragmatic and moral grounds for this point.

Practically speaking, if the level of evidence required were not "seeing the duty filled," everyone would be entitled to make the same assumption that it *might* be filled by someone and leave without filling it. There are numerous instances of just such cases occurring in fact. That is what the statistical studies reflect. Thus, pragmatic considerations require seeing the duty filled as the level of evidence required to rebut one's own duty.

Morally speaking, Sam 2 is under a duty to aid as soon as she recognizes that the emergency requires intervention. If five people all stand around for ten minutes, waiting to see who will make the first move, all five are violating the duty. This is not to say that one violates the duty if one does not have instantaneous reactions. People react to emergencies in different ways, and some are more clearheaded than others. But waiting for someone else to act itself violates the duty. Leaving the scene quickly so that someone else will be left with the problem violates the duty in the same way. Both actions take unreasonable risks with the victim's life. Both shirk responsibility on the blind hope that someone else will assume it. So these factors should be viewed as illegitimate excuses, not excusing conditions. Sam 2 violates the duty even if others are around, because her assumption that they will take care of it is irresponsible unless she sees someone do it.

Once one person assumes the obligation, everyone else is absolved from it, because there is then no more need. But until someone assumes the responsibility, everyone is under the same duty. If no one corrects the situation, all are equally blameworthy. The blame is not divided among them, so that each is, say, one-fifth to blame. It may be natural for people to feel less blameworthy or to feel that responsibility is diffused among many people. It may also be natural to wait to see if

anyone else takes the initiative. Such factors explain why the duty is so often violated, but they do not justify not meeting it. That is, the mere presence of others
does not rebut the duty, does not constitute a reasonable excusing condition.

The only point I shall make regarding the problem of violation is that the mere
fact that the duty is regularly violated does not show either that it is not morally required or that it is not generally accepted. The duty not to lie is almost universally
recognized as a moral prohibition. Yet it is regularly violated. Furthermore, it is regularly violated by people who accept it as a general prohibition. It does not follow
that it is not a duty, that it is not morally justifiable, or even that it is not generally
accepted. So the problem of moral failure is not exclusive to the duty to rescue.

Still, it might be asked, in terms of my criteria, in what sense are multiple witnesses uniquely positioned to help? If twenty people are on the scene, and all have
the same duty, then none, surely, is uniquely needed, or so it will undoubtedly be
argued. But I believe, on the contrary, that they are all uniquely positioned to help
as opposed to all the rest of society or the world at large. That is, even if there are
several people present, they are in a unique position to exercise control over a serious harm that cannot be handled by prearrangement, whether public or private.
There is no way such emergencies can be handled unless one of them handles it.
The circumstances have selected them all individually. That is why all witnesses
must respond to the situation as though each were the only one there. None can
rely on the assumption that others will act, precisely because no prearrangements
are possible. No delegation of duty is permitted by the circumstances. If it were, it
could be handled by other means.

This is why the presence of multiple witnesses does not vitiate the uniqueness
condition. Even if twenty people are selected by the circumstances to exercise control over a dire emergency, this still is not comparable to or reducible to any other
positive duties, which can be handled by prearrangement—by social mechanisms,
by special relations, by contract or consent. Unlike all other human needs, the special need discussed here can only be filled by a random stranger, and that makes
each witness uniquely positioned to assist, even if there happen to be twenty instead
of only one. It is necessarily individual, not social. Thus the presence of multiple
witnesses does not affect the duty at all. The duty is defeasible only if someone else
fills it in fact.

Multiple Victims and the Rights Question

While the defeasibility problem may be the most-discussed line-drawing issue associated with the duty of the good Samaritan, the question of victims' rights is the
most theoretically difficult. The toughest challenge seems to arise in cases involving multiple victims. Suppose three or four people capsize a boat, and all need
help. A single agent who is in a position to help has a duty merely to do what she
can. She does not have a duty to save all of them if she cannot do so without risk to
herself. Such a situation does not eliminate the duty, but it does point in the direction of some problematic features in terms of victims' rights, or at least features that
are thought to be problematic.

Some philosophers have argued that such situations undercut the idea that any victims could have a right to such aid from a stranger, and therefore show that the duty is not a perfect duty.[17] It may indeed, do precisely that in some circumstances, but the question is, Which circumstances, and why, and what follows for a general account of the duty? It certainly does not obviously follow, for example, that if the duty is not a perfect duty in unclear cases that it cannot be a perfect duty in clear cases either. Additional argument would surely be needed to make any inference in that direction. In any event, some paradoxical cases have been discussed with conflicting results in the literature.

Joel Feinberg has carefully analyzed this problem in a way that seems to me illuminating, so I will briefly review his position here.[18] He responds to the following expansion of Murphy's case.[19] Suppose, it is asked, that you are relaxing by a swimming pool when suddenly you see, not one, but two babies floundering at opposite ends of the pool. You can easily save one, it is hypothesized, but it is impossible for you to save both. It must follow that both babies cannot have a right to be saved by you, since it is impossible for you to save both of them. And since there is no distinguishing characteristic between the babies (from the point of view of a stranger with no special relationship to either), it makes no sense for one but not the other to have a right to be saved. It follows that neither one of them has a right to be saved. Therefore, the duty of the good Samaritan must be an imperfect duty that generates no correlative right on behalf of any victim. That means that even if the bad Samaritan makes no effort to save either baby, no rights have been violated.

Feinberg disagrees with the final conclusion. It cannot be, he reasons, that if there is one baby that can easily be saved, it has a right to be rescued; but if there is one that can easily be saved and one that cannot be saved, suddenly neither one has any right at all. That is just too paradoxical, he suggests, so it must be that at least one victim has a right that is violated in such a case. Nevertheless, it is no easy matter to explain the nature and foundation of such a right. Feinberg considers three possible views.

1. It may be that each (or every) victim has a right that the rescuer save as many as she can (without risk to herself, of course). If the potential rescuer makes no effort at all, the rights of all the victims are equally violated. The oddity of this view is that if the pool lounger rescues one baby, she will have met the right of the other (or fulfilled her duty to the other). Such a consequence seems less than ideal.

2. It may be that there is no right to a rescue attempt as such, but rather a right to equal consideration in such cases. This approach makes the right analogous to a distributive justice claim, and it would avoid the oddity of the first approach. But the second view has serious problems of its own. For one thing, it is not clear that equal consideration is an appropriate criterion here. So long as you save one of the babies (and cannot in any case save the other), it may not matter how you select which one to save. More important, if the bad Samaritan does nothing whatever, he treats both victims equally. That makes it appear that the rights of the victims are met by doing nothing whatever for any of them, but violated if one victim is saved for the "wrong" reason. But that consequence is even more paradoxical than the one with which we started.

3. It could be argued that only one baby actually had a right (or was wronged by the bad Samaritan who did nothing), namely, the one baby that would have

been saved if the bad Samaritan had made a reasonable effort. Under the circumstances, however, it is impossible to tell which one that would have been (since the bad Samaritan made no effort at all). This approach avoids the defects of both the other approaches, but it raises a new and different problem that may be even worse. All moral properties are commonly thought to have a characteristic called supervenience: that is, moral properties apply across the board unless there is some relevant factor that explains any difference in application.[20] Application cannot simply be random or arbitrary. It may not be subject to logical demonstration, but it should be subject to rational explanation of some sort. This characteristic is generally taken to be rather basic to any moral consideration. The big problem with option 3 is that by hypothesis there is no moral difference between the two babies. So this approach seems to violate the requirement of supervenience, a very serious deficiency.

Recognizing that each possible view has its drawbacks, Feinberg decides (with some apparent reservations) that the first is the best of the three, since its deficiencies are the least telling. I think that he is right, indeed, clearly right about all this. In fact, I think that his position deserves more confidence than he seems to express (although, of course, caution is a virtue in such sticky matters as victims' rights in paradoxical cases). Perhaps my explanation will help to bolster Feinberg's position and address his concerns.

First, it seems to me that we need to emphasize a little more strongly what the victim's right is a right to. It is not (as Feinberg and everyone else recognizes in passing) a right to be saved as such, but is a right to a reasonable effort. That is also true as applied to special positive duties (which unquestionably are perfect duties). If, for example, I am swimming in a pool with a lifeguard looking on, I have a right to the diligent and responsible effort of the lifeguard to watch over my safety (as well as everyone else's) and to respond professionally and conscientiously in an emergency. But I do not, and cannot, have a right to be saved as such. I cannot have that right, because saving requires not only a reasonable effort but a successful attempt, and success is something that cannot be guaranteed. Having a right to success would be like having a right to win. No one can have a right to win (a race, a contest, or whatever); one can have only a right to a fair chance. Similar considerations apply to a right to be rescued. No one actually has a right to be rescued; one can have only a right to a reasonable and conscientious effort on the part of an available rescuer. All this is true whether one victim is involved, or ten, or thirty.

In some circumstances (such as the original case of Murphy's pool lounger, for example), the task required is so simple that we should reasonably be able to expect the success rate to be very high, almost one hundred percent. But even in the clearest case possible (as Murphy's original case is constructed to be), one can imagine a freak accident that could make everything come out wrong. (Suppose, for example, that the pool lounger grabs the baby by its swimming trunks—a possibility envisioned in the original case—only to discover that the trunks are too large. The baby slips out of them and falls back in the water out of reach. The pool lounger cannot swim, and no one else manages to get there in time, so once again the baby is lost. Stranger things have happened.) The point is that success can never be guaranteed one hundred percent. Consequently, no one actually has a right to be rescued, strictly speaking, although they do have a right to a reasonable effort, if someone is available to make such an effort. The "right to be rescued" is just shorthand for all that, and everyone knows it.

Now, let's apply this analysis to the "two baby case" as a preliminary representative of any case involving multiple victims. What both babies have is a right to a reasonable effort on the part of any available witness to save them, if it is possible to do so without serious cost or risk to the rescuer. In most cases there is no way to know in advance how many could be saved (except for the general point that the more the rescuer is outnumbered by victims, the clearer it will be that all cannot be saved). So what does the two baby case require specifically? It seems rather obvious that the rescuer is required to save one victim as quickly as possible and then try to save the other. If it turns out to be too late (as we philosophers get to decide, by hypothesis, that it will) then the second child's right has not been violated, because the rescuer is already engaged in a reasonable effort to save them both.

It might be complained that this is small comfort to the child who does not get saved, and consequently that the second victim's right is not worth much. Indeed, it is hardly distinguishable from no right at all, and its correlative duty is indistinguishable from other imperfect duties. This kind of complaint is the basis for Feinberg's perplexity at the appearance that somehow by fulfilling the right of the first victim we have met our duty to the second. This is a valid worry, but I think that it is exacerbated by the philosophical practice of constructing hypothetical cases that enable us to assume a God's-eye view that is impossible for real people in real circumstances. We need to be always aware that we have privileges in philosophy that people do not have in real life, for example, the ability to foretell the future in Murphy's case. Don't get me wrong. I like hypotheticals as much as the next guy, in part because I love fiction. But I harbor no illusions about the drawbacks of either simply because I am enamored by the benefits of both. We philosophers provide ourselves with a level of certainty through the use of hypotheticals that may encourage us to draw conclusions that are entirely unwarranted.

Think about how our swimming pool saga would actually play out in real life. Let's suppose that you are out walking early one Sunday morning when you hear something, a cry, perhaps. From the sidewalk you can see someone flailing about in a backyard swimming pool. Fearing trouble, you rush to the pool and discover that there are two victims, perhaps an old woman and a baby apparently drowning at either end of the pool. (We have already admitted that strange things do sometimes really happen, so what if it really did happen? It is not beyond the pale of impossibility.) What would you do? More important, what *should* you do? (This isn't a hard question, is it?) You would and you should, of course, run as fast as you can to the closest victim (or if they are equally distant, to either one—just don't take up time deciding) and pull her out (assuming that you can reach her or you can swim, or whatever is necessary). I presume that you would also be calling for help at the same time (I certainly would be), but let's suppose that no one seems to be around or at least no one hears you or shows up to help, and by the time you do all this, you can see the baby at the other end of the pool sinking under water, having ceased to struggle. Would you—or should you—then say, "Oh, well. No sense making any effort for *that* one." Of course not! You would still run or swim or somehow get to the other end of the pool as fast as you could and try to rescue the other victim, even if you were afraid, terrified, perhaps virtually certain that it was too late. After all, how much time are we talking about here, two minutes? Five minutes? Emergencies happen fast. That is what makes them urgent. If you didn't even try to help that second victim, wouldn't you still be blameworthy if you thought that there was any chance at all that you might be able to save her? And isn't that just the same as if there were only one victim?

The one baby case and the two baby case would not in fact be very different in real life. You had better try to save both victims. You had better take that extra two minutes to run to the other end of the pool and fish out the second one, even if your heart is sinking while you do it. And that is precisely what you would do, or what any ordinary and reasonable person would do, because after all someone's life is at stake. So five minutes (or ten or twenty minutes) of your time is not too much to sacrifice for that. The important point is that you cannot know before the fact that it will be in vain. So you must try. As long as you try, you have violated no one's right to a reasonable effort. No one can have a right to more than that in fact. And whether you can succeed, you do not get to know until later—after it's all over.

Of course, we philosophers can always construct a case in which *we* get to *know*, by hypothesis, that it is impossible for you to save both victims. But in real life, either you know for a fact that you cannot save (or more generally, that there is nothing you can do to help) the victim, or you don't know.

If you know for a fact, or in any case you clearly and reasonably believe without a doubt that you cannot do anything for the victim, then it is already too late; you are not a potential rescuer; and the duty does not arise. Nor does the victim have any right against you. You are not witnessing an emergency, but a tragedy that has already been completed. If you had been there five minutes earlier, perhaps things would have been different. But as it stands (presumably through no fault of your own), you were not on the scene when you needed to be in order to have that duty. That's it. The circumstances did not select you.

On the other hand, if you are confronted by a situation in which you do not know for certain whether you might be able to save the victim, then it is worth a reasonable effort to find out. It is worth a try. That is exactly the duty you have to a single victim or two victims or four, just as long as it is not reasonable for you to believe that there is absolutely nothing you can do (at least without endangering yourself). Thus, it is not impossibility as such that is the limiting condition, but knowledge of impossibility. As long as that condition is not met, you have a duty to make a reasonable effort. And that is the only right that all the victims have against you. If you do nothing, then you have violated the rights of all to a reasonable effort, which it is your perfect duty to perform. On my view, then, the two baby case poses no serious problems at all. It is indistinguishable from the one baby case. The potential rescuer has a perfect duty to make a reasonable effort to save both babies, and both babies have a right to that reasonable effort.

Of course, as philosophers, we can always throw in another baby, if you will pardon the pun. If two babies are not enough, how about three, or five, or ten? At some point it will not be reasonable for you to believe that you can save all of them (or even do anything for all of them). At some point you will know that there is nothing more you can do. At that point (wherever it is) the case is certainly changed from a clear case to an unclear case. And at that point, it will surely be asked, hasn't the perfect duty been converted to an imperfect duty? And if the perfect duty simply turns into an imperfect duty at some unspecified point, doesn't that introduce the problem of the slippery slope that throws a cloud of uncertainty over the victim's rights in the first place?

My answer to all those questions is no. I don't think so. Here is why. It is true that the more victims you add to any case, the more *likely* it will be that the required task will be beyond the capacity of a single rescuer. But nothing in particular about the intrinsic nature of the duty (or its correlative right) follows from that. The duty is not tied in any necessary way to a question of numbers.

Suppose, for example, that a driver on a lonely road witnesses a calamity involving twenty-five people in a bus accident that no one else sees. The driver has a car phone. Every single victim has a right that he use his car phone to call for help. If he doesn't bother to do it, he has violated all their rights. He has a perfect duty to every one of them that can be filled with a single action. The numbers don't matter. What matters is whether there is some action within his control that addresses the harm.

The relevance of numbers simply goes to assessing the implications of exerting a reasonable effort in any particular case. It never undermines the duty to do so. But it looks like it does. The reason it looks like sheer numbers convert the perfect duty into an imperfect duty (thereby eliminating the victims' rights) is that the effect of exerting a reasonable effort to save, let's say, five people is likely to be rather different (namely, less effective) than a reasonable effort to save one. Furthermore, the way in which this often works is that the rescuer must select which victim will be helped first, which will be second, and so forth. That looks just like an imperfect duty in which a donor must select among many worthy recipients, none of whom can have a right to her donation. It looks the same, but it is not the same. Not ever.

Here is the difference. Imperfect duties are basically interchangeable with one another. They stand on more or less the same footing, and rely on the values and preferences of each potential contributor. Potential recipients may offer arguments to a potential donor to support one cause rather than another, but in the last analysis whatever the individual donor decides is acceptable. Whatever the decision, no one is entitled to complain. There is a sense in which the donor cannot be wrong, so long as she does her share in general. The only way she can be criticized is by evaluating her overall record. If she doesn't do enough on the whole, she can be criticized as ungenerous. How much she does can be evaluated, but what she does cannot be. Numerous causes exist that require contribution to continuing efforts to supply crucial needs or desired services. Individuals must decide for themselves how they will order their priorities for such giving. Consequently, the duty is an imperfect duty, and no one has a right to a particular donation from any particular party; hence, the idea that they are charitable causes, at least as applied to a random stranger.

The duty to rescue is clearly not imperfect in that sense. That is, it is not interchangeable with any other causes or recipients, and this is true whether multiple victims are involved or only one. That means that it is not an imperfect duty, but here is what makes it look like it is.

If multiple victims are involved in a single emergency, all are entitled to a reasonable effort on the part of an available rescuer to provide assistance that is within his control. They cannot have a right to more than a reasonable effort, or to anything beyond the rescuer's control. But if there are multiple victims, it may not be clear in advance what is within the control of the rescuer, or whether a reasonable effort on his part will be sufficient to save any particular one of them. Consequently, what is being determined within the context of that particular emergency is what is within the control of the rescuer and therefore what the implications of a reasonable effort turn out to be as applied to each individual victim. This factor, however, does not make the situation different in kind from the case of a single victim. For example, a rescuer might see someone drowning in the distance, try to get to him, and be unable to get to him in time. The victim's right to a reasonable effort would not have been violated in such a case. As long as the rescuer attempted to address the emergency, the victim's rights were met. That means that the duty "to rescue" in a multiple victim case is still a perfect duty owed to all victims involved to make a reasonable effort to assist them.

None of this analysis fits the paradigm of imperfect duties, however. If the duty to rescue were an imperfect duty, no one would have any right to any effort at all. It would be up to the potential rescuer to determine whether she had given enough on other occasions or intended to do so tomorrow. The duty would be interchangeable with other imperfect duties, and it would not be up to any of us to second-guess the donor over her choice of worthy causes. If she wants to support the symphony orchestra instead of saving someone who is dying in front of her, that should be quite all right with us.

But it isn't. And it shouldn't be. The duty of emergency assistance is not imperfect in that sense, because it is not imperfect at all. It is not interchangeable with other causes. The circumstances select a particular person as the only potential solution to a crisis. Such situations are not amenable to collective contribution over time, so they cannot be interchangeable with other charitable causes, no matter how worthy. Murphy's pool lounger cannot absolve himself of his obligation to make a reasonable effort to save the victim (or victims) who are drowning right in front of him by pointing out that he just gave a large sum to famine relief ten minutes ago, and therefore has contributed to saving numerous lives already. The duty of the good Samaritan is not generalizable or transferable in that way. Unlike all charitable causes, this need can only be met by the particular individual on the scene at the moment. Furthermore, the circumstances are so serious that ignoring them is not compatible with a basic respect for human worth. The requirements of justice that ordinarily compel only refraining from causing harm, in these special circumstances demand at least a minimal effort to intervene on behalf of the victim. Consequently, emergency victims have a right to a reasonable effort that is not vitiated by multiple victims, multiple rescuers, or prior giving to other causes.

4. Emergencies, Disasters, and Chronic Conditions

I have relied heavily in this analysis on the significance of special circumstances that directly confront or uniquely position some witness to exercise control over a clear, immediate, unaddressed need. It is not the victim who picks out the rescuer or the rescuer who picks out the victim, but the circumstances that pick out both and oblige the potential rescuer to act on behalf of the victim. These unique circumstances create a special relationship between the victim and the potential rescuer, thereby generating a hybrid form of a special/general positive duty that is limited both by circumstances and by the foundations of justice that ordinarily supply a rationale for only negative duties. It is time to clarify the features of the special circumstances that generate this obligation.

I think the best way to construe the notion of clear, immediate, unaddressed need as it relates to the duty of the good Samaritan is in terms of emergency. The *Oxford English Dictionary* defines *emergency* as "a state of affairs unexpectedly arising and urgently demanding immediate action." So an emergency, first, is something that turns up unexpectedly. It cannot be planned for; consequently, it cannot be socialized or even reliably delegated. It must be dealt with on the spot and on its own terms.

Second, it is urgent. It cannot be put off. It demands immediate attention to avoid dire consequences. Thus, it is an acute, specifiable event, which is short-term, in the sense that it must be acted on with dispatch or it will get worse, perhaps so much worse that if put off it cannot be corrected. These are the defining features of emergencies in general.

In addition to these general features we must add a third (noted earlier): The kind of emergency that generates a duty to rescue is so severe that it incapacitates its victim. It is not self-correcting; there is no reason to think that the victim can correct it; it requires intervention. In some cases it must be confronted immediately or it will be too late for anyone to correct it.

Finally, this emergency must be witnessed by someone who can do something about correcting the situation. There must be some act that is within the control of a witness that will in some way address the peril without endangering or overburdening the witness. These are the circumstances that generate a duty to rescue. The term 'emergency' would commonly be used to describe them.

The idea of an emergency as used here should be contrasted with that of a chronic condition. A condition is chronic if it continues or recurs over time. It may be mild or severe, but either way it is long-term or ongoing. Chronic conditions can be identified, studied, evaluated, and addressed by social action, private arrangement, or individual planning. Indeed, chronic conditions require continuing treatment over time. There are a great many very serious but generally chronic conditions that constitute social or personal problems. Poverty, disease, malnutrition, crime, and unemployment are common examples. Thus, a chronic condition may be devastating and debilitating, but still (unfortunately, perhaps) be "ignorable" in the sense that victims are able to live with it, deal with it, and, sometimes, correct it themselves.

An emergency, in contrast, is not ignorable in this sense. It stops the functioning of the victim in a way that necessitates outside intervention. Thus, an emergency in this context constitutes a specific demonstration of urgent, compelling, immediate need as opposed to long-term general need. This definition conforms to the idea of the duty being one of individual necessity and contrasts rather clearly with the ideas of chronic conditions or general hardship.

The distinction just drawn may not be quite as sharp as one might wish, however, since there are what could be called chronic emergencies. Certainly some chronic conditions may turn into emergencies or make some people more susceptible to emergency conditions than they otherwise would be. Victims of famine, natural catastrophes, and war are in a state of chronic emergency. Let us call these chronic emergencies disasters. In order to make clear the circumstances in which the duty to rescue applies, disasters must be distinguishable from ordinary emergencies. To analyze this distinction, let's consider a case.

Suppose you are presented with a televised appeal for little Juan in Honduras. Juan will soon die of malnutrition unless you help, the ad says. Certainly, Juan is a human being whose intrinsic worth is the same as that of any other person. The liberal individualist principle of respecting the value of every human being applies here just as it does in the case of the drowning baby or any other case. Furthermore, there is a sense in which you are being confronted with a specific case of clear need, and there may indeed be a duty of some sort to help out. But the conditions of this situation do not fit the duty to rescue as defined here in several respects.

First, we need to understand whether in fact this is an emergency of the sort we have defined. If this is not a case of impending death, but rather continuing hardship, it is a chronic condition and not an emergency. Making this evaluation is rather like deciding whether we believe the specifics of the ad. Juan, after all, is a representative of many children who are hungry and malnourished. The important point of the ad is not Juan's particular future, but the plight of hungry children around the world. We would not, I think, consider it false advertising if we discovered that Juan himself had been adopted and was no longer hungry. That information would be irrelevant because the ad is not really about Juan but is about a worldwide problem that calls for continuing, collective support. If that is the correct interpretation of the ad, it is clear that the focus is a chronic condition and not an emergency of the sort I have been discussing.[21] Consequently, there may be a duty to help out, but if so, it is not the duty to rescue. Why is that?

First, this is not really an individual, discrete event, in the relevant sense described earlier. It is really one piece of a general problem that requires collective action. You are not in a unique position to help. Your relation to Juan is no different from that of any potential donor the world over. It is not *your* help that is needed, but the help of someone, or more accurately, everyone. And that help is needed not specifically for Juan but for all the hungry children that his case represents. Thus, little Juan, while a heartbreaking case, stands in the same relation to you as do the potential recipients of all charities that provide serious or crucial services for mankind and that cannot function without continuing, collective support. Medical research for cancer or heart disease, rescue efforts for refugees, relief for the aged and destitute, to mention only a few worthy causes, can make the same claim on you as that made on behalf of little Juan. And we could construct the description in the same way as well. That is, we could pick out a particular instantiation of the general problem and present that piece of the problem in order to make it more real so that people can identify with it more readily. These kinds of cases fit the traditional notion of charitable duties. We all, presumably, should do our part with regard to them, but no individual can even contribute to all those in need, let alone *fill* such needs. So each donor must decide for himself as an individual matter how he will do his share.

There is a second factor that differentiates these charitable duties from the duty of the good Samaritan. The problems represented by the charities just mentioned have already been addressed by others at the level of the minimal duty relevant to good Samaritan cases. The fact that little Juan is on television shows that his particular case has been noticed and plugged into the social mechanisms we have for dealing with such problems. That is what would correspond to the duty to rescue. That does not mean necessarily that there are sufficient resources to care for Juan over time. Nor does it mean that every malnourished child has been noticed and included in the social effort as Juan has. But that is a different problem that will not necessarily be addressed by your contribution and that you are not yourself in control of.

We need to keep in mind the limits of the duty to rescue. It is not a requirement of enduring sacrifice, or of contribution to a worthy cause. It is, as I said before, a default duty that fills in the gaps of social organization. It might require one to initiate social action where it ought to apply or to correct a calamity for which social planning is impossible. But there is no question of initiating social action in Juan's case. Nor is what is needed a discrete act to allay an unanticipated crisis. The appeal made by charities is for continuing support for social action already in progress, as a means of addressing a relatively continuous need. It should be obvious that meeting this appeal involves a duty of a different sort from the duty to rescue.

The real question, however, has not been answered yet. As I interpreted it, Juan's case is a case of poverty—very serious poverty that includes hunger and malnutrition—but poverty nonetheless. Thus, it is not a sudden emergency but a chronic condition. It wouldn't take much, however, to make it an emergency (which is part of the point of such ad campaigns.) Serious poverty is itself a perilous condition, because it involves living permanently on the edge of disaster. One severe drought, and Juan's entire country could be overwhelmed by famine. Famine is an emergency condition in the sense that it incapacitates its victims. It is not ignorable in the sense discussed earlier; people cannot simply endure it. They will be killed by it unless they are assisted. It is not self-correcting. It requires intervention. Thus, most of the duty-generating conditions are met. So is the duty to rescue generated in such a case?

I believe that it depends entirely on the position of the potential rescuer. If you are the potential rescuer, just where do you stand in relation to little Juan, whose entire country is being devastated by famine? Are you on the scene? If you are on the scene, you could well find yourself in particular circumstances that are very much like those we have identified as generating a duty to aid. It would seem that the same criteria would apply (at least I cannot think of any reason why they should not in general), except for one. Given the extraordinary circumstances involved in a disaster, the restriction of minimal effort no longer makes sense to anyone directly involved. This is not to say that one is (ever?) obligated to risk one's life. Presumably heroism must always be beyond the scope of mere duty. But limiting one's duty to minimal cost or inconvenience is out of place in the middle of a disaster. Such circumstances pretty much take over the lives of all who are directly involved. Disasters generally stop "business as usual," so to think in moral terms that apply to ordinary life doesn't work very well.

All this simply underscores the necessity of making evaluations of disaster situations for those on the scene in a highly contextualized way. Even more than usual, what is required depends entirely on multiple factors in particular circumstances. Two points may be noted.

First, despite its large and collective character, a disaster is also made up of a multitude of individual situations. These could constitute discrete emergencies, thus confronting a given individual with a special circumstance that could require a specific act on the spot. Whether the duty obtained would have to be determined in the particular situation, basically using the criteria already laid out for more ordinary emergencies. Yet the decision is even more complex. Why are you there? Are you yourself a victim? Do you have a family to protect? Are you part of a rescue team? If so, special obligations may apply. And those special obligations may not only expand but also contract, or at least channel one's duty or ability to respond on the spot or in a spontaneous way to particular incidents. Whether an individual crisis requires you to stop what you are doing and deal with it right then yourself would depend completely on the specific individual circumstances, taking into account the general conditions and requirements of the disaster.

This leads to the second point to be noted. By and large, a disaster is a social problem. No individual can address it as a whole, or even deal very effectively with very many of its victims. A disaster requires an organized response, so the first duty of those on the scene would sensibly be to cooperate in the common effort. In that respect, the generalized problem created by large-scale social emergencies that we call disasters in effect socializes the duty to rescue into a duty to cooperate in a common rescue effort. Many disasters (perhaps most) must be dealt with in terms of public health measures, the construction of public shelter, and the distribution of public resources for food, medicine, blankets, tents, and so on. They cannot be dealt with as five hundred or five hundred thousand discrete individual emergencies, even though, or perhaps because, each individual within the general disaster is significant. Group measures must be adopted in order to meet the needs generated by massive calamities.

This point highlights the limits of the first point noted. Although it is the case that discrete individual problems occur within an overall disaster, that setting must always be taken into account. It would certainly be inaccurate to describe a disaster as though it were merely a series of discrete, individual emergencies. There is some significant relevant event that connects the individuals involved (whether hurricane, war, famine, etc.) which it would be extremely misleading to omit. For example to describe hurricane victims simply as homeless people would certainly leave out a material factor in their condition. They are not merely individual homeless people but an identifiable group with an obvious common connection beyond the fact of their homelessness. Dealing with such emergencies requires organized and cooperative group effort that may take precedence over some individual emergencies, or at least channel the manner in which they are handled. By and large, then, a disaster is a social problem, and the duties associated with it are cooperative, social duties. If you are on the scene of a disaster, your primary duty is to cooperate in its common relief effort. Beyond that, any individual duty is entirely dependent on the special context and cannot be evaluated outside of it. So the duty to rescue does not translate in any orderly way from individual emergencies to overall disaster relief at the scene of the crisis.

What about those who are not on the scene—which, of course, would be most of us. If you are not on the scene, then I would suppose that you are not in any special position to help. You would seem to be in the same position as everyone else who knows about the problem, namely, that of a potential contributor to a very worthy cause. You are not yourself in a position to rescue Juan or anyone else from the famine because you are not there. Consequently, the duty to rescue cannot arise because you are not in any special circumstances that generate it.

It appears, then, that the features of the individual situation are what pick out a particular individual and obligate him to act, apparently, on grounds of necessity. If you happen to be the one who is present in an emergency, you must act because someone must, and due to circumstances, you are the *only* one who *can* act. General disasters and chronic conditions do not fit this pattern.

5. World Hunger and Individual Obligation

I do not mean to suggest by my previous arguments that one need not contribute to correcting general disasters and serious chronic conditions. I am suggesting that if there is a duty to contribute to such worthy causes, it is not the same as the duty to rescue that I have been discussing here. Nor can it be derived simply by expanding the duty to rescue to cover all serious suffering wherever it may occur. In this final section I would like to round out the analysis by considering the views of Rachels and Singer that were noted at the beginning of this chapter. Assuming that the minimal duty has now been established and clearly defined, the central remaining question is why, if at all, are we justified in thinking that the duty to rescue is as minimal as I have suggested? Why isn't it a universal duty that is comparable in scope to negative duties? This is a question to which my analysis is particularly susceptible, since I have argued that the duty is a hybrid that combines the scope of a special positive duty with the foundation of a negative duty. Why should anyone agree with that? I hope that considering the strongest objections to my position will make that clear.

From a liberal point of view, freedom is always taken as a fundamental value. It is not the only fundamental value, however. It can be overridden and limited by other values, especially justice, and sometimes the general welfare, at least at the level of survival. But a commitment to freedom means that any obligation must be strongly justified. Singer and Rachels offer justifications for overriding freedom in favor of obligation on certain grounds.

I will deal with Singer's view only briefly, since I do not assume a consequentialist stance here. Singer uses a straightforwardly consequentialist form of justification, which has some serious drawbacks from a liberal point of view, I believe. For example, in the famous article "Famine, Affluence, and Morality," which I previously quoted, he begins his argument with the premise that if we are able to prevent something bad from happening without sacrificing anything morally comparable, then morally, we ought to do it. I think that a consequentialist (or at least a utilitarian) should be committed to that assumption, as Singer suggests.[22] But he then assumes that this premise is basically uncontroversial for anyone. I do not believe that is the case.

I suppose that most people would not agree to such a stringent moral requirement. While most people would agree that it is a good thing to prevent bad things from happening, most would claim that so long as they do not cause bad things to happen, they are not obligated to correct every bad thing that it is possible to prevent, no matter what it costs, as long as it does not contradict some other moral requirement to do it. Preventing every bad thing possible goes far beyond the bounds of obligation, to charity or virtue. While not everyone holds this view, it is surely much more common than the view proposed by Singer. Thus, his assumption that his initial premise is basically uncontroversial is clearly unwarranted. Since he offers no argument to support this initial premise, that would seem to undermine his argument from the outset. At least it seems to make its relevance to the project here questionable.[23]

Rachels, on the other hand, uses arguments that are directly relevant to our discussion. Rachels supposes (first) that if we accept obligations in one case (such as the obligation of the good Samaritan for which I argued in chapter 2), then we are bound to accept them in any analogous case unless we can provide reasons for distinguishing between them. Fair enough. It is to that end that he asks what you would do if a starving child were somehow in the same room with you. Surely, you would help her if you could. And more than that, you would consider anyone who thoughtlessly let her die to be a monster, wouldn't you? The answer for me (as I noted at the outset of this chapter) has to be yes. That is the position for which I argued in chapter 2. But then the question is, What is the difference between that child standing in front of you and little Juan, who simply had the bad fortune to be born in a different country?

I have made some preliminary suggestions about what the differences might be in the previous sections of this chapter. It is time to clarify and defend that position now. That can be done, I believe, by carefully considering Rachels's very trenchant arguments, which lead him to the conclusion that there is no morally relevant difference between the emergency that confronts you directly and the one that is far away.[24]

One of Rachels's (or Singer's) most controversial points is to deny the moral significance of the distinction between killing someone and letting him die. It is commonly supposed that letting something (bad) happen is not nearly as bad as making it happen or causing it to happen. Rachels denies this assumption, at least at the level of killing versus letting die. This is what has been called the equivalence thesis. It is the view that if all other factors are held constant, letting someone die as such is morally equivalent to killing him. It is not held that there is no difference of any kind (say, logical or causal) between killing and letting die, but only that whatever difference there may be, it is not a morally relevant difference. This thesis has generated enormous controversy for at least thirty years, and it is generally assumed that accepting it leads to the conclusion that Rachels (and Singer) suggest, namely, that we are as morally responsible for the deaths of those we could have saved by contributing to famine relief as we would have been if we had negligently run over them all with a truck.[25] This idea, of course, is highly counterintuitive, but Rachels supports his position with a powerful argument:

1. If there are the same reasons for or against A as for or against B, then the reasons in favor of A are neither stronger nor weaker than the reasons in favor of B; and so A and B are morally equivalent—neither is preferable to the other.
2. There are the same reasons for and against letting die as for and against killing.
3. Therefore, killing and letting die are morally equivalent—neither is preferable to the other.[26]

Premise 1 is a principle of rationality that cannot be denied without denying the basis for rational thought as well as moral reasoning. It has to be right. Premise 2 Rachels supports with the following argument. Consider why killing is morally objectionable. The primary reason is that the victim is deprived of a significant good: his life. But precisely the same thing can be said about letting someone die who could be saved. The victim is deprived of his life. Thus, premise 2 is established and with it the conclusion: killing and letting die are morally equivalent.

A number of responses have been suggested to rebut this argument, most of them not very effective. Rachels considers and dispenses with several that might have been viewed as the strongest contenders. Instead of arguing for or against the equivalence thesis here, however, I would like to consider more carefully what follows from it, especially in terms of the nature of general positive duties. Does it follow, as Rachels (and others) have suggested, that we all have a duty to give all we can to famine relief? I think that it does not. Here is why.

Whether or not killing and letting die are morally equivalent, positive and negative duty are not. There is at least one significant difference between them. Negative moral duties are universal, and their correlative rights are universal. We all have rights not to be harmed, coerced, or defrauded by anyone, and we all have corresponding duties to respect the same rights in all others. There is no problem with universalizing negative rights and duties, either logically or morally, or for that matter practically speaking. The reason that there is no problem is due precisely to the fact that negative duties are negative. They require forbearance, restraint, or restriction. Because of this, personal compliance with negative duty never requires resources. That is why they can be universalized.[27]

This is not to say that negative duties do not involve costs, of course. They do often involve costs. But the kind of costs involved do not require resources. Instead they typically deprive the actor of some advantage he would otherwise have. They require forgoing opportunities. You cannot commit fraud just to get ahead. That may cost you a lot, but it does not require resources to meet the duty. They require restricting one's impulses or emotions. You cannot strangle someone even though you are very angry. That may cost you some level of freedom, but involves no resources to meet the duty. Negative duties are, by definition, prohibitions or restrictions. Thus, they may involve costs, but not resources. Consequently, they are universalizable.

That is not why they are universal, of course. The universal character of negative rights and duties presumably follows from a commitment to the equal moral worth of human beings and the recognition that we are not entitled to intrude on one another in harmful and coercive ways. Justification for this basic core of morality is found in most philosophical theories, ranging from enlightened self-interest to social contract or utilitarian, and is widely acknowledged in practice (although not as widely as one might hope). In addition, negative duties need to be universal because they are highly individual. Each and every individual must comply. Negative duties are not defeasible in the way that the duty to rescue is, for example. It does not rebut my duty if you fulfill yours. On the contrary, if anything, it reinforces my duty if you fulfill yours. But even if you don't fulfill yours, I still must meet mine, except for the outer limit of an anarchy so profound that it eliminates moral life altogether. Outside of that one extreme case, we all individually owe all other individuals decent treatment in the form of compliance with negative duties. That is what makes them universal.

What makes them universalizable, however—what makes it possible to universalize them is the fact that they require no resources. Most of the time it requires nothing, quite literally, to meet all negative duties to everyone everywhere. You are (very probably) right now meeting your negative duties to the entire world without doing anything at all, without even thinking about it. The most it requires, on occasion, is restraint. Consequently, it is entirely possible (nor is it particularly overbearing) for all of us to meet these prohibitions universally.

Positive duties are very different. Unlike negative duties, positive duties always (or almost always) require resources of some kind or other. Meeting positive duties requires time, energy, effort, money, thought. Unlike negative duties, which can ordinarily be met without even a thought, positive duties stop your other activities, or fill up your life, or use up your money. Beyond their potentially intrusive and oppressive quality, however, the most significant moral difference between positive and negative duties is that positive duties cannot be universalized. You cannot meet even one positive duty universally.[28] That means that positive duties must always be defined in terms of a principle that delineates their scope and application. That is why it is commonly thought that special positive duties are based on natural or contractual relations. Whether that formulation is ultimately justifiable or not, it is a distributive principle that delineates the scope of positive duties in a manageable way that explains who has them and to whom they are owed, within limits that human beings can meet.

One problem with treating positive duties as equivalent to negative duties as such is that it leaves us without any distributive principle for the positive duty. One result is the impression or conclusion that we must simply keep doing all we can to prevent death from starvation until we cannot do any more. This issue is reflected in Rachels's discussion of a particular objection to the equivalence thesis.

Richard Trammel argued that a significant difference between killing and letting die is that negative duties can be fully discharged, whereas positive duties cannot be. Consequently, we can fully discharge our duty not to kill anyone, but we cannot discharge a duty to save everyone who needs aid.[29] Rachels correctly responds that this argument merely shows that the class of people we have a duty to save is smaller than the class of people we have a duty not to kill. And furthermore, if we cannot save someone, then we do not let him die.

All this seems right, but it raises two important points. First, Rachels's remarks reflect my observation that unlike negative duties, positive duties are limited in scope, but he seems not to recognize the significance of that point. The difference in scope is the difference between being universal and not being universal. That is a morally (as well as a logically) significant difference. It means that negative duties and positive duties function differently, in that positive duties must be defined in scope or reduced to imperfect obligation. There are two reasons for this require- ment. First, it is impossible to meet unlimited positive duties. Second, the value of individual freedom must be balanced against the principle of obligation. That is, first, if the principle is that you must prevent all the deaths that you can, then you must be free to determine which deaths you will prevent, given that there will al- ways be more than you personally can prevent. Second, the obligation to prevent death cannot be so onerous that people cannot determine how to live their own lives.

Here are two possible ways to interpret this point. Either the duty is an imper- fect duty of charity, or it is analogous to the duty to rescue that involves many vic- tims (as discussed in section 3). If it is the latter, it means that the potential donor is equivalent to the potential rescuer who must try to save both drowning victims even though it is likely that she will not succeed in both cases. Both victims have a right to a reasonable effort on the part of the potential rescuer, because a relatively small inconvenience on her part is their only hope to survive. Doing nothing in such cir- cumstances effectively denies the value of their lives altogether.

Is the call to contribute to disaster relief analogous to the duty to rescue? It is similar in that the victims' survival depends on the help of others. It seems to me, however, that there are several important differences.

First, unlike the potential rescuer, the potential donor to the cause of disaster relief is not in a unique position to help. You will be not a rescuer yourself but a contributor to a worthy cause. In this regard you are indistinguishable from every other potential donor in the world. While I have already noted that a potential res- cuer is not necessarily unique in the sense of being the only available person in- volved, even if a fairly sizable group of individuals could potentially be rescuers, each of those individuals is uniquely confronted with an immediate need that dis- tinguishes him or her from the rest of the world. Furthermore, the need in such cases is well defined in a way that is individually addressable. Recall that once the need is addressed by one of a group of potential rescuers, it rebuts the duty of all others. This is not the case with disaster relief precisely because no individual can address such needs. This reflects the fact that the duty to contribute is essentially so- cial. Unlike the duty to rescue, which is fundamentally individual, the duty to con- tribute cannot arise without prior social arrangement of some kind. It is precisely because some organized effort is in existence to address some ongoing and pre- sumably urgent need that a call to contribute goes out. There would be nothing to contribute to if there were no such social organization. That does not mean that there would be no need, of course, but there would be no good way for a random, unrelated contributor to address it. Thus, unlike the duty to rescue, the duty to con- tribute is a duty to participate in a social effort of some kind.

Second, there is no particular or specifiable individual that you as a contributor can help. Unlike the duty to rescue, which involves at most a definable group of specifiable individuals, usually just one or two, a disaster by definition involves masses of people. There is no particular individual that you help by contributing to disaster relief. Nor is any particular person denied help if you do not contribute.

It follows that you are not in control of such circumstances. There is no individual over whom you are in a position to exercise any control whatsoever. You are in control over making a contribution. That is all. What happens to that contribution after you make it is completely in someone else's control. Who will be saved by it or whether anyone will be saved by it is not up to the contributor. That is because no random contributor is in control over the actual circumstances or crises that occur within the disaster. And if you are not in control over any particular situation, then you cannot prevent it from happening. As Rachels recognizes, if you cannot prevent something from happening, then it is not appropriate to say that you let it happen. So even if killing and letting die are morally equivalent,[30] not contributing all you can to disaster relief is not equivalent to letting someone die.

This point reflects Rachels's observation that the scope of the duty not to let die is smaller than the scope of the duty not to kill. But the problem is that we have no principle to define the scope of the duty outside the duty to rescue as previously delineated. That problem constitutes a major difference between the duty to rescue and the duty to contribute to lifesaving causes. Unlike the duty to rescue, a duty to contribute to preventing death is ill defined. Remember that since these are positive duties, they must be clearly defined in terms of their scope and application. Yet it is not clear what is meant by a duty to contribute to preventing death, to whom it is owed, and why.

Let's suppose that we all have the duty. In this regard it can be universal. All people everywhere should prevent death if they can, let's say. That seems reasonable enough. But that is the easy part. What does it mean to have this duty? What is owed and to whom? The duty was formulated in the context of relieving world hunger, a very serious problem. It has been noted that every day many children die of malnutrition, starvation, and preventable diseases. Some of these children could be saved if more money were contributed to relief organizations or spent on foreign aid. Without any principle of limitation, that in itself can impose a greater burden than any individual could meet alone.

But these are not the only deaths that could be prevented. Adults die of preventable disease and malnutrition as well. And every year some elderly people die of exposure to heat or cold that could be avoided if better living conditions were provided for them. Shouldn't contributing to these causes count as preventing death?

Furthermore, if contributions to medical research had not been made, enabling the medical discoveries and other scientific research that have provided understanding of life-threatening conditions, many of the diseases we now consider preventable might not be preventable. Where would we be without the vaccines and treatments that turn deadly diseases into merely uncomfortable or inconvenient illness or, better yet, pieces of ancient history? Shouldn't contributing to lifesaving medical research count as contributing to preventing death?

What about contributions to organizations that help war refugees or fight political persecution? Aren't they aimed at preventing death as well as hardship and oppression? What about supporting prenatal programs to reduce infant mortality or programs to reduce violent crime? Aren't all these aimed at preventing death as well as injury and deprivation? In fact, most organizations do not aim exclusively at preventing death alone, nor do we think that they should. It is hardly a gift to provide a child with enough food to live but not enough to avoid brain damage or crippling physical deformity. So it would seem that contributions should not be limited strictly to the prevention of death alone. But if all these causes should count as meeting the duty, then it is very unclear in any individual case what the duty requires or to whom it is owed. Consequently, it must be within the discretion of any individual agent to determine whether, when, and to what extent it will be met. It seems to be an imperfect duty of charity that focuses on very serious needs. Other than that it is hard to say what exactly it requires. Unlike the duty to rescue, the duty to contribute to lifesaving efforts is ill defined, and because it is ill defined it is potentially oppressive. Indeed, it is impossible to meet. Duties of that nature are classified as imperfect duties and left to the discretion of the individual agent to meet or not in any particular case. It follows from all this, I believe, that the duty to rescue is significantly different from any possible duty to contribute to lifesaving causes of any sort, which shows that it is possible to distinguish the duty to rescue from all other positive duties, including the duty to contribute to efforts to prevent death. That duty, however it should be articulated, cannot be derived by universalizing the duty to rescue. The duty to rescue, since it is a positive duty, cannot be universalized. It is distinct from all other positive duties.

It also apparently follows, however, that not contributing to lifesaving causes at all is not blameworthy. That is why people say things like: It would be a good thing to give to CARE or UNICEF, but I am not blameworthy if I don't. Not at all. That is what bothers Rachels, and Singer, and Unger and others. And I must admit, it bothers me too. At the very least it seems too simplistic, too susceptible to abuse.

There are two possibilities for dealing with this problem. Either the duty is an individual duty, in which case it must be an imperfect duty of charity, or it is a collective social duty (or both). In the case of the former, it may be that we need a better analysis of duties of charity. What does it mean to say that implementing the duty is within the discretion of the agent? The agent has the final say. But agents are susceptible to moral argument and persuasion. Can it really make no difference what I contribute to as long as I give to something? Anything? Imperfect duties are supposed to be interchangeable. But what does that mean? The worthiness of a charity must be open to moral and rational evaluation. Giving to lifesaving causes cannot simply be equivalent to supporting the debutantes' ball, or the garden club, or the local ballet, can it? "I don't have to give to famine relief, because after all I handsomely supported the Little League this year." That doesn't have the right ring to it, somehow. But what exactly is wrong with it? There are many worthy causes that are not lifesaving causes. How should they be ordered? Should they be ordered? More work needs to be done on such evaluation, not in terms of obligation, but perhaps in terms of worthiness. Even if imperfect duties are a matter of individual judgment, individual judgments can be evaluated. This problem needs to be addressed but I cannot address it here.

If the duty is a collective duty, it is a special positive duty that must be justified by a principle that explains the source and limit of the obligation. I cannot say at this point that there is or should be a special positive duty to cooperate in a collective obligation to prevent life-threatening hardship. That would require a theory of special positive duty that provided both justification and limits. Yet the idea has intuitive appeal. It does seem to me that if there is a perfect duty to prevent such hardship, it has to be a cooperative special positive duty. The rest of this book is dedicated to examining the nature, scope, and foundations of special positive duties. To that challenge I will now turn.

II

SPECIAL POSITIVE DUTY AND NATURAL RELATIONS

Blood is thicker than water.

Proverb

What its children become, that will the community become.

Suzanne LaFollette

4

Family Obligations and the Implications of Membership

In liberal theory, special positive duties are said to be based on natural or contractual relations, and natural relations have always been taken to refer to the so-called biological connections of the traditional family. Of course, liberals didn't invent family obligation, nor have they accounted for it particularly well. Nevertheless, liberal social organization relies on the family. There is nothing unique about that. One of the main sources of affirmative obligation recognized the world over is family membership. It is probably the oldest and possibly the least-questioned form of obligation that human beings have (or think they have). It is much older than the idea of contractual obligation, and it is not particularly individualistic or apparently consensual. It is, well—just natural. Liberals have hardly disputed this, although one might think it contradictory to basic liberal principles of freedom and autonomy. Indeed, that is precisely the problem. The family, with its natural duties relatively intact, is without question the basic building block of liberal society. It is an interesting fact that liberal societies are built on the institution of the private family, but liberal theory reflects this structure very little.[1]

Historically speaking, in theory and practice, pre-liberal society was coherently hierarchical. Even the Greek democracies and the Roman republic applied the idea of self-rule and equal participation in government only to a small minority of the population. The subjection of slaves, women, and unpropertied freemen was justified by appeal to natural differences, as it was among the patriarchal tribes of biblical antiquity and in the highly structured feudal societies of the Middle Ages. Lords and patriarchs may in some sense have been equals, but everyone else was hierarchically ordered below them. All the world was ordered in classes; lords were subordinated to princes and princes to the emperor, and all this was justified as *natural*. Sir Robert Filmer's *Patriarcha* is considered by many to be the last great attempt to justify patriarchal hierarchy as the natural order of the universe, with natural duty, authority, and subordination following from it. This may not have been a defensible view, but it was a coherent one.[2]

The liberal challenge to the ancient patriarchal order denied the natural subordination of the sons to the father, indeed, of any man to any other (thus denying the basic presumption of the hierarchy of nature from which natural duties followed). Accordingly, an alternative justification for authority was needed. The answer (with many variations) was that obligation (or subjection) followed (only) from consent. If every man was born free and equal to every other, then no man could be subject to the will of another without his consent. Thus, economic obligation was contractual, and political obligation was derived from the consent of the governed. Family obligation, on the other hand, became a strange amalgam of free will and determinism, or contract merged with status. Familial duty was by and large maintained as natural. But classical liberal philosophers were ambivalent and inconsistent in their treatments of natural duty and family obligation, in their quest to refute the patriarchal authority of any man over any other while retaining it for all men over their wives and children. Having rejected the coherent hierarchies of Aristotle, Aquinas, or Filmer, liberal philosophers were stuck with the implications of an egalitarian theory postulated in (sometimes ringing) universal terms. "All human beings are entitled to life, liberty, and the pursuit of happiness." "Morality requires respect for the dignity of all persons." Any exceptions to such powerful basic principles would obviously require rigorous defense. That attempts to justify such exceptions fail miserably should be considered a virtue of the liberal position overall. That such attempts were made and their failure ignored is not surprising, given the social structures of the times. Indeed, every liberal philosopher (with the exception of Mill and the early feminists)[3] from the seventeenth to the early twentieth century argues or simply asserts that women should be considered exceptions to universal principles of freedom, and patriarchal authority should be maintained within the family.

Feminist philosophers have clearly demonstrated the inadequacy of classical liberal accounts of family obligation.[4] They need not be reargued here; but a few may be noted briefly for illustration. Locke, for example, after characterizing men and women as equal in parental authority, construes the marital duty of wifely obedience as a curious mixture of natural and contractual obligation. Since men are the "abler and stronger," women are naturally subordinate to men; consequently, disputes between man and wife should be settled in the man's favor. Furthermore, Locke is silent on the possible participation of women in the social contract. Thus, in a philosophical work explicitly devoted to overturning the patriarchal claims of fathers over sons (and thereby to assert the equality of all men), Locke pointedly supports the patriarchal authority of men over women because of their inherent inferiority. So it is only reasonable to conclude that Locke is supporting the status quo that excluded women from participation in contractual activities whether economic or political. Yet, according to Locke, women are (apparently) competent to engage in one (and only one) contract: the marital contract, which grounds spousal and parental rights and duties. This exception is necessary because on Locke's theory, contract is the only ground for legitimate obligation in the private sphere. One cannot be obligated (permanently) by birth. Yet, the content of the contract is (apparently) not set by mutual agreement, but by the natural subordination of women to men.[5] Carole Pateman rightly asks why, if a woman is incompetent to engage in any other contract, she should be competent to engage in that one. And if she is naturally subordinate (like a child, one supposes), why is a contract for subordinate status not superfluous in any case?[6] In fact Locke's discussion of this matter is very brief, a few paragraphs, although he spends an entire chapter on parental duty (which he construes as natural), all of which is typical of most early liberal accounts of family obligation.

Kant's treatment and difficulties are similar. Having argued that all human beings because of their rationality are entitled to respect as free persons, he remarks, essentially without argument, that women are not truly rational, are guided only by feeling, and are not capable of understanding principles.[7] Consequently, women in general . . . have no civil personality, and their existence is, so to speak, purely inherent.[8] Yet Kant construes marriage as contractual, a unity of wills (represented by the will of the husband, of course), which creates "a relation of equality as regards the mutual possession of their Persons, as well as of their Goods." He further argues that there is no contradiction between this equality and the legal recognition of men as masters of their households, given the "natural superiority of the faculties of the Husband compared with the Wife."[9] Thus, Kant, like Locke, claims women have no civil standing; yet they have standing to contract (only) for marriage, which makes them equal to their husbands yet makes their husbands their masters.[10]

Unlike the two previous views, Bentham's reasoning on this issue is not self-contradictory, just consistently bad. Since a man has physical superiority over his wife, Bentham argues, the law may as well preserve the status quo; otherwise husbands, having physical superiority, would always be tempted to disobey the law. Thus, the difficulties of enforcement may be avoided (and domestic tranquillity imposed?) by simply reinforcing the power of the strong. He also voices the pious hope that the interests of all might be considered in cases of conflict. He has little further to say, except that women are restricted in their affections to their own families (and so presumably cannot be good utilitarians).[11]

Even Mill (the first true egalitarian to be accepted within the liberal canon), while arguing for "perfect equality between the sexes," balks at challenging the sexual division of labor within the family. A man may pursue both a family and a profession, but when a woman chooses to have a family, she has chosen her profession (although her restriction should not be enforced by law).[12]

This summary should be sufficient to illustrate the inadequacy of classical liberal thought on the foundations of family obligation. Liberal philosophers rejected the traditional patriarchal grounding for obligation across the board in universal terms, but they tried to retain it within the domestic sphere alone, largely by asserting the natural incapacity of women for any other arrangement. This set of attitudes has been reflected in liberal political practices and social institutions, which still rely on the gendered division of labor within the family, although legal enforcement of this division has been very gradually removed.[13]

So within classical liberal theory a coherent account of family obligation is not provided.[14] Are these natural duties or contractual? If contractual, what sort of contractual theory accounts for them? If natural, how do they fit within a liberal framework at all?

Contemporary liberals have largely ignored the problem of family obligation, either by assuming the private domestic sphere to be outside the domain of political theory, or by taking the universal language of the classical theorists at its face value and assuming that family relations are voluntary and thus concluding that obligations are based on consent. But feminist philosophers have rejected both these alternatives. Feminists have been arguing that the personal is political since the late 1960s.[15] Susan Okin, more recently, argues specifically that the family is political because (1) power is of central importance within it; (2) it is legally constituted, created by political decision; (3) it socializes all people to gendered roles; and (4) the division of labor within it raises psychological and practical barriers against women in all other spheres of life.[16] Thus, given extensive feminist argumentation to the contrary over the past thirty years, assuming that domestic life is an inappropriate subject for political theory seems insupportable.

The second approach to the problem (taking universal language to apply universally) is actually a step in the right direction, but feminists have argued that it is inadequate without any acknowledgment of the gendered structure of institutions and their reliance on the sexual division of labor within the family. Political and economic endeavors depend on a supply of political and economic actors—citizens, entrepreneurs, and workers—who are produced, raised, nourished, and socialized in families, largely by the (unpaid) labor of women.[17] This sexual division of labor impairs the ability of women to participate in political or economic life, as well as their standing within the family as equal partners with their husbands. Thus, as Okin has shown, any adequate theory of justice must include an account of the family that addresses these issues.

Some critics have suggested that a liberal theory, being highly individualistic, cannot provide such an account;[18] Okin disagrees. She argues that although liberal philosophers have not yet provided an acceptable theory of justice within the family, there is no reason in principle that it cannot be done. I agree with Okin on this, and would add that developing a theory of affirmative obligation among family members should be seen as a part of this general project.

The question is, How can these positive duties be consistently accommodated within a liberal worldview? From a liberal perspective, natural duty is peculiar, anachronistic, and presumptively insupportable. To characterize these duties as narrow exceptions to liberal principles (as they are sometimes characterized) or as historical relics from a pre-liberal era is obviously inadequate. From that view it follows that family obligations cannot be justified within liberalism (at least without some highly questionable and generally antiliberal metaphysical presuppositions about inherent inequality among persons). On the other hand, to shift uncritically to the idea of individual consent, without accounting for the social context (and gendered structure of institutions) within which consent functions, raises criticisms of atomistic individualism and false neutrality.[19]

So the question is, What would a consistently liberal justification of family obligation look like? I will approach these issues by attempting to help fill in a hole that has attracted some attention in recent liberal scholarship.

1. On Membership

There is a good bit of current concern over whether liberal theory can accommodate adequately the social side of human life, the idea of individuals as members of communities, groups, and associations of various sorts. Accounting for family obligation fits within this general concern. Family obligation appears to be essentially social; family members seem to have obligations precisely because they are family members. Thus, confronting the problem of accounting for family obligations directly confronts the general issue in a particular context. The traditional confusion and current neglect of family obligation highlights two related deficiencies in liberal theory: first, the need to incorporate an account of the person as socially connected; second, the need to account for obligations that do not fit clearly within a model of individual consent. An adequate account of family obligation will require addressing these deficiencies. To approach these issues I will develop the notion of *communal membership*. First, I will outline the concept briefly. Secondly, I will explicate and test the idea within the contexts of specific family obligations.

A number of philosophers have suggested the idea of membership as a foundation for moral responsibility, but it has not yet been carefully developed within liberal theory.[20] It has traditionally been viewed as a concept more central to communitarian, socialist, or conservative thought than liberal individualism. But liberals have never denied the significance of communal association for human life and moral being, critics to the contrary notwithstanding. Liberal utilitarian theory has always focused on evaluating moral action in terms of the common good, for example. The point of social contract theory was and is to justify as well as limit social obligation. Furthermore, it is not only the individual as such who is protected by the liberal legal tradition, but the individual within the private family. Indeed, the private family is the backbone of liberal social practice. Unfortunately, as just noted, traditional liberal theory has not provided an adequate account of family obligations.

Recently this lacuna has become a source of concern. The social nature of humanity has become the preoccupation of many liberal thinkers, and great dissatisfaction has been expressed regarding the supposedly traditional liberal notion of the unencumbered self.[21] Indeed, more work is now being directed toward explaining family (and other social) relationships, responsibilities, and roles.[22] The analysis of membership offered here is intended to contribute to that effort.

In its weakest sense, membership simply refers to any intelligible grouping. If you are a member of some group it means that some feature of yours identifies you as connected to it in a way that makes it intelligible to describe you as falling within that group. If you are American, female, Christian, and black, for example, then you are a member of all those groups, and any combination of them. That is, it makes sense to describe you as connected to or identified with them. Membership also describes you as part of something larger than yourself alone: a family, race, faith, nation, culture, and so on. Many such characteristics, being blue-eyed, left-handed, short, or slim, for example, are rarely important for any purpose but still formally connect you to the set of all others having those characteristics. Thus, this weak sense of membership simply picks out particular characteristics that you share with others, that might or might not be significant for some purpose or other. Many of these features are not consensual at all, but you are no less a member of certain groups for not having chosen them.

There is also a more substantive sense of membership that follows from a more robust sense of a group. We hardly think that any obligations sensibly follow from being blue-eyed, and that may be because the group of blue-eyed people is only a group in the formal sense of being an identifiable set. It is simply not relevant to much of anything. On the other hand, being, say, an American will often be relevant to considerations, both moral and political, of obligation, right, privilege, duty, and so forth. That, it would seem, is because 'American' as a group denomination involves much more than simply a designation of all things that possess the characteristic of 'being American.' It involves a richer notion of group membership, and it is this richer notion that we are interested in here. I want to explore what is implied in being a member in this robust sense.[23] As a beginning I will briefly describe some elements that must be considered central to any substantive concept of membership. For convenience I will refer to this substantive concept as *communal membership*.

Some Elements of Membership

One very basic element of communal membership is what I will call the *reflexive identity* of community and member. Member and community are part of one another. Each makes the other into what it is, at least in some particular respects, so they must be analyzed together. A member is someone who identifies with something larger than himself or herself. A community is formed and constituted by a group of such members, who identify themselves and each other as constituent elements of the whole, and collectively define the nature of the community over time. It is the idea of being part of something that is most basic to the idea of membership.[24]

A second, and closely related, element of communal membership is the idea of *community expectations* (often called reasonable or settled expectations). Any community is woven together in a pervasive web of assumptions held by all and used by all to facilitate and enable human interaction, from the simplest transactions to the most intricate institutions. These expectations or assumptions are what specify the nature of particular obligations, as well as attitudes and beliefs about them. So what it is you feel yourself a part of—the nature of the community, as well as the specific roles within it—is largely defined by the common expectations of its members over time.[25]

A third important element is the idea of a shared commitment to, and *cooperation in*, the accomplishment of certain *common objectives* or tasks. The general idea is that a community is composed of certain constitutive tasks or common objectives that form its identity and ground its obligations. What makes a group a community, rather than a collection of strangers, is the common commitment of its members to certain communal objectives (such as liberation or equal rights) or tasks (such as arrangements for old age, for youth care and schooling, for national defense, public health, and so forth). It seems clear that the idea of participation in communal tasks or objectives is one important element of the idea of membership.[26]

Finally, a fourth element is the idea of *role*. The membership of specific individuals is often manifested in the form of roles, an idea that has been subjected to considerable analysis. While the notion of membership refers to the connection as such between an individual and an institution, the concept of a role specifies the manifestation of memberships in the form of particular positions or sets of responsibilities. Thus, obligations of membership can often (although not always) be explained as role responsibilities.[27]

These ideas—reflexive identity, reasonable expectations, shared communal objectives, and roles—will be operative in my analysis of what it means to be a member, and how obligations might be derived from, or at least profoundly affected by, and certainly motivated by, the idea of communal membership. If this analysis is to be useful for a liberal theory of obligation, it must be developed in a way that is compatible with basic liberal precepts. For example, a liberal view of family obligation should accommodate the liberal openness to many conceptions of the good. On the other hand, this range of options must fit within the parameters set by the basic requirements of justice and utility. I would like to develop these ideas further within the contexts of specific family relationships. Since relations among family members differ rather significantly, I will consider them in three representative groups or contexts: parental obligations, filial obligations, and spousal obligations.

2. Reflexive Identity, Socialization, and Voluntariness: A Look at Parental Obligation

Common attitudes about parental responsibilities have evolved over time and vary enormously with time and place. Yet within most societies the socialization and care of children in general is thought to fall primarily within the domain of the family. So we may be able to use this "natural duty" to illustrate the element of membership I have called reflexive identity. Developing this idea will begin an account of family membership. At the same time it raises some problematic issues for a liberal analysis of obligation. The question is, How can a liberal theory that respects the equal worth of individuals account for parental obligations?

The traditional approach, as noted earlier, was to construe natural duties as narrow exceptions to the general contractual thrust of liberal theory. There were a few family obligations, it was supposed, that are simply biological—that follow from nature, in other words. This position actually conceded that there was a germ of truth to the old status system of obligation, and assumed that it was confined strictly to the family—perhaps the nuclear family. That allowed a highly restrictive system of duty and subordination based on the natural trait of sex to persist alongside the rejection of duty and subordination based on the accident of birth in all other areas of liberal thought. This exception was never adequately integrated with the general principles of liberalism. Thus it is a very problematic basis of obligation for a liberal, yet an explanation of some sort is necessary, because family obligation is central to liberal society and so is the socialization of children.

Contemporary accounts, when they treat the issue at all, construe parental obligation as voluntarily assumed and up to individual parents to determine. While not incorrect in the abstract, this construction is much too simplistic, as Okin has shown. Individual consent without an account of social structures and institutional pressure is inadequate to represent family obligation fully. An account is needed that places individual decisionmaking in context.

While individuals are undeniably unique—they are not merely parts of communities—they are, nonetheless, fundamentally social.[28] An asocial or antisocial person is dysfunctional. It is through socialization that basic values, beliefs, attitudes, and habits are imparted and instilled. From beliefs, attitudes, habits, and values come character, personality, identity. This is not to suggest that individuals are determined by their social surroundings; but few would deny that we are all profoundly influenced by them.[29] This point is amply demonstrated by the highly gendered structure of presumed parental obligations. On the one hand, it shows the dangers of socialization (its tendency to be discriminatory). On the other hand, it shows that the power of socialization is effective. Children are socialized both to good and bad values. Either way individual consent is greatly affected.

All this simply corresponds to the basic general principles of modern psychology regarding child development and educational theory. I am not presupposing any unusual theoretical requirements here. It may be worth noting at this point that early liberal philosophers very generally agreed with these ideas. John Locke, for example, while formulating one of the most individualistic political theories ever articulated, also postulated that the human mind is a tabula rasa, a blank slate that derives knowledge entirely from experience. John Stuart Mill also acknowledged the significance of social influence on the formation of individual beliefs and values, as have many other liberals over the past two or three centuries.[30] Yet it is far from clear how such views can be accommodated within a highly individualistic liberal political theory, such as Locke's. Indeed, Mill's individualism in *On Liberty* is sometimes viewed as inconsistent with his social position in *Utilitarianism*. Questions of parental obligation raise these issues in a concrete context.

Since the first social influences in liberal societies are provided by families, and more specifically by parents, parental influence is rightly viewed as a matter of considerable responsibility. What is the responsibility a parent owes a child? Parental obligation, in the abstract, is fairly easy to formulate in terms of the point of the practice of parenthood. What is the point of parenthood? Presumably, it is, at a minimum, to produce a new member of the species who can survive and function in terms appropriate to its well-being as a member of that species. Accordingly, the first and most basic parental obligation is support and protection while it is needed. The first duty to a child is to keep it alive and in good health until it can provide for itself.[31] That leads naturally to the second obligation, which is to teach the child to function reasonably well within a social environment (since human beings are indisputably social beings) and to provide for itself.[32] That is, presumably, the whole of parental responsibility in very general terms.

As long as parents are the primary caregivers of their children, these obligations follow from the point of the practice. What does this imply? To provide care and support for your child is fairly self-evident. At a basic level it requires providing food, clothing, and shelter, the basic requirements for health and survival, as well as protection from danger (in other words, supervision). In circumstances of poverty or deprivation, meeting these requirements will not be a trivial matter. In affluent countries, most parents tend to exceed rather than fall short of this duty, far surpassing basic needs.

Now consider the second set of obligations, which is to make the child able to take care of itself. What this amounts to in different times and cultures varies dramatically. What was required to become or to be self-sufficient and socially well adjusted in fifth-century Rome differed a great deal from what was required in eighteenth-century England. What is required in twentieth-century Washington, D.C., is quite different from what is required in twentieth-century Brazilian rain forests. Obviously, particular requirements will differ with the needs of circumstance, and beliefs about these needs will also differ with education and theoretical development. Yet the obligations amount to the same thing: to do what it takes in your particular circumstances to support and take care of your child while and until you enable the child to take care of him or herself. What would that include?

At the most general level, self-sufficiency requires two sorts of skills. First, and most obviously, it requires the skills necessary to make a living. This requirement, as mentioned, varies culturally, but still amounts to the same thing in general terms. It is not that a child must be trained in a particular vocation, although in some cultures this may be necessary, but, more important, that he or she must acquire the social and analytical skills necessary to solve problems and provide some economically valuable service to society, enabling self-sufficiency in terms of economic contribution. This is an important point that should be emphasized. Self-sufficiency for a human being (almost) always means adequate economic contribution, and (almost) never means isolated individual provision. Human beings are social; consequently, these goods are highly socialized or culture specific.

That leads naturally to the second prong of the requirement, which overlaps the first: social adjustment. Given the nature of human life (while recognizing that it is technically possible to live as a hermit), any ordinary person must have basic social and moral virtues to enable him or her to get along in the world, both with and without regard to making a living. So all parents owe it to their children to raise them to be self-sufficient, socially well-adjusted, and moral.[33] That is what it means, in general terms in any society, to enable your child to take care of herself.[34] These are the obligations that follow from considering the point of the practice of parenthood in the abstract. They would be owed both to the child and to the society. The obligation to the child would be justified in terms of the well-being of the child, which is the point of the practice of parenthood. And since human beings are social, approximately the same obligations (to promote the health, morality, and social adjustment of children) would be owed to the community on the ground of social utility—or at least the requirement not to impair the common good.

All this very generally is what is meant by socialization—the process whereby children are made part of a community. And it is evident that beyond the duty to keep their offspring alive, the most basic parental obligation is to make the child a productive, cooperative community member. This aim is accomplished (whether consciously or not) by instilling the values and assumptions of the community in the child. Hence, the reflexive identity of community and member begins with early childhood interaction through the very mechanism of parental obligation—or at least community expectations about parental obligation. All this must be suitably qualified and justified by liberal theory, because the family is considered to be the primary socializing factor in childhood development in liberal societies.[35]

Of course, the more complex the social environment, the more varied the influences. In today's bustle of activity a child may receive considerable influence from nurseries, day-care centers, mass media, and public interaction at a very early age. This interaction develops a child's sense of normal life, basic values, and identity. Over time these influences shift and change in detail, and a person's ability for self-evaluation (it is hoped) grows and becomes more individual; yet it grows out of all the interactions that began in childhood that made the very identity of the child, and thus the adult, part of the community. It is this process of development that accounts for half of what I am calling reflexive identity. The other half refers to the fact that the community in turn is composed of the attitudes, actions, and interactions of all its members over time.[36] Communities are constituted by families interacting with and reinforcing the attitudes, habits, and values of one another. Internally, family interactions provide the first bridge, the initial socializing environment that connects the identity of the child with the identity of the community. Indeed, the duty of parents to raise their children to be well-adjusted economic and social contributors to their communities ultimately provides for the most basic elements of society as well as the identity and well-being of children. In a cohesive community, parents are in a good position to fulfill this duty (indeed, to desire to do what the duty requires even if it were not a duty) because parents are themselves community members. Their own values constitute the values of the community, and so the duty amounts to a mandate for parents to instill their own values in their children. Thus, one can see that the parent/child relationship illustrates the element of communal membership that I have called reflexive identity in its richest form—which is also to illustrate how individuals are essentially connected to one another within embedded and overlapping social groups or communities of various sorts and sizes, ranging from family to state.[37]

This whole process, while illustrating how individuals are essentially part of communities and how communities are essentially constituted by their members, also raises difficult questions for liberals, or so it is often claimed. These difficulties are of two sorts: metaphysical and moral. The metaphysical issues have to do with articulating a liberal conception of identity or self. Michael Sandel, for example, has argued that liberalism presupposes an atomistic view of an unencumbered self that precludes a coherent understanding of human persons as social beings with essential communal connections.[38] If he is right, how can a liberal acknowledge the sorts of social facts or agree with the sorts of psychological theories of human development that I have just outlined? To what extent is socialization compatible with liberal assumptions about individual autonomy and freedom? Can it fit within a liberal worldview, or a liberal individualist conception of human nature? Does it undermine liberal assumptions of autonomy and individuality? In other words, how can a communal notion of identity at the level I just acknowledged be compatible with liberal individualism at all?

The moral issues are as follows. Supposing that it is possible to explain how the idea of reflexive (or communal) identity is compatible with a liberal individualist worldview—how is that in turn related to obligation? How are communal obligations to be justified on liberal grounds? More specifically, the process of socialization is restrictive as well as enhancing, so how can a parental responsibility to socialize children to communal values be justified by or even compatible with basic liberal commitments to protect individual freedom, justice, and autonomy?

The first set of issues goes to the heart of critiques of liberalism as atomistic individualism. To see how the idea of reflexive identity is compatible with liberal individualism, one has to consider what liberal individualism means and why it tends to generate such criticisms as those of Sandel. As I briefly noted earlier, classical liberal scholars such as Locke and Mill did not deny the influence of community or family on the development of individual beliefs, attitudes, values, or intellectual development in general. (Indeed, they both clearly believed that instilling liberal values in children was crucial to the development of a good society.) Certainly, contemporary liberals, having the benefit of current psychological and sociological theories of human development, do not deny such influences. Yet liberals insist that communities are composed of individuals, and that this point is morally significant.

So what does it mean to make such a claim (or for that matter, to deny it)? In what sense are we individuals (while acknowledging that we are all socialized to be members of communities)? What does the presumption of individuality amount to? Among liberals it stands for the idea that we are not fungible, replaceable, or interchangeable with one another. Each of us is unique. Whatever our similarities, commonalities, shared interests, beliefs, attitudes, and expectations, no two individuals are alike. Each one counts, as Bentham insisted. Each is significant in his or her own right, as Kant eloquently argued. This moral thesis is the heart of individualism, but it is in no way incompatible with community membership or reflexive identity, even of the rich sort associated with socializing children (unless it is claimed that such socialization actually does make us interchangeable). Nor is it incompatible with communal obligations, although it would certainly limit their scope according to the requirements of justice as respect for the significance of the individual.

Justice would preclude the sacrifice of individuals for the common good or the good of some other group or individual. At least it would impose limits on the nature and extent of such sacrifice. For example, a minority may lose out to a majority vote on some issue of public policy, such as where or whether to have a park or a social service of some kind. But there are limits on what can be decided by vote that are intended to provide minimal protection from discrimination and abuse of power by majorities to individuals and minorities. Justice is the basis of such limits. So the liberal commitment to the significance of individuals sets limits or parameters on the *kind* of community that is legitimate, but it does not eliminate community obligation or deny communal influence on individual identity. Thus, the mere assertion of individuality does not seem to be a problem. Indeed, it would seem that those who seek to deny the significance of individuality have a more controversial position to support than those who seek to defend it.[39]

Where then does the problem (if there is one) lie? Liberals do not simply assert that individuals are morally significant but also that they are autonomous. This is the claim that seems to draw objection. In what sense are we autonomous if we are essentially communal? What does the claim to autonomy mean? To claim that people are autonomous is to say that they are self-legislating, capable of evaluating circumstances, consequences, behavior, and values; capable of individual thought and decisionmaking. Autonomous individuals are not *determined* by their history or culture, even if they are influenced by it, and so they are to that extent and in that respect free and responsible for their acts and choices. This is not to claim that our lives are devoid of influences, or that we are free of influences. That would be a naive and foolish view to hold; yet it seems to be attributed to liberals by critics who claim that liberalism presupposes an atomistic view of human nature that postulates each human being as radically disconnected from all others.

The views that seem to draw the most fire in this regard are those that rest on the methodological foundation of the social contract. Hobbes, Locke, and Rawls, for example, all presuppose a hypothetical situation composed of rational decision-makers, devoid of the influence of state and community, coming together to choose principles that will govern them in the future. Without delving into the critiques of social contract views, I would suggest that this approach to moral theory presupposes nothing about human identity except that human beings are individuals (they can be individuated) and that they are not determined by their social surroundings. Denying either of these assumptions eliminates any moral responsibility whatsoever. The social contract methodology also presupposes that the requirements of morality can be rationally ascertained. That may be a debatable presumption, but (a) what is questionable about it is not any particular view of human nature, and (b) denying it makes any moral theory questionable. So the metaphysical presuppositions seem minimal. Rawls, for one, explicitly denies that he is formulating a metaphysical view.[40] I would further point out that not all liberal views rest on this methodological foundation. Bentham and Mill, to cite two prominent examples from the early liberal tradition, do not formulate their theories in these terms. Ronald Dworkin and Joel Feinberg, to cite two prominent contemporary liberals, do not either. So why should the criticism be applied to all liberalism in any case?

It sometimes seems to be suggested that the mere characterization of persons as autonomous decisionmakers itself implies atomistic individualism or radical disconnection. But I see no support for this view. 'Autonomous' means self-legislating, not disconnected or uninfluenced. It does imply free choice. That much is required; but even determinism is not precluded for a compatiblist. So again I would suggest that the metaphysical presuppositions of liberalism itself are rather mild, and therefore those who seek to deny them should have the burden of proof. At the very least, there are insufficient grounds to conclude that liberalism as such entails atomistic individualism and, consequently, insufficient grounds to conclude that liberal individualism is incompatible with communal influence or commitment.

But what of the moral question of obligation, parental obligation in particular? There are three issues at stake here, all of which I will deal with only briefly, since they (or analogous issues) come up again in the next section and the following chapter. (1) Why is there any parental obligation at all? What justifies it? (2) Why is it an obligation of membership? (3) In what sense is it liberal?

The traditional answer to the first question was biology, or destiny. Parental obligation, indeed all natural duties, simply followed from human nature, the order of God for all men to rule and protect their families and for all women to obey their husbands and serve them, as well as the duty of all human beings to be fruitful and multiply. This was the idea of status in its most restrictive and question-begging form. Since liberals argued against this idea in all its applications except family, we should be presumptively suspicious of applying it to family as well. But if parental obligation is to be justified, is there a liberal alternative to the idea of status or biology?

The obvious liberal alternative would be some version of consent. Parental obligations are voluntarily assumed, rather like contractual obligations. People choose to become parents; cause themselves to become parents; cause their children to exist; and therefore are responsible for the consequences of their actions and choices. That reasoning would be a consistently liberal justification for parental duty, but it has definite limits. In particular, it implies that parental obligations should be voluntary in fact. That means that first, in many societies today and most or all societies for most of history, this justification was not available. Second, it means that institutional structures and socialization (e.g., by gender) should not be so profound as to preclude free choice. Nevertheless, it seems right. It simply suggests that there was (or is) no liberal justification for parental obligations of the restrictive form traditionally based on status or gender. So it should be no surprise that family obligations were construed as remnants of an earlier status system of obligation. That is what they were.

The point is that they need not be. Liberal justification for parental obligation is available, although it (predictably) liberalizes the institution of parenthood. For example, restrictive roles based on gender as such should not be supportable on liberal grounds, since they violate the basic requirements of justice to respect the self-determination of all persons. That much is very clear. It also implies that no one should be forced to be a parent, although that issue is highly complex—too complex to be explicated here. Still, it provides a sketch of what a liberal view of parental obligation would be.

Why should this be considered an obligation of membership, rather than a contractual obligation? The answer (although it will need further articulation) is that parental obligations, on a liberal model, may be voluntary in entry, but parents do not get to define them. The obligations follow from being part of (or reflexively identified with) a community (in the form of an institution, or association of like-minded members or participants with similar assumptions) that is defined by the reasonable expectations of its participants. The reasonable expectations of the community set the norms of behavior and common practice and thus determine what is normal and acceptable and excellent. Complying with such norms as a matter of parental obligation does not fit the usual model of contractual obligation. The idea of membership obligation seems to capture it better. What you consent to as a parent is to be a member of an institution or participant in a practice defined by institutional norms.

That parental obligations are defined by the community is evident if one considers just how varied such obligations might be. Suppose that you lived in a tribal society in which the old people took care of the infants and toddlers, while the young adults worked in the fields. Your parental obligations would seem to be much different in such a social arrangement from what they would be if the institutional organization were otherwise. Since members of the community reasonably rely on one another to cooperate in such practices, they generate obligations—unless they are patently unfair, oppressive, or irrationally unproductive. A liberal commitment to diverse lifestyles and social experiments requires openness to a very wide (though not unlimited) range of such communal arrangements. Thus, the point is not that liberalism itself generates parental obligation, but that community membership falls within the moral parameters set by liberal values. Parental roles are justified as long as the institution that defines them is justified by the requirements of justice and utility. Yet, in liberal societies participation in the practice of parenthood should be voluntary in entry.

The one special issue that arises in this context is the moral justification of socializing children. The conflict arises between socializing children to accept and support the values and traditions of the community on the one hand, and teaching them to be individual thinkers who can and may challenge and criticize the values and traditions of the community on the other. This does create a tension of competing commitments within liberal thought, and it does qualify or limit the extent or sort of socialization that can be justified, but (contrary to some conservative claims) it does not eliminate or contradict commitment to communal values or the socialization of children within communities as such. The liberal value of tolerance allows for a fairly wide range of such commitments to be determined by individuals within communities. Consider an example.

Suppose that you are a committed Muslim (or Christian, or Jew, etc.). Do you have an obligation to raise your children to espouse your values? Many Muslims would certainly say yes. So if your religious commitments include a commitment to instill your beliefs in your children, then you do have that obligation. That obligation is derived from being a member of the Muslim community (not from liberalism). Does liberalism contradict any such obligation? Presumably not, but it does qualify it in the following respect. Insofar as your communal (in this case religious) beliefs include a commitment that contradicts universal values of justice and tolerance, they cannot be compatible with liberalism. For example, the view of some traditional communities that women are inferior and appropriately restricted in their activities would not be compatible with liberal commitments, although the rest of their beliefs may be perfectly acceptable. This acknowledgment of liberal values will indeed eliminate obligation to some communities altogether if the central organizing principle of the community contradicts universal liberal values. A Satanist community committed to human sacrifice would be fundamentally incompatible with liberalism. A Nazi society committed to the annihilation of certain races or discrimination against all races but one would be fundamentally incompatible with liberalism. That does not mean that such communities could not exist within a liberal society, but that a member of such a community could not also be a liberal.

Most communities, however, are perfectly, or largely, compatible with liberalism, although not mandated by it. This is ensured by the principle of tolerance. So, for example, you may be obligated by your communal commitments to teach your children to be, say, Buddhist; and even to teach them that Buddhism is the one true religion, and that the world would be a better place if all people were Buddhist. You may even be committed to teach them that they should try to persuade all people to be Buddhist, and liberalism would contradict none of this. What you cannot teach them (consistently with liberalism) is that all people *must* be Buddhist, no matter what they believe or desire; that they can be forced to be Buddhist; or that anyone who is not Buddhist is worthless, despicable, less than human or unworthy of respect, consideration, justice, or decent and humane treatment. Such views would violate universal principles of tolerance and justice.

I do not mean to make light of the difficulties involved in this issue. The marketplace of ideas inherent in liberal tolerance can be (and has been) very destructive to some traditional insular communities, such as those of the Amish, the Shakers, and certain indigenous tribal peoples. These issues can be and have been discussed and analyzed within liberalism as well as outside it, so I will not address them further here.[41]

My only suggestion is that liberalism is bound to incorporate tensions since it stands for diversity, dialogue, and freedom. Acknowledging obligations based on community membership complicates the analysis, but provides resources as well. This should be no surprise for a liberal. Life is complicated and embodies tensions, even contradictions (at least apparent ones) that must be negotiated in terms of competing interests and commitments. Acknowledging that many obligations are defined by community expectations and justified by mutual reliance on communal practices provides a better explanation of those obligations than assertions of status obligation derived from the cosmic order on the one hand, or declarations of disconnected individual consent on the other. Such layering of individual obligation through community membership is not contradicted by liberalism, although it is limited by liberal principles and values. It provides the best account of parental obligation within a liberal framework.

3. Communal Tasks and Institutional Justification: Some Thoughts on Filial Obligation

Historically, a concern common to all societies and their members has been to make some arrangements for old age or other infirmity or dependence. In many traditions the family was the locus of addressing this need. So the care of parents was (and still is) often considered to be the obligation of their children. These customs might vary considerably from one culture to another, but nearly all develop some kind of social norm for how such needs are to be handled and who will be obligated to deal with them. So obligations to parents (especially given recent changes regarding them) provide us with a rather good illustration of the element of communal membership that I have suggested as a commitment to communal tasks or objectives. As noted earlier, communities are defined by their common objectives.

The obligation to care for one's parents (if it exists) provides a clear case of nonconsensual obligation. In fact, this obligation is very often voluntarily assumed, but the fact that it is often assumed merely shows that it is widely recognized. It does not show whether or not people have such an obligation if they do not assume it. The claim that people do have an obligation to care for their parents can be denied, so the major question to be asked here is, What, if anything, justifies such a claim? Why should people agree that they are obligated to care for their parents?

The most commonly offered ground (besides the claim that God willed such an arrangement) is the idea of debt or reciprocity. We owe our parents our existence, and very probably our well-being also. In most cases parents provide their children with material comforts, at least subsistence, education, and upbringing necessary for an independent and successful life. It might be said (and has been said) that all you are you owe your parents. So a debt may be owed for reciprocal support when support is needed. The obligation to care for one's parents is justified because it is fair, or so it has been argued.

There are, however, a number of objections to be considered regarding this argument. The first is the same problem that has plagued a similar argument suggested by both H. L. A. Hart and John Rawls as a basis for political obligation, an argument commonly associated with Rawls's principle of fairness. In essence, it runs as follows. If a group of individuals sacrifice (or restrict themselves) to obtain mutual benefits, then those who do so restrict themselves are entitled to equal (or at least equitable) sacrifice on the part of all those who share in the common advantage thus derived. The intuitive idea is that all who enjoy a common good should share the burden necessary to obtain the mutual benefit.[42] Notice that this reflects the general rationale embodied in the idea of communal tasks as well as the notion of mutual reliance. Obligations are generated by a common — or social — commitment to certain communal objectives.

The biggest objection to such an argument is that it obligates (and therefore restricts) people without their consent. Suppose you do not want the benefit? You cannot refuse it. You cannot resign from the group (without leaving the country, and perhaps the burden cannot be avoided even then). So you must contribute to a joint venture (by hypothesis to your advantage, but) without your consent.[43]

The same objection holds against an obligation to your parents based on fairness. To put it tritely, you did not ask to be born. Nor, in all probability, were you consulted regarding your upbringing and education. In fact, many of the greatest benefits you may have received from your parents (such as, for example, a well-disciplined, clean, and orderly life) you surely did not ask for and very probably did not want at the time. Since these gifts were entirely unsolicited, why should a debt of reciprocal action be generated?

At the very least it must be recognized that certainly where parental obligations are voluntarily incurred (as is commonly the case in many societies today), filial obligations cannot be construed as analogous to parental ones. Duties of children to parents cannot be viewed as direct corollaries of parental duties to children.[44] Nor can they be accounted for by debts of gratitude for good favors done by parents, since that would undermine the idea of parental duty. (Parents, presumably, are not doing their children a favor to raise them; they are doing their duty.) And such a view would otherwise make the obligation highly variable with individual circumstance. (Some children might owe nothing or revenge rather than gratitude.) It is also implausible to view obligations to parents as a special case of duties of charity or beneficence, since duties of charity impose only minimal burdens.[45]

Overall, the moral foundations for filial duties remain unclear and largely unpersuasive. As a matter of fact, most children do remain committed to their parents, and that is, no doubt, a good thing. Whether they are blameworthy if they do not do so is most likely an individual matter. It is not clear that children as such owe their parents a debt merely in virtue of the relationship in itself—at least not in contemporary societies that provide alternative social arrangements for elder care.[46]

I suspect that if such a duty can ever be justified, it can only be justified institutionally. That is, it will be a commitment to a particular institutional arrangement that will justify filial obligation in general, if anything does. I am not saying that institutional commitment explains why people actually assume obligations to care for their parents, or do care for them in fact (whether they assume an obligation to do so or not). Most people care for their parents because they love them, or at least care about them or respect them and do not want them to suffer. Many have a feeling of connection or identification, which generates an attitude of responsibility, even if the relations could not be described as loving or even respectful. There are old and powerful traditions that reinforce the feeling of obligation to care for one's parents (and possibly other family members such as siblings, grandparents, etc.) even in the absence of love or respect. All these are common motivating factors that explain prevalent attitudes, but do not self-evidently justify moral obligation without consent.

The question is whether people are blameworthy if they do not assume the responsibility to care for their parents, and if so, why or under what circumstances? Despite the reservations just noted, I think that social practice is relevant here, although not decisive or irrebuttable. In a society in which all social arrangements are made in terms of private families, and the settled expectations of the community are that children are to care for parents in old age, it may be reasonable to assume that people do have such obligations and are blameworthy if they intentionally do not meet them, just so long as the burdens are distributed in a reasonably equitable way, and the restrictions are necessary for the benefits produced, especially in terms of the flourishing of the community and all its members. That is, as with parental obligations, I would suggest that filial obligations are justified only if the institutional arrangement is justified.

This is not to say that historical family arrangements were morally justified, since they were often highly discriminatory and unreasonably restrictive. My only point is that this need not be so. As part of a society that met the minimal requirements of justice and freedom, arranging social structures in a way that provided for needed old age benefits by relying on private family obligations rather than, say, provision of the village or state, would be perfectly reasonable, and consequently justifiable. I suspect that a variety of social structures might potentially be compatible with a basic commitment to freedom and justice. Unlike certain radical reformers, I do not believe that families are irretrievably unjust. That is, I think that the minimal requirements of justice could be met by a state, even if it were arranged in families.[47] If this were the case, then social practice would provide a moral (as well as a social or legal) justification for recognizing the prevailing obligations, since people in general would reasonably rely on their fulfillment, and would conduct their lives accordingly.

Theoretically speaking, I suppose that this simply amounts to a reaffirmation of Rawls's principle of fairness on institutional grounds, whether it succeeds on social contract grounds or not. Where people arrange their lives, making sacrifices for mutual benefit, as long as those arrangements meet the basic requirements of justice, consent is not required to generate cooperative obligations. Being part of the institution does that.

Practically speaking, what would such an obligation amount to? I believe it would simply mean that if parents provide the benefits of ordinary family life to their children, assuming in good faith that they in turn will be provided for in their old age by their children as is the common practice of the community, then it is wrong for their children not to comply with the common practice, even if they happen to be ungrateful.

Should such an obligation be irrebuttable? I do not think so. That is, for example, if the institution in general is fair (as it would have to be to be justified) but the individual case is not, then the moral obligations should be undermined. It hardly seems reasonable to suppose, if the institution is presumed fair, that any obligation to care for an abusive parent or an absent one could be maintained morally. The presumption of fairness supposes a certain reciprocity: mutual cooperation in an institution that produces mutual benefits. If the parent does not meet the initial conditions, then the subsequent obligations cannot arise.

The moral reasoning does not really seem that difficult in principle. There is, of course, no such thing as a moral proof, but a reasonable interpretation of the requirements of fairness does provide support for the idea that obligations to care for parents could be justified within certain institutional structures.

The practical considerations attached to such an idea, however, appear impossible. That is the big problem. Who would determine whether the parent's conditions had been met? Would it be presumptive? What would count as abuse or absence, and who would decide that? Should it be total absence, severe abuse? If society made such evaluations, how could it assess abuse in private, which often goes undetected? If social mechanisms of evaluation were meticulous enough to detect all or most cases of abuse, how could it avoid egregious violations of privacy? On the other hand, if the evaluation is to be made by the child, how accurate is it likely to be, and how would it be raised? Should the claim be raised after the child has grown up? How would that be evaluated?

In fact, social structures are unlikely to be able to handle individual deviation from social practice in private. Most likely, social structures will be powerful and rigid, without accommodating deviation, or they will reduce largely to a weak presumption favoring parental support assumed by children as a matter of individual conscience. The former amounts to a flat rule that children care for their parents. The latter amounts to obligation based on consent, tempered by the expectations of the community. The former view is oppressive. The latter is somewhat similar to the conclusions drawn about parental obligations that combine requirements of membership with an important element of consent. But there is one significant difference.

In the case of parental duties, the relationship itself is ideally consensual—it may be entered or avoided—even though the duties attached to the relationship once entered are largely set by social practice, or community expectations. Furthermore, this obligation seems to be morally justified if the institution is justified. That is, if the social institution meets the general requirements of justice and equal freedom as required by the liberal tradition, then greater than minimal (or negative) duties are justified by membership in the institution.

In the case of filial duties, the relationship is not ever consensual, since one is born into it. Yet the obligations seem to be justified in much the same way, that is, by evaluating the justice of the institution. Making such institutions compatible with the liberal commitment to maximal freedom would presumably require the adoption of the least intrusive institutions possible. Historically this has meant the restriction of governmental power. Libertarians still use this ideal to argue for small government, and indeed the commitment to freedom is a crucial one. However, in the context of filial duty, I think that the liberal argument should run exactly opposite to the libertarian thrust against government. That is, once we recognize (as many liberals have in various contexts) that private arrangements can sometimes be more oppressive than governmental or collective ones, it can make good sense, on grounds of freedom (as well as utility), to argue for the pooling of resources to handle otherwise private problems socially. This option is especially important where the relationship itself is not consensual.

Recognizing the practical difficulties noted earlier, as well as the great diversity of family arrangements, some writers have recently argued that social solutions to problems of elder care, and to issues of distributive justice between age groups, are more workable and fair than individual solutions are likely to be.[48] This is not to suggest that one precludes the other. Rather, it is to allow individual families to work out their own arrangements within supportive social institutions that are calculated to be fair to the population at large. Formulating such institutional structures is an exceedingly difficult task, since ideas about what is fair to the population at large vary considerably. But then, so do ideas of individual filial duty. Indeed, Norman Daniels, for example, argues that filial responsibility will be encouraged by supportive social institutions. And social arrangements for the accomplishment of communal tasks are appropriately determined by vote, since that should reflect common commitment or lack of it.

What we see happening in the United States and many other countries today is the progressive socialization or communalization of the task of elder care. If we are to trust public opinion polls, this development is in accord with and in response to public agreement on moving in the direction of a social response to this need.[49] That is, public or at least collective provision for elders is apparently desired, both by children and elders, even though much elder care is still provided by children.[50] This desire is easily understandable in terms of the modern concern for providing choices. If alternative provisions are available for elder care (public or private insurance, pension plans, retirement and nursing homes, etc.), then children are not obligated to make such provisions, although they are still free to do so. Nor do parents have to rely on their children, although they may accept arrangements freely offered. Thus, alternative institutional structures make personal arrangements voluntary and thus more compatible with a liberal social philosophy. Yet it is clear that the institutional arrangement providing for communal objectives (such as elder care) is what generates personal obligations with regard to those objectives or makes them optional.

This discussion illustrates several aspects of the idea of communal tasks or

shared objectives that I have claimed are a basic element of community membership. Elder care is a task or objective the accomplishment of which must be addressed by some sort of institutional practice. (So, for that matter, is child care.)
Such needs can be met in various ways, obviously. For example, appeal could be
made to the resources of the nuclear family, extended family, clan, tribe, village,
city, or state. Institutional arrangements might be formal or informal, that is, le-
gal/political, or social/moral.

From a liberal perspective, any such arrangements are acceptable, as long as
the basic requirements of justice and utility are met. People determine their own institutional arrangements, and it is the necessity for cooperation and mutual reliance
within particular institutional structures that justifies the obligations of community
members. Thus, membership sometimes justifies obligations even within liberal
societies.

4. Community Expectation and the Function of Role: Spousal Obligations and Marital Contracts

Obligations to spouses today look contractual, but are they? Does individual consent account for marital obligations? Contemporary liberal perspectives assume
that it does. It is the nature and scope of that idea in the present context that I
would like to examine here. The interesting questions are: (1) Taking the marital relationship as formally contractual, how well does the idea of contractual obligation
(or explicit consent or agreement) explain spousal obligations? (2) To the extent
that spousal obligations are not explained by consent, why are they not? and what,
then, justifies them within a liberal framework?

Assuming that you agree to marry, what is it that you agree to, and how do you
know what your obligations will be? The contract, such as it is, is exceedingly
vague. Exchanging vows to love, honor, and cherish one another hardly gives people a clear idea of the specifics of their contractual obligations, if that is what they
are. By way of comparison, considering the wedding vows to define marital obligations would amount to entering a partnership in which the articles of institution
contained virtually no information except who the parties were. Odd sort of contract, when you think about it. You get to know (1) who your partner is, (2) that you
both promise not to assume any other partnerships of that type, and (3) that you will
both maintain an extremely favorable attitude (love) toward one another, permanently, and no matter how much any or all other conditions might change. First, we
must ignore the fact that item 3 as a vow is impossible for any human being to keep
at will or as a matter of commitment. You can try to love each other forever, or hope
that you will, but only if you are lucky will you both succeed; so we must ignore the
problem of impossibility that would void any ordinary contract. Second, if the vow
is the contract, it tells you nothing (useful) about what your specific obligations are.
As a real contract, it would be void for vagueness. Should we ignore that, too? Let's
do.[51]

It might be noted here that some people now write their own vows. (These are
of no particular legal effect—that is, the legal effect is exactly the same as if they
used traditional vows—but possibly some special moral obligations could follow

from them.) In any case, all specially written marital vows that I have ever heard were just as vague and poetic as the traditional ones. I have never heard the bride and groom exchange specific lists, such as: the party of the first part promises to do the cooking, shopping and laundry. The party of the second part pledges to handle the child care, cleaning, and recordkeeping. I take it that such an exchange at the marital altar would be viewed with horror or hilarity, which shows that it would be considered inappropriate. In fact, the public vows today do not define the obligations of the contract or rather the relationship. They are instead simply declarations of love and commitment in general. There is not and is not supposed to be any specific content to them whatsoever.[52] In fact, the current legal effect of marriage (vows) is to change the legal status of the parties from single to married, and thus to trigger certain legal consequences. But this phenomenon tells us little about the personal obligations of the parties that are the heart of the marriage.

That does not mean that there is no specific content to the agreement, however. It does not even mean (necessarily) that the details are left free to be worked out by the individual parties in private. What actually lays out your specific obligations (if anything does) is social practice—the settled expectations of the community, as mentioned earlier in more general terms regarding parental and filial duties. The reason people know what they are obligating themselves to do is that they grow up in a society that engages widely in the practice of marriage, and so everyone understands, more or less by osmosis, what marital obligations are.[53] They are in fact specified by the settled expectations of the community, by and large in the form of roles.[54]

As with most social practices, these change over time. For example, not more than two and a half decades ago in the United States, the settled expectations for men and for women were quite different in marriage. Roles were sharply divided and rather clearly defined. Among other things (oversimplifying a bit), men were expected to support the family financially, but not to care for it domestically. Women, on the other hand, were expected to care for the family, but not to support it financially.[55] There was very little freedom to deviate from these roles, even though the marital relationship itself was viewed as consensual. That situation illustrates that the marital roles of spouses during the twentieth century in the United States (and many other countries as well, of course) were consensual in the sense that one consented to enter them, but not in the sense that individual parties were free to define them.[56] Indeed, the function of settled community expectations (that is, the way they work) is to make it difficult even to think of deviating from them.

Community expectations set the bounds of what is normal. Perhaps I can use some current expectations about spousal obligations to illustrate how community expectations function to inform attitudes and assumptions about obligations in general and especially family obligations in the form of roles. In order to do so, I will dwell on certain social practices at some length. The fact that assumptions about domestic roles and relations are currently changing may enable us to question and understand them better than we could in other times when such assumptions were settled and thus virtually invisible.

Two or three decades ago, normal roles in marriage were clearly defined, and socially dictated, despite the fact that marriages were considered consensual. Such roles are not nearly as clear at present, which means that individuals have more freedom to negotiate their personal arrangements, if it occurs to them to do so, which it probably doesn't most of the time. That is, evolving social standards or community expectations do not necessarily dissolve into unfettered personal choice or matters of taste. Instead they often disintegrate into conflicting social standards. Thus, because there is much less guidance as to what specific arrangements and obligations should be, there is much more room for misunderstanding, miscommunication, disparate assumptions, and disagreement about them. All this may account for some (though certainly not all) of the marital problems and failures that are so widespread and prevalent today. Since community expectations are more unsettled, spousal obligations are less clear and more open to controversy, instead of being merely a matter of individual agreement. To illustrate, consider two major changes or challenges to spousal obligations and marital roles that have occurred in recent decades.

Economic arrangements are becoming increasingly unclear for spouses in certain respects. Some couples now set out prenuptial agreements. These are almost always entirely economic settlements, frequently preserving prior property or future rights, such as pensions as separate property. Despite these special qualifications and limits (which are further evidence of unsettled community standards),[57] the general presumption is still, however, that a family is an economic unit, and that spouses are economically responsible to and for one another.

What has changed in this regard is that in a majority of families today, both spouses are economic contributors. Community expectations are completely up in the air, however, as to the economic role or obligations of women. Men are still expected to be breadwinners without question, but social expectations about the economic obligations of women are confused and conflicted. While some, especially younger generations, expect women to work in the public sphere, others expect them to be domestic. The result is that women are widely viewed as working "because they want to," or as providing "supplementary income" at their own discretion, but not because it is their responsibility to do so. This view badly represents the economic situation of the average woman. Very few women work as a hobby.[58] And while it is true that most women earn less than their spouses, to characterize their income as "supplemental" reflects more strongly the male role of breadwinner (which is longstanding and still intact) than the more recent female role of economic contributor.[59]

Traditionally, the breadwinner was the sole supporter of the family—ideally, that is. In fact, the majority of the world population was never able to meet that standard except in the United States, Canada, and parts of Western Europe after World War I for about ten years, and after World War II for about twenty-five years. Most families (that is, a majority) were, and still are, working-class families, and most working-class families have not survived and cannot not survive on a single income, except for the short periods of time and in the places just mentioned.[60]

Still, the standard of aspiration was the sole breadwinner, who was supposed to support the entire family unaided. Where necessary, the breadwinner's income (the basic or primary income) was supplemented with the contributions of grown children, or not-so-grown children, or the "homework" (e.g., income from taking in laundry, sewing, or boarders) provided by his wife, and only as a last resort the work of his wife outside the home. A working wife was traditional evidence of an inadequate breadwinner. Hence the lingering attitude today that a woman's income is "merely supplemental" and, frequently, that she works "because she wants to" and not because her family needs her contribution, since that would reflect badly on her breadwinner.[61]

The sole breadwinner standard was never a reasonable standard, since (a) the majority of the population was not in a position to meet it for most of history; (b) a significant minority has never been able to meet it, and was always discredited by it for no good purpose; (c) it separated and rigidly structured roles without regard to the preferences of those who filled the roles; (d) it necessitated discounting the economic role of women no matter how significant it was or is in fact; (e) it generated prejudice against all women as economic actors; and (f) it is now clearly outdated and detrimental to both men and women most of the time.[62]

Nevertheless, the male breadwinner role was (and still is) the community standard for marital roles of spouses, and it cannot be changed by fiat, legislation, or even moral argument, but only by social evolution. That it is still the standard is illustrated by many forms of evidence: for example, the absence of sociological investigation or public opinion polls asking whether men should work, in the face of continuous sociological studies and public opinion polls asking whether women should work. It is often asked whether working mothers harm their children; but no one asks if working fathers harm their children.[63] A recent report noted that although in 31 percent of dual income families the wives were the primary breadwinners, only a tiny fraction of their husbands elected to stay home with the children. This situation, it was suggested, exists because men and women defined masculinity in terms of being a good provider.[64] Analogously, a single man measures his self-esteem in large part by his work accomplishments maximally (often by how much money he makes) and minimally by his ability to support himself.[65] The independent breadwinner standard is not optional for men. All men are obligated to conform their behavior to these powerful and settled community expectations that go to the very definition of masculinity. This is a clear example of a settled norm manifested in the expectations of the community.

The obligations of men within the family, however, are much less clear. Traditionally, housekeeping and child care were decidedly outside the scope of male obligation, but that norm has been rather vigorously challenged in recent decades. The result is that it is now conceivable that a man might sweep a floor in his own home or even change a diaper without being considered deranged. But in fact, behavior has changed very little, and certainly a man's self-esteem does not depend on his participation in child care and housekeeping responsibilities. What has changed is how people talk about the issue. It is now widely conceded that a man should "help out" with the household chores, or even do "his share" around the house, points that certainly would not have been acknowledged thirty years ago, but this attitude hardly imposes a responsibility (in fact "help out" implies no responsibility) and indeed, responsibility has remained largely at the talking stage with little change in behavior indicated.[66] This is an example of a community standard that is being challenged and discussed, and is therefore visible as a social arrangement rather than an edict of nature, but is not yet really unsettled. The community expectations may be questioned, but they haven't changed.

By contrast, the general norm (or community expectation) for working women has changed continuously over the past thirty years. Female participation in the work force has more than doubled since 1950, and attitudes toward work have changed among women. A majority of women today expect to work permanently and consider this situation normal. Work is not a sign of lower-class status for women as it once was. Even the number of working mothers with preschool children has risen dramatically since 1970.[67] In the 1950s it was considered shameful or tragic for a mother to work outside the home before her children had reached maturity. Today working mothers are more commonly accepted. One point of institutional evidence for this observation in the United States is provided by recent trends in public opinion about welfare. In order to receive welfare benefits today, it is argued that mothers of even preschool children should work for pay if they can. But when welfare was instituted in the 1930s, it was precisely because it was believed that mothers ought not to work outside the home. The idea of welfare (Aid to Families with Dependent Children) was to enable women who had no breadwinners to stay home with their children "as all normal women would if they were able to." This evidence shows that, unlike the male breadwinner standard, community expectations (that which is assumed to be normal) have begun to change in regard to married women or, more specifically, mothers working. Indeed, it would appear that women are now expected to work in the public sphere.

On the other hand, uncertainty and outright hostility to mothers who work is continually expressed in various quarters.[68] While arguing against welfare, no one suggests that poverty-stricken working mothers will not also be held to a full-time standard of housekeeping and child care. Backlashes and hostility to working mothers are evidence that the old standard that middle-class women are first and foremost obligated to provide the primary care for their families is alive and well (and it follows that poor women are stuck, as always, being deficient because they cannot meet the standard). Continual expressions (often in print or other media) of uncertainty and guilt among working mothers are evidence that the old standard of domestic responsibility is still accepted. A woman is the primary domestic caretaker. If the obligation is not adequately met, she is responsible and she feels guilty.[69]

In the face of changing expectations about working women, the intact domestic standard shows that the expectations of the community can be contradictory and oppressive. Surveys show that young women have internalized the work accomplishment standard in large numbers. Most young women today do not *aspire* to be homemakers, although many assume that they will be. They also expect to be self-supporting.[70] Men are no longer expected to support women after divorce. Alimony is largely a thing of the past. Even child support is widely defaulted by many absent fathers.[71] Women are no longer considered innately dependent. In fact, they are being assimilated to the male work accomplishment standard on equal terms, except that they are still being held to the domestic caregiver standard as well. Women are supposed to compete with men on an equal footing in the public sphere, but women are also socialized to be sexually attractive and domestically responsible—to be good wives and mothers. The new standard of self-esteem is being assumed, but the old (incompatible) standard is not being denied. Thus, community expectations can be contradictory, oppressive, and unfair.

Still, community expectations define the roles of spouses, and even though at some periods those expectations may become rather confused, or even contradictory, they do not simply capitulate to personal choice without constraint. That is, the disintegration of community standards does not automatically lead to indifference about the matter, but leads rather to arguments over what is normal, as well as to uncertainty, guilt, and conflict. On the other hand, it also enables norms to be seen as norms rather than as imperatives of God or nature, or invisible altogether.

These various evolutionary changes illustrate how roles and attitudes about obligations are set by common assumptions that are often referred to as the expectations of the community, if they are recognized at all. Often they are invisible, which makes them even more powerful than when they can be seen. These community expectations, seen or unseen, retard individual choices, by defining the nature of roles, the basis of self-esteem and normal behavior, and even supposedly basic characteristics of human nature, such as masculinity and femininity. These assumptions can be highly restrictive. On the other hand, they also facilitate human interaction, at least in the sense of simplifying it, by enabling individuals to anticipate what it is reasonable to expect in many situations, because those expectations are pre-arranged by settled roles and practices. Obviously, social life would be impossible without norms.

In the context of spousal obligations, the norms just considered illustrate that community standards can change greatly over time, and the more unsettled the community expectations are, the more freedom individuals will have to set their own unique commitments. Yet even in the most chaotic of times, social expectations and assumptions will still be strongly operative in basic institutions. Marriage simply is a social practice. It is constituted by community assumptions. Such assumptions rarely dissolve or fade away into nothing (unless the social practice itself becomes obsolete, as, for example, with knighthood). They are replaced or challenged by other assumptions. When assumptions become unsettled, it simply means that they are more open to challenge than usual, thus more subject to evaluation and change. Still, they always form the background against which individuals form their opinions—either in agreement with or in rejection of the common norms, as they see them.

So spousal obligations, even in unsettled eras such as our own, are largely set by the expectations of the community rather than by private contract or truly individual agreement. Even where the norms are unsettled enough to allow considerable individual variation, personal preferences and attitudes are themselves profoundly affected by community assumptions. Marriage just is a social practice, and it is social practice in the form of community expectations about roles that explains presumptions about spousal obligation, as opposed to private agreement, for the most part.

Yet, in general, the marital relationship itself is considered consensual, that is, one that people enter voluntarily. Historically, this element of voluntariness was thought to distinguish obligations of contract from those of status, as well as to distinguish relationships of freedom from those of bondage, and this still seems to be a useful distinction to retain, with the following qualification. When one considers the social practice—the community expectations that inform spousal obligations—it seems clear that consent takes place within a social context that may significantly complicate and constrain it.

What this qualification points to, in a preliminary way, is the fact that even when relationships are consensual (in the formal sense of voluntary entry), consent alone may not account for the specific obligations that fall within them. That is, consent (at least as applied to general responsibilities that follow from the acceptance of a position) is a highly complex notion that needs to be integrated with the community practices that flesh out the relationship or institution to which the consent applies. This point will be examined at some length in chapter 7 on professional obligations. For now, one can see that as accepted, spousal obligations may vary a great deal from place to place or time to time but are nevertheless primarily generated, defined, and explained by social practice—the settled expectations of the community, even though the relationship is considered consensual because entering it is consensual.

This account explains beliefs about spousal obligations, but what about justification? As a preliminary position, I will suggest that in this context, as in those of parental and filial obligations, the obligations of the role are justified on liberal grounds only if the role is justified, that is, if it meets minimal requirements of justice and utility. Given the potential for community expectations defining roles to be oppressive or discriminatory, it is important for a liberal view to evaluate the role itself, and not merely the individual consent to enter it. By acknowledging individual agreement as embedded in social practice, the evaluation of the social practice as well as consent is required. While not claiming that my brief remarks here constitute an adequately supported analysis, I hope in the next chapter to build on the foundation laid here.

Considering obligations of individual family members to other individual family members, one can see that the elements of membership—reflexive identity, community expectations, role assignment, and communal tasks—function to produce beliefs about family (or so-called natural) obligations. These elements explain our beliefs about natural obligations much better than either ideas about biology or status, on the one hand, or consent alone, on the other hand, can do. The assumption that you have the obligations you were born into is no longer compatible with contemporary world views, and our recognition of diverse social practices and divergent moral beliefs about family obligations undercuts claims of biological necessity about them. From a liberal point of view, if obligations do not follow from biological necessity, then they must be justified on moral grounds. Yet, the standard liberal notion of contract or individual consent alone is inadequate to account for family obligations. Instead, as I have shown, they must be explained in terms of participation in social practices that are themselves justifiable in terms of utility and justice. I have suggested briefly that the form of justice appropriate to this context is justice as reciprocity, which could be developed in terms of the ideas of mutual reliance or cooperative support. To develop these concepts further, I will turn now to the question whether this analysis of "natural" duty as obligations of membership can be applied to the family as a whole.

5

Family Membership
and Reciprocity

Liberal theory is fiercely individualistic; yet liberal societies seem to acknowledge, and even rely on, obligations to the family. We need an explanation for this. How does family obligation fit within the individualistic framework of traditional liberal theory? In chapter 4 I developed the theoretical notion of communal membership to provide the beginning of a liberal explanation of family obligation based on a review of three important and basic family relations and widely accepted obligations that appear to be based on or associated with them. These, of course, do not exhaust family relations or obligations, but they do provide a reasonable representation of them as broadly acknowledged and central to liberal social practice.

The idea of cooperative communal membership, I want to suggest, may offer a better explanation for what traditional liberal theory has generally referred to in passing as natural duty—and contemporary liberal theory has largely ignored or subsumed under the abstract idea of individual consent. Construed in terms of cooperative communal membership, family obligations become more flexible, more accommodating to social connection than accounts of individual consent have been, and more compatible with liberal presumptions and perspectives than traditional duties of status or biology could be.

Assuming that a liberal account of family obligation is critical to any adequate liberal theory of affirmative obligation, I have tried to show how the idea of membership may contribute to our understanding of basic obligations that individual family members may owe to other individual members. I would now like to expand on this analysis by considering how or whether the idea of membership can account for family obligation as such. In this chapter I will consider two conceptions of family obligation that are clearly collective (that is, not individual) as well as apparently not consensual (at least in the usual sense). I will call these conceptions *family in the abstract* and *family as household* and distinguish them here as terms of convenience. I do not suppose that these exhaust all possible conceptions of family, or that obligations to them are necessarily justified, but suppose only that they are conceivable, distinguishable from one another, and widely acknowledged. These will be the objects of interest throughout this chapter.

Although family obligations are not considered central to liberal thought, they are central to liberal social practice, and thus, I hope, may provide some valuable insights for an account of affirmative obligations within the liberal tradition. In the first section I will examine the nature of these two conceptions of family. In the next section I turn to the issue of justification to explore the basis for acknowledging obligations to family on liberal grounds. Finally, I will consider in a tentative and preliminary way what all this might mean for a theory of justice as reciprocity and how it might fit within the liberal tradition.

1. Obligations to Family As Such

It is not inconceivable to owe something or to have responsibilities to the family that do not translate automatically to its individual members. Where that is the case, you may be referring to what I will call family in the abstract. I use this term to refer to a traditional idea or ideal that alludes to a family name or genetic line, the boundaries or members of which extend over both space and time. This is the extended family in the largest sense. Easy examples are famous families, such as the Romanovs, the Windsors, the Rockefellers, or the Kennedys. But there are many humbler examples, of which many, if not most, people find themselves a part, and this is rather like being part of an institution.

The other sense of family, which I will call family as household, is an aggregate or group of actual (living) members, who are closely associated in fact by living arrangement and commitment, for better or worse. Households may include any couple or small group who live together and share resources over some period of time (which is generally expected to be permanent) as a matter of commitment or vow. An extended household may include children or other relatives who are grown and do not live in the same house but still maintain close ties.[1] The extent of such households may vary a great deal, and borderline cases between a household and family in the abstract are unavoidable. Nevertheless, the core case is the household that lives together: a committed couple, or a parent and child, with a few reasonable extensions, and this arrangement can easily be distinguished from family in the abstract. As I shall use the term, a household is a small group, closely associated by living arrangement and commitment, whose members consider themselves a family. Family in the abstract, in contrast, is an idea that refers to an extended group whose members are traditionally thought of as genetically connected but more accurately are connected by the group's legal recognition as a family unit most typically based on biology, marriage, or adoption.[2]

Both family in the abstract and family as household are often considered to be owed things. If you have such obligations, you are obligated to "the family." For example, you may be obliged to conduct yourself with a certain amount of decorum or a certain standard of morality or virtue, so as not to bring shame, dishonor, or embarrassment on "the family." You may be exhorted or expected to work hard, to excel, or to do particular things (such as preserve traditions, attend gatherings, or not move away) for the sake of the family, where the family is the group as a whole or, even more than the present group, a continuing entity. You might be singled out as a special representative or functionary of some sort: the leader, promoter, protector, provider, negotiator, judge, or counselor of the family, and because of your special qualities or position have special obligations and possibly special privileges as well, all of which relate back to the family as a whole. Thus, it is evident that certain expectations or assumptions of the family fill out the content of particular family obligations, as long as the general parameters are compatible with larger patterns of social expectations about family life in general as developed in the society within which the family is embedded. This involves the notion of community expectations discussed earlier, as that notion applies in the context of the family as a group. These expectations form the content of family members' beliefs about their obligations. Whether the obligations are justified I will take up later. Here I would just like to consider what sort of obligation would make sense as applied to these two conceptions of family.

Responsibility to family in the abstract must be calculated to perpetuate or promote the good of the group as a whole, or the abstract entity—the idea with which the members identify. This latter is often construed as a blood line and relates to the perpetuation of inherited characteristics, both genetic and social, and sometimes material as well. A family may be identified with certain material possessions such as a house, an estate, heirlooms, or land. It may be identified with an enterprise such as a business, a farm, or a profession. Family in the abstract generally includes genetic inheritance ("He has the Whitlock chin!"), traits of character ("Well, aren't you just like a Brisbane—stubborn as a mule."), and often the perpetuation of certain values, lifestyles, or other commitments. ("That simply is not the way Westmores do things, dear.") Obligation to family in the abstract refers to any or all of these things, which are symbolized, I believe, by the idea of perpetuating or identifying with a family name.[3]

Obligation to household, on the other hand, largely refers to promoting the common good of the members. Explaining what the common or aggregate good is in the case of families is no easy task. (Of course, it is no easy task in other cases either.) The moral maxim that ideally motivates family as household obligations, I think, should be something like the following. Each family member should be accorded maximal benefits relevant to his or her individual characteristics and compatible with maximal benefits relevant to all others. This formulation represents the idea that the foundation of ideal treatment for family members is at least equitable in principle. However, in application, even ideally, it may be rather unequal. For example, a child with special talents or abilities may be and should be provided with special opportunities to develop them. On the other hand, a child with special handicaps may be and should be provided with special treatment to overcome or deal with them. All members of a household may be obligated to sacrifice greatly to accommodate special problems or opportunities of a particular member in special circumstances, or even over time. The point is that the aggregate good of a household must somehow accommodate the special needs of its individual members, as well as the identity of interests and obligations that they seem to share.

This is a difficult idea to capture, but it is no more difficult for a liberal theory than any other. In fact it seems to me rather well represented by Ronald Dworkin's conception of justice, which requires affording each member of a group equal concern and respect.[4] This conception at least represents the idea of equity just articulated. The element of group membership might be explicated in terms of the legal notion of "jointly and severally" held interests.

For example, a person might accept (or refuse) a particular job for the sake of the family, where that refers to the good of any and all members of the household who would be affected by such a decision. "I did it for my family" on this use simply means that I did what I did because I, and my family (or at least the adult members of it), believed it was in our common interest for me to do it. This decision would involve my evaluating the interest of the group jointly and severally—that is, as a whole, and in terms of each individual, including my own interest as part of the group—as opposed to thinking about what my interest might have been if I were not part of the group. Maybe the new job would be a great opportunity if I were single, but not for my whole family, or vice versa. It is the good of the whole group, jointly and severally, in the long run, and as a continuing entity, that is my obligation to my family as a household.

Thus, the challenge is to come up with a conception of the common good that manages on the one hand to capture the identity of interests and the identification of members with the whole, and on the other hand to represent the significance of each individual's interest adequately. I think this is what Mill had in mind with his idea of the aggregate good—a concept that has gotten an awful lot of bad press, and deservedly so if it treats interests as simply additive.[5] I don't suppose Mill's view to be so simplistic.

The problem of representation, especially for a liberal theory, is that individuals do not dissolve into unity like drops in an ocean. They retain their individual significance like threads in a tapestry. Every thread counts, individually and in its own right, but you cannot represent the tapestry simply by adding up the threads. The challenge is to account for the tapestry without losing sight of the significance of each thread within it. That is my notion of the common good as applied to household. If, indeed, that is not compatible with Mill's notion of the aggregate good, than another articulation will have to be found.

To do things for the sake of the family in the abstract is not quite the same as doing things for the common good as I just used that term. At least we seem to encounter an extended notion of family obligation for the common good that includes an extra element. This is rather like being obligated, or doing things for the sake of the state, the nation, the race, or the faith, in that all these ideas entail more than the sum of the good of their constituent members. I am not sure what exactly the difference is. Perhaps it is merely that family in the abstract persists across generations, whereas household does not. Thus, the former becomes associated with an abstract idea that is symbolized by the family name and that is not reducible to the sum of its current living members.

Thus, justifying obligations to family in the abstract cannot be accomplished by a simple appeal to the common good, or to equal concern and respect for its members. At least not directly. Furthermore, family in the abstract is a slippery notion that may dissolve altogether if pressed. For purposes of determining obligations, who constitutes the group? Is it all one's ancestors and descendants, or is there a statute of limitations? Perhaps all living relatives only—but even then, what is the standard of connection—everyone with the same family name? That's clearly inadequate, even by traditional standards. As Sir Henry Maine observed long ago (without drawing any conclusions from the point) the traditional dynastic or hierarchical family is founded on a legal fiction that is incoherent under close scrutiny.[6] Even so, the traditional idea of family in the abstract persists, more or less as I described it earlier, despite our inability to define its boundaries clearly.

All this means that justifying obligations to family in the abstract will be more difficult and more problematic on a liberal view than ordinary obligations to household are likely to be. Despite this difference, however, I would like to examine whether obligations to household or to family in the abstract might be similar in nature and foundation, and indeed, similar in important respects to the ideas I explored in the previous chapter. What sort of obligation would this be, if justified? I will suggest that we call it an obligation of cooperative communal membership. Membership defines its nature. It is derived from and determined by family connection and commitment. The reason you have this sort of obligation (if you have it) is that you are part of something that requires cooperation; you belong to something larger than yourself, with which you are partly identified. You are connected. We are all connected in one way or another, and these connections form part of our identity. Family obligations come with family connections, and in general they are obligations of mutual reliance and cooperative support. (I will have more to say about this shortly.) Quite unlike universal obligations of noninterference, family obligations are complex, layered, and often affirmative. They may include obligations to intercede for the benefit of other members, and include affirmative obligations large and small, as set in detail by the expectations of the family. Merely not causing harm is entirely inadequate to account for family obligations. Promoting the common good, especially if construed as maintaining the conditions needed for the good life or the flourishing of the family, however, comes pretty close.

Beyond the general description of cooperative support, and mutual reliance, the nature of your particular obligations depends on the nature of your membership. Such obligations will be affected by your personal characteristics, by your level of involvement, and by the character of the family relations your particular family has, as well as by the expectations of the broader society within which the family is embedded. Some families may generate extensive particular obligations; others may have few. For example, some families, whether extended or nuclear, may observe holidays or birthdays in a formal way, others not at all. Some will exchange (and expect) gifts, frequent phone calls and visits, and any number of other particular activities. Other families may do very little of this sort of thing. Whatever the variation, each member knows what her membership entails, generally because she grows into it. Thus, she knows what is expected, and she largely expects the same. As mentioned, membership is part of identity. You are to conduct yourself "as a member," you are to think as a member, act as a member, identify yourself as a member. This is not only a matter of explicit teaching, which may or may not be involved. It is also simply the way children grow up and develop their worldviews. This is not to say that family membership (or membership of state, race, or faith) defines your whole being, since most of us hold more than one membership. But the nature of your membership defines the nature of your responsibility, or at least your beliefs about it, as evolved in the expectations of the family.

I have attempted to describe in the past few pages roughly how this works and some of the things it would include. I would emphasize here that while particular ideas about obligations vary considerably from family to family, a great deal is also standardized by role and custom, for better or worse (often worse, as observed in the previous chapter), but in any case to some extent as a matter of necessity. As noted earlier, families are embedded in societies, so even if your family customs and expectations differ quite a bit from those of your next-door neighbor, they will reflect the society from which you take your assumptions. Family expectations are layered on community expectations, constituting an extensive web or network of assumptions and obligations that define and connect individual identities through relationships to institutions.

To sum up: this connection or attachment of human beings that I am calling communal membership is the foundation of social life and the source of common beliefs about obligations, including perhaps as a paradigm, family obligations. They are derived from family connection and commitment, from being part of something larger than oneself, and from identifying oneself (partly) in terms of it. Described most generally, these are obligations of mutual reliance and cooperative support, toward the accomplishment of communal tasks or objectives. They are often affirmative and are sometimes extensive and exacting, far exceeding universal obligations of nonharm and noninterference. The particular manifestations or interpretations of these family obligations are defined by what are considered the reasonable expectations of the family, and are understood as a matter of common practice, tradition, or role. They do not appear to fit the paradigm of individual, consensual obligations; yet they form the bedrock of liberal society as based on the private family.

It is not hard to see in a very general way how community expectations form interlocking networks of belief that structure, influence, and limit individuals' assumptions and even their considered judgments about their obligations (as well as about most other things). The big question for a theory of liberal responsibility is how community expectations relate to *justified* obligation (not simply people's beliefs about obligation). Is community expectation itself a foundation for obligation? It is often thought to be so, but one must consider why, if at all, such a foundation should be accepted; what conditions must be met to make such a foundation compatible with liberal commitments; and what other grounds should be considered for justifying family obligation as such.

2. Justifying Family Obligation

The foregoing considerations show that family membership is widely believed to generate obligations. But are these beliefs justified, and if so, why? Historically, family obligations were described as "natural duties" and left largely unanalyzed, but as duties of cooperative communal membership, there is no reason that they could not be subjected to the same sort of analysis that other social relations and institutions have been given. For example, utilitarian theory could evaluate them in terms of the promotion of the common good. A social contract theory could analyze them according to what rational individuals in a fair bargaining position would choose (or in whatever terms the social contract was formulated). A Kantian could consider them in terms of potentially universalizable maxims, and so on.

What is distinctive about family obligations, from a liberal point of view, is that they are special duties (that is, not universal), often affirmative, and apparently at least sometimes involuntary and possibly sometimes collective. Consequently, any such duties must be clearly articulated in terms of foundations and limits that do not violate basic liberal commitments to respect individual freedom and justice. The question is whether any justification is available for family obligation that can meet this standard. Several possibilities can be considered.

Biology or Status

The traditional idea of natural duties rested on the notion of biology (generally interpreted as status): the assumption that there is a natural order of life that specifies the obligations of human beings in terms of their birth. This ordering of obligation (as well as position, rank, privilege, etc.) was also thought to correspond to natural abilities and instincts or preferences. Well-known examples include the ideas that nobility was conveyed by blood and that slaves (or serfs) were naturally unsuited to be free, as well as the assumption that men were the natural masters of their families and women were inherently domestic and deferential. The basic idea was that given natural differences in races, classes, nationalities, and genders, it was right and proper that obligations and privileges should reflect and correspond to the order and hierarchy laid out by nature.

Not much, if any, of this general position seems defensible today. Indeed, much of the traditional liberal agenda was aimed at dismantling the status system of rank and privilege, assuming moral equality among all men. This goal was part of the revolutionary fervor that transformed both the political and economic landscape of Western civilization from the seventeenth through the nineteenth centuries. Aristocratic birth was seriously challenged as a foundation for political or economic privilege, at least in the form of legal barriers to the freedom of others. Yet family obligation based on status or birth was hardly questioned until the twentieth century. Is the idea of natural duty, or family obligation based on status, defensible on liberal grounds? Let's consider what that would mean.

I examined this question as applied to the obligations of individual family members to other individual members and found it to be generally inadequate. Obligations to spouses can hardly be traced to biology. The common-sense explanation is much more like the idea of contract (although, as I noted, this too has deficiencies, at least as a complete account). Parental and filial duties can only be accounted for by biology or instinct if adoptive parenthood, communal care, and similar arrangements are ignored. But these alternative arrangements seem too common and too effective to dismiss, especially as "un-natural." The idea that family obligations are grounded or specified by natural instinct or universal preferences is undercut by the wide variety of societal and personal arrangements that emerge when personal freedom is allowed.

Finally, from a liberal point of view that emphasizes a commitment to the freedom and equal moral worth of all persons, a consensual arrangement will always be preferable to a nonconsensual one, thus providing two strikes against justification on grounds of status or biology as one of the most restrictive foundations possible for any obligation. Since empirical verification of biological instincts or the hierarchy of nature among human beings has not been forthcoming, the presumptions for equal treatment of all persons and against restrictive grounds for obligation should militate against assuming obligations of status in liberal theory. Consequently, other grounds are clearly preferable.

Furthermore, from a liberal perspective, even if there is a natural tendency to favor one's own family, there is no reason to suppose that any obligation should necessarily follow from that. A liberal concern for justice in the form of equal treatment might well argue for neutralizing any such tendency rather than reinforcing it. To so argue would be analogous to arguing that social arrangements should undermine rather than reinforce the human tendency to violence, vice, or discrimination. It would also parallel earlier liberal arguments that hierarchies of class should not be entrenched by law. The latter assertion seems particularly true of collective obligations to family in the abstract, which are suspiciously similar to class hierarchies of exactly the sort traditionally opposed by liberals. Indeed, such concerns raise questions as to whether traditionally accepted obligations to family in the abstract can actually be justified on any grounds compatible with basic liberal commitments. Perhaps they can be, but it seems clear that a powerful justification would be needed to overcome liberal presumptions that favor individual freedom and equity, whereas the least viable of all possible justifications from a liberal perspective is status. Thus one might argue that preservation of family in the abstract is necessary, say, to reinforce human moral qualities that are needed to protect the common good over time or across generations. It is hard to see why this would be true in contemporary society, but suppose it were. It is clear that it is appeal to the general welfare and not to biology that justifies the obligation. So, even if there is a natural instinct to preserve one's family name, no obligation follows from it as an intrinsic good; obligation follows from it only if it is instrumental to some other good—such as the flourishing of the entire community. In contemporary society, however, there is no reason that individual survival or the common good requires social organization by dynastic biological family, and insofar as this is not necessary, it has long been opposed in principle by a liberal perspective that favors less restrictive alternatives. Thus, it seems likely that obligations to family in the abstract from a liberal point of view must be purely and individually consensual. That is to say, it appears that there can be no obligation to family in the abstract as such. If obligation on the basis of biology is rejected, obligation to family in the abstract is rejected along with it.

Obligations to family as household, on the other hand, seem more likely to be open to justification on other grounds (such as the common good) that are much more straightforward and more liberal, as I will discuss more fully in the next few pages. If so, then the more controversial foundation of status is not needed to support them.

The idea of obligations based on status or biology, then, is not compatible with other liberal commitments, unless controversial metaphysical assumptions about human nature and the hierarchical order of life are accepted on faith. Thus, the idea of biology or status is a very unlikely ground for justification of any obligations within a contemporary liberal theory, even if this idea has been uncritically accepted in liberal societies. The important point to be noted here is that the traditional idea of natural duties simply will not do as a liberal foundation for obligation of any kind. This rejection eliminates any liberal justification for obligation to family in the abstract as such, and requires us to find a more viable basis of justification for family as household. It is time to consider what such justification might be.

Consent

While the pre-liberal paradigm for justifying obligation was status, the liberal paradigm for justifying all affirmative duties, other than family duties, was consent. Can family obligation as such be justified by individual consent? Is it voluntarily assumed? I hope that the consideration of the features of membership in chapter 4 made clear why feminists object to this idea as too simplistic. As applied to individual family members, I have shown that the distinction between membership and consent is not quite clear, since communal membership profoundly influences the parameters of consent. So, these considerations lead me to divide the question. That is, given our analysis of spousal, parental, and filial obligations, it appears that the idea of consent itself could arguably be construed in at least two different ways. This point is important because it has to do with evaluating the voluntariness of consent. Given that social influences are always more or less present, when should they and when should they not be said to eliminate the voluntariness of consent?[7]

One way to construe consent is in terms of the (more or less) straightforward assumption of obligation that we see exhibited in attitudes about filial obligations in the United States and many other countries today. Specifically, a common attitude is that if people have obligations to care for their elderly parents, it is because they agree to do so. (This, of course, may not be all that is involved in individual cases, which may vary enormously, and may include feelings of debt, gratitude, love, etc., and all this illustrates that voluntariness is a matter of degree.) The important point is that if someone does not choose to assume this responsibility, the state will not require it by law, and social standards are so ambiguous and conflicted that they cannot be said to impose serious social sanctions or condemnation in such cases. Furthermore, in terms of public policy, the burden of elder care is becoming increasingly socialized, which means that parents need not (necessarily) depend on their children for survival.[8] This point is crucial, for it changes the institutional arrangements, the actual need, and the community and individual expectations about how the need will be accommodated normally. In such a social environment, obligations to parents are best described as voluntarily assumed. If that is the case, it is consent that justifies them.

The second sort of consent is much more indirect, and is exemplified by attitudes about spousal and parental obligations. As noted earlier, what is consensual in these cases are the relationships. Assuming that (or at least to the extent that) one becomes a spouse or a parent voluntarily, one thereby assumes the obligations that go with the relationship, but does not define those obligations personally. The obligations of role are socially defined. In these cases, I have suggested that elements of consent and membership are combined. Consent alone cannot explain these obligations adequately, since the reason you have them is that you are in the relationship to which they are attached, and not that you consented to each obligation individually. Furthermore, consent alone cannot justify these obligations, since (unlike obligations assumed by consent) something must justify the social construction of the role or institution that specifies them. Thus, the obligations must be justified by whatever justifies the social institution or role within which they function.

I have suggested that from a liberal perspective such justification would entail meeting minimal requirements of freedom, justice, and utility. How would this be evaluated? As a preliminary proposal, the following considerations seem appropriate. Affirmative obligations might be justified as tending to promote the common good only if they are not oppressive or unfair. Promoting the common good can be assessed in standard ways, such as weighing the relative burdens and benefits associated with the role or institution, and so forth. There is an enormous literature on how to assess utility. Presumably, such evaluations could be made in this context at least in a general way. A practice or role could be judged oppressive or unfair if less restrictive alternatives were realistically available and not used, or the burdens associated with the practice or role were not equitably distributed. Such considerations, I believe, articulate the major commitments of the liberal tradition in terms that could apply to affirmative obligations in general and family obligations in particular. Such a process of evaluation seems necessary if, as I have suggested, family obligations as such cannot be explained or justified adequately by individual consent. I think that they cannot be.

For the sake of debate, consider the following argument to the contrary. Family connections are rather like those of nationality, race, or faith. It is obvious that one's genetic family or race is not voluntarily acquired. It is less obvious but still true that one's nationality and faith are not voluntarily acquired. We are born into all these things. Of course, it could be argued that all of them can be renounced. Nationality and faith can be renounced explicitly. Race and family cannot be eliminated in quite the same way, but they can nevertheless be renounced, at least arguably. You can in effect turn in your membership, sever your connections, at least your conscious connections, and eliminate the significance of any of these things in your life. That is, psychologically one may cease to identify with any of these things, at least in terms of personally acknowledging their significance, as long as they are replaced by something equally important, or so it could be argued. To the extent that this is possible, if you do not reject your membership you thereby accept it. You tacitly consent. Can such an argument justify family obligation?

The argument has some force in certain particular circumstances (namely, those in which a person's life and behavior really do indicate tacit agreement in fact). As a general argument for family obligation as such, it has two major problems. First, it fails to give adequate recognition to the enormous difficulty of renouncing such basic and profound connections as nation or family. To do this one must first be in a position to conceive of the choice. That is, one must first have the vision to imagine things to be other than the way they are. Without proper background, such vision may not be possible. And the more deprived the background is, the less likely is the possibility of imaginative vision. This possibility is also profoundly affected by the strength of community standards, of course. The stronger and more pervasive the expectations of the community, the less likely it will be that anyone can think otherwise. Where community standards are solid, they will be virtually unquestioned, so the idea of consent cannot even arise. At one time, for example, it was unthinkable (for a woman, at least) to consider living life outside of marriage, or to decide not to have children within a marriage. Such decisions would have been considered evidence of abnormality or immorality or both. But the issue would rarely come up, because part of the foundations of identity and self-respect were built into participation in marriage and childbearing arrangements. You simply were not a normal adult until you were a parent. Similarly, the very idea of living outside a traditional family may be virtually precluded by strong communal structures and assumptions that insure not only compliance but assimilation. Social conditioning is ordinarily set up to retard deviance. The most effective means to retard deviant behavior is to eliminate the possibility for deviant thought. Obviously, then, community expectations or standards may retard the ability to envision alternatives. The point is that under the right conditions, this obstacle to individual choice can be profound.

Now, suppose that obstacle is overcome; even if imaginative vision is there, one must still have the strength to give up whatever it takes, or pay the cost of making the vision a reality. If the change is a basic one of the sort I have been discussing, not many are strong enough to effect the change even if they can envision it. Furthermore, many who could change are not willing to because the price is too high. One has to give up too much, endure too much hardship, prejudice, loneliness, or condemnation. We should be wary of counting acquiescence to that kind of pressure as consent.

Suppose for the sake of argument that it is viewed as a form of consent: a sort of grudging consent. It is acquiescence as opposed to agreement. But then obligations are often like that. If you agree with the enterprise attached to the obligation, then it is rather like paying the price for what you want. That amounts to consent, arguably. It is agreement "on the whole" or "all things considered." You agree, at any rate, that what you get is (more or less) worth the price of getting it. At least, it is arguable that if you did not think so, you would not agree and would not participate. That is the argument.

This view, unfortunately, is compatible with some highly coercive social relations. Often it is not that one agrees with the obligation, agrees willingly to assume it, or even agrees with the enterprise it is intended to promote, but instead it is that the obligation or enterprise comes attached to other things that are too important, too valuable, to give up. So the person grudgingly acquiesces in assuming the obligation. I think that acquiescence should not count as consent. Henry David Thoreau went to jail rather than pay taxes that supported what he considered an unjust war. Ralph Waldo Emerson (and most other citizens) were not willing to do that. I do not think it follows that Emerson (and all the others) consented to the war or to the obligation of paying for it. The price of objecting can be very high. If the price is high enough it is tantamount to coercion, not consent.

All these points, I think, show that consent is a problematic foundation for justifying obligations of family membership (although it should not be ruled out altogether, because it will apply in individual cases where there is agreement in fact to obligations that do not contradict the requirements of justice). Given that most individuals are raised in families and gain their sense of identity, values, and self-esteem through family relations and their sense of a normal life from family living, just how reasonable is it to suppose that obligations can be freely assumed or denied in such circumstances? As noted, at a preliminary level, it seems inappropriate, indeed, false to suppose free choice in a social situation that precludes the possibility of imagining a situation or practice to be other than it is. If that basic level is transcended, free choice is closer to being a possibility, but it will still be questionable where the costs of exercising it are so high as to go far beyond what we could reasonably expect an ordinary person to meet. At a certain level, a form of consent is operable in many family relations. That is, the relationship is voluntarily entered, initiated, or assumed, even if the obligations are not. Still, postulating tacit consent to such obligations is questionable as a justification for them because family membership is not voluntary in the first place and although renouncing one's family (or any family) to avoid obligation is theoretically possible, practically speaking it is extremely difficult. To use the language of duress in legal theory, it may be a price too high to reasonably expect anyone to be able to pay. It is not the sort of choice that we can reasonably expect a person to be able to make.

A second problem with the tacit consent justification of family obligation is that it is not clear that one can always eliminate family obligations even by renouncing one's family connections. Consider, for example, the obligation of a man to support his family. (I formulate the example this way because, as stated, this obligation is very widely, almost universally, acknowledged; roles of women may be in upheaval, but the male breadwinner role is still firm.) Does a man voluntarily assume this obligation? Well, yes and no. He voluntarily acquires a wife and children (at least we are assuming that this is voluntary), but does he voluntarily assume responsibility to support them? Ask yourself this: How could he avoid it? Not shirk it—some men might simply neglect the obligation or fail to meet it. That does not mean that they do not have it, or even that people do not think they have it. The question is, How could they avoid having it? The answer, I think, is only by avoiding the relationship. Is that conclusion too quick? Couldn't a man avoid the obligation by special agreement with his (future) wife? That is, couldn't a man and woman agree in advance that neither is financially responsible for the other? They could; but it would not be an enforceable agreement as applied to children. The law would not recognize it, at least, not in virtue of the agreement alone. It is not clear that social standards are that flexible either. That is, men (or women) may be socially condemned for how they treat their spouses, even if the spouse agrees or acquiesces in the mistreatment. So, in this particular context, suppose that a man and woman agree not to have children. They use contraceptives, but she finds herself pregnant despite them. She discovers that she cannot bring herself to have an abortion; then she realizes that she wants to keep the child. He cannot avoid the obligation to support his child, no matter what she agreed to in advance. Nor can he avoid it by avoiding a legal marriage, that is, by simply cohabiting, although that makes the obligation socially and legally less clear. So legally and socially, this obligation is virtually unavoidable. What about morally?

Overall, the justification of obligation depends on the general social institutions and the living arrangements of the couple and not on any formal agreement between them in and of itself. That is to say, although consent should probably be presumptive or prima facie justification in personal relations, it is not conclusive: for example, it does not follow that the consent of a man's wife would relieve him of the obligation to support his family, since it is clear that formally consensual relations can be oppressive or unjust. Even if a woman were willing to sacrifice herself (and perhaps risk the well-being of her children) for her husband, her consent would not make it moral to take advantage of her. So the obligation appears unavoidable.

Similarly, as I noted earlier, given current social structures, if a woman has a child, she is obligated to provide its primary care. This remains true no matter what private agreements may have been made between husband and wife. Imagine a situation analogous to the example just discussed. A man and woman agree not to have children, but she finds herself accidently pregnant. He finds that he does not believe in abortion, and then realizes that he cannot give up the child, so he promises that if they keep it he will assume total responsibility for all child care and any additional housekeeping requirements generated by having it. He fully intends to keep this promise, but he finds that it seriously conflicts with his obligations at work. The domestic responsibilities are distracting. They impede his concentration. His boss is unsympathetic to the time constraints of child rearing. In order to advance, he needs to work overtime or bring work home with him. He doesn't have the time or the energy to meet these conflicting obligations over time, so gradually he does less and less around the house. His wife, on the other hand, is socialized to meet these obligations and consequently finds it intolerable to leave them unmet. She feels guilty. And she gets blamed for being a bad mother. Remember, no one asks if working fathers harm their children. So she finds herself doing double duty. And after all, someone does have to care for the child. It cannot simply be neglected. So is there any way she can really avoid the obligation to care for it? I don't think there is.

If a man and woman produce a child, even if they did not intend to, they are both obligated to support and care for the child unless alternative institutional arrangements (such as adoption or collective support) are available and utilized. Furthermore, if either parent is not willing to give up the child, the other parent is obligated to contribute to its care and support unless alternative institutional arrangements are available. So I ask again: Is this obligation voluntarily assumed?

I suggest that it is not; but of course, it does not follow that the obligation is necessarily unfair or unreasonable. Whether it is fair or reasonable or not depends on whether constituting the social institution of marriage and parenthood in that way can be justified on grounds of justice and utility. Even if it can be so justified, it seems to me misleading to call the obligation voluntary. Why? If a man acquires a family, he automatically acquires the obligation to support it. If a woman acquires a child, she is automatically obligated to care for it. Is that consenting to obligation? I would say that the obligation is fixed by the position; entering the relationship (or position) is what is consensual. Thus, the consent element here is rather attenuated.

Such special obligations are easily explained (by consent) in cases of truly voluntary memberships, but realistically they are crucially tied to institutional arrangements and socialization mechanisms—the expectations of the community. The interesting feature of family (or racial or national) membership is that initially you do not or may not voluntarily join, and when you do voluntarily join (initiate the membership) you cannot necessarily quit. The assumption is that you join forever. No one asks to be born, but many an adult child has found it necessary to assume the obligations of caring for an elderly parent. As I have shown, a parental relationship may be irrevocable. You can ignore being a parent, but you cannot really cancel the fact that you are one, as many parents today find when, long after they assumed their obligations were over, their children return to the fold in periods of hard time. Spousal relationships are now much more tenuous, but they are intended to be permanent and, depending on the circumstances, may generate permanent obligations. To call these obligations simply consensual does not reflect the subtleties of life. Thus, you may initiate these memberships voluntarily, but not hold them voluntarily (since you cannot necessarily retract your consent even if you change your mind in fact). What makes these relations and the obligations that follow from them truly voluntary or not are the institutional arrangements within which individual consent is exercised.

All these considerations do indicate, I think, that individual consent is not an adequate ground to account for family obligations. Consent cannot fully explain or justify them as such, although it is not irrelevant. We can say that it is normally sufficient in particular cases, but our considerations of community membership should make us leery of any automatic presumptions, and consent is not a necessary condition for justified family obligation. So it would seem that any adequate justification of family obligation in general would require a broader account that includes and qualifies the notion of consent as one of its elements but does not rely on it exclusively.

Debt

Another possible justification for family obligations, at least one that is often informally suggested, is debt. This justification is sometimes proposed to explain obligations to family in the abstract, and is often applied to household obligations. You might possibly owe a debt to your family, at least a debt of gratitude in a particular case. If you do, owing a debt to family in the abstract would be like owing a debt to your alma mater, your country, or your home town, perhaps, or so it might be suggested. But debt depends on particular circumstances, and it is hard to see how it could possibly apply to family in the abstract. Indeed, most extended families are so loosely organized that owing a debt to one's family in the sense of, say, one's family name could hardly come up. For example, it is hard for me to imagine that I might owe "the Smiths" (the family of my father) something, or why I might owe it. My father, yes; the Smiths, no. Furthermore, unless the family (in its abstract form) is incorporated in such a way as to provide decision procedures that enable it to engage in corporate action (a pretty rare sort of family organization, I'd say) it is not the sort of entity that can act, and therefore it cannot do anything to generate a debt. Thus, debt to family in the abstract is a nonstarter.

Generally, a debt is owed to a particular person (an intentional actor), so most likely, whatever you owe, you owe to some particular family member, or perhaps to the members of your household jointly. It is your grandfather who spent his Saturdays helping you build models. Your aunt always had a kind word. Your brother set you straight when no one else would. Your household together got along on less so that you could go to school. Some of the obligations you have to them are grounded on debt—the receipt of benefits. As mentioned earlier, you may have received the benefits long before you were old enough to be competent to consent to a debt. But it does not follow, I think, that no debt is generated. Why should that be?

Such a notion certainly is not a standard version of debt, for example, one that would be legally enforceable, especially since the benefits I am discussing were, presumably, gifts. They were not bestowed in order to generate a reciprocal benefit. But it still does not follow that there is no debt of gratitude.

I know that my parents do not believe that I owe them anything; but I certainly think that I do. This set of attitudes is very common (and should be, in my opinion). Statistics in the United States show that 80 percent of elder care is provided by the family and especially the children of the elderly person.[9] Why do so many children take care of their elderly parents? For many reasons; one major reason is that people feel a debt of gratitude to their parents. At the same time, a recent survey showed that most elders (75 percent of those surveyed) felt that their children did not owe them anything, and preferred not to impose any burden on them.[10]

All this, of course, is as it should be. That is, it is just the way debts of gratitude ought to work. If parents expected a return for services rendered, the parental relationship would not correspond to the one we ordinarily associate with our model (at least our current model) of parental love. If children did not (ultimately) feel gratitude for parental services (and love), it would surely indicate a serious flaw in their character (or a serious flaw in our current family relationships, or both, perhaps). Of course, individual family relationships and experiences vary widely, but unless we are indeed suffering a frightening level of personal family disintegration, some amount of filial gratitude must be appropriate in at least a majority of families. If so, a debt of gratitude to parents is often appropriate (though often is not always).

These considerations seem most applicable to household obligations, especially between parents and children, but one might also consider siblings. To do so may illustrate how coincidental is the notion of debt. If you and your brother have shared life experiences you might well owe him a debt of gratitude, as I suggested earlier, based on your past interactions. If, on the other hand, you and your brother go your separate ways at an early age, and he shows up a derelict on your doorstep after twenty years of no contact, is your obligation to him no different from what it would be for any derelict? If you have an obligation to him (and you may not, morally speaking, but if you do), it cannot be based on debt. In fact, it could only exist simply because he is your brother, that is, because of the connection of family membership (since we already rejected biology). The reason (as cause) for most people thinking that they have such obligations is that social practice or tradition profoundly affects our individual attitudes, and these should not be discounted as social forces. Whether you are justified in ignoring or denying such forces or claims of family obligation depends on the general institutional arrangements and the reasonable expectations of the community. If you are a member of a community that reasonably expects such obligations to be met, as part of an institution that is not unjust, then you cannot morally deny them.

Can such obligations, even to siblings, be justified as such? I think they might be under the right circumstances, but not as debts of gratitude. Debts of gratitude are specific (i.e., depend on particular relationships and experiences) and can be owed to anyone—friends, associates, colleagues, benefactors. Because of the common arrangement of social structures in families, there is a high correlation between debts of gratitude and family relationships, but there is no necessary connection. So, debt, like consent, may justify particular obligations to people who happen to be family members, but debt does not justify family obligation as such. Does anything?

Membership

I have suggested that being part of a cooperative arrangement that is itself justified may generate obligations attached to roles that constitute that arrangement, practice, or institution. These are what I am calling obligations of cooperative communal membership. Family households are intimate forms of social organization that may be justified on grounds of justice and utility, which in turn would justify certain obligations of family members as such.

If these are obligations of membership specifically, then they should be justified by features that are intrinsic to that idea or uniquely related to it. Obviously, it is not membership as such that justifies any duty. As noted earlier, one can be a member of all sorts of groups (e.g., all blue-eyed people) that have no moral significance whatsoever. One can also be a member of a group that is unjustified or immoral (e.g., membership in a slave society cannot generate an obligation to be a slave). So the only memberships that justify obligations are those that meet two requirements, as follows.

1. The membership must be minimally just. It must not contradict the basic liberal commitment to freedom and equal treatment or fairness. I have made this point repeatedly, so I will not dwell on it here. Suffice it to say that positive duties do not override negative duties. Thus, duties of membership do not contract the scope of justice; they expand it.[11]

2. The membership must be cooperative. (Being blue-eyed requires no cooperation.) Otherwise, the notion of duty does not arise. Thus, the sort of membership that is relevant here is a cooperative arrangement that is organized to meet some need (in a way that is not discriminatory or oppressive).

I have so far considered membership in terms of four elements: reflexive identity, communal tasks, common expectations, and roles. What do they tell us about the justification of family duty? The central motivational factor and the most general explanatory element is, I believe, twofold or conjunctive, as follows. (1) What I have called the reflexive identity of community and member is basic. If you have an obligation of membership (rather than some other kind), it must be because you are a crucial part of some larger entity that is itself justified. (2) What justifies it is being organized around some communal task or institutional objective. The community is defined or constituted by its members in terms of common commitments that require cooperative participation. This is the key. And it is why, when I considered the obligations of particular individual roles (of spouse, parent, or child) in every case, ultimately I had to consider the justification of the institution that generated or fixed the role. In each case, the obligation is justified only if the role is justified, and the role must be justified as part of an institution that specifies it.

I suggested earlier that institutions that involve affirmative obligations could be justified in terms of justice and utility, but that suggestion, of course, needs a great deal of explication. It seems reasonable to suppose prima facie that institutions can be justified as tending to promote the general welfare just as long as those institutions also comply with the requirements of justice. That is, when considering the organizational structure of social institutions, both utility and justice are obviously relevant. Utility is served if at least one person is better off and no one is worse off, or more generally, when benefits outweigh losses on balance. Estimates of utility are necessarily impressionistic in a context like this one, but of course, the basic idea is that an institution or practice serves the cause of utility if it improves the general welfare overall. Thus, in order to justify family obligation as such, the claim must be that society on the whole is better off for being organized around individual private families with particular obligations attached to them as such. For example, one claim might be that society on the whole is better off if children are raised by individual persons who are committed to them individually (and perhaps officially) for life (that is, by parents), rather than say, by the state, as a normal course of events. This is not an indisputable claim, but it is, I believe a basic presumption of liberalism. If the claim is reasonable, it can serve as a prima facie justification for parental obligation as such (if, as mentioned before, the institution on the whole is justified).

Since in terms of utility the gains of some may be bought with the losses of others, however, evaluations of utility must be bounded by the requirements of justice. Justice is relevant here in (at least) two ways. It is relevant, of course, in the standard sense of imposing negative duties to respect persons as individual human beings. Justice imposes the boundary conditions on utility that require institutional obligations to be the least restrictive alternatives that are reasonably available, and to be distributed according to minimal standards of fairness.[12] Thus, justice, being universal, prohibits the mistreatment of individuals in this area of life as it does in any other. You cannot morally treat family members worse than the minimal standards imposed by justice on all of us. Justice as respect for persons applies everywhere, but that is not all that justice requires.[13]

There is also, I want to suggest, an affirmative aspect of justice that is particularly relevant to the context of family obligations. It can be developed, I believe, in terms of the concepts of *mutual reliance* and *cooperative support*. I have mentioned both these ideas before, and now I would like to consider them in more detail.

Grounding special positive duties on mutual reliance supposes that people can (at least sometimes) be obligated to one another because they rely on one another. When are you obligated to people because they rely on you? Presumably, only when they are entitled to rely on you. What would generate such entitlements? In contract law the idea is that if you allow someone to rely on you to his detriment, you are obligated to make good on your agreement, at least to the extent of his losses.

Does this apply to family relations?[14] In a certain respect it does, except that family obligation has an added element that makes it distinct from the usual construction of reliance in contract.[15] If you allow family members to rely on you, you are, of course, morally obligated to make good on what you have led them to believe. This would be true for a friend or colleague as well, and would tell us nothing about family obligation as such. But if you are part of a family, your family members may be entitled to rely on you in certain ways, not only because you have allowed them to rely on you, but because of your role, or the place you hold as part of the family. Furthermore, you are entitled to rely on them in analogous ways. What that points out is that mutual reliance is intrinsic to a family relationship: family members are entitled to rely on one another precisely because they are members.

I have already noted that people commonly believe that they have such obligations, and they accept or comply with them because they are embodied in community standards (mutual expectations) that largely go unquestioned. It is easy to see why socialization and immersion in a culture and community environment will tend to result in common expectations such as this. The question is, Should the very existence of mutual expectations be viewed as justifying obligations to comply with them?

I believe that the answer is not absolutely, but presumptively, yes, if and only if the institutional organization is not unjust. As I have shown, there is nothing about settled community expections that implies a just organizational structure. Furthermore, community expectations are necessarily restrictive to some extent, and can be highly oppressive as well as discriminatory, even though it is community expectation that informs us of predominant beliefs about obligations. So community expectations must be evaluated in terms of the values presupposed in them and the character of the institutions that follow from them. I will tentatively suggest that a plausible concept for making such evaluations could be developed as the *reasonable* expectations of the community. This phrase is commonly used in law, but the idea I have in mind is more exacting than some legal usage. In some legal usage, reasonable community expectation simply means settled community expectation (whatever that expectation may be), which is what I am arguing is inadequate in this context. Nevertheless, the idea of reasonable expectation is a normative standard (as opposed to a description of what most people happen to think). It refers to what it is reasonable to think; and that could, and for present purposes should, include a moral element that incorporates the requirements of justice. It is not *reasonable*, it could be argued, to expect community members to adhere to unjust institutions, but if community expectations are reasonable (and therefore not unjust) then the obligations explicated by them are justified. Thus, reasonable expectations of the community should be viewed as rebuttable presumptions in favor of an obligation to comply. This should be so as applied to family obligation, I think, for two reasons: both utility and justice support it.

Any society needs some basic institutions and relations in which mutual reliance or, in other words, trust is the norm. This norm may be met or not in particular cases, but as a norm it is the standard by which success of social cooperation is measured. Trust is so life-enhancing that in terms of utility alone it should be a norm in as many areas of life in which it is possible to instill trustworthiness. A society devoid of trust is an inhospitable environment for human interaction. But trust is a very high standard, so it may not be possible or realistic as a norm, as a reasonable expectation (rather than as an ideal) in many areas of life.

The family, however, is particularly appropriate for the application of this norm because it is small, intimate, and enduring. Family members are able to know one another well, to interact over time, and to reinforce the mutuality of the trust they share. The family is also a primary location for the transmission of values to children. If the value of trustworthiness is important for social life and the general welfare, then providing a model and standard of trustworthiness for children in family life may be the most potent source of moral instruction available for future generations. Furthermore, individuals in intimate circumstances are particularly vulnerable to one another, so a greater level of trust is needed, and this fact can serve as a greater incentive to be trustworthy, especially if the reliance appropriate to family life is recognized as mutual. A family without trust is dysfunctional.

Thus, it appears that family (as household) is constituted by a common commitment of mutual reliance. That is the kind of institution it is. What, on this conception, is a family, after all? It is a permanently committed, small and intimate, cooperative group. What distinguishes a family from a group of roommates (for example) is that family relations are intended to be permanent and maximally cooperative. Roommates' relations, in comparison, are usually temporary and may be only minimally cooperative. Family ties are not arrangements of temporary convenience. The idea behind family is that the relationships endure. Enduring relations need trust. Family (as household) is intimate and cooperative in that it is a small group that pools resources, and shares household arrangements. At least to the extent necessary to make those living arrangements work, it is necessarily a cooperative association. That leads to the substantive manifestation of mutual reliance that I am calling *cooperative support*. I would now like to explore that related idea very briefly.

A household is the epitome of a shared enterprise. Where people not only pool their resources but merge their lives, then a common sharing of burdens is most appropriate. Thus, the idea of communal tasks mentioned earlier is exemplified here. The distribution of these tasks will not be equal; instead they are borne by those most able or most available to bear them. Even so, both fairness and the common good demand that everyone has some share in both the burdens and benefits. As long as you are a part of this common enterprise, you have an obligation to contribute to it, to share the common tasks as needed and in terms of your ability. This obligation is not the same as one based on debt or contract, which are obligations that follow from a prior act or event. Rather, it is based on the fairness and value and even the necessity of common contribution to an ongoing enterprise of which one is a part. The central feature is mutual participation. Communal association is constituted by the cooperative contribution of its members; it forms the substantive manifestation of their mutual reliance. Mutual reliance, as I just explained, is the foundation of trust that should be central to any ongoing relation of intimacy and daily interaction that are, if not necessary, certainly preferable for family living. The norm for family relations should be a relation of trust—that is, of mutual reliance. But trust is manifested in various ways: substantively, cooperative support is a primary manifestation of the communal living arrangements that constitute a household, and an expression of the trust that is generated by mutual reliance. Thus, like mutual reliance, the obligation of cooperative support in family relations is founded on the requirements of justice as well as utility. It is, in fact, merely a substantive manifestation of the same idea.

There are, of course, many variations on this theme, but this is the paradigm of family living: trust and cooperation are crucial for ongoing, intimate association. It should be obvious that in such circumstances it will be highly detrimental to the functioning of the group and all its members if they cannot rely on one another in mutually understood ways. Thus, undermining mutual reliance in ongoing family relationships fails to comply with utility.

It also violates justice. Not only is the general welfare harmed by the erosion of good family relations (although it is), but also the trust of another is betrayed by the failure to uphold reasonable reliance on mutual expectations. The direct and primary victim is not society at large but the individual who was betrayed. The betrayal of trust is a violation of justice.[16]

For this reason, I suggest that reasonable expectations of mutual reliance should be treated as presumptive evidence of obligation. They may be rebuttable in particular circumstances, but the burden of rebutting them should be on the person who rejects the common expectations. Unless such a rebuttal is forthcoming, reasonable expectations are reasonable and necessary for daily life and human interaction, and they generate obligations to particular individuals on which those individuals are entitled to rely. Violating such reasonable reliance is a violation of special positive duty—something that one owes to particular individuals by virtue of a special relationship—and thus it violates justice.

Consequently, it appears that mutual reliance can justify duties of family membership. Why should that be? I have argued that it is because family as household is constituted by a common commitment of mutual reliance. In fact, the element of mutual reliance in family relations is so rich that it leads to affirmative obligations that I have referred to as obligations of cooperative support. These obligations expand the general liberal requirements of justice in terms of special positive duties to the family. These family obligations are widely acknowledged, indeed, are relied on in liberal social practice. In liberal theory they have been merely referred to as natural duties. I hope the account offered here in terms of cooperative participation in a communal institution provides a fuller and richer explanation.

3. Some Preliminary Conclusions: Justice As Reciprocity and Liberal Obligations of Membership

The important implication of all this is that family obligations, as I suggested earlier (in chapter 1), are actually duties of justice (as well as mandates of utility). They are not, however, duties of noninterference (or, for that matter, duties of respect, if that means noninterference). A duty of respect responds to the individual need to be recognized as a separate entity of worth. It reflects the dignity of human beings as individuals, each one unique and intrinsically valuable in his or her own right. It is premised on the value of the human capacity for self-legislation and consequently protects the integrity of rational agency in the form of free, autonomous choice. These are all significant values, but they are inadequate to account for all the needs of human life or even for all the requirements of justice. Not all duties of justice are alike. Not all duties of justice are negative.

Special positive duties are also duties of justice. Like universal negative duties, they are perfect duties—specifiable obligations owed to particular individuals. Failing to meet them violates the rights of those individuals to whom they are owed. Unlike universal negative duties, special positive duties are limited in scope and affirmative. The best justification for these affirmative obligations in the context of family relations is mutual reliance, or in its substantive mode, cooperative support. The aspect of these duties that needs to be highlighted is their connection to the idea of fairness in terms of mutual contribution to cooperative endeavor. Mutuality is central to both notions. Therefore, I would like to explore the possible connection between these ideas and the notion of justice as reciprocity.

Justice as reciprocity is an ancient idea; in fact, it has been argued that reciprocity is actually the oldest of all concepts of justice.[17] It is without question much older than its individualistic Kantian counterpart, but oddly it is not widely discussed in contemporary literature except in its negative form as retribution.[18] Aristotle considered it the appropriate form of justice in matters of exchange.

[I]n associations for exchange this sort of justice does hold men together—reciprocity in accordance with a proportion and not on the basis of precisely equal return. For it is by proportionate requital that the city holds together. Men seek to return either evil for evil—and if they cannot do so, think their position mere slavery—or good for good—and if they cannot do so there is no exchange, but it is by exchange that they hold together.[19]

Reciprocity is concerned with the idea of appropriate return—the idea of like for like: good for good and, traditionally, evil for evil. (At least one contemporary philosopher has argued that the virtue of reciprocity does not entail returning evil for evil;[20] and virtually all moral traditions have treated this relation as more complex than strict retaliation in kind, whether affirmative or negative.) In any case, in its affirmative mode, the general idea embodied in reciprocity is the idea of mutual and fair or proportional contribution.[21] From reciprocity is derived the notion of desert, a central moral concept that is directly connected to fairness—the idea that people should receive what they deserve. Within the context of cooperative endeavor, if people should receive what they deserve, they also should contribute their fair share. As Aristotle treats it, reciprocity reflects the human need to interact socially and cooperate, to transact business in terms of mutual exchange, or even to foster relationships of mutual advantage.[22] This form of justice, he claims, holds men together, and responds to a basic inclination to return like for like.

Consequently, the ideas of mutual reliance and cooperative support fall, I believe, within this general domain of justice. The idea behind them is not self-sacrifice or altruism, or respect for individual integrity as such, but mutuality of contribution and collateral trustworthiness. They are, consequently, the basis for building relationships of cooperation and responsibility as well as mutual respect. Most important, perhaps, the ideas of mutual reliance and cooperative support as reciprocity or appropriate interaction are inherently social concepts that apply to all transactions but are especially conducive to the promotion of ongoing relationships. They provide the basis for reliable human cooperation, the ground rules of social intercourse, and interrelation.

Thus, unlike duties of respect, which focus on and protect the autonomy, individuality, and separateness of persons, duties of reciprocity are the building blocks of social interaction and personal interdependence. Although they have not been featured in liberal theory for the most part, being overshadowed by an emphasis on duties of respect, these duties of interaction have always been acknowledged in liberal theory and central to liberal social practice.[23] Of course, duties of reciprocity are in no way incompatible with liberalism, and they can (I am suggesting) provide an adequate liberal explanation of family obligation as duties of membership in the form of mutual reliance and cooperative support. I think that it is time to reorient the focus of liberal theory to highlight these neglected duties of reciprocity that in fact have always been so central to cooperative liberal institutions and practices. Family obligation is a good beginning point for this project, since family relations are paradigmatic of ongoing, cooperative endeavor. One can see that construing family duties as obligations of membership, necessary for continuing and cooperative communal association at an intimate level that is fundamental to liberal society, provides a basis for setting boundaries on individual freedom that is compatible with liberal presumptions in a way that was never true of traditional ideas of natural duty.

I find that liberals seem to be of two minds regarding the nature of family obligation. Some regard it as absolutely fundamental. From that perspective, it may be that any discussion that attempts to justify family obligation in terms of something else is misguided. This view suggests that family membership may be more basic than any other social relation or moral value on which we might attempt to justify obligation. This is not to claim that family obligations override universal negative duties or other obligations, such as contractual ones. It is to suppose that other grounds for obligations are not rich enough to capture the strength and extent of family obligation. For that it may be best to look to the nature and value of family itself, as an institution. Although this would not be my own approach to family obligation, for those who do hold this view, I believe it can be accommodated in the present account in the following way.

Philosophers sometimes talk about natural necessity. In fact, they used to talk about it a lot, but today it is considered to be a concept that should be used very sparingly and with great caution. I agree with that view. As an embattled, liberal feminist since the seventies, I am exceedingly suspicious of any claim of natural necessity whatsoever, since it has always been used against women. Yet I would not claim that there is no such thing at all. H. L. A. Hart, for example, who is a pretty down-to-earth, modern legal positivist, with little inclination toward legal explanations based on natural law, nevertheless reasonably recognized that some common features of law are related to very basic human characteristics and conditions — natural necessities — such as having limited resources and basic needs.[24] Pretty reasonable. In fact, it would be quite unreasonable to deny it. So let's agree that natural necessity does exist, at a very fundamental level, and with some trepidation, I will suggest that it might not be out of place here.

Human beings cannot survive (at least cannot survive as human beings) with only the so-called neutral relations and negative moral proscriptions of the state, the species, or the planet. If, somehow by magic, we had universal adherence to all negative duties; if all proscriptions not to harm others were universally observed, but there were no other obligations or commitments, we would all die — or turn into a different sort of animal. Human beings are social creatures. We need affection, companionship, love, intimacy. Without the intimate relations of friends, lovers, parents, and children, we could not maintain our humanity at all (much less universal duties, which would be the first to go). We require support and sympathy. But more than that, we need a foundation of connection and commitment (which is occasionally suggested as one explanation for why even abused family members will sometimes remain in bad conditions rather than risk being alone without those connections).

This account of family obligation as natural necessity does not supersede justice. On the contrary, justice provides the standard for measuring these relations and obligations, for assessing what they ought to be like — minimally, that is — for setting limits and boundaries. Justice can invalidate particular family arrangements — tyrannical, discriminatory, or oppressive ones — but it does not justify the institution of the family itself, according to this view. Natural necessity does that. Families, in the form of intimate, long-term, supportive associations, provide basic relations and values that human beings need. And these are insured by obligations of membership.[25]

But how can obligations of membership, on this construction, possibly be compatible with the central premise of liberalism, which is the significance of individual freedom and autonomy? The answer is that they cannot, unless the institution of the family meets the basic requirements of justice to individuals; it cannot be discriminatory or oppressive. But there is nothing about social organization in the form of families that *must* be discriminatory or oppressive, or at least I am willing to suppose that that is true. So social organization in terms of private families is not necessarily incompatible with liberal moral commitments even if the justification for families is natural necessity.

The private family is the fundamental unit of liberal social organization. This is reflected in legal institutions, moral assumptions, and social customs that instantiate the liberal presumption that takes the private family as the most basic element of a free society. The idea behind organizing free societies around a commitment to the private family is to place the basic unit of social organization outside the control of central government and beyond the range of centralized authority, while yet recognizing that human beings are fundamentally social.[26] That is, liberalism is not (and never has been) premised on social organization based on isolated individuals, but instead is premised on small group organization rather than large group organization as the strongest protection of individual freedom.

Despite traditional analytical deficiencies, it is clear that family obligations (generally without consent) are now and always have been accepted as part of the basic institutional arrangements of liberal society, and acknowledged within liberal theory. Once that fact is recognized, it shows that liberalism has never been as atomistic as its critics allege. Family obligations as natural duties were acknowledged by all the classical liberal thinkers, as well as, recently, by John Rawls's theory of justice, which is constructed around heads of families as contractors in an original position determining basic principles of justice by which all would later be bound. Thus, families have always been central to liberal theory (or at least presumed within it) as well as essential to liberal social organization in fact.

Therefore, at least some involuntary affirmative obligations have always been accepted by liberals as necessary to liberal social organization. The idea of family as a social institution necessarily includes obligations at least some of which are not based on consent, and none of which are based on a full-blown notion of individual consent that would correspond to quasi-contractual ideals often highlighted within traditional liberal theories. In fact, liberal theory has never treated family obligation as derived from consent. Natural relations were always contrasted with contractual ones.

What then, accounts for these obligations? Historically, of course, they developed from obligations of status, which were predominant in pre-liberal societies and which liberals opposed in other contexts (such as commercial and political spheres). Why did obligations to family remain separate when everything else was being absorbed within the framework of contract? And more important, viewing them as distinct—not covered by consent—can they be justified within a liberal view?

Family obligation remained the bulwark of liberal society, and must remain so, because the private family on some formulation is necessary for liberal social organization. Without the idea of a privately initiated, intimate social unit as the basis for any larger political organization, there can only be truly atomistic individualism (which is untenable and nihilistic) or some form of directly communal, thus centralized, organization (which is perfectly plausible, but not liberal if it is the only option). Liberal principles, even (or perhaps especially) if considerable central organization is allowed, must be protected by reserving the basic choices and relations of personal life, as well as basic beliefs and attitudes for the individual direction of private citizens within the seclusion of private family life.

Of course, no such explanation for the existence of the private family within liberal society was ever given, historically, as far as I know. Traditionally, the family was simply viewed as "natural" and consequently as an exception to the general liberal focus on universal, negative duties of noninterference, on the one hand, or (affirmative) obligation by consent (usually in the form of contract) on the other. This traditional view is at least superficially plausible because reliance on family as a foundation for some duties provides at least the appearance of two basic requirements for coherently ascribing positive duties: definition of scope and justification.

Affirmative family obligations are not impossible to meet, because they are confined in scope to a small, manageable, and specifiable group. Family members can be identified, so one's positive duties can be reasonably limited. Without some such limitation, positive duties become incoherent because they become impossible to meet. And beyond this conceptual requirement, a liberal commitment to freedom requires that one's affirmative obligations be strictly limited in this way, so family obligations appear to meet that liberal requirement.

While family obligations are in fact well defined in scope, their justification as "natural" is much more questionable from a liberal point of view, as I have argued. Unless controversial metaphysical assumptions about natural inclinations and preferences, as well as natural differences between men and women, are maintained against all evidence to the contrary, positing natural duties as biological requirements is hard to square with the liberal commitment to individual freedom. On the other hand, I have tried to show that shifting uncritically to individual consent without accounting for the social context within which consent is exercised is inadequate as well. So, biology (or nature) is an unacceptable foundation altogether, and consent alone is inadequate as a liberal foundation for family obligation.

But I have developed two possible justifications of family obligation that are, or could be, compatible with liberal commitments. One is the idea of family organization as natural necessity that I just explicated. That is to say, one way to construe the traditional notion of natural duties is as a reflection of the human need for enduring relationships of mutual commitment and support at an intimate level. To do so is to recognize that human beings are not atomistic individuals, not isolated nomads or reclusive hermits in ordinary circumstances, but social beings who need and want, who seek out and cultivate, the cooperative companionship supplied by a few lifelong, or at least longstanding and committed, relationships.

Human beings, one might say, tend to live in families, as certain other animals tend to live. The comparison illustrates the point that the traditional idea of natural duties, based on natural relationships, need not reflect anything more controversial to liberal theory than the idea that human beings, naturally, are best served by small group organization of some sort that can protect private life and thought from centralized government, and that can provide enduring relationships of commitment and mutual support that human beings seem to need at an intimate level. These sorts of values—connection, commitment, support, love—can only be provided by a small, intimate group founded on assumptions of mutual reliance and cooperative contribution. This view would support the traditional language of natural duty in a manner more compatible with general liberal presumptions than the usual notions of biological necessity or status were ever able to do. And it presumes nothing more controversial than the minimal idea of natural necessity articulated by H. L. A. Hart forty years ago and widely acknowledged by liberals since then.

But even these presumptions are not necessary, since family duties as duties of membership can be viewed (as I suggested earlier) as necessary for liberal social organization itself, that is, as a hedge against atomistic anarchy on the one hand and totalitarian central planning on the other. This foundation for family obligation as duties of membership entails only the presumption that liberal social organization requires the recognition and support of small, intimate, private, cooperative groups (families) as well as their protection from state interference as a restriction of state power over individuals. This approach reflects the idea that the liberal insistence on the private family as the cornerstone of democratic society is overall a protection rather than a restriction of freedom. It is a protection, that is, against centralized power.

Either of these approaches "socializes" liberalism by eliminating supposedly atomistic assumptions, by complicating the predominance of obligation by consent, and also by broadening the idea of liberal justice to include considerations of reciprocity that undergird relations of ongoing, cooperative social interaction—in this context, particularly in the form of liberal obligations of membership that account for special positive duties to family. None of this thinking is in any way incompatible with traditional liberal presumptions; it simply refocuses them in a way that highlights and explains obligations in terms of the longstanding liberal commitment to the institution of the private family. Thus, it provides a framework for developing a consistent liberal conception of family obligation in terms of family membership. Furthermore, a liberal conception of family obligation cannot be formulated, consequently liberal social organization based on the private family cannot be justified, without appeal to an account more or less like this one. Appeal to consent alone is inadequate. Appeal to biology is not liberal. Thus, acknowledging cooperative communal membership or cooperative participation in social institutions at a basic level is necessary for a liberal justification of positive duties to the family.

III

SPECIAL POSITIVE DUTY AND CONTRACTUAL RELATIONS

The movement of the progressive societies has been uniform in one respect. Through all its course it has been distinguished by the gradual dissolution of family dependency and the growth of individual obligation in its place. . . . Nor is it difficult to see what is the tie between man and man which replaces by degrees those forms of reciprocity in rights and duties which have their origin in the Family. It is Contract. The word Status may be usefully employed to construct a formula expressing the law of progress thus indicated. . . . [W]e may say that the movement of the progressive societies has hitherto been a movement *from Status to Contract*.

Sir Henry Maine, 1864

6

The Complexity of Consent
in Legal Theory and Practice

Since before the time of Sir Henry Maine the notion of contract has fascinated philosophers and lawyers alike. As Maine pointed out, English lawyers realized early on that the idea of contract could be made to account for virtually every political and legal obligation.[1] Contract came to be viewed as the foundation of all law, and even morality. So rich is the idea that philosophers since Hobbes have used it to justify state power and explain what constitutes legitimate authority. In recent years versions of the social contract idea have been used to explain the requirements of justice and moral responsibility as well as political obligation.[2]

One of the reasons for the popularity of this precept is that it fits so well with, indeed it embodies, the spirit of nineteenth-century individualism—the pervasive presumption of modern Western civilization and the foundation of liberal society. Affirmative obligations, on this view, are the result of the free choices of autonomous individuals. The key to contractual obligation is consent.

But what is consent? What choice is free? And what does it mean to construe it as the voluntary interaction of autonomous individuals? These are the issues that need exploration in order to provide a reasonable analysis of special positive duties as based on contractual relations, which have long been regarded as the centerpiece and explanatory paradigm of affirmative obligations in liberal theory. In the next two chapters I will examine these questions in the basic contexts of contractual and professional obligation.

In this chapter I will begin with the context of contract law itself. Can the idea of contractual obligation be explained adequately or justified by the intentional agreements or exchanged promises of the parties alone (the traditional view), or does contractual obligation involve a broader range of considerations, and if the latter, what do those considerations include? This is an important area of investigation, because there is a peculiar interaction of law with morality occurring within it. Contract being a legal concept, it is striking that moral theory and practice should so often be patterned on this legal model. Conversely, contract law itself represents the development of a distinctive moral view, which is all the more peculiar for its avowal of value neutrality. It is, in effect, the morality of neutrality. In this respect it is particularly representative of the predominant worldview of modern liberal society, one distinctive characteristic of which is precisely value neutrality. We moderns have espoused this position as our personal tragicomic foible, having confused it with tolerance, on the one hand, and with science, on the other. It is the phlogiston of modernity, and at its heart is contract law. Nowhere is there a better developed view of obligation as the free choices of autonomous individuals neutrally monitored by impartial institutions. So it is important to consider how this development has proceeded.

1. Contract Theory and Legal Practice: Doctrine and Debate

The basic idea behind the classical view of contractual obligation in its simplest terms can be easily stated. Contractual obligation is that which is voluntarily assumed in exchange for a benefit in return. You do not have a contractual obligation unless you agree to it, and if you agree to it, you have it—you are bound, precisely because you agreed. Both in legal and in moral theory, this idea is the essence of the traditional view of contractual obligation. In law, however, this simple idea has undergone some rather complex developmental permutations. What, then, can legal theory and the practice of law tell us about contractual obligation?

It is sometimes "explained" or postulated that the civil law of obligation is divided into two categories, with contract law on one side representing obligations that are voluntarily incurred, and tort (and restitution) law on the other side representing obligations that are imposed by law. Contract law merely enforces obligations incurred by consent. Tort law, by contrast, imposes obligations derived from community standards: the reasonable expectations of the community. With that traditional conceptual framework in mind, what does contract law tell us about obligation by agreement?

The first general lesson about agreements derived from the practice of contract law is that they are often broken. People change their minds; they back out of their agreements for an astonishing array of reasons, both good and bad. As a lawyer, one thing that you can probably count on is that by the time you finish drafting the document (possibly before) at least one of the parties will have changed his mind about at least some part of it. Another thing you can probably rely on is that no matter how carefully you draft it, at least one of the parties will have misunderstood or misconstrued at least one of its terms or implications. Despite the fact that a majority of contracts are adhered to by the parties involved, there are an enormous number of ways in which special agreements can go bad.

If that were not true, why would we need lawyers to draft our agreements for us? Why couldn't we just do it ourselves? Contract lawyers are supposed to do (at least) four things for us. (1) They are supposed to clarify the terms of the agreement and eliminate misunderstanding so that the agreement is real and, more specifically, so that the agreement is in fact what the lawyer's client thinks it is. (2) They are supposed to anticipate all the things that could possibly go wrong later, even supposing the good faith of both parties at the outset—all the reasons either party might have for changing her mind—and spell out what happens in the event of such change. (3) They are supposed to protect their clients from being defrauded, tricked, overpowered, and so on, by people of bad will. (4) They are supposed to see to it that if anything goes wrong, the contract will be legally enforceable.[3] That is, we might say, contract lawyers are professional pessimists, thus providing a very important service, given the vicissitudes of human nature.

This in turn explains why we have contract law. Basically, agreements must be kept in general, and not only among friends, families, and neighbors, but among strangers, or else modern life as we know it would come to a screeching halt. Modern contract law developed in response to the needs of expanded social (and particularly commercial) interaction.[4] The developments of modern social and commercial life make it necessary that strangers (as well as friends and neighbors) be able to rely on one another within certain cooperative ventures that contribute to their mutual advantage at some level. (In fact this mutual benefit can be extremely unequal, and thus unfair, but I will discuss that problem later.) Social development beyond a small community level requires the cooperation of strangers. People have to be able to rely on one another in ongoing ventures, and they cannot realistically do so without some means of reinforcement. General living experience teaches us that, unfortunately, many human beings are weak, selfish, capricious, short-sighted, often greedy, and even sometimes dishonest and malevolent. Besides, circumstances always change, and people are not always good at anticipating those changes, and are not much inclined to sacrifice themselves to their former commitments once their new circumstances have made their old agreements disadvantageous to them. This is life. People always need to make agreements, and later need to break them. So agreements have to be reinforcible, or else it would be irrational to make them, and life would consequently be primitive.

If your only agreements are made with your family, friends, or neighbors, within a relatively static society, then there are many avenues of social reinforcement: moral, social, or personal pressure. You will have to think twice about breaking your agreement with your neighbors if you have to continue living next door to them for the rest of your life, and who knows, possibly wind up related to them by the marriage of your grandchildren later on. On the other hand, your neighbor will have to think twice about holding you to the agreement if circumstances truly justify revising or postponing it, for all the same reasons. Furthermore, people in close and continuous association have reason to make their agreements minimally fair or at least defensible to the rest of the community. Thus, the butcher can afford to extend your credit right now if she knows you, and knows that your circumstances are bound to be better next summer, and besides there is no one else to buy meat from when you want it later, and the whole community is going to know whether you pay your debts. They will also know, of course, whether the butcher's terms are fair. And you are both better off by being able to trust each other. There are many sources of reinforcement for bargains at a personal level. But once you move from friends to strangers, those sources are gone, and so is your bargain. Hence contract law.[5]

Contract law extends the range of rational interaction by making cooperation possible among strangers, or so it is often argued. This extension is accomplished by providing the reinforcement that is necessary to make people keep their agreements most of the time or pay for the losses if they don't. This makes it rational for people to rely on one another even when they are strangers.

So, implied in the very existence of contract law are several basic ideas: people need to be able to cooperate to advance mutual interests. In order to cooperate, people need to be able to rely on agreements, that is, to rely on others keeping their bargains. But in fact people often break their agreements, or at least have reason to. So agreements must be reinforced or insured, so to speak. People must be held to their word, or required to pay for losses incurred by breaking it, unless there is some very good reason for not holding them to it. Therefore, people are obligated in general to keep their agreements—at least legally obligated. All these ideas are implied in the existence of contract law or, in other words, in the existence of a body of co-ercive rules that enforce agreements.

Does it follow that people are morally obligated to keep their agreements? Not from the fact that they are legally obligated to do so, of course. People were once legally obligated to return runaway slaves to abusive owners (and for that matter, runaway wives to abusive husbands). I assume no one was morally obligated to do so, although perhaps many people thought they were. Law, it is well known, does not necessarily correspond to morality, at least not in its particulars.

What it does correspond to more or less, however, and must correspond to in general, are the predominant social norms and mores. This must be so, at least in democracies, for two reasons. First, law is enacted or developed by members of the community, so it necessarily reflects the assumptions, values, and beliefs of those who enact or develop it. Judges and legislators are themselves, after all, part of the community, and they are generally responding to the needs of some community members. Second, if law deviates far from predominant beliefs (for better or worse—for example, as the result of a very farsighted reformer) it will not generally be obeyed, and it will be almost impossible to enforce.[6] Prohibition law in the 1920s is a good example of this problem, as are the early integration laws, which were first subverted completely and which ultimately required National Guard action to enforce.

The study of law can provide us with many insights about social mores and human nature, as well as interpersonal interactions and needs—with some qualifications. In general, law is a slightly delayed reflection of social norms that predominate in a society. It will almost always be a little behind current needs and values, unless they are longstanding. And in a diverse society, it will leave out certain segments (especially the least powerful or least noticeable). Law reflects the bottom-line commitments of those who comprise the legislatures and law courts, as they perceive the needs of society. This is generally the same group—the middle to upper class—that (unconsciously) sets the social norms, or the standards of aspiration of what is normal or accepted or good. So, law can tell us a lot about dominant social standards, including perceived needs and problems, among which is the need for cooperative interaction that relies on agreement, and the problem of human susceptibility to break agreements if they become inconvenient.

As I have just laid it out, one might think that contractual obligation is founded on the social need of cooperative enterprise or the more personal need of mutual reliance in agreements. This, however, has not been the dominant theory in Anglo-American law.

2. The Will Theory and Its Critics: Evaluating Consent

Since the nineteenth century, contract doctrine has been dominated by what was originally called the *will theory*, which has been reformulated in a powerful modern form as the *promise principle*.[7] This theory has always focused on the significance of individual freedom, autonomy, and responsibility for one's words and actions. The autonomous person is self-legislating, able to formulate his or her own rules and act according to them. Respect for the dignity of the individual requires noninterference with the decisions of free and self-legislating adults. Accordingly, the will theory defines a contract as a meeting of the minds, an agreement to which the parties are bound precisely because that is what they themselves intended. Thus, a contract is an exchange of promises, and contractual obligation arises from the combined will, or intentions, or promises of the parties. Contract law merely enforces what the parties have in effect legislated for themselves.

Basic contract doctrine today reflects this theory, with one slight but significant adjustment. That is to say, there is an element in standard doctrine that is not accommodated by the will theory, even though this element has been a feature of legal contracts for centuries. The dominant theory of contractual obligation (as reflected, for example, in current textbooks and legal opinions) is that a contract is an agreement *with consideration*. In other words, it is an agreement that involves an exchange of value, that is to say an agreement that each party has a reason to keep that was itself a feature of the bargain.

This is a very basic point that lawyers hardly think about unless they are first-year students or reach the level of high theory. For the layperson, however, it is important to realize that the law of contracts is not about the enforcement of a promise as such. A bare promise, or a gratuitous promise, is rarely enforceable by law, and certainly not as a contract. A contract is an agreement: a promise made in order to get something (possibly a reciprocal promise) in return. These are the only promises of interest to contract law.

So not all promises are enforceable. Only those promises that are exchanged for value (or consideration) will be backed by law. But, it is pointed out, the court will not presume to reevaluate the adequacy of consideration. It is up to the parties themselves to determine the value exchanged. Thus, the court will remain value neutral. As long as the parties deem that a value is exchanged, the court will not presume to second-guess them as to the worthiness or fairness of it, according to this theory. It is up to the parties to determine the value of their bargains for themselves, without the interference of the court.[8]

Thus, contract law has stood for individual freedom, independence, and in general the noninterference of government. The court should not presume to monitor the agreements of competent adults, who should be considered capable of negotiating their own bargains and being held to them. The court is and should be neutral with respect to the content or value of private agreements. It is simply to enforce the manifested intentions of the parties. Such is standard contract doctrine according to modern texts and from the perspective of the will theory.

As stated, this is a clear and elegant theory, which is the foundation of basic contract law even today. Very basic contract law. It must be recognized that this doctrine is "supplemented" by an enormous array of subsidiary theories of obligation, caveats and qualifications, extensions and limits, both inside and outside of contract law. In fact, the "supplementary" elements of contract law are so extensive and important that it has long been argued that the will theory is inadequate to explain contractual obligation, that the foundation of contractual obligation is not the enforcement of mutual promises, or the united will of autonomous parties, and indeed, that there is no single founding principle that can account for all contractual obligation.[9]

There is much to be said for these criticisms. Even a cursory glance at a current text in contract law will provide a summary of grounds to support them. One leading text, for example, discusses seven theories of obligation.[10] The primary theory, of course, is "agreement with consideration," but also discussed are obligations arising from detrimental reliance (or promissory estoppel), unjust enrichment, promises for benefits received, tort limitations—such as liability for defective products that cannot be disclaimed by agreement—and statutory warranties, such as those set out in section 2 of the Uniform Commercial Code on the sale of goods, which are also binding without regard to the promises of parties. The appearance and growth of these supplementary doctrines has led some commentators to suggest that the law of contract, especially as characterized by classical theory, is disappearing as a separate field of law. For example:

> Speaking descriptively, we might say that what is happening is that "contract" is being reabsorbed into the mainstream of "tort." . . . With the growth of the ideas of quasicontract and unjust enrichment, classical consideration theory was breached on the benefit side. With the growth of the promissory estoppel idea, it was breached on the detriment side. We are fast approaching the point where, to prevent unjust enrichment, any benefit received by a defendant must be paid for unless it was clearly meant as a gift; where any detriment reasonably incurred by a plaintiff in reliance on a defendant's assurances must be recompensed. When that point is reached, there is really no longer any viable distinction between liability in contract and liability in tort.[11]

The significance of this point for present purposes is that it claims that contract law is moving in the direction of tort law in a particular sense. In what sense? Tort law is (among other things) the enforcement of obligations that reflect certain basic community standards of fundamental fairness, without regard to individual agreement or consent, whereas contract law was claimed to be value neutral: simply the enforcement of the intentions of the parties as manifested in their exchanged promises, whatever they happened to be. Whether or not contract law is being absorbed by tort law, the important point is that the courts have developed doctrines of fairness and flexibility over the past century—either within contract law or in tort and restitution doctrines that apply to contract cases—that make the treatment of contracts more like that of torts in the sense of respecting, responding to, and attempting to articulate community standards of fairness and honesty.

The courts do not enforce all agreements, even with consideration. A contract will not be enforced if it is found to be unconscionable or against public policy, for example, or the result of duress, possibly including economic duress, and these considerations sometimes translate into the inequality of the exchange itself. Furthermore, there are limitations for fraud, concealment, misrepresentation, sometimes even innocent misrepresentation, as well as certain accommodations for impossibility of performance, mistake, impractibility, and frustration. Thus, the exchange of promises, to be enforceable, must be made within minimal (and they are minimal) limits set by community standards or social values of fairness, reasonableness, and honesty. Agreement or exchange of promises, even with consideration, is not sufficient for legal enforcement.

On the other hand, agreement in the form of exchanged promises is also not a necessary condition for affirmative obligation. Relief is often available to parties who have reasonably relied, to their detriment, on the assertions of others, even if there is no enforceable contract. This is the idea of promissory estoppel, which is recognized in all law courts, and in section 90 of the Restatements (1st & 2nd) of Contracts.

Similarly, a party who receives a benefit at the expense of someone who did not intend a gift may be required to return it, or pay for it, even in the absence of an enforceable contract. This is the doctrine of unjust enrichment, or quasicontract, which is actually an equitable doctrine of restitution rather than a contractual obligation as such. Yet it is clearly applicable to failed (or unenforceable) contractual agreements, even if the fiction is maintained that no contract is involved, and a strict separation of contract and restitution is insisted on for theoretical elegance. There is no question that such remedies are available within or without a contract.

So, as a description of Anglo-American law in fact or in practice, an exchange of promises is neither necessary nor sufficient for affirmative obligations enforced in law, and thus, classical liberal will theory cannot explain legal practice. This, I take it, is the point of critics such as Grant Gilmore, Lawrence Friedman, and P. S. Atiyah.

In addition, the observation has been made that twentieth-century contractual agreements are often neither as consensual nor as individual as classical theory would suggest.[12] Max Radin, for example, has pointed out that there are (at least) two ways in which a contract can be compulsory: it can be compulsory in entry, or compulsory in its terms. With the rise of mass contracts, and standardized contracts, he argues, the majority of contracts today are not negotiable in their terms. One may accept or reject them, but they are not open to revision. Decisions are made and terms set that determine conditions for great masses of people who are not in a position to negotiate terms individually. Labor contracts, for example, are often negotiated for very large groups. Insurance contracts and mortgage rates are standardized. And some of these arrangements have the effect of a monopoly. It is useless to go to another vendor, since terms are fixed across the market. And, by the same token, there are numerous fields of business (public utilities, banks, and common carriers, for example) that are highly regulated and to that extent not in control of their own terms.[13]

Furthermore, he argues, there are many contracts that people are not free to decline to enter: for example, public utilities and liability insurance. Thus, he concludes, the nineteenth-century picture of the negotiated contract that manifested the intentions of two individuals, who were free to set their own terms to mutual advantage or to decline altogether, actually represents a rather small percentage of the interpersonal transactions of the population today, even if (or perhaps especially if) confined to commercial transactions alone. Contracts typically are neither as consensual nor as individual as the classical theory suggests.[14]

It is often further argued that classical contract theory supported a judicial policy that reflected the dominant economic view of the nineteenth century, namely, the idea of laissez faire.[15] This view has been widely criticized as reinforcing the status quo, entrenching the wealth of the wealthy and the power of the powerful, and allowing the quick and the strong to take advantage of those in weaker bargaining positions.[16] Thus, Friederich Kessler:

> Society, when granting freedom of contract, does not guarantee that all members of the community will be able to make use of it to the same extent. On the contrary, the law, by protecting the unequal distribution of property, does nothing to prevent freedom of contract from becoming a onesided privilege. Society, by proclaiming freedom of contract, guarantees that it will not interfere with the exercise of power by contract. Freedom of contract enables enterprisers to legislate by contract and, what is even more important, to legislate in a substantially authoritarian manner without using the appearance of authoritarian forms.[17]

There is no question, historically speaking, that the classical will theory in its most austere form resulted in outrageous injustices that prompted the courts to develop or reinstitute the equitable—or what I, for convenience, called supplementary—doctrines in order to address considerations of substantive fairness and honesty that limit the original theory. Not that the judiciary itself was necessarily quick to respond to the needs of justice or social change, or united in doing so. One of the most infamous periods in Supreme Court history occurred during the late nineteenth and early twentieth centuries, when its development of the constitutional doctrine of "freedom of contract," backed by the reasoning of the will theory and the motivation of the free market, led it to block progressive labor and legislative reforms initiated for the benefit of workers exploited by big business. In fact, the famous line of cases dealing with this issue (often called the *Lochner* line) clearly illustrates the change of judicial rationale from nineteenth-century atomistic individualism to the social experimentation that developed during the twentieth century. Although many lower courts had moved away from the atomistic view by this time, striking down a minimum wage law as late as 1923 we find the U.S. Supreme Court reasoning as follows:

> There is, of course, no such thing as absolute freedom of contract. . . . But freedom of contract is, nevertheless, the general rule and restraint the exception; and the exercise of legislative authority to abridge it can be justified only by the existence of exceptional circumstances. . . . [A] statute which prescribes payment . . . solely with relation to circumstances apart from the contract of employment, the business affected by it, and the work done under it, [i.e., a minimum wage law] is so clearly the product of a naked, arbitrary exercise of power that it cannot be allowed to stand under the Constitution of the United States.[18]

The general rationale that supported this view was stated in its clearest form in a 1915 case that restricted a state legislature's power to prohibit an employer from requiring an employee not to be a member of any labor union as a condition of employment—the infamous "yellow-dog contract." The Court reasoned as follows.

> As to the interest of the employed, it is said by the Kansas Supreme Court to be a matter of common knowledge that "employees, as a rule, are not financially able to be as independent in making contracts for the sale of their labor as are employers in the making of contracts for the purchase thereof." No doubt, whenever the right of private property exists, there must and will be inequalities of fortune. . . . [I]t is from the nature of things impossible to uphold freedom of contract and the right to private property without at the same time recognizing as legitimate those inequalities of fortune that are the necessary result of the exercise of those rights.[19]

This view epitomizes nineteenth-century assumptions about free will and market value, but it was by this time out of step with predominant views, which had developed over a thirty-year period in response largely to the concern to promote labor reform. By 1934 the Supreme Court view changed substantially:

> So far as the requirement of due process is concerned, and in the absence of other constitutional restriction, a state is free to adopt whatever economic policy may reasonably be deemed to promote the public welfare, and to enforce that policy by legislation adapted to its purpose.[20]

By 1937 the Court had reversed its policy completely, denying that the basic rationale it had previously articulated had any legitimate basis in the Constitution:

> [The violation of the due process clause alleged by the appellant] is deprivation of freedom of contract. What is this freedom? The Constitution does not speak of freedom of contract. It speaks of liberty and prohibits the deprivation of liberty without due process of law. . . . Liberty under the Constitution is thus necessarily subject to the restraints of due process, and regulation which is reasonable in relation to its subject and is adopted in the interests of the community is due process.[21]

This change of rationale is reflected in a greater acceptance of limiting and alternative doctrines that restrict, extend, or socialize obligation by agreement in various directions. Yet the conceptual paradigm of contract law remains strongly tied to the nineteenth-century model, thus generating considerable debate and disagreement.

So overall, there are two major sorts of criticism directed toward the traditional theory of contractual obligation. One is descriptive: it fails to represent or explain adequately twentieth-century legal practice, or the practical experience of real people in a highly organized modern society. The other is normative: it reflects a nineteenth-century laissez faire economic theory that ignores the inequality of bargaining situations and allows the powerful to prey on the disadvantaged.

Now, what does all this tell us about the legal model of obligation by agreement, especially in terms of the voluntary choices of autonomous individuals? One thing it does is illustrate rather nicely the development of a predominant attitude about individualism and obligation in this country (and in England with slight vari-

ations) during a certain period of time. By studying legal history (in the form of judicial opinions and legal treatises) we can observe in the late eighteenth and early
nineteenth centuries the rise of a certain mode of highly individualistic, as well as
abstract and even formalistic thinking—a commitment to a market theory of value,
and a declining interest in the content or fairness of the bargain, all expressed as an
increasing reluctance to restrict or monitor the range of individual interaction: the
morality of neutrality at its apex. And then we see the relative decline of this attitude a century later, although the decline is not uniform; that is, there is much controversy, both rejection and defense, of the old paradigm. This process occurs—as
always in the common law—incrementally, in response to new situations, new
problems, newly proposed solutions.

Early on, the courts adopt a highly individualistic stance to deny aristocratic
privileges, certain traditional privileges associated with land ownership, and other
restrictive practices (some based on traditional notions of fairness, such as the idea
of a "just price") associated with an earlier, more static social and commercial life,
in order to promote enterprise and to reflect emerging ideas of freedom and self-
reliance. Of course, since it replaces one form of domination with another (namely,
an aristocratic power structure with an entrepreneurial one), this new freedom is
quickly abused, raising new problems (or perhaps old problems in new forms) to
which the courts must then respond (sooner or later) by instituting doctrines that
limit and direct or even equalize the total freedom of the contracting parties.[22]

Some of these doctrines can be explained in terms of protecting the free
choices of the parties. Prohibition of fraud, concealment, and misrepresentation
can certainly be explained that way. You have not made a free choice if you were
deceived about the nature of the choice you were making. Fraud is a form of coercion. Even mistake and duress may fit this rationale, although they are more problematic because it is not (ordinarily) the other contracting party who causes your
mistake or duress, even though she may take advantage of it. Yet, mistake and
duress do restrict the freedom of one's choices, at least on the same rationale just accepted for fraud.

Once you are on this path, of course, it is clear that freedom is a matter of degree to be interpreted in terms of the magnitude of the impediments to its exercise.
This was, indeed, a popular theory of freedom among certain prominent philosophers of the nineteenth century (Bentham and Mill, for example). Yet the courts
have had problems with this rationale, because on the one hand, not enough fits
into it (it is too narrow) and on the other hand, too much fits into it (it is too broad).

What about the doctrines that simply do not fit, or apparently do not fit, the
free choice of autonomous parties paradigm? Some of them are separated out of the
conceptual domain of contracts. As noted earlier, some can be viewed as supplementary doctrines of tort and restitution, or as statutory limitations. Remaining doctrines that do not fit (e.g., consideration) are generally argued to be wrong by doctrinal purists, or perhaps they are anomalous historical remnants, or minor
exceptions. Even if such arguments are accepted, however, some things cannot be
covered—most notably, perhaps, detrimental reliance. But possibly it too can be
bent (it will have to be badly bent) to fit the traditional paradigm.

All this illustrates the complexity of contract law, even if the doctrinal paradigm is accepted as a generalization that contractual obligation is obligation by agreement. Simple consent will not do as an explanation of legal contracts, although it is one central and significant element. It is not even clear what consent would mean standing alone in the contractual context, since it was never necessary or sufficient for transactional obligation even in the heyday of nineteenth-century will theory. There have always been elements that the paradigm could not cover; thus, the model is too narrow.

In what way is the model too broad? Many sorts of obstacles are potential impediments to freedom. Which ones should be recognized by a court, and which should not, and for what reasons? The exercise of freedom cannot tell us that. One form of restriction is as restrictive as another. Should we make no distinctions among them? My mistake may misdirect my choice just as much as your fraud does. Either my poverty or your misrepresentation may be equal impediments to my freedom. Should the court not distinguish among them?

The protection of one person always restricts another. (If it didn't, no protection would be needed.) There is no such thing as absolute freedom. Anarchy (lawlessness) is generally a restrictive condition. Freedom (of certain kinds) is protected by law, which is itself a restriction of freedom (of other kinds). Protection of your interest in freely walking the city streets restricts my freedom to jump out of an alley and viciously punch you in the knee (being short). One interest is legitimate and the other is not, we say, but protecting either restricts the freedom of the other. The law must decide whether to protect my punch or your knee. Either way, as far as the value of freedom is concerned, it restricts one and enhances the other. The protection of freedom itself cannot negotiate that.

How to decide? Various principles may be used: fairness, security, efficiency, the common good. From the perspective of the parties, the issue will always be a matter of fairness (even though the case may be decided on other grounds), and fairness is not always as clearly separable from freedom as we would like to think, since injustice is usually oppressive. Analytically we can separate the two, as Michael Sandel has noted. We can always ask, "But is it fair, this agreement that they have made?" Conversely, "Did they consent to it, this fair arrangement?" Neither guarantees the other.[23] They are conceptually distinct.

But in daily life in practice, their coincidence is striking (although not surprising). It may not be impossible for someone to agree freely to injustice, but it would be far more common to acquiesce with reluctance. The fact that a bad deal is the only deal I can get does not make it a good deal, or a fair deal, even if I agree to it, and certainly not merely *because* I agree to it. It just makes it better than no deal at all. And if I agree, because I have no other viable option, is that a free choice? We can make it a free choice by definition, but it will not feel like one. If I am coerced by circumstances, it may restrict my choices just as much as if I am coerced by a person. Does my poverty restrict my choices? Of course it does. It eliminates practically all of them. Certainly most courts do not want to include my hard luck as a condition of enforcing a valid contract. But if the foundation of contractual obligation is free choice, it is not clear why they shouldn't. You cannot distinguish among types of restriction on the basis of their impediment to freedom, for that is what they all have in common.

But court decisions also restrict freedom; that is, they protect one interest by restricting another. Was the Court supporting the free choices of autonomous individuals in *Coppage* (the 1915 case just cited) and retracting it in *West Coast Hotel* (the 1937 case)? I don't think so. *West Coast Hotel* simply represents a more complex notion, or a different notion, of what counts as free choice. Coercion comes in many forms, and is not easy to articulate, much less address. It is coercive for the courts (or the legislatures) to oversee the agreements of private parties—to tell people what they can or cannot agree to. But government is not the only source of coercion. Private parties can and do also coerce one another in all sorts of ways on a regular basis, and the fact that they manage to come to some sort of agreement does not guarantee that one of them was not forced into accepting terms that were seriously objectionable to him or her. The problem is that all this is a matter of degree. Coercion is a matter of degree, which only reflects the fact that free choice is a matter of degree. A great many perfectly good contracts (perhaps most) contain some terms that are at least mildly disagreeable to one party or another. That is what negotiation is about. Presumably those contracts are not coercive. So where along the continuum do they become coercive? At one end of the scale the court is protecting the free choice of one party from the coercion of another. At the other end the court restricts the free choices of both parties by substituting its own judgment for theirs. Somewhere between these two poles the court must draw a line, but at what point, by what deciding factor, do the choices stop being free? The court must decide which form of coercion is worse—government coercion or private coercion. Is there any good formula for doing that? Well . . .

3. Recent Debate: Consent or Reliance?

There seem to be, very roughly speaking, two main camps on the issue of the proper foundation for contractual obligation, or at least I find it convenient to treat the field in that way for present purposes. The two camps are comprised of those who defend established doctrine in terms of traditional theory, and those who oppose it. The crux of the theoretical difference is the extent to which a commitment to respect for individual autonomy in the abstract is thought to require the enforcement of promises as such, or on the other hand, whether the courts should be available to assess claims of unfairness that require the evaluation of actual circumstances in particular contexts. This issue has been crystalized in the debate between P. S. Atiyah and Charles Fried.

Atiyah has argued that the classical will theory (as well as its more recent defense as the promise theory) fails utterly to account for the complexity and diversity of contractual circumstances and legal doctrine. There is no single principle or paradigm that will account for all contract law. Rather it is "a set of rules . . . concerning the creation of obligations in which the law itself has refined and made use of the concept of a promise."[24] Promise alone, however, cannot explain it. Indeed, he points out, bare promises, or gratuitous promises, are seldom enforceable. It should be recognized, he notes, that gratuitous promises are not typical. Most promises are given to induce a promise or act in return. That is, most promises are given for reasons, and those reasons are significant. It is precisely that fact that has long been recognized in law, as symbolized in the doctrine of consideration. Accordingly, only promises "for consideration," that is, given for a reason, for something of value, constitute a contract. Atiyah argues that the doctrine of consideration (the idea that there must be an exchange of value), while much in need of reform, nevertheless embodies a useful set of rules by which the courts have determined the enforceability of contracts over time.

> Consideration means a reason for the enforcement of a promise, or, even more broadly, for the recognition of an obligation. . . . Nobody can seriously propose that all promises should become enforceable; to abolish the doctrine of consideration, therefore, is simply to require the courts to begin all over again the task of deciding what promises are to be enforceable.[25]

But even an exchange of promises with consideration is neither necessary nor sufficient for obligation, he acknowledges. The principles of contract law should be broad enough to include equitable doctrines that protect parties from loss due to detrimental reliance or unjust enrichment, and so forth. Indeed, it is the fact that people often rely on promises, and must rely on them, that most often provides the best explanation of why and to what extent they should be enforceable. But on the whole, since no single principle accounts for all contract law, the enforcement of contracts must sometime be evaluated in terms of the reasons for which they were made.

Fried has argued, to the contrary, that the promise principle is still the best account of contract law, both normatively and descriptively.[26] The basic principle that provides the foundation of contractual obligation, he claims, is "Keep your word." Noting that a liberal society requires maintaining respect for the person, property, and decisions of individuals, he observes that individual needs and purposes also make cooperation necessary. The basic moral question, however, was how to secure cooperation without using others or being used by them; how to insure cooperation without violating autonomy. Thus, the idea of a promise, as a commitment to cooperate, was a crucial moral discovery that enabled individuals to bind themselves by means of their own autonomous choices. By the use of a promise, free individuals came to understand that they could secure cooperation without losing freedom by trusting one another to keep their commitments. Thus, free and autonomous persons can bind themselves by their own acts of will, or promises.[27]

One question, of course, was, How can this be so? That is, how can persons, by promising, become morally obligated? How can they acquire a moral obligation that they would not otherwise have, in effect, by saying or acknowledging that they have it? Fried's answer (following John Searle, John Rawls, and many others) is that promising is a social convention. The moral obligation of a promise arises because a promisor intentionally invokes a convention, the very purpose of which is to provide moral grounds for another to expect the promise to be performed. And it is this promissory obligation that provides the foundation and justification of contractual obligation.[28]

What is the essence of this "new" or at least updated debate? It turns on the following two questions: (a) Should contract law be viewed as a mechanism for implementing the liberal principle that freely made commitments of autonomous individuals should be enforced: Are you bound by your word? (b) Does current contract law in practice (at least in its main lines and principle doctrines) reflect this principle?

I believe that Atiyah amply demonstrates that the short answer to (b), despite Fried's ingenious arguments to the contrary, is no. Contract law really is not uniform enough for the answer to be otherwise. As a descriptive view of legal practice, the promise principle has the same serious deficiencies that the will theory had. Atiyah provides a long and devastating list of mainstream doctrines of contract law that the promise principle really cannot satisfactorily cover.[29] The most obvious is the doctrine of consideration—the basic principle that the law does not enforce bare promises. There is, of course, no contract without consideration. It is a basic element of contractual obligation. Fried, naturally, acknowledges this point, but he argues that consideration is itself an incoherent doctrine and an anomalous remnant of an earlier era that is today reduced to a mere formality. Besides, there may be good reasons to suppose that bare promises ought to be binding.

This argument, however, simply makes Fried's theory an ingenious normative view, not an accurate descriptive one. Whether the doctrine of consideration is a good legal doctrine, or even a coherent one, is irrelevant to the demonstrable fact that it is an operable one. Nor is it new, on the one hand, or declining, on the other. It is a central element of contractual validity; it has been for a very long time; and it looks to be firmly entrenched for the foreseeable future. It is true that in many cases it is a formality; for example, exchanged promises are themselves taken to be consideration, and no inquiry is made into their relative fairness or adequacy. And it is historically true that a requirement of consideration is a remnant from the past. Yet, as long as consideration remains a basic element of a valid contract (relic or not, formality or not), it stands for the proposition that contract law is not about promising as such. And other doctrines that are less central but still part of contract law further support this point. For example, if contract law were about commitment as such, it could never tolerate the doctrine of efficient breach: the idea that if you can make a better profit by breaking your contract and paying the other party's losses than you could by keeping the bargain, then you may break the contract. Specific performance (or at least expectation damage) is not the general rule as it would be if the governing principle of contract law were "Keep your commitments." Thus, descriptively speaking, contract law is not about commitment as such, but about cooperative exchanges—often, perhaps, exchanged commitments. If there is any unifying thread that runs through contract law, cooperative exchange is closest to it. But that is not a principle. It is just an empirical generalization, a statement of subject matter. Nor does it generate any single principle, as far as I can tell. This is reflected in the contemporary debate over expectation damages, among other things.

It is argued (by Atiyah, for example) that if the foundation of contractual obligation is the promise itself, then the logical damage award should be for the amount of the promise, or in other words, expectation damages. (Fried thinks so too.) However, outside of strictly commercial contracts, expectation damages are not usually awarded. In fact, since the famous article by Fuller and Purdue, it has been rather widely held that the main function of contractual damages is to protect against loss due to reliance.[30] Expectation damages, even when awarded, may be a substitute for reliance losses, which may be harder to measure or prove. Certainly in some cases reliance losses are all that will be covered. But why, it is asked, should reliance be the standard, if promise is the foundation? There is no uncontroversial answer, which shows that trying to subsume contract damages under any single principle will unavoidably distort a sizeable body of law.

There are other problems as well. Surely, detrimental reliance (as noted earlier) is not explained well as the enforcement of promises. The mitigation rule (the rule that one may not simply "sit on" a broken contract, collecting the full amount of the original agreement without trying to mitigate damages) may vitiate the force of commitments altogether. And the notion of efficient breach flies in the face of an ideal to keep one's word. Thus, the descriptive difficulties that plagued the will theory as applied to twentieth-century legal practice make the promise principle similarly problematic. But what about its normative force?

As a normative view, Fried's theory is one of the most powerful statements of contemporary individualist values in a form applicable to contract law. There is no question that respecting the decisions of autonomous individuals is central to any liberal view. (Perhaps it should be noted, however, that libertarians differ greatly from moderate liberals over what they believe follows from that commitment.) All liberals are generally opposed to paternalism, so overseeing the agreements of consenting adults should be presumptively suspicious. Yet, as noted earlier, restrictions on contracts are most often intended to enable one party to protect himself from the coercive tactics of the other. That is not paternalism.

The normative debate between traditionalists and progressives (such as Fried and Atiyah) is often characterized as turning on the question whether the courts should monitor the fairness of agreements or respect the autonomy of the parties — as though it must be one or the other but not both. This characterization of the issue, however, seems flawed. In what sense is the court necessarily monitoring agreements or being paternalistic if it considers the fairness of a contract case? No one claims that all contract cases are cases of overseeing the agreements of private parties. The claim seems to be that the court is only monitoring the decisions of the contractors if it undertakes to reassess the values of the parties in terms of the fairness of the bargain. That in turn seems to be translated into whether it is legitimate for the court to consider background conditions, or the relative bargaining strength of the parties. But why is that, as opposed to any other consideration, paternalistically monitoring agreements? Remember, parties always initiate contract cases, so the court is never involved unless one party seeks it out. That means that at least one of the parties is unhappy about the deal. If that unhappy party can convince the court that he was coerced into the agreement, that he was taken advantage of in some way, then protecting him from that coercion is not monitoring his decisions, even if, given the nature of the case, it necessitates inquiring into agreements of competent consenting adults. It cannot be that any and all such inquiry is paternalistic, or else all contract cases would be paternalism. Virtually all contract cases are, after all, about the agreements of competent consenting adults. If, then, a party's background conditions are relevant to her claim of coercion, why should they not be allowed?

Perhaps a better formulation of the relevant questions might be as follows. (1) Should the court be available to evaluate a claim by a party who, having made a commitment, later feels he or she has good reason to be allowed to retract it? (2) What kinds of reasons should that party be allowed to raise as relevant? Question 2, the relevance of background conditions, is what I have just been considering. As to question 1, does hearing such an appeal violate that individual's autonomy? That has been suggested (by traditionalists, including Fried), but it clearly does not do so. Holding a person to his or her first choice without appeal to defend the possibility of a change of mind supposes not autonomy but infallibility. There are certainly other grounds for holding someone to his or her commitments, most obviously concern for the other party, but respect for autonomy is an inadequate explanation. As Atiyah has queried, why should respect for autonomy require a commitment to one's first choice rather than one's present choice?

This is not to suggest, however, that commitments should be taken lightly. Not at all. It is only contemplated that a commitment might on occasion be reassessed for good reasons. That is not a controversial position.

What kinds of reasons? That is the source of major controversy. In very general terms, the answer is acceptable reasons are those that fit the particular case within doctrines developed by the courts as relevant considerations: such as duress, unconscionability, mistake, fraud, and so forth. Many of these judicial doctrines are supported by theorists on both sides of the contemporary debate (e.g., by both Fried and Atiyah), although their reasons or grounds for support are different, and thus their conclusions are different. For example, some argue that free choice alone is the only ground. Some argue that fairness is also relevant. Some argue that free choices and fair choices are not as neatly separable as we would like to think.

The real nub of this dispute is whether these legal relations (that is, contractual relations) are best accounted for in terms of individual interactions alone, or whether the relative circumstances of the parties must sometimes be considered as well. Can each transaction be viewed as a discrete item, so to speak, or must it be considered within a social context? This, of course, is the same dispute as that between the libertarian and the moderate liberal (or, for that matter, the libertarian and the socialist). Thus, the problem with the so-called autonomy view is not that it focuses on the significance of autonomy (for moderate liberals do that as well) but that it assumes that autonomous choices can be dealt with in the abstract. As a result, it does not adequately represent the social environment that enables individual cooperation to occur in the form of binding commitments that could be called contracts in the first place.

It is interesting that in defending an updated (and much improved) but still very atomistic version of traditional will theory, Fried finds it necessary to rely fundamentally and specifically on the fact that promising gives rise to moral obligation because it invokes a social convention that makes it binding. Now where would we be without the social convention? Respect for individual freedom and autonomy alone cannot account for this.

Nor can it explain twentieth-century developments in contract law or in economic life that are not as individual or consensual as the traditional model suggests, developments pointed out by Friederich Kessler and Max Radin as long ago as the 1940s. Surely, economic life has not become less structured and interdependent since then.

The problem, as Lawrence Friedman has explained it, is that the autonomy model is highly abstract or formalistic:

> Basically, then, the "pure" law [autonomy model] of contracts is an area of what we can call abstract relationships. "Pure" contract doctrine is blind to details of subject matter and person. It does not ask who buys and who sells, and what is bought and sold. . . . Contract law [on the autonomy model] is abstraction—what is left in the law relating to agreements when all particularities of person and subject-matter are removed.[31]

Thus, contract law as abstract theory cannot take account of background conditions, or social change. This means that often it cannot take account of individual circumstances, for example, in a way that might allow individuals to explain why they might change their minds about their commitments due to changed circumstances or in light of pertinent new information or experience. Nor can it adequately accommodate social changes that might make such contextual factors relevant to legal decisions. Finally, it cannot account for unequal bargaining power that might reasonably be considered to make a contract unfair and coercive.

I began this chapter by asking what contract law or theory can tell us about contractual obligations. Obviously, the normative debate within contract theory reflects the ongoing debate in political theory between libertarians and moderate liberals or communitarians.

But what about legal practice itself? Legal practice, I have shown, must be viewed as incorporating a collection of doctrines apparently intended and designed to facilitate cooperative interaction for mutual benefit, by individuals or groups with different ends, most generally by agreement, and within the parameters set by minimal social values of fairness and honesty.[32] As it stands, contract law in practice does not support an atomistic view of individual transactions, nor does it support a single, unique theory of contractual obligation. It clearly implies an obligation to keep agreements of some mutual benefit, unless they violate minimal standards of fairness and honesty, and includes an obligation to take responsibility for inducing reliance of others in response to one's words or conduct, whether a specific agreement is involved or not. Of course, it can always be (and sometimes is) argued that certain doctrines are wrong, but if we take the law as it stands, all the implications above are included in it.

So, if we look to contract law itself to tell us about the nature of affirmative obligation arising out of cooperative exchanges, we get a picture that is rather more complex than simply "obligations follow from individual agreement or consent as such"; and we will find this picture even more complex as applied to generalized responsibility, such as professional obligation—to which I will now turn.

7

Consent and Role in Professional Obligation

Besides family obligations, professional obligations or obligations of employment are the single largest and most uncontroversial source of affirmative obligation that human beings have. Family obligations and work obligations fill most people's lives. Unlike family obligations, however, professional obligations are considered to be contractual and therefore ordinarily justified by appeal to consent. That is, it often seems to be assumed that professional obligations, being contractual, are binding because you agreed to them. A look at American law, however, shows us that it is more complicated than that.

What I want to explore here is what consent amounts to as applied to circumstances of generalized responsibility in employment or profession. Just what does the appeal to voluntariness tell us about these obligations of role? How does the notion of reliance figure into such circumstances? I want to evaluate how the notion of contract handles or interacts with the idea of membership in the form of role in the professional context. Occupational role is clearly relevant to professional obligation.[1] Yet it is not clear that the idea of contract alone explains this feature of occupational duty, despite the historical assumption that it does. I will argue here that professional or any ongoing obligations of employment are best explained as combining two forms of obligation—obligations of contract and obligations of membership (in the form of role responsibility). More generally, I want to show that the idea of consent is much more complex than it is commonly portrayed, and not as completely voluntary. Just as the idea of role or membership in family obligation is not devoid of the influence of consent, the idea of consent in contract is not devoid of the influence of role or membership. While there are significant differences, there are also important commonalities between family obligations and professional ones.

1. Justifying Professional Obligations: Consent or Reliance?

In general, recognizing that people do a great variety of things for a living, we could describe this span of activity as ranging from very clearly specified duties (e.g., deliver the package, or polish the silver) to very vague and generalized responsibilities (e.g., treat the sick, or report the news). Professions tend to be at the vague end of that continuum, along with other occupations that may or may not be considered professions, depending on whose view you adopt. What I am primarily interested in here are the obligations attached to any of the occupations that fall along the vaguer half of the continuum, and more generally, obligations that continue over time, whether we call them professions or not. All people who have such occupations incur general responsibilities and obligations by virtue of a role or position that they hold, and these obligations are construed as contractual. I want to understand what that means. It seems clear enough that these professional or occupational obligations are at least in one sense voluntarily assumed. Namely, the reason that you have the position or role is that you agreed to it. You voluntarily entered the relationship or assumed the position. Furthermore, you can, presumably, leave the relationship more or less at any time—subject, of course, to your meeting (or making some other acceptable arrangements for) all specific obligations that you have already incurred within the general role.[2] Since you can leave, if you don't leave, you voluntarily remain. Consequently, your obligations are voluntarily assumed.

Yet, it's not quite that simple, is it? Just as the terms of many contracts (e.g., for insurance, or utilities) are not open to negotiation (as I noted in chapter 6), neither are many of the terms of most employment contracts or the responsibilities of many professional positions. You can accept or reject the position, but you do not (usually) get to define it. Who does? Professional positions in general are defined over time by the profession in terms of its purpose, and by the reasonable expectations of the community as to the nature and extent of the services the profession is to provide. These definitions are not open to negotiation.[3]

In the case of employment contracts, the employer defines the position, basically in terms of what he or she needs done. Obviously, this is not going to be open to negotiation. Why in the world would an employer hire anyone to do a job that does not need to be done? So, as an employee, you may be able to negotiate some things, such as your pay, but you do not for the most part get to define the duties or obligations of your position. What this means is that an employment contract—whether a job or a profession—is a package. You can accept or reject the whole package (in terms of the duties involved), but you cannot change the contents. Thus, most probably you will like some parts and dislike others. If you are unlucky, you may dislike or disagree with all of it, although you are willing to accept the package for the pay. Is that consent? It is indeed consent to perform the duties of the role that is accepted. Is that all there is to it?

Suppose that I join the staff of Acme Company, which has policies X, Y, and Z. I need the job, and policies X and Y seem okay to me, although Z seems pretty questionable. I don't like it, but I take the job, so I guess I consented to Z. Suppose that after a while Z gets changed for the worse, perhaps even against my own interest, or against my personal beliefs or principles, to Z'. I am specifically opposed to Z' but not enough to change jobs or quit without another job. Perhaps there is a general trend in which all firms are moving to Z'. It will be useless for me to change jobs. Did I consent to Z'? Did I assume an obligation to perform Z'? Is there a difference between the two? Suppose I lead a campaign against Z′ but get outvoted? Or privately I do my best to turn people against Z′ and do every little thing I can to undermine it (not being in a position to do anything bigger). Did I still consent to Z′, just as long as I don't quit my job in protest? If I hold a position, presumably I acquiesce in all its aspects (that I do not fight against and win). Is that what consent means? Surely I do not *freely* choose what I oppose. At least that much must be granted. This is the problem of the employment package.

Furthermore, if we are talking about ordinary employment, many people do not have much of a choice about the work they do, and some have no choice at all, but they are (I assume) still obligated to perform the duties of the job they have accepted. That is to say, if the job you have is the only job you could get, you still incur the same obligations as you would if you had other choices. Isn't that right? If so, it looks like choice is not necessary to the existence of the obligation. In what sense is this obligation voluntarily assumed?

Of course (in theory and in philosophical discussion) it can be argued that you always have the choice to decline any job whatsoever, even if you cannot get another one. This point is reminiscent of Jean-Paul Sartre's argument that human beings are radically free because they are free to commit suicide should they decide that is the right choice. Both statements are true, and are even useful as illustrations of the moral point that we are all ultimately responsible for our own lives. But they seem to me unpersuasive as a description of human choices. Are you responsible for what you do? Yes. Is it because you consented to it when you had no other choice (besides suicide or starvation)? I hope that there is a better explanation than that.

In ordinary life the consent view of employment obligation is at least sometimes misleading, I think, because in fact you do not have a choice not to work, unless you are among the 0.2 percent of the population who are so wealthy that gainful employment is no longer required. Even a sizable number of these very wealthy people must work, sometimes even harder than other people do. It is said that the Rockefeller children didn't get away without working, for example; nor did the Vanderbilts. So where does that leave the rest of us? The truth is that not working is not an acceptable choice. You will be harshly condemned for taking it. Imagine writing home to your folks:

> Dear Mom and Dad,
>   I am really tired of my job here in Middletown, and I can't find anything else, so I've decided to become a hobo and ride the rails. Yes, it's the romantic life for me. I think I can become a proficient panhandler, sleep under the stars, and eat my beans from a can.
>
> Love, X.

Do you think your mother will write back saying, "How nice, dear; we are so pleased that you have finally settled on a vocation"? Can you imagine your friends' conversations? "Have you heard the latest? X quit work to become a hobo." "You don't say. What an interesting choice. X is bound to meet a fascinating group of people that way. And what an opportunity to travel!" I don't think so. Your friends would be appalled; and your parents would have you in therapy before you made it out of the city. And all this is what would happen only if you were single, rather well off, and had no specific commitments and responsibilities, such as a spouse or children.

Beyond the general condemnation received for not working, the real restriction is even more basic. Most people could not seriously consider such a choice at all, because our socialization process is so effective in this respect that our own self-esteem would not allow us to contemplate such a choice, long before we considered whether anyone else would condemn us for it.[4] Nor is such social conditioning unjustified; it is absolutely necessary for the basic functioning of any society that at least most of its members contribute productively to the general wealth. Nor is that unfair, as long as all contribute, or as long as rewards are connected to contributions. So working is not really optional, is it?[5]

More fundamentally, and obviously, not working is not a very attractive choice, given its consequences. Most people feel that they must have a home, shelter, food, and at least some minimal level of security. This is not considered unreasonable, but normal and even socially productive. Most of us would like to know where our next meal is coming from, and many of us must meet obligations to others, which means that we must have enough money to pay for these things. At the bottom line, that means that we must work. Is that consent? Not in my book, if you will pardon the pun.

That is to say, it seems to me that Radin's observations about contract law (as noted in chapter 6) apply to a great many human interactions, and certainly to employment, which is not as consensual or as individual as we tend to picture it. That is not to say that it is not consensual or individual at all, but life is more complex than theory tends to represent it. Virtually no one has the option not to work. Very few are able to be self-employed, and virtually no employee defines the duties of his or her position, even when it is a professional one. Yet, despite the attenuated nature of consent in the case of employment, we are all obligated to perform the duties of our positions. At least I am willing to assume that we are. The question is, Why? What justifies the obligation? Does agreement provide the best explanation here?

It seems to me that in this context, the basis of the obligation must be construed at least partly in terms of the idea of reliance. The reason that you must perform the duties of your position is not (or at least not only) that you consented to them but that other people are relying on you to perform them. It is reasonable for others to rely on us to meet the obligations associated with our positions, and that reliance is crucial for social cooperation and interpersonal interaction in general. As long as we hold a particular position, we allow others to rely on us in that capacity. This concept has considerable potential to explain the nature and scope of occupational obligations, as well as why we have them.

It is not usual, and often is not possible, for all the duties of a position to be fully specified (or listed) in a contract. Even if they were, I have tried to show how it is entirely possible and not uncommon to hold a position part of which requires you to perform duties you disagree with and would change if you could. Although it is not exactly false to construe these obligations as consensual, that hardly seems adequate justification for them. Nor is it as helpful as explaining and motivating them in terms of reliance. In terms of explanation, the idea that other people reasonably rely on you to perform the duties associated with your position can explain why you must perform a particular task that is part of your job, even though you may specifically object to performing that task and even may have lodged a formal objection to doing so. Explaining or justifying your obligation in terms of consent is rather strained and unhelpful in that sort of circumstance, even though it is not exactly false. This sort of case illustrates the complexity of consent in some circumstances. Your consent to assume the position as a whole conflicts with your rejection of some part of the package. Merely claiming that the former overrides the latter is unhelpful at best and is certainly misleading. At least part of what needs to be captured is the integrated nature of the practice within which the consent operates. The notion of reliance in the context of cooperative interaction heads us in that direction.

Understanding the complexity of consent and reliance becomes increasingly important as social and economic interaction become ever more interdependent and specialized. Increasing recognition of this situation is apparent in evolving legal doctrines and business practices: the disappearance of caveat emptor, the rise of warrants of merchantability, guarantees, licenses, implied warranties, product liability, professional malpractice suits; the proliferation of codes of ethics, professional schools, and state board exams for trades and professions. All these reflect our increasing need and awareness of mutual reliance. We are becoming a world of specialists, and we must be able to rely on one another in the twenty-first century in ways that are simply incompatible with the nineteenth-century caveat emptor mentality. It doesn't make sense anymore in most situations to say, "You're on your own." It isn't accurate. It isn't fair. It isn't even efficient. So mutual reliance is the emerging value of our time. And it is reliance that best explains obligations of employment or occupation.

I am not claiming that consent plays no part. I do not mean to characterize all employment as forced labor simply because some have few choices, and none have unlimited freedom. I am only suggesting that a simple analysis of consent alone is not sufficient to explain employment obligation. After all, it is a mistake to characterize consent as all or nothing. It is not the same in all contexts. Agreeing to be a part of a complex, ongoing project hardly seems the same as an individual undertaking. Assuming a role the characteristics of which are socially fixed is hardly the same as agreeing to perform a specific task. In some circumstances one has extensive control over all aspects of one's activity, in other circumstances much less.

Consent is not a simple, unitary concept. It stands for at least two different things. It may stand for an act—let's call that acceptance. Or it may stand for a psychological state—let's call that agreement. As a psychological state, it is a matter of degree. As opinion polls now often reflect, one may strongly, moderately, or weakly agree or disagree with most anything. Is one who strongly agrees more obligated than one who only weakly agrees? Obviously not. Furthermore, consent (as agreement) is usually partial in complex enterprises such as employment. You may agree with some parts, or tasks, or policies and disagree with others. Are you only obligated to comply with what you agree with? Obviously not. So consent as agreement—as a psychological condition—is entirely inadequate to account for obligation in most occupational settings.

On the other hand, consent as an act—as acceptance—is a trigger concept. It is all or nothing. It puts you in the position you are in with all its aspects included. That means that you may accept what you disagree with. Is that possible? Of course. It happens all the time. I have just been exploring the tension between these two concepts in the past few pages. What that exploration illustrates, I think, is that in the occupational context, at least, people very often (perhaps most often) accept what they disagree with because they do not have control over changing it. But having control over events, circumstances, or conditions is ordinarily considered to be a very strong factor in being responsible for them. It does not follow, of course, that people are not obligated in such circumstances or that consent plays no part in their obligation. It is a crucial element, but given the features just discussed, it functions in a particular way that ought to be represented.

A better explanation of the nature of the voluntariness or consent component in employment is usually that it is agreeing to be a participant in an ongoing venture over which one does not have full control. This is something like joining a team in several respects. Ordinarily, what you consent to is a role or position comprising certain duties that fill a need within a larger entity. You consent to play a part, which you yourself do not get to define. I will expand on this shortly. As to the present point, the metaphor of joining a team provides a reasonable representation of the way in which consent usually functions in regard to occupational obligations. It is consent without full control. This is certainly one form of consent, and a very common one in real life, but it hardly conforms to the paradigm suggested by traditional contract theorists or by the picture drawn in most philosophical accounts.

Am I saying that consent is not important here? Not at all. It is absolutely crucial—but why? It cannot be because it indicates actual agreement or commitment in fact, since obviously it does not in some cases. It is important because it is a trigger that indicates to others that they can rely on you. By your consent you invite reliance. So the question in my view is not whether consent is important, but why. Thus, I do not want to overstate the lack of consent in employment. While almost none of us have a choice not to work at all, many of us do have a choice regarding what kind of work we will do, at least within some limits.[6] Certainly professionals fall in this group. Nobody has to be a doctor or lawyer, for example. If you feel that your profession requires you to perform immoral acts, you can quit and (very probably) find other employment. This would not be an easy choice, but it would be a choice nonetheless.

Even here, however, I would like to enter a word or two about the complications of real life, even for (at least some) professionals. First, it should be recognized that people invest in professions. They invest their time and energy and commitment and creativity; in other words, they invest their lives. The longer that investment has accrued, so to speak, the harder it may be to give up, and the fewer other choices one may have. We should recognize, for example, that age discrimination is still the rule informally, despite legal regulations against it. A professional person who finds new practices morally unconscionable (or realizes too late that old ones are), after having been in a field for many years, may find him- or herself in a serious situation that is not so different from that of the individual who seems to have no choice about a job. Admittedly, a difficult choice is still a choice. (Of course, if you are too old to avoid age discrimination, you may be eligible for early retire-ment—I wouldn't count on it, though.) In any case, choosing to quit, to give up one's profession, may carry extremely high costs that may undermine one's ability to meet other obligations. That is not to say that there is no choice here, but only to point out that real choices are seldom as simple as they appear in abstraction. One choice and obligation is seldom disconnected from other choices and obligations, and consequently cannot be considered in luxurious isolation nearly as often in practice as it is in theory.

Second, giving up one's position on moral grounds is not necessarily the best moral choice. Presumably, working to change the offensive practices would be bet-ter, and you may well be more effective in that endeavor if you remain within the field than if you quit. This is the package problem I mentioned earlier. It is rarely all or nothing; bad things are balanced by good things. All things considered, you may decide to stay, which will leave you accepting, or even performing, acts or carrying out policies with which you disagree. Even so, you may believe that you can do more good by staying than by quitting. And you may be right. No doubt, such reasoning can be and is used as an excuse. But it can also be true. If you decide to stay in circumstances like those I just described, you will be faced with professional duties that you find morally questionable, and possibly to which you explicitly object. This raises the issue of conflicting duties, a difficult set of is-sues that I will consider further in section 3. For now, it is easy enough to see the problem.[7]

Overall, explicit individual consent alone simply is not the best explanation of professional obligations. Reliance is needed as well. If you hold a professional posi-tion, it is both reasonable and necessary for others to rely on your performance of commonly recognized obligations associated with that role or position. The world has become a highly specialized place. People must rely on one another, as experts, to provide services of widely divergent sorts. In general this is unavoidable, a matter of necessity, and a fact of modern life.

At least sometimes you have obligations just because of your position (whether you agreed to or agree with the specific duties or not) because you took the posi-tion, (i.e., accepted it in the minimal sense described earlier) or, perhaps more im-portant, because you *hold* the position, and since you hold it, it is reasonable for others to expect that you will meet the requirements of the position as set by the profession and the community. Furthermore, it is necessary for them to be able to rely on your doing so. And all this is true whether you had a choice or not, that is, even if it was the only opportunity you had.

2. Professional Membership and Professional Obligation

Within the contractual realm, as I have just noted, the level of reliance necessary for a cooperative venture may vary enormously, from a long-term fiduciary relation-ship on the high end to an arm's-length bargain for delivery of fungible goods at the low end. Thus, even our rather broad description of contractual obligation does not fully capture the professional relation between an expert and a client, except in a very abstract way. That is, it does not distinguish a professional relationship (or even an employment relationship) from any other contractual relation. And more generally, it does not distinguish an ongoing occupational relationship from a unique transaction. For example, it does not distinguish a doctor/patient relation from a promise to deliver goods on a single occasion. Such distinctions and differences can be explained (if at all) only by the *content* of the particular contract involved, and very frequently not by that either, at least in any helpful way.

The question is, How does one capture what is professional in a professional relationship, or what is implied in a responsible ongoing occupation? The idea of contract as such, at least contract as consent alone, does not seem to do that, much less does it helpfully cover the ongoing relations between an employer and an employee, even though these are all contractual relations, and very significant and common ones. The idea of reliance, however, if it is fleshed out and combined with consent, has the potential to provide a fuller account.

I shall consider the employment relation, since it is the broader category of which the professional relation is a part. The concept of reliance functions naturally here, although it does so in a particular way that needs exposition; similarly the notion of consent. I noted earlier that the consent component within this context is rather like that of someone who joins a team or agrees to participate in an ongoing project or enterprise. Thus, within the employment context the contractual obligation might be construed helpfully as implying a membership obligation (as I discussed in chapter 5) because the contract is a contract of membership, so to speak. What the contract does is make one a member by agreement. At least, I take it that this is what it means to "join" an organization or enterprise. You become a "staff member," or a part of the "administrative team," for example. You become a participant in an ongoing cooperative enterprise. Indeed, businesses and corporations frequently use just such language with regard to employees, although I would not want to press that point, since it can be and is sometimes used to manipulate employees.

The point is, there is a clear and unavoidable sense in which any employee is a member of the organization that employs him or her. If you are employed by an organization, you are unavoidably part of that organization. So the consent component of the contractual obligation in employment can be viewed as related to or at least compatible with the idea of membership.

The concept of reliance obligation, I want to suggest, just is another name for, another way of referring to what I am calling membership obligation, or at least part of it. I believe the two concepts are overlapping.[8] What I have labeled membership obligations are obligations of mutual or reciprocal reliance (i.e., obligations of cooperative endeavor). Consequently, to analyze the idea of membership just is a way of unpacking the concept of mutual or reciprocal reliance, and of determining the obligations that follow from it. So I shall now examine what it means to have an obligation of membership in the context of employment or profession.

First, there is a minimal sense of identification, as just mentioned, which is a necessary condition of employment and of obligations of membership. It is the sense in which employment makes you a part of something larger than yourself, an organization, institution, profession, or enterprise. This holds without regard to your attitudes, tendencies, customs, or anyone else's. If you are employed, you are part of the enterprise or institution within which you are engaged. In this minimal sense you are identified with it as part of it, whether you like it or not.[9]

Beyond that minimal sense, identification is more variable. There are two ways, as a start, in which one can be identified with an occupation: internally and externally. Neither, I think, is necessary, in the way that the first (and minimal) sense is for employment. Psychologically, many (perhaps most) people do identify strongly with what they do for a living, particularly if they do it for some length of time. But someone might take a summer job, or a part-time job, and not identify with it. That is primarily because they do not think of that activity as the main thing they do, or as a goal in their lives, and so on. It is just something they do "on the side." But usually people identify rather strongly with what they do for a living over time. At the same time, it should be recognized that some people feel alienated from their jobs, hate their work, feel that they should be elsewhere. Insofar as that is true, obviously, they do not identify with, and might even be described as rejecting any identification with, their occupation. However, many people (probably a majority) identify internally with what they do for a living over time. People become what they do.[10] That is, occupation plays a significant part in the self-image of most people, though not always or necessarily.

Externally, people are often identified with their occupation by other people or by society at large. This tendency is very common and very old. In ancient literary sources, such as the Bible, for example, people are very frequently identified by reference to their occupations. They are shepherds, or fishermen, or soldiers, or whatever. Since (at least in the Bible) these references are frequently of no particular relevance to the story, they seem merely to reflect the common tendency to identify people by what they do. So you may reject being identified with your job, but other people are likely to identify you with it anyway. Like self-identification as a psychological phenomenon, this is just a general tendency, although a very common one. It has an effect on community expectations about you, just as self-identification has an effect on expectations you have for yourself. I will return to this point shortly. For now, at least the minimal sense of being part of something obligates you in a cooperative endeavor to some extent.

This concept can be filled out by considering a second and obvious implication of joining an organization: you adopt a certain common task of that organization as your own. At the narrowest level, this is necessarily true. The job you accept defines your task, and the accomplishment of this task is an objective that you share with your employer. The more broadly the objective is defined, however, the more controversial is the assertion that you accept it, merely by accepting the job. But, even if you disagree with the overall objective of your employer, it is nevertheless undeniable that you are participating in the accomplishment of that objective (unless you are engaged in sabotage).

Are you obligated in any broader way to support the overall objective of the organization you join because you join it? That is a hard question. I doubt that a uniform answer is possible across the board. In an employment context, it is like asking whether an employer is entitled to expect loyalty or commitment. Ideally, in a perfect world, the answer might be yes. In the real world, a very qualified and tentative "sometimes" is surely the strongest claim that could reasonably be made.[11] At the narrow level, however, you are obligated to meet the specific responsibilities of the position you accept. That task you are committed to. So, as long as you are doing your job, you are obligated to participating in a common task or objective of the enterprise at that level.

Third, this task or objective as applied to you will be defined as, or in terms of, a role. Employment is a fairly clear context of role responsibility. It is not merely that professionals and employees are part of some larger entity; they play a particular part, a role, that is defined by the profession or the employer and the public over time, and that provides the basis for professional responsibilities and the reasonable expectations of the public in general and clients in particular.

Thus, finally, community expectations will be directed toward you (by clients, customers, fellow workers, associates, etc.) that reflect your role or position. As I mentioned earlier, since you hold the position, it is reasonable for others to assume that you will fulfill the obligations associated with it, indeed, to rely on you to do so. Role and expectation are interactive in an interesting way. Each is influenced by the other. Expectations are generated by public perceptions of the role, which in turn affects the role itself, which in turn may modify expectations. Reasonable expectations and role are the two elements that define the content of these obligations as obligations of membership.

All these elements together—your acceptance of a common task or objective, defined in terms of a role, as well as the reasonable expectations, or reliance of others on you to perform it—define and justify your obligations of membership, and fill in the content of your contractual obligation in the employment context.

Obligations of membership in general are not necessarily well defined. They are obligations that people have in virtue of being part of something larger than themselves alone, but not necessarily any particular part. In fact, one of the problems associated with defining and analyzing duties of membership may be their possible vagueness. But duties of occupation are usually duties of role, and so will almost always be fairly well defined in terms of basic understandings about the role or position within a given practice or institution. One who has a role has a particular part to play, and this will always be true in the case of professions. So although a written contract may not specify in detail the obligations consented to, understandings of business practice and professional responsibility will do so. Thus, filling in the idea of contract as consent with the idea of obligations of membership or mutual reliance provides a richer account of the scope and content of professional obligations, or what is consented to and why.

A greater problem within the context of professional obligation, as mentioned earlier, is the problem of conflicting duties. Considering this problem will refine our understanding of the scope and limits of professional obligation.

3. Professional Dilemmas and the Priority of Negative Duty

It is in the area of professional obligation that questions of the conflict of positive with negative duty are most commonly raised. These are frequently expressed in the following form. Do professional obligations or the requirements of professional life supersede ordinary morality, or do they release the professional from the requirements of ordinary morality, that is to say, negative duty?[12] There is a considerable literature on this issue in the field of professional ethics and its various specialized subfields: legal ethics, medical ethics, business ethics, and so on.[13] Some difficult questions are raised within this topic of conflicting duties. As a doctor, committed to promoting health and preventing suffering, should you lie to a weak patient about the perilousness of her condition? As a lawyer, sworn to represent the interests of your client, should you destroy the credibility of an adverse witness you know to be truthful? As a journalist, committed to reporting the news, should you invade the privacy of an ordinary person to pursue a story you think is in the public interest? Should positive duty sometimes override negative duty?

There are arguments on both sides of the issue. On the one hand, it can be noted that basic requirements of ordinary morality are supposed to be universal and binding, not conditional to position or context. On the other hand, special obligations of profession can create very difficult conflicts that appear to necessitate suspending the requirements of ordinary morality in certain circumstances.

My own view is that negative duty is presumptively, rather than absolutely, overriding, and therefore there will be occasions when special circumstances may require actions ordinarily considered immoral. Furthermore, these circumstances frequently involve clashes between two duties of justice, although positive and negative. However, negative and positive duty should be compatible most of the time, unless there is a flaw in the institutions involved—which, of course, there may often be. Indeed, I would suggest that the persistence of conflicting duties is presumptive evidence of flawed institutions.

The point is, negative duty is justified as a minimal and universal requirement of human interaction. Special duties (including professional ones) are justified by the requirements of the institution or relation that relies on them. If the institution or relation commonly requires the violation of negative duty, then there is something wrong with the institution. Thus, conflicts will arise from time to time due to special circumstances. But any conflict of professional obligations with negative duties (or ordinary morality) should raise some serious questions about the particular obligation, especially (a) whether a certain action is the only way to meet it, and (b) if it is the only way, whether such a duty should be a requirement of the profession. If it is a correct and unavoidable requirement of the profession, then (c) you have a genuine dilemma that must be considered as an individual case.

Nor is there likely to be any single principle or formula that can be used to settle the question, since dilemmas by definition cannot be satisfactorily resolved. There will, no doubt, be a number of considerations that presumably are relevant and should be taken into account in such cases. You would certainly want to cause the least harm possible. Given your fiduciary relationship, you must necessarily weigh very heavily the fidelity you owe your client. You might also want to consider the values and expectations of your profession. But none of these considerations will, in the last analysis, decide the issue for you, and ultimately, I believe, the existentialist characterization of such circumstances is correct. If your situation is in fact a conflict of two genuine duties, there will be no real solution, just two bad choices. You must make your decision and take responsibility for it.

It should be apparent, given the dramatic way in which I just characterized this kind of situation, that it should be a relatively infrequent occurrence. It will be one of those unfortunate extraordinary circumstances that must be dealt with on its own terms, and lived with later. In light of this extreme conclusion, let me return to the first two points, mentioned but left unexplored earlier.

As to (a)—Is a certain action the only way to meet the obligation?—the first thing a professional must do is seek to avoid the dilemma. One must consider whether there are other ways to meet the obligation, or other ways to handle the situation. Sometimes there will not be, but it does not follow that professionals are not bound by ordinary morality. We would need to see a convincing argument for that. Ordinary morality is minimal morality. It is generally construed as what is required of all human beings just by virtue of being human. Professionals might be required to do more, but profession alone cannot require them to do less, since they are still human beings, and are still dealing with other human beings. If professionals are excused from minimal requirements of morality, then there must be a moral argument to justify that. "My job requires this" is not itself a moral argument (e.g., a hit man could use it) nor is "I don't make the rules; I just play by them." But there are serious arguments on both sides of this issue.

The strongest arguments favoring an exemption for professionals from ordinary morality are, of course, always put in terms of the difficult circumstances of the particular profession, and the futility of refusing to accede to them. For example, Monroe Freedman has outlined the difficulties facing criminal defense attorneys, especially when defending the indigent accused, who has few alternatives and must rely heavily on a court appointed attorney.[14] In such circumstances the lawyer may begin by pleading innocent a party she knows (or has every reason to believe) is guilty. She may then find it necessary, on behalf of her client, to undermine the testimony of a truthful witness, to risk putting her client on the stand, knowing that he may commit perjury, or to supply him with information or advice to which he is entitled that may tempt him to commit perjury. Furthermore, she may not be able to inform the court of perjured testimony, or withdraw from the case, without seriously prejudicing the position of her client or breaching her duty of confidentiality to him. Thus, criminal defense attorneys may find themselves in a position that would ordinarily be described as collusion to misrepresent or deceive. While not lying herself, if she represents a guilty party, she is hired precisely to provide the most skillful defense possible of a proposition she may know to be false. And she does so as an officer of the court, sworn to participate in the search for truth. Most people find this situation troubling.[15]

Freedman certainly does not take the matter lightly, but he argues that such conduct is justified by policy considerations that require it. The maintenance of the adversary system, the prosecution's burden to prove guilt beyond a reasonable doubt, the presumption of innocence, the right to counsel, and the obligation of confidentiality are among those policies.

I do not presume to have an answer—a real solution, that is—to this very difficult problem, but it may be useful to consider some doubts raised by Freedman's very able defense of the idea that certain professional obligations (at least those of the criminal defense attorney) sometimes override ordinary morality, and consequently that professionals are sometimes justified in conduct that would otherwise violate basic moral requirements.

First, I wonder why we should suppose that professional obligations should be viewed as such strong moral requirements that they actually justify conduct that ignores what would otherwise be morally required, rather than at most excusing such conduct? Freedman characterizes the countervailing considerations as policy considerations. Why should policy considerations be taken as so weighty as to nullify morality altogether? A stronger moral consideration might be the right of the client, which justice requires to be respected, and given the special relation, the lawyer owes a perfect duty to her client—in fact, a fiduciary duty—which makes that claim very strong indeed. But what exactly does the client have a right to? He has no right to commit perjury. He has no right to collusion to illegal acts on the part of his lawyer. But he does have a right to competent legal counsel.

Is this situation an example of the dilemma that I mentioned earlier? If so, it seems to warrant the idea of excuse at most, rather than justification. Justification means that what the attorney does is right, all things considered. There is nothing wrong with the conduct at all under the circumstances. Excuse, on the other hand, recognizes that the conduct is wrong, but that it was unavoidable, and therefore should be condoned. That may better describe the unfortunate position of the defense attorney. The conduct is apparently wrong, but the attorney has no better choice. At least, given the arrangement of the institution (the current adversary system), the only other choice available would also be wrong. That description better captures the dilemma, if that is what it is, though it certainly doesn't solve it.

Second, doesn't this dilemma suggest that something is wrong with the institution? If the adversary system is what requires this conduct, then presumably we should want some strong justification for the institution that indicates that the same ends could not be accomplished without the violation of basic moral requirements. It would seem that we ought to be searching for some better way to handle this public goal. But we do not seem to be doing so. Thus, my answer to Freedman, such as it is, leads back to my second point, point b.

As to (b), it may occasionally be the case that professional responsibility will conflict with ordinary morality in fact. I believe that moral dilemmas do occur, but they ought not to be common. This state of affairs cannot be a matter of ordinary professional practice. It cannot be an everyday occurrence. If it is, it means that you are stuck in a profession that is requiring you to perform presumptively immoral acts on a continuing basis, in the interest of a crucial service performed by the profession for society. There can be such "professions," espionage coming easily to mind. But we don't think of spying as an honorable profession, do we? Spies sacrifice their moral integrity to a cause. If the responsibilities of your profession compel you to violate ordinary moral requirements on a regular basis, it indicates that you are engaged in an immoral profession, hopefully for an extraordinary objective, or that the profession has been misorganized under an immoral principle or purpose. Any profession or occupation that actually requires its participants to violate principles of ordinary morality on a regular basis could, it seems to me, have at least three rather untoward tendencies.

First, such a requirement may well threaten the character of those professionals who are required to behave immorally (or maintain the view that they are justified in ignoring basic moral requirements). Since the time of Aristotle it has been rather widely recognized that our character is produced by our habits. Identification with one's profession is often very strong. Indeed, it has been observed that "one's professional role becomes and is one's dominant role, so that for many persons at least they become their professional being."[16] We should hardly be surprised if it turns out that many people cannot compartmentalize their attitudes so well as to practice dishonesty and manipulation in one institutional context but not in any others. Richard Wasserstrom suggests, for example, that the predominance of lawyers in the Watergate scandal illustrates precisely this point. Their actions in the cover-up were surely an illegal extension of their fiduciary obligations but were not different in kind from the ordinary duties Freedman describes as belonging to the defense attorney in common practice. It is easy to see the slippery slope that may lure lawyers to debase themselves by rationalizing immoral conduct not different in kind from the (otherwise) immoral conduct they are excusing themselves from already.

Second, a professional requirement to regularly violate basic moral principles could undermine the general commitment to such principles over time. If, for example, a significant segment of the population is actually excused from a requirement of honesty (shall we say all lawyers, politicians, diplomats, labor negotiators, and business executives, to take a random sample of fields that have claimed to be so excused), how is honesty to be maintained as a general value? Who would not be exempt in one capacity or another?

Perhaps it is worth noting that such conflicts are almost always about honesty or the invasion of privacy.[17] The question is generally, Do professionals really have to be honest? This is a remarkable question, when one considers that one of our strongest requirements or greatest needs in contemporary society is to be able to trust our professionals, or for that matter, to be able to trust one another. With the proliferation of professions, is a professional exemption from honesty a good basis to maintain honesty as a general social commitment, a virtue of public life at all?

Third, if a profession, as a group, must violate ordinary morality on a regular basis as a matter of professional obligation, it may impair or even ruin the reputation of the profession as a group over time. Even if this supposed violation of morality is a false or exaggerated perception, it can seriously undermine public trust and professional reputation. Lawyers, as a group, for example, are held in very low esteem, morally speaking, in public opinion in this country. They always seem to be at the very bottom of opinion polls, along with used car dealers and snake oil salesmen. They are not considered trustworthy—unless you pay them, perhaps. They are not honest, at least according to public opinion.

In the same vein, broadcasters and other journalists are widely perceived as intrusive, argumentative, and sensationalistic gossips who do not respect the privacy of anyone and are not particularly concerned about the harm they cause individuals in their pursuit of news. Such perceptions are often unfair but not without some basis in truth. And the truth they reflect is contained in the moral dilemmas faced by such professionals regarding whether to violate ordinary morality for the sake of professional goals, coupled with occasional reliance on these dilemmas as an excuse for questionable conduct. We should not consider that no price is to be paid for such reliance.

As I said, these assessments are often unfair, or at least overdrawn. Members of professions need to recognize that we are all responsible for all the members of our group, the reputation of which, unfortunately, is often biased by its most flamboyant and not necessarily most virtuous members, as well as its most spectacular problems. To return to the example of lawyers, why is it that the reputation of the entire profession seems to be so dominated by images of criminal trial attorneys and corporate hired guns? Criminal trial attorneys do face some terrible moral dilemmas that in fact throw into question the adversary system itself, but why should that problem be taken as representative of the profession as a whole when the majority of lawyers are not primarily trial attorneys at all, and those who are are not primarily criminal attorneys. Nor do most lawyers hold powerful positions within international corporations. But then you can't make a TV series out of some trustworthy individual who spends the better part of the day methodically researching cases, meticulously drafting documents, or attentively filing forms, and the rest of the day writing carefully worded letters. Surely that's not what lawyers do as a rule. We want to think that they are more like the attorneys on television's *LA Law*, which at least had the virtue of giving a generally positive image. But even the good guys on *LA Law*, which is just pretend after all, may not be able to counter the reputation produced by the more spectacular and notorious hired guns in real life, who at least appear to be willing not only to take any sensational case just to prove they can win, no matter what the truth might be, but also to justify this conduct as a special requirement of their profession that supersedes—exempts them from—the requirements of ordinary morality.

I believe the general position of trust that is inherent in the idea of a profession is undermined if its members violate basic morality, even if—or perhaps especially if—they excuse themselves from these requirements. Public cynicism must be generated by such conduct. How trustworthy is a person who is capable of being immoral for a cause, even a good cause, even his client's cause? If someone is able to put aside the requirements of morality in one context, why not in another? If for one good reason, why not another good reason, or even a somewhat less pressing reason? Why not for mere convenience? For utility? For profit?

Such questions reflect the point I just mentioned about the character of professionals who engage in professional activity that violates ordinary morality. Perhaps it is possible to compartmentalize one's moral values and habits in the way that would be required to meet such obligations on a regular basis, and still maintain personal integrity, but if so, such compartmentalization does not correspond to common attitudes about morality, psychology, or character in general. Common beliefs about moral character seem to construe it as more integrated than that. Violating ordinary morality is generally viewed as a sign of a weak moral character. It is a flaw, or so it might be reasoned.

On the other hand, it might be reasoned, if it is not a flaw, then it is not a flaw for anyone. Why should we suppose that only lawyers are able to compartmentalize? Postulates of human psychology and morality should presumably apply across the board. That is, it seems reasonable to suppose that the points just mentioned could be viewed as functioning in the alternative. If ordinary morality is necessarily violated by some group in a professional capacity, then either the members of that group must be of questionable moral character, or the value that is violated is conditional—it may be overridden by anyone on a regular basis for certain reasons, such as professional need.

I do not mean to suggest that moral reasoning is all or nothing—that it requires either absolutism or relativism. On the contrary, I think the moral position I outlined earlier is a defensible one. Moral dilemmas do occasionally occur. In extraordinary times (such as war, perhaps) they may even occur often. Extraordinary circumstances may require extraordinary responses (that may reflect the breakdown of moral and social systems). That is not relativism. But if you are violating ordinary morality as part of a professional service in daily life, you cannot characterize that as extraordinary. You are not violating morality as a response to some extraordinary circumstance; you are violating it for a living. It is your profession—or part of it. That sounds morally questionable to me. Nor is it justified by utility, since it necessarily undermines public confidence not only in you, but in your profession as a whole (which was my point c). One question is, Why does it do that?

Basic professional responsibility, as I showed at the beginning of this chapter, is founded on the value of reliance, even as a contractual relationship alone. This should hardly come as a surprise. The ultimate professional relation is a fiduciary relation—that is, a relation of trust. A professional is supposed to be someone you can trust. The whole idea of hiring professionals is that you ought to be able to rely on them. If they represent themselves as professionals, then it is (or should be) reasonable to rely on them in their professional capacity. That is part of what it means to be a professional. And certainly reasonable reliance is a primary source of enforceable obligation in both contract and tort law. That fact should tell us that it provides a very firm foundation for strong obligations. But what does it mean to deserve to be the object of such reliance, such trust? What does it take to earn it—to be worthy of it?

These questions lead us to consider what it means to be a responsible person in a professional context. A professional assumes responsibility for accomplishing a certain task or goal, or for protecting a certain interest for the client. Often (although not necessarily) responsibility is assumed because the client is unable to do it personally. This disability may be due to simple time constraints, but more often it is due to a lack of knowledge, skill, or ability. In either case, the client is dependent on the professional. That is, the client must rely on the professional in a rather strong sense.

People hire professionals so that they can rely on them in this strong sense in a certain capacity that is specified by the role of the profession. Thus, the first and most distinctive characteristic of professional responsibility as such is that professionals must be competent in the profession. They must be the experts that they hold themselves up to be. Professionals should have some special qualifications. They must have mastered some special body of knowledge or skill through education or experience or both.

Thus, a professional must be competent (or expert) in the field. But that still is not enough, I think, although people (who are clients in need of the service) may be forced to settle for it. Yet it is not enough, because reliance is a synonym for trust, and trust is not rational without some level of honesty—the higher the better, in fact. You have no good reason to trust a professional who is either incompetent or dishonest. In either case, since you are dependent on this person, you are in a vulnerable relationship, and it is not a relationship of trust, at least not in the sense of rational or reasonable reliance. Without both competence and honesty, the client is at risk. Thus, professional responsibility requires both competence and honesty, or the relationship between the professional and the client is not one of reasonable reliance or trust.

But if the profession itself requires the violation of ordinary morality, a natural corollary will be the erosion of general confidence in that profession. No profession can regularly violate ordinary morality and not have a reputation as doing so. No profession can engage regularly in manipulative or deceptive practices and retain a reputation for honesty. Professional conduct reflects on all members of that profession presumptively, and illustrates a further aspect of the communal nature of morality and perceptions about it. For this reason, institutions must be structured in a way that will not require participants in them to violate the basic requirements of ordinary morality or, in other words, negative duty. If such violation occurs with regularity, it indicates a flaw in the institution or practice.

The general upshot of all this is that a clear limit on the scope of special positive duty is negative duty, and this is true despite the fact that special positive duties are duties of justice. Indeed, the fact that both special positive and negative duties are duties of justice creates very serious problems if the two conflict in an individual case. At an individual level, one may be faced with an existential dilemma that has no right answer. This is one reason to acknowledge that negative duties are presumptively but not absolutely overriding. It is also a reason to acknowledge that institutional structures that generate special positive duties should be evaluated in terms of their correspondence with the requirements of negative duty. Dilemmas of duty cannot be corrected on an individual level, but it does not follow that positive professional duties can justify otherwise immoral conduct. Instead, the conflict of professional obligation with the requirements of ordinary morality should be taken as presumptive evidence of a flawed institution in need of reorganization or correction.

4. Explicating Reciprocal Duties: Two Forms of Trust

The preceding sections should make it clear that the traditional contractual model of professional obligation based on explicit consent or agreement must be complicated a great deal if it is to account for actual practices of employment or profession. Clearly, ideas of consent and reliance as a foundation for contractual obligation in this context are not entirely distinct and exclusive of one another. Both play a part in explaining complex obligations that together constitute an occupational role, which one accepts as a package under a variety of conditions, ranging from fully free to severely constrained. Consent in this context is like joining a team. It is consenting to play a part, and to be a part, that is, to be a member, of an ongoing enterprise over which one does not have full control. It is also consenting to allow others to rely on one to fulfill the obligations attached to that role.

Obviously, then, the idea of role is crucial to these explanations, and yet it is not clear that either consent or reliance, as traditionally construed, can adequately accommodate that concept. Role, as a concept, is extraneous to the notion of contract. Standard theories of contract cannot account for it. Yet it is central to obligations of profession or occupation. The idea of role is intrinsic, however, to the notion of membership as developed in chapter 4. In that construction, obligations of role are obligations of membership in the form of reciprocal reliance. That is, I want to suggest that it is helpful to consider these obligations as incorporating elements of membership as well as contract. The question is, How do the ideas of consent and role interact within a professional context, and can the formal structure of liberal theory provide a framework for accommodating these interactions? Let me sketch briefly here an outline of how these elements might fit together.

Summing up the explorations of the previous sections, one might say that a contract for professional services is an agreement that creates at least a minimally consensual relationship of mutual reliance for reciprocal benefit (frequently between parties with different ends).[18] At least, that is a reasonable preliminary statement that follows our considerations of contract law in chapter 6 as well as the interactions of consent and reliance just considered. It also distinguishes a contractual obligation from an obligation of membership as such.

Obligations of membership are duties of connection in a common pursuit or relationship by parties with a common source of identification. These duties are derived from connection: from being part of something with which one is partly identified (one's family, nation, or religion, for example); they are fleshed out, or developed and defined by the reasonable expectations (or common assumptions and beliefs) of the community over time; and they are justified if the institution or practice they comprise is justified, all things considered.

Duties of contract, in contrast, are duties of cooperative interaction by parties of any sort, frequently, but not necessarily, with different ends, and usually (but not necessarily) with different connections. There is no intrinsic connection between contracting parties, as there is with members of a common institution or practice. Very often contractors may have nothing apparent in common other than the contract. In fact, one useful way to view a contract (or contract law) is as a device that extends the range of rational reliance or cooperation to strangers. On the other hand, this point should not be overstated, since contracting strangers do have more connections than meet the eye. They are not totally disconnected, since all contracting takes place within contexts that provide rules and practices that enable such transactions to take place. All contracting takes place within a complex and, at this point, highly developed structure of legal, social, and commercial practice or custom that actually makes contractors rather connected indeed, even if they are strangers to one another. These connections form the background conditions that make the contracts possible.

Yet, the difference (between a duty of membership and a duty of contract) is that preserving or supporting these background connections is not the object of the contract, nor the point of the obligations that follow from it, whereas the common connection, or relation of membership, is itself a part of the object of obligations of membership. One object of family obligation, for example, is supporting and nurturing the family itself. Furthermore, the interests, values, or even the identity of the members are not always clearly separable (which is not to say, not separable at all) from the well-being, values or identity of what they are members of. But the identity and interests of contractors are surely separable from the background conditions and connections that make their contracts possible. Suppose we represent this difference by referring to duties of membership as duties of common connection and duties of contract as duties of interpersonal cooperation.[19] This description represents what distinguishes them.

What they have in common is the value of reciprocal reliance. Duties of membership and contract are both founded (at least in part) on reliance, since both participation in a common relation and cooperative interaction by diverse parties require it. Webster's Dictionary defines 'reliance' as 'trust'. To be reliable is to be trustworthy. Conversely, it defines the verb 'to trust' as 'to rely or depend upon'. Yet, oddly, this close association of the two terms is not always noted. Charles Fried, for example, in arguing against reliance as a foundation of contractual obligation and for the strength of promising in that capacity, repeatedly refers to the value of trust to justify his promise principle.[20] But why doesn't that just reintroduce reliance under another name? It may be that he has in mind a focus on honesty, and that is indeed an important aspect of trust. There is no question that deception in the form of fraud or false promise undermines trust. But what does that amount to, other than the fact that people cannot rely on the deceiver? Of course, there are various ways of being unreliable. Dishonesty is only one of them. So it might be assumed that reliance is a broader category than trust, and so includes too much, perhaps. But that is incorrect, for all the ways in which it is possible to be unreliable are the same ways in which it is possible to be untrustworthy. For example, one can be negligent and therefore unreliable or untrustworthy, but not dishonest. Honesty is a narrower concept, but trust is essentially synonymous with reliance, and so I will use them interchangeably.

Virginia Held has used the concept of trust in approximately the way I intend to use it here, I believe.[21] Trust, she argues, is a social value that must be supported by a proper environment. At least minimal social conditions must be met, since trusting the untrustworthy is not virtuous, or even rational. Trust is an interactive value. It must be fostered. It is for this reason that it is best captured as a form of justice as reciprocity in cooperative interactions. To be a value at all (rather than a pious hope) it must be reciprocated. The more it is undermined socially, the harder it is to maintain individually. Even individually (that is, between two individuals alone), trust must be built. It must be earned over time by mutual adherence to standards of reliability. It must be deserved. The more untrustworthy the general environment, the harder it is to accomplish this. If community standards of honesty are strong, each individual within the community has an easier burden of proof. For example, if members of a society are normally scrupulous about telling the truth, then it is not unreasonable to assume that a particular individual within it is also being truthful. But if there is no such community standard, then each individual bears the entire burden of providing evidence of trustworthiness alone. If the environment is bad enough, it may not be clear how to get that started at all. Thus, reliability must be reciprocal in order to produce trust.

Trust is absolutely crucial for cooperation (as Held also notes), which in turn is critical for either contractual or membership relations. Since cooperation without trust is seriously impaired, the virtue of trustworthiness must be cultivated. And if trust is needed for cooperation, how much more is it needed for relationships of common membership? Thus, we can characterize both duties of membership and duties of contract as duties of mutual trust or reciprocal reliance. We might construe this as two forms of trust: the trust required for common connection, and the trust required for interpersonal cooperation.

Both of these can be distinguished from negative duties, in that negative duties are founded on respect for other individuals as unique and significant in their own right. They are commonly characterized as duties of noninterference, and thus can reasonably be described as duties of separation, as well as respect. Duties of respect protect individuals as such from the harm or interference of others. We can think of them as forming a shield around each person, enclosing each individual within a protective barrier that no one else is entitled to penetrate. Thus, negative duties are duties of separation.

This description provides a clear contrast with duties of trust, as duties of connection and cooperation. Negative duties of respect for persons protect the integrity of separate individuals; positive duties of trust or reciprocal reliance form the groundwork of human interaction and social cooperation.

Yet all three duties appear to be derived from justice, that is, to be based on respect for persons as autonomous individuals on the one hand, and on mutual trust or reciprocal reliance on the other. While duties of respect and noninterference have been a central focus of liberal theory, duties of reciprocity, especially in the form of mutual trust, have been much less considered. Yet, these are values based on the requirements of justice. It is justice that requires us to pay our debts and keep our promises. But it is not the justice of noninterference and respect for autonomy. It is not the justice of separation, but the justice of interaction. Some theories have tried to explain these duties of promising and paying debts in terms of the duty of noninterference, but these accounts are always awkward; and that is because noninterference is the wrong aspect of justice with which to explain positive duties. These duties are founded on the affirmative aspect of justice: the justice of interactions, of reciprocity and reliance and trust. But they are no less duties of justice for that. This affirmative side of justice is badly in need of further analysis. We need to understand the weight and scope of duties of reciprocal reliance. This brief sketch at least explains how the duties are related to and distinguished from one another.

Let me sum up briefly the points of this chapter: Professional obligations are traditionally considered contractual and thus justified by consent. Yet in circumstances of general responsibility of profession or employment, the appeal to voluntariness or autonomy tells us less than one might hope. When one holds a responsible position (as in profession or employment), the position itself is constituted as a set of obligations in the form of a role. Since others must, and do, reasonably rely on occupational specialists to meet the responsibilities associated with their positions, whether or not these specialists freely choose the position or its full complement of attendant obligations, the idea of reliance must be included in any adequate explanation and justification of occupational obligation. Furthermore, the fact that obligations of role are constituted by cooperative practices and institutions makes the form of reliance that is relevant to them mutual or reciprocal reliance.

This is not to say that consent is not relevant. The nature of the consent component in employment is usually that of agreeing to be a participant in an ongoing cooperative venture over which one does not have full control, like joining a team. Ordinarily, what you consent to is a role or position comprising certain duties or general responsibilities within a larger entity. That is to say, you consent to become a member of that larger entity and in a particular capacity or role. You consent to play a part that you yourself do not get to define. All this shows that the ideas of role and membership are crucial elements in an adequate account of occupational obligation. But how do consent and role (or contract and membership) interact within the context of professional obligation? They combine the following elements:

1. Duties of contract, which I construe as obligations of cooperative commitment for reciprocal benefit by otherwise unrelated parties, perform a central explanatory function.
2. Duties of membership, which are obligations of common connection by parties ordinarily identified with one another by role or objective, are also necessary factors.
3. Both of the above are based on mutual reliance or trust, which I develop as an element of justice as reciprocity in cooperative interaction.
4. Both can be distinguished from negative duties as duties of separation or respect for individuals as such.
5. While negative duties protect individual integrity, positive duties of reciprocity or mutual trust form the groundwork of personal connection, human interaction, and social cooperation.
6. Negative duties presumptively override special positive duties, although not absolutely in every case. Dilemmas can occur that must be decided in context, but they should be rare.
7. If professional obligations conflict with negative duties on a regular basis, such conflict indicates a flaw in the institution or practice that defines those professional obligations.
8. Finally, despite their differences, all these duties are derived from justice, based either on respect for persons or on reciprocal reliance.

Acknowledging this analysis of professional (or occupational) obligation also reinforces the view that an adequate liberal theory cannot rely on an atomistic social vision, even as the basis of contractual obligation, the paradigm of traditional liberal theory. Simple models of individual consent alone are much too narrow to accommodate the complex features of any ongoing contractual relations (that is to say, most actual contracts), as the longstanding debate over consent and reliance in legal theory attests. And when we move to the context of professional or occupational obligation (surely a very large component of contractual obligation), we find that these cannot be explained without reference to some account of cooperative communal interaction such as that provided by analysis in terms of communal membership and role relations. I have suggested one such analysis here. Adopting it or anything like it "socializes" liberal individualism, just as incorporating a serious liberal account of family obligations will do.

Thus, providing even the beginnings of an account of special positive duties in terms of the traditional categories of natural and contractual relations—an account that attempts to accommodate actual liberal social practices and institutions—requires a cooperative social vision that eliminates atomistic individualism as a viable foundation, and broadens the concept of justice to include ideas of reciprocity as well as noninterference. This is an important point. It shows that standard traditional liberal categories of affirmative obligation (namely, natural and contractual relations) cannot account for special positive duties if they are construed in traditionally narrow terms. Now, these categories can easily be, and often are, interpreted more broadly, just as I interpreted them more broadly here. My way is surely not the only way to accomplish this broader interpretation but however it is done, it will require a liberal foundation that relies on a cooperative rather than an atomistic vision of social life and human nature, as well as a concept of justice that explicitly includes the requirements of cooperative social interaction.

The positive side of justice, and the cooperative element of special positive duty, that I have been discussing here have been much neglected by the liberal tradition, and this neglect causes a gap in the ability of liberal theory to account adequately for obligations that are in fact commonly recognized and relied on in liberal societies, including familial and contractual duties. It also has affected the liberal analysis and understanding of obligations that are even more controversial than those I have been discussing so far: namely, political obligations. In the next two chapters I will consider how it affects a liberal theory of political obligation to found it on a presumption of cooperative interaction—membership in a common endeavor—as well as respect for individual integrity.

IV

POLITICAL OBLIGATION AS SPECIAL POSITIVE DUTY

It was Jefferson's purpose to teach the country that the solidarity of Federalism was only a partial one, that it represented only a minority of the people and that to build a great nation the interests of all groups in every part must be considered. . . . To insure the . . . rights [of freedom] a government must so order its functions as not to interfere with the individual. But even Jefferson realized that the exercise of the property rights must so interfere with the rights of the individual that the government, without whose assistance the property rights could not exist, must intervene, not to destroy individualism but to protect it.

Franklin D. Roosevelt

8

Justifying the Obligations of Neighbors and Citizens

L iberal individualism was first the discovery and then the presumption of modern Western civilization. Countries and constitutions were founded or re-
formed by its ideas. Freedom is its watchword, and the recognition of human rights
(at least to noninterference) its great achievement. Classical liberal theory focuses
on the significance of every person as a unique, autonomous individual. Every person has moral worth according to this doctrine. Everyone counts.

As a result of this pervasive presumption, liberal moral theories that try to account for social obligations or accommodate competing interests tend to view societies as aggregates of individuals.[1] Both utilitarian and social contract theories traditionally view societies and approach moral justification in this way. For some
purposes this approach works very well; for example, it underscores the significance
of the individual person as a moral unit and thereby sets in motion the impetus
toward universal human rights. But there have also been some shortcomings, since
the focus on individuals may tend to undermine the recognition of the necessity of
social cooperation. Thus, some obligations are not handled well this way, and some
relationships are not best represented this way. Family relations and obligations are
a good case in point. Community obligations might be another. Moral theories
have encountered great difficulty justifying political obligation resting on a vision of
society as an aggregate of presumptively unrelated individuals. Some important insights have been gained from the individualist perspective, but it has produced
some unfortunate blind spots as well.

Even freedom in the form of individualism has not delivered on its promises,
or at least the promises made in its name. Think of the high hopes for it in the eighteenth and nineteenth centuries, expressed in doctrines such as Adam Smith's invisible hand. We didn't need a planned social policy, it was thought. All we had to
do was give individuals the right and the protection to pursue their own interests,
and the common good would just naturally follow.[2] Everyone would be better off.

Similar presuppositions explain how John Stuart Mill managed to argue for
both justice and freedom on utilitarian grounds, a feat that is rather more difficult

to accomplish today.[3] It is not impossible; there are still believers in the invisible hand. But many of us have lost that particular faith. The question now is not how to protect freedom and rights simply, but how to promote the common good and meet the requirements of distributive justice without sacrificing personal freedom and individual rights. Thus, the question for the moderate liberal has become how to coordinate what are now often perceived as competing goods: individual freedom and social justice.

That is the modern idea of the social contract following Rawls.[4] This idea has been and is a rich and illuminating one. But it too has limits. One of them, it seems to me, is its exclusive reliance on the classical individualistic idea of contract. As a foundation for moral responsibility, the traditional notion of contract is at once a strength and a weakness.

The heart and soul of the classical idea of contract is, as I have noted, individual consent or agreement. While it is true that the law of contract itself has a difficult time explaining such theoretical embarrassments as compulsory contracts and mass contracts in terms of individual consent, these can be viewed legally as derivative notions, parasitic on the conceptual core of contract, which relies on agreement, or so it is often argued. Indeed, if you subtract the idea of agreement from the legal concept of contract altogether, nothing remains to distinguish a contract from a tort. Agreement in some form is central to the legal concept.[5] But, unlike the legal theory of contract, the philosophical social contract is not really about consent at all. It is about the obligations we *would* agree to *if* we were rational and, perhaps, moral. In other words, it is about the obligations we *ought* to agree to or, to put it more bluntly, the obligations we justly ought to have whether we agree to them or not.

That's what bothers libertarians. Robert Nozick and other critics of Rawls have rightly pointed out that a hypothetical contract is not a contract; constructive consent is not consent.[6] Philosophical social contract theories (unlike legal contract theories) are really engaged in a project of justifying obligation without consent. I think that's all right, myself. That is, it is a legitimate project, within limits. But, of course, constructing your model of moral justification in terms of contract leads naturally to the kinds of criticism leveled by libertarians. If individual liberty is the fundamental moral value and consent the justification to limit it, then justifying involuntarily acquired obligation by appeal to an imaginary contract can hardly be expected to satisfy anyone who is not already inclined to agree without argument to such limits. Thus, the social contract approach to political obligation tends to reinforce the libertarian view by accepting its atomistic presuppositions. So the question remains: how, if at all, can a moderate liberal position on political obligation be justified?

1. Positive Duties and Liberal Justification: A Social State of Nature

The general problem with which I am concerned here is that the pervasiveness of the individualist perspective creates a blind spot regarding any affirmative obligations that are not individually and voluntarily incurred. Collective obligation cannot be handled well within this view (as illustrated by the theoretical problems with mass contracts in law and political obligation in philosophy). And although non-consensually incurred obligations are not presumed illegitimate altogether, they are discounted. That is, they are either named, bracketed, and ignored, as with family obligations; or they are analogized to contractual (and therefore supposedly consensual) obligations, as with political obligations viewed through the social contract. All in all, justifying political obligation—the affirmative obligations of neighbors and citizens—is apparently a difficult task for liberal theory, especially in its traditional form.

If such obligations exist, and if they are special positive duties (as I will argue), they are both less clearly recognized or accepted by people in general and conceptually more amorphous than most special positive duties. Although they are owed (if at all) in virtue of a special relationship (e.g., as members of a community or political body), it is not always terribly clear who owes them or to whom they are owed, since the relationship may not always be well defined. This feature, coupled with the fact that the size of the relevant group may be very large and its articulation vague (e.g., all citizens—or inhabitants?—of a nation, or possibly the "general public"), raises the question of whether or how these duties (if they exist) are truly distinguishable from universal duties, or general positive duties, or, practically speaking, what such a distinction would amount to. That is, in what sense is the form of these duties consonant with the formal requirements of special positive duty as a class?

It is true that a basic feature of special positive duties is that they are owed by determinate parties to other determinate parties by virtue of some special relationship or transaction. The class of relevant agents and recipients must be specifiable. Furthermore, they are perfect duties: they generate correlative rights. But these formal requirements cause no particular problem, even if the class should be very large. As long as we are referring to specific political bodies, the scope of the duty as a special positive duty is not hard to articulate in terms of membership in a cooperative community: a city, state, or nation, for example. Citizenship rolls are or can be very specific, and insofar as they are, the class of relevant parties is or can be determinate. There can, of course, be unclear cases, but there can be unclear cases in the realm of contract or family as well. We do not view that as undermining the existence of special positive duties altogether. So the scope of application poses no particular formal problem.

Nor is it a *formal* problem to view such duties as perfect duties with correlative rights. Having such duties simply means that acting on them is not within the discretion of the agent, and that others are entitled to the agent's performance of the duty. In the analogous case of universal negative duties, we do not hesitate to say that all human beings have rights to be treated in certain ways, and that consequently, all human beings have perfect duties to the entire world to behave in certain ways that respect those rights. So formally or theoretically there is no problem applying perfect duties to very large classes of people. The difficulty that arises in applying the case of perfect positive duties to large classes of people is practical. The duty must be possible to meet. Yet it does not follow that no such positive duties are possible. Indeed, many liberals over time have explicitly recognized and tried to justify such duties.

John Stuart Mill, for example, acknowledged and argued that in addition to preventing harm, the coercive power of the state could legitimately be used to require each citizen to bear her fair share of the burdens necessary to insure the general welfare.[7] Of course, it might be argued that Mill was not particularly concerned about rights and, as a utilitarian, was committed to promoting the general welfare without regard to its effect on any particular individual. All that may be true, but it does not undermine the point that Mill (a liberal, without question) argued for the obligation of all citizens to share the cost of promoting the general welfare, and he argued for this as a perfect obligation on a par with (or actually as a part of) the obligation not to cause harm. It may also be worth noting that Hobbes, Locke, and Rousseau all argued for extensive political obligations based on the idea of the social contract, which included at least the affirmative obligation to pay taxes, as long as the conditions of a (minimally) just state were met. These were special positive duties, not owed to the world at large but only to other members of the state or community.

More recently, H. L. A. Hart explicitly characterized obligations derived from cooperative endeavor as special positive duties and noted that special rights are created not only by deliberate choices (such as promises or contracts) but also from what he calls mutuality of restrictions. The basic idea is that when persons restrict their liberty in order to cooperate in a common endeavor for mutual advantage according to rules, all have a right to a similar sacrifice on the part of all others who benefit from the common endeavor.[8] He adds: "the moral obligation to obey the rules in such circumstances is *due to* the co-operating members of society, and they have a correlative moral right to obedience." (Emphasis in original.)[9]

This is clearly an articulation of perfect obligations with correlative rights derived from a notion of justice as reciprocity—justice arising out of cooperative endeavor. Many other prominent liberals have made similar arguments. The most notable, perhaps, is John Rawls, who paraphrases from Hart to articulate the rationale for his principle of fairness:

> The main idea is that when a number of persons engage in a mutually advantageous cooperative venture according to rules, and thus restrict their liberty in ways necessary to yield advantages for all, those who have submitted to these restrictions have a right to a similar acquiescence on the part of those who have benefitted from their submission. We are not to gain from the cooperative labors of others without doing our fair share.[10]

These are special duties, political obligations owed to members of cooperative communities as such, and not to the world at large. They are contrasted with natural duties, which are owed to the world at large and without regard to institutional affiliation or social practice. And they are duties of justice with correlative rights.[11] So, it is fair to say, I think, that there is no particular formal problem associated with political obligation as special positive duty, and it is a position often espoused by many liberals throughout history and in the present.

What is a problem is that the content of such duties is not self-evident. In comparison to family duties or professional duties, for example, what the duties of citizens or neighbors are does not follow easily, obviously, or uncontroversially from the nature of the role or relationship, or from actual agreement or consent. So while most people may agree that they have some responsibilities as citizens, for instance, they disagree radically about what those responsibilities are. For example, some people agree with moderate liberal policies to tax well-off citizens to provide programs of education, opportunity, and support for the less well-off, on the theory that the people at large or, in other words, the state owes all its members a fair chance for a decent life. But others deny any obligation to contribute to such "redistributive" policies, which are really just a violation of private property rights, as they see it. Thus, the content, or extent and limits, of an abstract affirmative duty of citizenship is not clear.

Finally, the justification of this sort of duty seems to be particularly tricky for liberal theory, as is evidenced by the often brilliant mental gymnastics both traditional and modern liberals have gone through in an attempt to ground political obligation, or even the obligation to obey the law. Liberal societies have in fact always recognized and relied on the obligations of citizens and community members, but liberal theory has never managed to explain adequately why they should. This is a point often noted by conservatives and communitarians alike, which should be and often is a focus of the moderate liberal.[12]

Having argued in the previous chapters that both family obligations and obligations of contract are often most plausibly viewed as a blend of factors of consent and factors of communal membership, I would now like to apply this analysis to the obligations of neighbors and citizens. What does it do to an analysis of social obligation to blend or augment the foundation of consent with that of membership in a community? Does community membership extend the grounds of social obligation? I shall argue that it does. A preliminary question, however, is whether such a move can be justified within a liberal framework of analysis. I believe that it can be, as I will shortly try to explain.

Within liberal theory, special positive duties are generally considered to be derived from natural or contractual relations. Obviously political obligations are not obligations of family, and it is not generally thought that analogizing them to family duties provides a promising model. At least traditional attempts to do so among ancient theorists, such as Plato, yielded rather oppressive accounts of the relationship between citizens and states. The state was compared to the authoritative father of a patriarchal family, and its citizens to his dutiful children. This, of course, will not be a popular model among modern liberals, all of whom stress the significance of individual autonomy and freedom, and despite the fact that there are some insightful comparisons of families and states within Plato's theory.

Some feminists have recently pointed out that one obvious problem with this view lies in its picture of the family. If the family model were different (e.g., nurturing rather than dominating) then the model of the state that follows from it would be different as well. This is an important point that provides some very useful insights and has the potential for development in interesting directions.[13] I want to pursue a somewhat different path here, but a related one, as should become clear in what follows.

As currently conceived, a family model of political obligation has always been problematic for a liberal theory: hence the popularity of the social contract. Many different social contract theories have been proposed to justify political obligation or explain what would be required to legitimize authority, the most recent and currently predominant attempt being that of John Rawls. Social contract theory (like all philosophical theories) has its strengths and weaknesses, both well known. Its strengths are commonly thought to be that it features the protection of individuality, freedom, and justice, and that it is compatible with diversity, with tolerance for a plurality of values.[14] It assumes no single vision of the good society and thus provides a maximal respect for individual choice.[15]

Two strong arguments have recently been leveled against approaching political obligation with the social contract model, however. First, it creates the illusion that political or social obligations are voluntarily assumed, when usually they are not. There is no contract in fact. If there were, we would not need a hypothetical one. And it is not the case that I am only obligated to comply with the political and legal requirements I happen to agree with. Second, it is said to be individualistic to the exclusion of the social nature and life of humankind. Alistair MacIntyre, for one, has argued that social contract (as well as utilitarian) theories treat society as a conglomeration of self-sufficient individuals who just happen to find themselves in the same place. This, as he says, is both an inaccurate picture of society and an inadequate foundation for morality.[16]

As a foundation for political obligation, social contract theory has its problems. On the other hand, as a limiting and explanatory theory, I would argue, it has great merit.[17] Furthermore, it is not supportable to hold that atomistic individualism is inherent to social contract theory. That is merely one current interpretation of contract among some philosophers in particular. As I have shown, other interpretations are also available that emphasize the cooperative function of contracts and their inherent connection to the idea of mutual reliance as well as consent. While this is still an individualistic notion, it is not asocial or atomistic.

Adjusting the Framework

I will suggest that a common-sense understanding of social or political obligations is that they are founded in membership in the community (although I recognize that this is not an idea that is generally associated with liberal theory). Individual human beings function best in communities; we do not survive well in isolation. Also, any community requires the participation and resources of its members at some level in order to function and flourish, or even to continue to exist. This idea has been recognized since before the Greeks. Communities require support. They are not dead, even when they are static. That is, they are, in a sense, living entities that come into existence, grow and flourish, decline and stagnate, revive or die. And the condition of the community affects the condition of every individual member within it. Thus, there is a reciprocal relation between communities and individual members of them. Communities are not buildings and roads. They are groups of people who are connected in one way or another. In that regard communities are somewhat comparable to families.

Political membership is not the same as family membership. There are important differences, but that does not mean that they are not both forms of communal membership. We are all members of many different groups, and those memberships may not have very much in common, but at least some of them have communal implications: they require cooperation for mutual benefit. That is, different memberships may have very different features, and thus require commitment and participation of different sorts. As I have shown, family memberships and their consequent obligations may vary enormously, as do professional memberships and obligations. Yet, there are certain common elements: the reflexive identity of community and member, the development of community expectations or standards, the assumption of shared tasks or cooperative endeavors, and the distribution and specialization of duties in the form of roles. Political membership fits within this model, showing that, although its content in particular cases must be determined by the character of the special relationship (as with any special positive duty), political obligation has the same formal structure as other special positive duties based on membership, such as family and profession. With that recognition, it seems to me that the traditional formulation of special positive duty as founded on contractual or natural relations can now be corrected.

Admittedly, in the liberal tradition affirmative obligations have always been viewed as grounded in natural or contractual relations: special relations of family or contract. But if we suppose instead a modest adjustment: that special positive duties are based on contractual relations or communal memberships, rather than contractual relations or family memberships, we would have a much more workable framework that better corresponds to the actual practices of both early and contemporary liberal societies. Just to restate this idea, I am suggesting that the traditional liberal framework mistakenly apportions special positive duties between the foundations of contractual and natural relations, when it should be divided between contractual relations and communal memberships. Natural relations (i.e., family relations) are only one subset of the larger category of communal memberships, which would include many other memberships—most important, citizenship, or in other words, political membership.

It is easy to see that once you set up your categories as dividing all special positive duty between family or contract, you will have trouble fitting in political obligation, because in using the narrower category (of family) instead of the more appropriate broader one (of communal membership), you left political obligation out of the basic framework. Thus, an adjustment seems warranted to coordinate the theory with the practice of liberalism.

I do not think that this reconstruction does violence to basic liberal theory, because I do not think that liberals ever intended to leave political obligation out of the basic framework. If they did, why would they spend so much time and intellect formulating ingenious devices like the social contract, apparently in order to explain how political obligation does fit in liberal theory after all? Of course, some traditional liberals may not have intended to include political obligation as special positive duty, but then why the analogy to contract? Political obligation is a form of special positive duty because it follows from the communal relationship—the common necessity for cooperation. If you have this obligation, it is because you are a citizen or a community member that you have it.

At a small communal level this is obvious. Why are members of a tribal society, for example, obligated to participate in the common good? Because the community cannot survive or at least cannot survive well without such participation, and individuals survive even less well alone. Survival is basic, and for human beings it requires cooperation. Beyond survival arises the moral requirement of fairness that limits the distribution of burdens and benefits. It is not fair for some to profit from the cooperation of others without contributing as well, since all do worse alone. Fair cooperation is morally obligatory.

If this idea of community obligation were institutionalized, it could explain, to pick an extremely unpopular example, when and why you are obligated to pay your taxes. Assume for the sake of discussion that taxes in some form can be justified, and therefore that you may sometimes be morally (not just legally) obligated to pay them. If so, on this view, you are obligated because (and only if) it represents your fair share of the burden necessary for the common good or continuing existence of the community. So taxes are justified, first, because (or only if) they are necessary for the accomplishment of cooperative communal objectives without which everyone would be worse off, and second, because (or only if) they are fairly apportioned.[18] Of course, figuring out what is included in the common good (what we all have to pay for together) and what constitutes a fair apportionment are horrendous problems. Nevertheless, we can see what justifies community (or political) obligation: the necessity for communal cooperation, and fairness. You are part of the community, so you are obligated to contribute your fair share to the common good.

At this level, consent as such has little to do with determining or justifying obligation directly.[19] However, it is useful as a rough gauge of both the common good and fairness. Thus, the value of hypothetical consent theories, pretty obviously, is to try to figure out what is included in the common good and what contributions to it would be fair. One way to approach that very difficult problem is to ask yourself: Now, in a fair bargaining situation that guarantees free choice, what would reasonable people agree to? The fact that you can give arguments that reasonable people would agree with or accept, is evidence that the institutions and distributions are fair, and promote the common good. Thus, the value of social contract theories is to provide criteria for determining the scope and limits of obligation or authority. I will have more to say about this issue later. For now, I think that it helps to show that political obligations fit into liberal theory in the form of special positive duties of communal membership, which addresses the issue of foundation (rather than scope).

I do not claim that my reformulation of the doctrine of special positive duty is the only way to account for political obligation. But it is one way (as I will try to defend in the next two sections), and adjusting the framework as I have suggested here seems to make liberal theory more coherent and comprehensive, in that it shows where something fits in, that didn't obviously fit before. There is a sense in which what I am suggesting is not particularly new. It is just a different way of looking at what has long been practiced.

Finally, I do not think that this idea about obligations of membership is incompatible with social contract theory or with utilitarian theory, nor would it supersede them. Quite the contrary. It is nothing more than a focusing device for utilitarian theory, especially rule utilitarian theory, which I think it would reinforce. And for social contract theory, understanding and justifying the obligations of cooperative community members is precisely the point of the contract. To use a Rawlsian framework, for example, it would be quite surprising if representative members of the original position declined to recognize basic obligations of community membership at some level, since community membership is a basic good, or process requirement, for the functioning, indeed for the existence, of community at all. What possible reason could anyone have in the abstract (i.e., behind the veil of ignorance) for rejecting it? In fact, the very idea of a social contract presupposes cooperative community membership.[20] This is not to say that there will not be any controversy about its scope and content, but some basic requirements of community membership are both supportable and necessary on either social contract or utilitarian grounds. Indeed, determining (justifying and limiting) the obligations of community membership is exactly the point of any utilitarian or social contract theory. So I think that those committed to either of these abstract moral theories should not be opposed to obligations of membership, since they are not incompatible, and instead seem to provide a foundation for political obligations that can be refined and limited by appeal to further principles.

If we recognize that political obligation is grounded at least partly in community membership, then utilitarian or social contract theories might be used to determine the scope and limits of it. But I will draw on a different theoretical device here, precisely because it has often been a centerpiece of classical liberal or libertarian theory.

A Social State of Nature

Since the time of Hobbes, the idea of constructing a picture of human character in a state of nature has intrigued philosophers of diverse backgrounds and predilections. The state of nature format is used to derive the authority of the legitimate state from basic features of human nature and morality. The idea is to speculate about what human nature would be like if we stripped away artificial features imbued by social influence, and to imagine human life outside the framework of a coercive or authoritative state. The point of the exercise is to show why a state is needed, why it is essential for human social life, and consequently, what purpose it must serve, what form it must take, what limits it must observe in order to be legitimate.

If we consider important examples of this enterprise, it is pretty clear that the features of a state of nature depend entirely on the human values and character that are plugged into the framework. For Hobbes a state of nature is a state of anarchy— a war of egoistic individuals whose only salvation lies in their ability to recognize that their rational self-interest will be served by agreeing to a social contract that sets up a sovereign who can guarantee peace.[21]

John Locke's picture is rather different: less chaotic, since the inhabitants of his state of nature are generally guided by the natural law of moral conduct imprinted by God on the minds of men. And yet insecurity of enforcement and uncertainty of individual judgment lead again to the need for a social contract, but this time one limited by the natural rights of life, liberty, and property already bestowed on them by the moral law in the state of nature.[22]

Almost one hundred years after Locke, we find Rousseau's state of nature—an idyllic vision of noble savages living peacefully in their natural goodness, uncorrupted by the structures of power and property that would otherwise enslave and debase them. Yet, Rousseau's innocent forest dwellers, for all their innate goodness, are premoral and unfree, being unreflective, and it takes a state with a social contract to make them fully moral beings.[23]

Moving to contemporary philosophers, Robert Nozick recently constructed his twentieth-century state of nature as a consideration of voluntary associations set up to preserve peace and private property with maximal freedom and minimal obligation, by which he means to show how individuals in a series of voluntary choices would move from a state of nature to a minimal, and no more than a minimal (or night watchman), state. The picture he paints is vaguely Lockean, voluntarily cooperative in general, without invoking either the egoistic anarchy of Hobbes or the idyllic goodness of Rousseau.[24]

Thus, one problem with state of nature theories (as the examples show) is that they are compatible with vastly divergent interpretations and claims, depending on the theory of morality and human nature that informs them. Among state of nature theories we find debate over whether it is possible to separate human nature from social environment (since Rousseau denies this possibility and the others apparently affirm it); or whether morality is objective (Locke) or conventional (Hobbes); or whether the state is limited in power (Locke and Nozick) or virtually absolute (Hobbes and Rousseau). Obviously none of these questions is settled by state of nature speculation in and of itself.

Yet each view has its insights. Hobbes, beginning with purely individual premises, provided the classic argument for the negative function of the state: the protection of peace and order. Hobbes recognized the dark side of human nature, and in so doing, he made clear that the most basic function of a state is to protect human beings from one another—to keep us from degenerating into our lowest form. In his pessimism he erroneously assumes that absolute power and only absolute power can prevent conflict. But his insight still stands: human social life requires peace and order in general that must be protected by the collective power of the state from the darker instincts of individuals.

Locke provides a more balanced representation of human nature. While he recognizes the potential threat of evil and of conflict resulting from it (that, after all, necessitates the social contract), he also acknowledges a moral side to human psychology. Although there is a dark side to human nature, it is not the only side. Human beings are also capable of believing in and living by moral principles in much of ordinary life. Morality is not created by the state. It resides in the moral significance of every individual, and a legitimate state cannot exceed these bounds of morality as set by universal human rights. Thus, the insight of Locke underscores the significance of individual human rights, although he fails to acknowledge the importance of community standards for maintaining and reinforcing such moral values.

Three hundred years later, Robert Nozick seems to recapitulate Locke's strengths and weaknesses. On Nozick's view, the premise behind the project is that the limit of social obligation is set by what individuals would otherwise accept by voluntary arrangement. This is a compelling (even if rather undemocratic) view, because again it underscores the moral significance of every individual. Unfortunately, following Locke, it relies on an informal social and moral life for which it provides no account. Thus, Hobbes, Locke, and Nozick all seem to fall prey to the critique of MacIntyre: they seem to assume that moral life can be accounted for as an aggregate of unrelated individual lives, a serious shortcoming.

Rousseau, on the other hand, focuses specifically on the power of social institutions to mold, educate, or corrupt human attitudes and values. Thus, the great insight provided by Rousseau is that individual personality cannot be strictly severed from its surroundings. We are too influenced by the institutions and communal relations of which we are a part to be able to consider individual identity in isolation from them. Unlike the other state of nature theorists, Rousseau begins with isolated individuals and ends with an organic community. But Rousseau loses the individual in the organic unity of the state. Merging with the general will, the individual disappears as a significantly discrete moral entity. This is a fatal flaw that undermines the purpose of the project to accommodate the significance of individuals, and yet the insights of Rousseau's work cannot be denied. So there are insights and deficiencies in each theory of the state of nature. There is cause for caution in the use of this theoretical approach.

Still, there is an intuitive appeal to the exercise. Its assumptions are in the right place. It presumes that the power of any individual over anyone else—at least in the form of state power as legitimate authority—must be justified in terms acceptable to those over whom that power will be exerted. It denies the moral efficacy of force in itself. It denies that might makes right. And it denies hereditary authority as such, at least in the form of a divine right to rule. Appeals to the common good, to justice and necessity, are needed for justification. Reasons must be given for the exercise of power or the restriction of freedom that citizens across the board might plausibly be expected to accept.

I would like to suggest a version of state of nature theory based on the idea that there is no evidence whatsoever that human beings ever did live or ever could live their lives as solitary individuals at any time. Without communal cooperation, there is no human life—at least if human beings are considered essentially rational and reflective. As Hobbes so eloquently observed, without cooperation there is no science, no art, no education, no agriculture, no commerce. One can easily extend the point. There is, in fact, no time for the luxury of human reflection at all. There are only prehuman, premoral individuals scratching out an existence by what they can forage or kill in isolation. What makes human beings human is our capacity to educate our young, to preserve and build on our past discoveries to make life better, more secure, more comfortable, more safe in the future. This can only be accomplished in cooperative communities that foster social values that enable common endeavor. Even the family, the smallest unit of human social life, is a communal unit. There is no morality without community. There is no reflective human life without social life. The only reason that we can imagine such individual life is that we abstract what we take to be the essential features of human identity and morality, which are derived from the socialization process of cooperative living, and we import these features into an imaginary environment that has no way to account for their appearance or preservation. Thus, individuals truly in a state of nature devoid of community at any time are not human beings at all.

If we imagine what prepolitical human nature could be like, therefore, it is more plausible to conceive of it in terms of small-scale social collectivities based on families, tribes, or clans—that is, on informal communal groups cooperating in the common interest to meet common needs. The nature and organization of such groups could have been, and no doubt were, extraordinarily diverse. Yet all were in some sense cooperative communities. The isolated individual is a deviant picture, not a representative of ordinary or typical or even normal human life.[25]

Is there a point to such atomistic representations, despite their inaccuracy? Certainly there is, in terms of representing the significance of individual interests. But even for that purpose, insofar as such pictures fail to capture the requirements of cooperative interaction, they incorporate a flaw that must ultimately prove fatal. That human beings must cooperate in the common good is a truism that distinguishes us from solitary animals, and describes a basic element of being human. Consequently, such a fundamental feature must be included in any adequate political theory.

The fact is, the idea of individualism of the atomistic sort is only made possible by a highly sophisticated political structure that enables individuals to live apart from their families and fellows if they so choose, by engaging in an extremely specialized political and economic system that provides for common needs with the illusion of isolation constructed by the formality of its institutions. All this requires constant cooperation, which may be overlooked or ignored because it can be impersonal. Thus, the foundation of individualism lies not in presuming isolated individuals in a state of nature but in showing how communal beings would or should move to a recognition of individual significance within (or without) the facilitating institutional structure of an authoritative state.

That said, I believe that the most effective version of a state of nature theory should focus on the motive and justification for moving from an informal, prepolitical or extra-legal group to a formal institutional structure—from a community to a state.[26] If it weren't a matter of coercion, what would be the point of such a move? Why would or should community members do it? What does a state accomplish for people that an informal community cannot, or vice versa? With these questions in mind, I would like now to consider one view of the evolution from informal to formal social structures and the consequent obligations of neighbors and citizens.

2. Informal Associations and Communal Obligations: The Demands of Reciprocity

A state of nature can be hypothesized over a range of forms and for a variety of purposes. One can suppose a Hobbesian state of nature that presumes the worst in human character. There is much to be said for considering the worst case scenario since this is what one would want political organization to protect against first and foremost. Still, a vision of total anarchy would be unable to account for the fruits of social cooperation, and it is unreasonable to base political obligation on a supposition that no one would ever cooperate with anyone else unless coerced or threatened. So it seems preferable to keep the worst case in mind but not to construct the state of nature entirely on that basis.

On the other hand, a Rousseauian best case scenario that presumes natural human goodness is far too optimistic to be supportable, and misses the useful point of liberal pessimism as a mechanism of protection. Like the worst case scenario, it has its point and should be kept in mind, but doesn't serve my purpose. Since my purpose is to examine the possibility for communal obligation within and without a legally authoritative state, I will imagine the state of nature as an informal (that is, prelegal or extralegal) community, such as a neighborhood, in order to explore the idea of communal obligation as neighborly duty.

Neighborly duties have fallen on hard times in recent years. I think we must acknowledge that they really are not recognized much at all in modern societies at this point. But neighborly duties were once a paradigm of communal obligation. Are obligations generated by community membership as such? Well, one might think so, at least at some level, but recognizing them seems to depend on identifying with a community, and communities change over time. Today the idea of community seems to have relocated itself to nongeographic entities, especially the workplace. We have the corporate community, the professional community, the academic community, the business community, and so forth. But the old idea of a community that referred to a geographical location where people lived seems to be fading into the past. We are no longer neighbors in a normative sense, or so it seems. This change may reflect the disintegration of traditional values feared by conservatives, or it may reflect changing social organization, or both. Whatever it is, exploring the demise of the neighborhood may provide us with a vehicle for examining informal social obligations.

Who is my neighbor? A lawyer asked that question a long time ago, but it is not clear to me that the question was ever answered helpfully. True, as Jesus informed the lawyer, we are all neighbors, as we are all "brothers" or all children of God. That is an important ideal. But it is not a good description of the world. Descriptively, I suppose, a neighbor is simply someone who lives rather nearby, but historically there was a normative element to it, the universalization of which was the point of the parable that Jesus told the lawyer. It is that normative element that seems to have dissolved in modern life.

Historically, especially in small town and village life, neighbors were very important. They seemed to function something like an extended family (and might often have been extended family, for that matter); or perhaps they were analogous to what today might be called a support group. They provided information and assistance of various sorts. Many tasks were done communally by neighbors, which brings in a significant common work element. A collateral effect of this common work element—this cooperative accomplishment of communal tasks—was the inclusion of all (or nearly all) members of the community in the work force, and thus the employment of (virtually) all members within the communal economy. This was not a matter of kindness. In a simple economy, all community members are needed to provide for the common welfare. No one who is able to work is excluded from participation (nor are any free to decline to participate). The more complex the economy, the more latitude there is for deviation from this norm, but there was not in fact much deviation from it for most of human history. Unemployment is a fairly modern "luxury" that preindustrial societies could not afford. During the predominance of the status system of social organization, for example, one's job (or position) came with the status, so to speak. People were born into their jobs. A surplus of labor was quite rare (although not nonexistent) until the population explosion and machine age of the nineteenth century. Historically, beggars were outcasts, not community members. Everyone else had a job to do. Everyone was part of the communal economy. Thus, the first feature of neighborly duty would be cooperation for the accomplishment of communal tasks. This feature seems to hold up whether a worst case or best case scenario is imagined, since it seems to be a necessity for communal life without a state. Supposing a best case would yield natural cooperation for the common good, since that (greater productivity, security, and comfort over what one could produce alone) is the point of communal living. The worst case actually requires even greater cooperation, since defenses against other marauding communities or individuals, and enforcement mechanisms for internal cheaters and freeriders, would be necessary (as well as cooperation to overcome scarcity and natural adversity). So cooperation for communal tasks would be required in any state of nature. Neighbors in the state of nature had to cooperate.

Neighbors also seem to provide a certain congeniality of environment, even friendship, or at least integration or inclusion, whether or not it is congenial (as sometimes, presumably, it would not be). As with family, whether you get along with your neighbors or not, you would be part of the group. You would not be alone; you would not be a stranger. Neighbors also produce community standards, unconsciously and organically, by formulating and fostering common expectations. And as part of that phenomenon they also provide moral (re)enforcement and preserve traditions. Participation in this mental or moral "community environment," this set of communal expectations, would be the second function of neighbors. And this holds whether a worst case or best case scenario is imagined. These two functions together—cooperation in communal tasks and participation in community standards or moral expectations—constitute cooperative communal living.

Given these two functions, what follows about the obligations of neighborliness? Communal duties (of which neighborly duties are just one variety) on a common-sense view, are those necessary to uphold (and perhaps even promote) the community. They are fundamentally duties of cooperation and mutual support. That is, I would suggest, that they combine the two forms of trust (the trust needed for ongoing cooperation and the trust needed for common commitment) that I discussed earlier in connection with professional obligations. Trust as needed for cooperation requires reliable participation and interaction in communal tasks or objectives as defined by the reasonable expectations of the community.

The trust needed for common commitment or mutual support in the context of neighbors would require courtesy and civility. This is not so strong or personal an obligation as that associated with friendship or family, but it might provide conditions within which friendship could occur or family could flourish. It is about providing an environment or ambiance of community, a certain sharing or at least inclusion. Neighborhood in the normative sense extended the area in which you could feel at home. Thus, the obligation of neighbors would include the recognition of other neighbors as belonging there, and thereby being part of something. That is what creates a neighborhood and makes individuals members of it, rather than just separate residents. Mutual recognition makes neighbors out of strangers, and creates neighborhoods, that is, communities, out of geographical locations. It requires a certain sort of behavior and a particular attitude, a certain level of concern or attention. If you had a duty of common commitment or communal membership as a neighbor, it would be to participate in that sociomoral environment. Participating in that shared concern or attention would maintain the conditions of trust that were needed for communal cooperation.

In what sense would these neighborly duties be duties? I believe that they would be rather standard moral duties. That is, morally speaking, they are expected by and necessary to the well-being—indeed, as one can now see, to the very existence of the community. It was a certain sort of attitude and behavior, as I have tried to show, that made you a good neighbor. (That is why the good Samaritan was a good neighbor, no matter where he was from, and, of course, universalizing that attitude and behavior, that level of concern and support, was the point of the parable.) This behavior would be a moral duty, for it would be expected and required by the community and justified as necessary for the well-being and existence of the community and all its members. If you did not conform to the standard, you would be a bad neighbor, which is something like being a bad person. In other words, you would be morally condemned by your peers. That is the way moral requirements work, and so, at least functionally, this would be a moral duty.[27]

Would it be a perfect duty? (Remember that special positive duties of family or contract, standard special positive duties, are perfect duties. They are derived from special relationships and attached to rights.) Would neighbors have rights to the cooperation and support of their fellows? That does not really seem like the correct way to put it, since the focus here is not on entitlement, but responsibility. Nevertheless, it would be reasonable for neighbors to expect neighborly conduct from their fellow community members. In that regard I suppose a particular individual, or several of them, might justifiably feel wronged as a result of the failure of a neighbor to meet the appropriate standard of conduct. And I have already mentioned that (moral or social) sanctions would be attached to such failures. By and large, however, the duty seems more communal and perhaps more holistic than perfect duties are usually construed to be. At least some of the time, the duty seems to be owed to the community at large and over time. It is not a one-shot deal, as they say. One swallow does not make a summer. One act does not make you a bad or good neighbor. It is continuing conduct over time, and thus more cumulative and more communal than acts usually associated with rights tend to be construed.

Besides, communal relations are more like family relations, where the idea of rights is really less appropriate than we rights-conscious moderns tend to make it out to be. There is a sense in which once you have "descended" to rights talk in communal or familial situations, you are already in trouble—you are already violating the spirit of community and family. That does not mean that individuals have no rights in these contexts, however, or are not entitled to respect in them. Far from it. But these contexts are more informal and integrated than, for instance, contractual ones, and so rights cannot work the same way. The requirement of noninterference, for example, is certainly not as clear in such circumstances. Family members may have a duty to interfere on behalf of a loved one; and friends and neighbors might have similar duties, at least at a certain level. I am not talking about coercion here, but pressure, influence, advice. Actions that would otherwise be considered prying, or invasion of privacy, or meddling are not always inappropriate for family, friends, or even neighbors in the normative way that neighbors used to or could be imagined to function. Yet it does not follow that friends and family members need not respect one another's autonomy. Quite the contrary. So, at least rights as noninterference do not function the same way in all contexts, and there cannot be any formula for understanding how they work in a communal situation, I think, because it is actually too individual, in the sense of being too personal. That may be precisely what is wrong with (at least a focus on) rights in this context. Rights are too formal, too impersonal, too abstract.

Yet we have no reason to suppose that there are no rights among community members, any more than there are no rights among family members. So, after due deliberation, perhaps I can begin to answer the question. Are neighborly duties in our imaginary informal community perfect duties? Certainly not in the way contractual duties are, but in much like the way family duties are.

And what about the fact that some such duties seem more oriented to the community than to particular individuals within it? Are those perfect duties? Only if it is useful and justifiable to suppose that groups can have rights, which it probably is. Group rights have been recognized in law for some time. Townships, municipalities, clubs, and corporations may all have rights and duties. These are the clear cases. Some philosophers (Plato or Rousseau, for example) have also argued for the recognition of moral rights or duties for certain groups. More recently, Peter French has argued that moral responsibility should be ascribed to corporations.[28] Others have argued for moral rights to reparation for certain groups, rights to equal treatment, rights to equal opportunity. While such positions are often controversial, they are plausible positions for which reasonable support is provided.[29]

In chapter 5 I argued at some length that obligations may be owed to one's family or household as a group. Sacrifices that are warranted by the common good cannot always be explained adequately by reference to the separate individuals within it. Does that mean that the family itself has rights? No, it means only that the family as an entity stands for the common interest of all its members jointly. In an informal setting such as family or community, the language of rights is awkward, in ways I have already discussed. But that has to do with the informality or intimacy of the setting, rather than whether a group or an individual is involved. As I suggested earlier, it does not follow that there are no rights in such contexts. Quite the contrary.

So, bearing in mind all these considerations, I would be inclined to say that although they do not fit the standard paradigm, communal duties are perfect duties, since they follow from special relationships and impose specifiable obligations to which (moral) sanctions for violation attach. If that view is accepted, it expands the notion of a perfect duty to include duties corresponding to group rights, and to obligations that are more informal and perhaps more generalized than those usually seen to characterize rights. I think there are reasons to favor such a move, as I will try to show in the next section. Furthermore, as I suggested in the previous section, viewing social obligation as a perfect duty is not anything new or particularly controversial within liberal theory.

Are these duties of benevolence or justice? As I will argue shortly, I believe both values are implicated. These duties cannot be accounted for by benevolence alone, because they are primarily about requirements of trust and reciprocity. These are duties of cooperation, not charity. Yet, the common good seems to be the point of them. It is the flourishing of community members as community members that motivates these duties, even though justice (as reciprocity) requires them. Since none of this changes when the duties are institutionalized, I will address this issue in the next section. But for the moment I want to return briefly to our saga of declining neighborly duties to explore another issue, the central issue for state of nature theory: What is the point or justification for moving from informal communal living to the formal institution of an authoritative state?

By the mid–twentieth century, neighborhoods, in the communal form I just described, were disappearing in many places for many reasons. Neighborhoods exist within highly organized formal states that have taken over many of the functions neighbors once performed. People were becoming more mobile. They didn't know their neighbors, didn't grow up with them, and didn't necessarily think of their residence as permanent in the same way that permanence was once viewed. Shopping malls defeated local stores, thereby eliminating one source of neighborly interaction. School busing eliminated another with the demise of the neighborhood school. Automobiles and mass transit made commuting a way of life that fragmented community organization. Entertainment changed: many people started watching TV instead of socializing with neighbors. And the clincher was the mass exodus of women from the home and into the work force.

As a result of all these social changes, the centrality of the home as a location of community (beyond a nuclear family level) has receded, and people do not recognize their neighbors as members of any particular group with which they share a common identification or connection. Indeed, they may not even know each other at all. Neighbors are now often strangers. Therefore, such neighborhoods are not communities, which means that there cannot be any communal obligations to them, because there is no group, no community to have an obligation to. You might in certain circumstances have an obligation to some particular individual who happens to live near you, but not because he is your neighbor. There is no connection between the two of you, in terms of geographical location, unless one is recognized. This phenomenon illustrates an interesting feature of informal groups or communities. Their existence is created and maintained by the mutual recognition or identification of their members. One reason for formalizing a group, therefore, might be to stabilize its existence. In the absence of some such formal feature, there is no obligation without the informal identification that creates the community. Thus, neighborhoods are not typically communities (at least not most of them), and neighbors have no affirmative obligations to one another as they once had, simply because none are recognized.

Is this a loss or just an interesting evolutionary phenomenon? It can certainly be characterized as a loss. Some people describe it, or experience it that way. The feeling of community, if anything, is what has been lost, but along with it, safety and cooperation in upkeep may be impaired. Buildings are now defaced, littering is common. There is no communal pride of ownership, or so it is often complained. And people do not feel as safe as they once did. It was recently remarked to me that when we were children we played on the streets without concern, and on Halloween we roamed the neighborhood at night, going house to house trick-or-treating. But now children are much more closely monitored. After school they are enrolled in programs and lessons. On Halloween going from house to house is not considered safe. People used to live in neighborhoods that were communities, but now they are not. People no longer feel connected or responsible to one another where they live; consequently, they no longer feel at home or even safe there. Trick-or-treat is gone, for we live in neighborhoods of strangers. The loss, if it is real, of a minimal standard of civility, congeniality, or safety is indeed a problem. The point here is simply to illustrate the attitude and values associated with community.

On the other hand, it is all too easy to be nostalgic about some little piece of a very idealized and thus largely fictional past. Highly integrated, small-town neighborhoods were not necessarily all bluebirds and roses. Being obligated personally to help everyone you know is hardly a benefit. It can easily consume all the time you have, and even if you dedicate all your time to it, you may, nevertheless, be unable to address all the problems. Of course, if everyone is involved and doing her share, that will help. That is the best case, the ideal. Even then, without formal organization, what you can accomplish personally will be very limited. Large problems and lofty goals will be out of reach. Furthermore, even if the entire community is completely involved in the general welfare, that will not reduce the potential invasion, or at least restriction, of privacy. It is all well and good to be included, helped, supported, and reinforced. But if this takes place where you live, it also may mean that you are being monitored, "guided," observed, and restrained. So, the requirements of community can absorb not only all your time but all your space as well. Obligations are burdens. It is not a loss to eliminate burdens. So, if the needs of community can be met in more effective, less intrusive ways, then eliminating oppressive social arrangements is generally and reasonably considered a good.

It is easy to see that human beings living in cooperative communities are not only better off than they would be living in isolation, but that the conditions necessary to produce what we now consider human life—that is, rational reflection and moral responsibility—are impossible for humans to produce in isolation. Without communal living we have only premoral, prereflective, and thus prehuman beings. Yet there are clear deficiencies associated with living in small informal communities. In particular, the informal community is limited in its ability to provide for the common welfare and it oppressively restricts individual freedom. So the informal community is better than isolation, but even in the best case it is far from ideal for individuals. Consequently, if the institutionalization of communal responsibility as political obligation can increase the welfare of its members and decrease their oppression, it can be justified on grounds of both utility and freedom. In considering such a move, however, from a state of nature point of view, a legitimate state cannot undermine the basic function performed by the cooperative community that provided the conditions for rational reflection and moral responsibility—that is, for truly human life in the first place. To these considerations I will now turn.

3. Formal Association and Duties of Citizens: Justifying Political Obligation

Political organization legalizes power, formalizes decision procedures, and institutionalizes many tasks of the community, thereby transferring the duties of neighbors, or at least some of their duties, to the state or formal government. But what does it mean to do that? Just how does it transform communal obligations, and what, if anything, justifies it? I said earlier that communities (at least in a form they must take in a state of nature theory) perform two sorts of function. First, they serve as a labor pool for accomplishing certain communal tasks or objectives.[30] I'll call these economic goods. Second, they provide an environment of inclusion and maintain communal standards of responsibility and morality that enable some level of trust or cooperation to pertain among the participants in that set of tasks. I'll call these sociomoral goods. Communal obligations are those necessary for the performance of these two functions for the cooperative accomplishment of these two sorts of goods. Without these basic goods, there can be no human community, and without community there is no human life.

On the other hand, village life can be both oppressive and economically insecure. The economic power of a small community (while greater than that of a solitary individual) is necessarily limited. And the latitude for individual diversity, privacy, and freedom within a small community is necessarily limited as well. If the institution of state authority can accommodate these inadequacies, it could potentially be justified by the increase of social welfare and individual freedom that it provided its citizens. So the question is whether (or under what conditions) the state can correct these communal deficiencies without undermining the foundations of human life provided by communal living. To examine this question, it is necessary to explore how the institution of state authority affects the two sorts of goods provided by the informal community.

With regard to the first set of goods, formal organization is a powerful way to handle *certain* concrete communal tasks or economic needs. In fact, if the objectives are large-scale public goods—providing for the national defense, public health, public education, public security, and so on—it may be the only way to accomplish them. At the same time, however, there are limits to the economic efficiency of central organization, and its blessings are definitely mixed. Bureaucratic states are famous for their inefficiency, and, morally speaking, while some economic problems are solved by pooling resources, others are created by formal organization. Most significant among these moral problems perhaps, is the problem of distributive injustice or economic exclusion. Despite such problems, however, the power of large-scale economic organization to produce wealth is undeniable. Whether this must be state (or legal) organization is a separate question.

With regard to the second set of considerations, political organization cannot replace the social goods of interactive support and civility, much less community standards of responsibility and morality, because these are social and personal byproducts of communal interaction, whereas political organization is, at least to some extent, impersonal and formal. Consequently, it may even contribute to the erosion of the social goods. I will return to this point shortly.

Consider first the accomplishment of the economic goods and the obligations and tasks associated with them. How does institutionalizing state authority affect these goods and obligations?

Institutionalization transforms both the object and the form of these communal responsibilities. First, it shifts the *object* of the mutual responsibility of individual community members for one another directly to a surrogate entity: the state. Second, it shifts the *form* of the responsibility from time to money.

Instead of community members being directly responsible to participate personally in communal tasks, they pool resources and pay a specialist to handle the problem or service (such as military defense, child instruction, police and fire protection). For example, you need not halt your life to go immediately to help flood victims in the next town. Instead you pay taxes to the state fund from which specialists (such as the national guard) are paid to help flood victims. Thus, specialization is almost always the most efficient and least oppressive way to accomplish such tasks. This is certainly what we have learned in the private sector, and communal tasks of a concrete nature are no different. Of course, which tasks should be regarded as communal is still an open question.

In addition, citizens may pay for communal goods that they could not otherwise afford separately (such as libraries, museums, parks, municipal buildings). Or they may enable some to provide goods that require special talent, training, and time that is not generally available (such as scientific research, technological invention, or artistic development). That means that instead of being directly responsible to one another for participation in all communal tasks, citizens are responsible to contribute their fair share of money, which they gain by providing a specialized service to the community, to the common pool (the state treasury, or common wealth). This arrangement substitutes property for freedom or money for time, and is potentially much more efficient than individual effort for the accomplishment of concrete economic objectives, especially if society is organized to insure that all contribute their fair share and none are necessarily overburdened by structurally conflicting obligations.[31] This arrangement also provides for the performance of a greater diversity of tasks and consequently the possibility of more choices among citizens. Furthermore, it greatly expands the potential size of the group, and thus the size of the pool or amount of resources (in terms of both capital and labor) available for accomplishing tasks. That means that it provides economic power and thus more economic security and diversity overall. Both points, if met, of course, make it particularly attractive from a liberal or utilitarian perspective.[32]

Significantly, however, such organization also changes the nature of the community. In fact, it changes the character of the group so much that it could be argued that it cannot be and should not be considered a communal association any longer. This is an important point that I will discuss in the next chapter. For now it is sufficient to note that even a large and formally bureaucratic state remains cooperative, since specialization requires mutual reliance.

Finally, institutional formalization also necessarily introduces a layer of bureaucracy as needed for organization and enforcement of participation or contribution, and the mechanisms for representation and decisionmaking that we call government—legislatures, parliaments, courts, and executives or administrators. Thus, the society becomes highly specialized, bureaucratized, compartmentalized—more economically powerful, in some ways more varied, in some ways more rigid, and certainly less personal. These are changes necessarily introduced by institutionalizing state authority. Problems associated with these changes place constraints on the kind of state that can be justified. This issue will be addressed specifically in chapter 9.

For now, what features would favor justifying the authoritative state? To what extent is law necessary over or preferable to the informal interactions of the cooperative community? The best case scenario that could be drawn for the informal (or prelegal) community is that it can be cooperative, fair, loving, inclusive, supportive, and peaceful. Even in this best case, however, it will necessarily be economically weak and thus vulnerable to any natural or human disaster, hardship, injustice, or misfortune. Furthermore, the informal community cannot afford (much) individual diversity or deviation from its defining standards and norms since its very existence is maintained by continued adherence to such norms. Thus personal freedom and privacy can be allowed only within those rather narrowly circumscribed boundaries. These are significant deficiencies.

Paradoxically, the introduction of law (and thus state authority) is the only way to correct them. But this introduction must be made cautiously. To obtain a Hobbesian peace at the price of freedom is to incur a greater cost than can be justified. To obtain freedom at the cost of the general welfare is also too great a price, since obtaining the general welfare is the point of communal living. In any case, the introduction of law is necessary to increase either freedom or the common good, although it also has the capacity to restrict both.

Consider first the general welfare, the economic goods of peace, security, comfort, and pleasure. From an economic point of view, broad ranging cooperation and specialization are efficient mechanisms of productivity. Pooling resources is unquestionably the most effective approach to most economic problems that take the form of large concrete communal objectives. Indeed, it may be the only way that large projects and services can be provided. And as the general prosperity of modern industrialized nations attests, specialized participation in the production of common needs can provide abundance. Furthermore, large-scale organization places economic goods on a more secure foundation in the following respect. The provision of basic goods and services (such as education, health care, national defense, emergency insurance, disability and old age support) can be built into formal institutions founded on a very broad base (or large pool) rather than depending on a small, informal community or personal loyalties that may dissolve or be overwhelmed in times of hardship, trouble, or change. Such insurance makes individuals more independent as well as more secure. Thus, large-scale organization, specialization, and cooperation has the capacity to increase economic power and consequently personal security, comfort, freedom or independence, and the general welfare.

Such cooperation and specialization need not be legally mandated across the board, much less governmentally orchestrated as such. That is, at least in theory, large-scale cooperation that produces economic strength and abundance can be provided by the voluntary exchange of the free market. However, the free market does not exist in a vacuum. As noted in chapter 6, any move to large-scale economic interaction entails cooperation among strangers, and rational cooperation among strangers requires the legal enforcement of contracts, prohibitions against fraud, misrepresentation, theft, and various forms of coercion and violence. Hence, the introduction of law and the justification of what has been called the minimal state follows from the economic necessity to cooperate with strangers or be restricted to the economic weakness and general vulnerability of the informal community. This much will be true whether the beginning point of analysis is the isolated individual or the informal community of section 2.

Now consider the value of freedom. A state can be less oppressive than the prelegal community in several respects. The specialization of tasks makes it potentially possible to cover all tasks without overloading individuals. The great virtue of replacing time commitments with money commitments is efficiency, which increases freedom. A state does not necessarily alleviate individual overload, but it can do so if social institutions are properly structured. Furthermore, a diversity of tasks potentially increases individual choice. The more diverse a society, the more choices individuals in it will have both economically and personally. Consequently, the diverse state can be less intrusive than the cooperative communal village discussed in section 2. (It can also be more intrusive, given its higher development of technology; but there is no political or structural reason or social factor that makes it inevitably intrusive as is the case in a small informal community.) Given the impersonality of formal economic and political organization, every individual need not be personally involved with every other person in the community. Specialization and formal institutions provide a compartmentalization that allows individuals to keep their private lives private, and their personal associations at least more voluntary than they otherwise would be. This means that individuals have more choices and consequently more freedom. They can be involved or not as they choose. On liberal grounds this is another plus. So it seems clear that at least the minimal state can be justified both on grounds of liberty and the common good.

Perhaps it should be noted that the minimal state is not really all that minimal. Once you have government you have government. Consider for a moment what is introduced merely by the acceptance of the minimal state (that is, a state that enforces contracts and prohibitions against harm, such as force, theft and fraud). As Henry Shue and James Sterba have pointed out, negative duties must be enforced, and enforcement creates costs.[33] I would add that not only must negative duties (and contractual duties) be enforced, they must be defined, interpreted, clarified, coordinated, adjudicated, and recorded because what our negative duties (and contractual duties) are in any particular circumstances is not self-evident. Consequently in the minimal state we need not only police (and other such enforcement mechanisms) but courts, legislatures, administrators, executors, magistrates, and their support systems. In other words, we need government. Some such services—certainly some administrative and possibly enforcement functions—could be privately rather than publically provided. Where that is possible it would be desirable (preferable to state action) both on grounds of efficiency and freedom. But, first, it is not possible to provide basic governmental functions (such as courts and legislatures) that must be answerable to the public in that way, and second, where it is possible to handle administrative and enforcement services privately, such services will still usually require oversight mechanisms that guarantee answerability, since voluntary compliance with high standards of honesty and fairness cannot rationally be presumed. Regulation and oversight are costly, and many services ordinarily supplied by government (such as prisons) are not directly susceptible to the ordinary qualitative pressures of competitive consumer appeal. So the government of the minimal state would not be as little as it is sometimes imagined, although it would be much smaller than the government that we have.

Furthermore, if we add into this equation the governmental institutions and practices necessary for the enforcement of contracts in a sophisticated economic system (assuming that arguing for a minimal state does not entail accepting a minimal economic system), the size of government necessarily takes a discernible jump. Global markets and international corporations will not be handled in a simple village meeting. Complex economic transactions generate complex legal issues, corporate negotiations, international treaties, trade agreements, labor agreements, environmental agreements, the regulation of resources, the exchange of securities, world banks, monetary supplies—all involve law. That law must be legislated, adjudicated, interpreted, administered, identified, recognized, and enforced by government. It is naive to suppose that this will not entail complex and fairly extensive mechanisms and institutions of state. Without legal recognition, stocks and bonds, corporations and treaties, indeed every sort of contract is just worthless paper with useless stuff written on it. The interactions of securities exchange can hardly be analogized to the haggling of a couple of guys bartering an appel for a pear at a corner fruit stand. Thus, complex economic activities imply complex and fairly extensive legal arrangements, and all that entails extensive state institutions. Maybe there is no such thing as a little government.

Still, the government required here could be much smaller than government in fact is, and I presume that those legal arrangements and the governmental organization required to support them that I have been describing as necessary for economic exchange needed to promote the general welfare and personal freedom (beyond the economic weakness of the prelegal community) would be justifiable by appeal to these values, and would still be viewed as a minimal state. So it appears that at least the minimal state can be justified by appeal to increased freedom and welfare that is made possible only by the formalization of some communal functions.

But can the governmental functions necessary for the enforcement of negative and contractual duties be accounted for by the negative function of law alone? It would seem pretty obviously not, since legislation, adjudication, regulation, and oversight, plus those administrative and enforcement mechanisms that are not plausibly handled by the private sector (if any) and those public goods that cannot be privately provided (such as national defense or environmental protection, perhaps), are all costly. Such common costs must presumably be borne by all citizens through taxation. So some affirmative obligations on the basis of citizenship or community membership must be justifiable even if the discussion is restricted to the idea of the minimal state. Consequently, the distinction between the so-called minimal state and the so-called welfare state is a matter of degree and argumentation. It is not a distinction between imposing positive rather than only negative and contractual (or voluntarily assumed) duties.

I presume that given the liberal commitment to the value of freedom (and since the potential increase of freedom is one of the two basic grounds for justifying the state) every governmental extension should be individually justifiable. (That is, liberals should be suspicious of increasing government.) The primary function of the state is protective or facilitating. The state is facilitating when, even though it may necessitate some restriction, greater freedom will result from legalization of an activity. Contract law is an obvious example. Taxation to provide impartial courts for settling disputes is another. The state is protective when it prevents individuals or groups from harming one another, or when one branch (or agency) of government prevents another from harming people or otherwise abusing power. Public security by provision of police protection is one example. Laws against discrimination and mechanisms for enforcing such laws are another example. Within such constraints the state can be justified, and with it the political obligation, both affirmative and negative, to cooperate in the common good.

Communal obligations or positive duties, are generated by membership in the community as necessary for the survival and welfare of the group and all its members. Those obligations can be transferred to the state in the form of political obligation through the institutionalization of the informal community, just as long as the conditions that provide for moral life and individual welfare are improved rather than undermined. If the formal organization of states provides for the increase of individual welfare and freedom, at least certain positive duties to the state are justified. That is, the affirmative obligations owed to the state can be derived from the obligations one would have in a state of nature by adjusting for improvements provided by the state. (The obligations owed to the institutional state should be less demanding that those owed in a state of nature, or it would be irrational to move in that direction.)

What sort of duties are these? They are duties of reciprocity or cooperation for the common good. Thus, these duties are not based on benevolence or sympathy (although sympathy in the form of fellow feeling would certainly be a good thing for any community to have). The basis of the duty of citizens is not fellow feeling but reciprocity. It is cooperation that is required. This might be construed either in terms of necessity or fairness, depending on the context or circumstances. That all should contribute to the general welfare can be a matter of necessity. If one considers a primitive tribe or an impoverished nation, it is doubtful that the very existence of the group (including all its individual members) can be maintained without the cooperative contribution of all its members. However, if the group manages to develop and flourish to the point of not needing the contribution of all members merely for survival alone, then the basis of requiring communal contribution becomes the fairness of reciprocal arrangements. There is a level at which mutual cooperation of the members is always needed by the group. That is, as the economic power of the group develops, the aim becomes not mere survival but the general welfare, at least in the form of increased security and comfort of its members, and ultimately in the form of increased freedom of its members. Without cooperation these developments cannot be accomplished. All this has to do with what I earlier referred to as the cooperative accomplishment of economic goods.

The traditional liberal position has been that the justifiable function of the legitimate state is largely defensive—its purpose is to protect individuals from the abuses of other individuals. I do not mean to deny this position, except to suggest that the justified defensive function extends further than is acknowledged by atomistic individualists, and to point out that the defensive function of the state is itself a cooperative endeavor. The defensive function extends beyond protection against individual force, theft, and fraud to protection against the use of power to organize institutions (economic or social, as well as legal) to the unfair disadvantage of community members who may be powerless to defend themselves against unfair arrangements and distributions of burdens and benefits. This claim is not anti-individualistic, since it is specifically aimed at acknowledging the significance of every individual in the structure of social institutions as well as individual transactions. Nor is it a new position. Mill, Hobhouse, Dewey, Rawls, and Dworkin all espouse this version of liberalism—a version that includes both the protection of individual freedom and the requirement of distributive justice in the form of cooperative affirmative obligations for the accomplishment of economic goods.

Cooperation is also necessary for the maintenance of moral standards or the sociomoral goods discussed earlier. Although some deviance from moral standards can be tolerated (and the larger and more institutionalized the group, the more diversity can be accommodated), by and large, moral standards do not exist without common commitment. So cooperation in economic goods and moral goods is necessary to the welfare of the group and all its members. The basis for requiring this cooperation is the fairness of mutual cooperation for mutual benefit. Thus, the foundation is the justice of reciprocity.

I want to suggest here that political philosophy has developed too sharp a contrast between the requirements of justice and the requirements of utility. The two are not always as distinct as they are often portrayed as being. The reason for this separation is that the focus of individualism has tended to pit the group against the individual (often for very good reason) and to focus the requirements of justice in terms of protecting the individual from the group or from other individuals. This perspective is what is commonly considered the justice of respect for individual autonomy. It is the justice of noninterference—and involves what I have described as duties of separation: presumptively overriding, negative duties. These are important, indeed, crucial concepts for any liberal theory.

Yet they do not provide a complete picture of the requirements of justice. As John Rawls and others have been concerned to show, justice is also applicable to the structure of social institutions and to the evaluation of cooperative interaction. Individuals must be protected from the group, but they must also function together within it. Individuals must be protected from one another, but they must also cooperate for the common good. Fair cooperation is a requirement of justice. It is embodied in the ancient concept of justice as reciprocity. It is the foundation of positive duties of neighbors and of citizens.

As I noted earlier, however, these duties of communal cooperation, these duties of neighbors, are only transferred to citizens—as political obligations—if the conditions necessary to human moral life produced by the cooperative community or state of nature are maintained in the institutional state. Unfortunately, it turns out that there are also two substantial drawbacks associated with formalizing communal tasks: the rise of distributive injustice and the decline of civic virtue. The two are not unrelated.

The general problem is that communal life has different dimensions—an economic dimension—and a sociomoral dimension. Consequently, traditional informal communities provided for two different needs: cooperation for the accomplishment of concrete communal tasks, and the maintenance of an environment of identification with and commitment to the group that fostered interpersonal trust, reliable cooperation, and responsible participation. The best way to meet the first need is by political and economic organization, specialization to avoid individual overload, and the pooling of resources to enable all needs to be met. But this increased efficiency, ironically, allows for greater distributive injustice and even the exclusion of some community members from economic participation altogether, because all members are no longer needed merely for the production of basic necessities. And the formalization of communal life appears to undermine identification with and feelings of responsibility to the community—the sociomoral goods—that make cooperation possible in the first place. This looks a lot like a Catch-22, but it is premature to draw that conclusion yet. In the next chapter I will consider the two problems I have identified in moving from informal to formal associations. Doing so will provide grounds for setting the scope and limits of affirmative political obligations.

9

Articulating the Scope of Political Obligation

The power of cooperation and the destruction of division have been part of the universal common wisdom for thousands of years. Yet our cooperation in the common interest is limited. That is primarily, I will suggest, because we refuse collectively to take responsibility for common problems; and this in turn is because we have as yet been unable to identify adequately with each other as groups to agree that our social problems are in fact common problems. Our collective refusal leaves social problems on the backs of charitable individuals, but large-scale social problems cannot be solved without collective efforts. In this chapter I will argue that this refusal to cooperate collectively in the common good is a form of irresponsibility, indeed a form of denial. So long as we deny our common responsibilities, we will cause ourselves individually irresolvable problems.

Visionaries over the years have tried to point this out to us, among them certainly Tolstoy and Dostoyevsky, Hannah Arendt and Simone Weil, as well as others. But the vision of universal responsibility that they advocated seems too utopian for human realization, and is counteracted by powerful images that are antagonistic to it. In what follows here I will describe how the twentieth century has been dominated by two central images, both exemplifying collective irresponsibility. This focus may not be surprising for an individualistic tradition, but it places serious limits on the liberal capacity to construct an adequate account of social responsibility. Indeed, this collective irresponsibility, or lack of communal cooperation, is often blamed on liberal individualism with its emphasis on justice as noninterference and affirmative obligation based on a contractual model of autonomous consent.

By considering the theoretical framework and the basic institutions of affirmative obligation in liberal society, especially institutions of family, profession, and contract, I have tried to show that the liberal tradition is much richer and more diverse than any picture ever suggested by the notion of atomistic individualism. Both liberal theory and liberal society have always included and required more cooperation, mutual reliance, and trust than was ever captured by the atomistic image. Thus, the atomistic picture must be expanded by the idea of communal membership and ultimately political membership. Just as we are family members and members of professions, so we are members of communities and nations. We are part of them and they are part of us. As members, we are each identified with our origins and national heritage. These identifications can be highly complex, but they are no insignificant part of who we are. And altogether we constitute the political community of which we are a part. In the previous chapter I argued, first, that human beings are innately communal, and that communal living provides us with the material security and social environment that enables the rational reflection and moral development that we identify with being human. Communal obligations are those that are required to maintain these necessary conditions for human existence. Second, I argued that political obligation (or state authority) can be justified only if institutionalizing communal tasks improves social life without undermining the communal goods necessary for human development in the first place. There I suggested that the material power of large-scale economic coordination, since it depends on sophisticated political organization, could provide a prima facie justification for cooperative political obligations. That is, it potentially justifies acknowledging political membership.

So, subject to the qualifications of communal goods just noted, we are all political members, and since a political community is necessarily a cooperative endeavor, as members we have obligations to cooperate in certain communal tasks. The question is, To what extent or with what limits? When do obligations follow from such an association? Various theories have been formulated to address this question. One currently popular and useful theory is the social contract. To suggest that political obligations are based on consent would simply be inaccurate, and of course, that is not what a social contract theorist is saying. The point of the social contract is to show which obligations *could* be justified by showing what (rational) people *would* consent to *if* they were in a condition of choice that also required the cooperation (or mutual reliance) of all members of the group. The assumption is that people would not agree to what is unfair to them if they have a choice. Surely a reasonable assumption. What this thought device shows are the scope and limits of justified obligation. It is a method of ascertaining the parameters set by respect for individual justice, but it is not the foundation of social obligation.

The foundation for political obligation is the need for communal cooperation in the common interest. If there were no such need, there would be no point to social obligation. The fact that we are social beings means that we must cooperate at some level or suffer the consequences. But the question is, How far beyond the minimal should (political) obligation extend? The social contract is one good method for articulating such limits, because it starts with the presumption of individual freedom. That means that it is set up to reflect the requirements of individual justice, which is critical to any theory of political obligation. But it is not everything. Another crucial aspect of human life is the necessity for communal cooperation, and a narrow focus on individual justice *may* not sufficiently acknowledge that. In fact, the contractual approach to political theory is not incompatible with a focus on communal cooperation. On the contrary, as I argued in chapter 6, contracts and contract law are evidence of and manifestations of communal cooperation. Nevertheless, a certain (mis)interpretation of the contractual approach to political theory leads to the abstract idea of atomistic individualism.

In my view, the liberal tradition presumes political membership (with or without the social contract) and thus is not really compatible with atomistic individualism. Yet the image persists. I think it is time to replace it. This is the image that causes the deficiency in liberal theory. For the twenty-first century, I will suggest, we need a new collective vision of cooperative individualism. I will try to explain why we need such an image, in what it would consist, why it is not impossible to achieve it, and finally, why a liberal individualist should accept it.

Let me begin where I left off. In chapter 8 I suggested that to be justified, there are two ways in which a state must maintain the benefits of communal cooperation that produce the necessary conditions for rational reflection and moral agency or, in other words, for human life. These might be construed as moral integrity and economic inclusion. These two features raise two potential problems for the institutional state, moral fragmentation and distributive injustice, that could undermine political obligation on the model that I have been developing here. Addressing these problems will articulate two limits on political obligation based on this model.

1. Acknowledging Membership and Socializing Individualism: Collective Responsibility and Economic Exclusion

In 1879 Henry George pondered the poverty and unemployment he saw all around him, describing the problem in terms that sound remarkably current:

> The present century has been marked by a prodigious increase in wealth-producing power. . . . At the beginning of this marvelous era it was natural to expect, and it was expected, that labor-saving inventions would lighten the toil of the laborer; that the enormous increase in the power of producing wealth would make real poverty a thing of the past. . . . [T]hese have been the hopes. . . . It is true that wealth has been greatly increased, and that the average of comfort, leisure, and refinement has been raised; but these gains are not general. . . . I mean that the tendency of what we call material progress is in nowise to improve the condition of the lowest class in the essentials of healthy, happy human life. Nay, more, that it is still further to depress the condition of the lowest class. The new forces, elevating in their nature though they be, do not act upon the social fabric from underneath, as was for a long time hoped and believed, but strike it at a point intermediate between top and bottom. It is as though an immense wedge were being forced, not underneath society, but through society. Those who are above the point of separation are elevated, but those who are below are crushed down.[1]

George was not alone in these observations, particularly throughout the nineteenth century. While optimistic reformers, such as John Stuart Mill and Adam Smith, predicted that poverty (and perhaps even disease) would soon disappear from the civilized world in the wake of scientific and technological progress, social critics, such as Charles Dickens and Émile Zola (not to mention Karl Marx), described the hardship that progress produced. The harshest effects of this tendency have been softened in this century, but in principle the problem has not changed a bit.

In 1995 two economists (Robert Frank and Phillip Cook) reidentified precisely the wedge so trenchantly described by George. In a book called *The Winner Take All Society* they have pointed out that the wedge effect, far from disappearing, has intensified during the 1980s and 1990s, at least in the United States. The average CEO now makes 225 times what the average worker makes. This in a time when working wages stagnated after 1979 and massive layoffs due to corporate downsizing and technological innovation made job insecurity a palpable fear.[2] This is certainly George's wedge with a vengeance.

The trend being analyzed by Frank and Cook is the increasing income and wealth disparity not only between groups (the poor and rich, or the bottom 10 percent and the top 10 percent) but within groups (the rich and richer, or the top 10 percent and the top 1 percent.) For example, it is a matter of public record that over 61 percent of all income gains from 1977 to 1990 went to the top 1 percent of American families (a group whose average yearly income was $438,000). The wedge isn't hitting in the middle any more. The authors explain this trend as the effect of technology (machines and computer programs can do more and more of what people used to do) and the developing practice of "free agency" (superstars at the top bargain for more and more of the pie by jumping, or threatening to jump, from one corporation to another).[3] Is this phenomenon an exemplification of deregulated capitalism and atomistic individualism run amok? Perhaps. It is certainly a source of both criticism and self-congratulation. Like most economists, Frank and Cook are (rightly) reluctant to construe the economy as a zero sum game. The "pie" is not necessarily a fixed amount; we can all do better or worse together. Yet they acknowledge that if a corporation is paying top dollar to its top executives (where top dollar means millions of dollars per annum), it will have to keep the margins everywhere else pretty tight. It is not hard to see that the less paid out for labor, the more there is left for stockholder dividends and executive benefits. Thus, the condition of the top and the bottom cannot be construed as entirely unrelated, despite the optimistic projections of sanguine supply-siders.

Kevin Phillips described all this, within the context of American history, as a cyclical process reflecting changes in governmental power and politics. He argues that the 1980s (the decade that increased the income of the top 1 percent by up to $150 billion per year as the annual income of the bottom and middle class actually declined) was the third era in which Republican policies concentrated vast wealth in the hands of a few. The two previous Republican heydays (as Phillips calls them) were, of course, the 1920s and the Gilded Age of the late nineteenth century. In all three eras Republicans presided over probusiness governments that initiated less regulation, high interest rates and low tax rates that produced boom cycles marked by conservative ideologies in which the rich got richer on a crest of debt and speculation. The downside of all three periods was also similar, including stagnated wages, collapsing farmland value, the decay of older industries with its resultant layoffs and job insecurity, and even a recurrent increase of homelessness.[4]

What does all this tell us? First, it supports the claim that social structures can cause harm. How a society is organized matters to the life chances and opportunities of its individual members. Even without formal barriers, the social structure sets the odds.

Second, as mentioned and argued in the previous chapter, it supports the idea that we are all members of an economic community that is not adequately captured by the idea of atomistic individualism. We need not presume a seamless web in which every act is affected by every other in order to support this point. We need only acknowledge that some acts affect the range of options available to others, and that governmental and business policy decisions are among the acts that have such effects. There can hardly be any doubt, for example, that probusiness and antibusiness environments can be politically fostered or constrained, and that prolabor and antilabor environments can be politically enhanced or retarded as well. Furthermore, individual decisions and transactions do take place within some such environment and are greatly affected by the environment within which they take place.

These conclusions surely cannot be very controversial, and yet they provide strong support for the idea that all citizens of a state are not isolated individuals, but members of an economic community, and this economic community is not entirely separated from its political environment. Thus, the economic and political community is essential to and intrinsic to the nature and welfare of the state. The political and the economic are two dimensions of one and the same community.

The further point illustrated by the trends just discussed is that people are greedy. Nearly all of us, probably. Maybe not quite all. There were Albert Schweitzer and Mother Theresa. But we tend to label such people saints, thereby distinguishing them from ordinary, normal people, and indicating that we don't expect ordinary, normal people to behave that way. It is admirable if they do, perhaps, but we don't expect it; and that is at least partly because we know that we are all greedy. Of course, some people are more greedy than others, (apparently a lot more) just as some are more ambitious than others, or more dominating than others. But probably all of us are susceptible to the vice of greed. And a consumer-focused economy does not help to retard that tendency, nor does a market theory of value that measures people's success or even their worth in terms of their material assets. If self-respect and public honor are measured by how much you have, you will always be confronted by others who are better because they have more.

The result is that most people don't share much, especially with strangers. In terms of probabilities it simply is not reasonable to expect it. This is nothing new, of course. The aristocratic standard of noblesse oblige imposed a very modest obligation on the rich to "be sensitive to the needs of the poor." Nor is there any evidence that the nobility tended to exceed this minimal standard—or even to meet it on a regular basis. And the middle class has not been any more forthcoming. The institution of the Elizabethan poor laws that imposed a responsibility on each township to care for the poverty-stricken within its own boundaries is evidence that townships were not assuming this obligation very well without legal encouragement to do so. There is also considerable evidence that the poor laws were followed grudgingly and even evaded when possible, much as similar requirements are evaded today. For example, apparently townships often encouraged their poor to move elsewhere, just as in recent times cities have occasionally been "caught" providing their homeless citizens with one-way bus tickets to other cities.[5] It is always tempting to ship one's problems to someone else if possible. While this is not illegal, it doesn't suggest a very high standard of communal responsibility, or much sympathy for the problem of poverty.

In fact, there never has been much sympathy for the poor, or even the working class. In the history of industrial development, one can read repeated testimony before parliamentary and legislative committees by manufacturers and entrepreneurs who swear that they will surely go out of business in no time if required to pay more than twenty-five cents an hour (or whatever minimum wage was proposed) or to provide even minimally safe equipment or working conditions, much less widows' pensions, or almost anything at all.[6] Every tiny improvement for workers has been consistently met with cries of immanent bankruptcy by owners. Without the leverage of labor unions and protective labor laws, there is no reason to suppose that wages or working conditions would have progressed at all beyond the horrors described by Dickens. And there is no reason to suppose that without constant vigilance such horrors would not swiftly return.

Most people don't want to believe this last point, but it seems to be true. For example, it has recently been noted that since the deregulation of business instituted during the 1980s, the incidence of sweat shops has increased in the United States.[7] One would like to believe such a development could not occur at the end of the twentieth century in a supposedly civilized society. But there it is. Sweatshops have increased in number. Homelessness also increased during the same decade. And we are too greedy and too busy and too self-centered to care enough to prevent it. So, clearly, without constant vigilance, some will be excluded from economic participation altogether. Unemployment is and has been a constant problem during the entire twentieth century.[8] Some workers are excluded from economic participation. Other workers, who are not excluded from participation entirely, to use George's metaphor, are "crushed down by the wedge of progress." They are included in the work but not the profits. They work but cannot make a living.

In an unregulated capitalist economy, this situation can only get worse. After all, consider the function of management: improving efficiency. At least in theory, managers should always eliminate as many jobs as possible and offer the lowest wages possible to get the work done with the greatest efficiency and profit. That is what managers are for, at least on any current understanding. As technology decreases the need for workers, wages and job security drop. This means that higher profits are concentrated in the hands of fewer people; the workers' share declines as their bargaining leverage declines, and some will be excluded from participation altogether. This point is also reflected in current economic trends. For example, recent figures from the U.S. Budget Office show that 98.7 percent of the economic growth since 1983 was gained by the top 20 percent of wage earners. That means that 1.3 percent of the economic growth was shared by 80 percent of the work force.[9] Since the cost of living always rises, when wages remain level as these figures indicate, it means that the purchasing power of 80 percent of the population is going down. Apparently a rising tide does not lift all boats.

Such exclusion from the means to make a living cannot be acceptable on a principle of fair cooperation among members of an economic community. This point should be obvious, at least within the context of the thesis of this book. According to the argument of the previous chapter, a primary reason for communal association in the first place is material security, which certainly includes economic security—a better chance to make a living and insure it over time, to reduce both worry and hardship. If one loses economic security, one primary reason for moving from an informal community (or state of nature) to a state is undercut. In other words, the conditions of legitimacy on (at least, my version of) a state of nature theory of justification for state authority are violated. If one is excluded from the means to make a living, it is like being denied membership in the economic community.

Mine is not the only liberal theory that would reject such economic conditions. Rawls's social contract theory would certainly reject them as incompatible with the second principle of justice. A utilitarian theory would reject them as incompatible with a commitment to the common good, presumably, although perhaps not as obviously as Rawls's theory would. The only liberal theories that apparently accept such economic exclusion are atomistic libertarian theories, such as that of Nozick or possibly Locke. If my argument is correct, however, a state of nature theory must include an account of individuals within cooperative communities that provide the conditions necessary for rational reflection and moral evaluation or, in other words, the conditions essential for distinctively human life. Atomistic theories fail to provide an account of these conditions and consequently offer an inadequate grounding for the state.

Most libertarians use one basic argument, with many sophisticated versions. That basic argument is as follows. (1) Since freedom is the fundamental value, voluntary arrangements are always better than coercive ones—which is not an unreasonable starting point. (2) Requirements enforced by the state are coercive—which is basically true. (3) Therefore, state action and state power should be restricted as much as possible. Clearly a valid argument, but the operative phrase is "as much as possible." Even libertarians recognize that a minimal state is necessary to prevent some individuals from harming others. The question is, What counts as harm? Does economic manipulation and deprivation of the sort I have just been discussing—conditions that at least some call economic injustice—count as harm? Is an economic structure that exploits 80 percent of the population and privileges 20 percent a harm? That is a source of continuing dispute. On an atomistic Nozickian view, for example, it does not count as a harm. On my view, it does. Furthermore, my argument is that any view that accounts adequately for the social/economic/political system as an integrated environment must count economic exclusion as a harm, because it is expulsion from the economic community that was a primary feature of communal living. To be justified, a state cannot eliminate the benefits of communal life that are central to human survival and development.

It should also be noted that there is more than one source of coercion. Not only states are coercive; individuals and groups in the private sector are also often coercive in their interactions. A corporate layoff, for example, can hardly be characterized as a voluntary transaction on the part of those who are dismissed from their jobs. Is such an act coercive? Well, it certainly is not voluntary. Whether it is coercive or not actually turns on one's theory of coercion. But it should be noted that if coercion is not equivalent to 'not voluntary,' then it drives a wedge through the premises of the basic libertarian argument. Perhaps the argument can be reformulated, but it illustrates my point in any case, because it makes clear that coercion is a moral or legal term that must be decided by determining people's rights and duties on other grounds.

I discussed this issue at some length in chapters 6 and 7, where I argued that the determination of whether state regulation or oversight is appropriate in particular contract cases will always be a matter of judgment that balances one source of coercion against another. It is not true that contractual cases involve free agents conducting purely voluntary transactions, on the one hand, versus the interference of the coercive state, on the other. That simply is not an accurate picture of contracting or contract law as such. In fact, the courts are often engaged in determining which form of coercion is worse — public coercion or private. It is always a balancing act. The state protects the freedom of some by restricting the freedom of others. It protects the interests of some by denying the interests of others. To borrow terminology from Ronald Dworkin, this is often a matter of policy rather than principle. All the arguments given in chapter 6 for treating contract law as often involved in determining policy, of balancing the interests of the parties, apply at least as well to issues of labor and management, the regulation of business, and the distribution of economic burdens and benefits.

All this leads, I believe, to the conclusion that state action as regulation of economic arrangements or compensation for unfair ones is sometimes warranted to correct the excesses and injustices of individual transactions between private parties with unequal bargaining power. Is it reasonable to expect that powerful individuals in their private transactions will voluntarily accept a smaller share of the profits in order to distribute profits more broadly to less powerful individuals (workers) or to include more participants (a larger work force) in the economic enterprise? Obviously, it is not. But if not, then an atomistic theory of political justification is either based on a pious hope of fair cooperation that has no plausible chance of voluntary realization, or it assumes a harshly Darwinistic perspective that fails to meet even the most basic Hobbesian requirements for a legitimate state. If individuals will not voluntarily meet the requirements of a minimally just society, then the state must reinforce those requirements by law and public policy, in the same way that it enforces the requirements of contractual obligation rather than leaving compliance to the good will of the parties.

Although it is no doubt an unpopular position to take these days, I believe this line of argument leads to a limited version of the much-maligned welfare state, that has as a matter of fact generally been supported by most liberals at least since the New Deal. My argument shows why liberals are justified in holding a limited version of that position. Why? Liberalism stands for individual freedom, but also for justice in the form of economic inclusion. Thus, economic regulation to insure fair interaction among unequal participants and compensation for the failure to achieve fairness are merely extensions of the defensive function of the state that all liberals (and libertarians) recognize.[10]

Beyond the mechanism of economic regulation, redistributive taxation for economic compensation may be the least intrusive and least restrictive mechanism for complying with the requirements of economic justice, and thus protecting the freedom and security of most of the members of the economic community. It is surely less intrusive than central planning or state ownership of industry, for example. Private enterprise allows more freedom. Yet, to maintain a minimal standard of fair cooperation, to comply with the principle of reciprocity, a state must provide its citizens with a fair opportunity to make a living if it is in a position to do so.[11] That is a fundamental function of cooperative communal living. The free market cannot be expected to provide this. Business leaders certainly will not. The big winners of the economic lottery will not voluntarily deplete their millions to provide economic security or public goods and social services needed by the population at large. Such guarantees must be provided by or at least insured by the state, for no one else is answerable to the people at large.

Ordinary middle-class and working people did not profit from the recent economic recovery in the United States. Those profits were concentrated in the hands of the top 10 percent of the population, which did not use it to create jobs. Obviously, citizens cannot necessarily look to the private sector of a state for economic fairness or even concern for the common good, at least not as a matter of voluntary action. That means government action is both necessary and more fair than hoping for voluntary cooperation or the magic of the invisible hand. The welfare state may not be popular, but it has stood for a commitment to the general welfare of *all* the people—and this is a commitment that the private sector cannot be expected to have.

Thus, the best case for a state to meet the economic obligations (of providing a living) for all its members is to provide full participation (that is, full employment) and at least minimally equitable compensation (a living wage) for participation. The problem is that achieving this goal in a free market economy might require prohibitive regulation of private enterprise that would be incompatible with a liberal commitment to freedom. Given the dual commitments to freedom and economic justice, the goal of economic equity should be accomplished by the least restrictive alternative. Thus, the amount of regulation that can be viewed as compatible with a commitment to freedom cannot be expected necessarily to produce economic justice effectively.

With the (inevitable) failure to achieve either full participation or equitable distribution of benefits (in the form of a living wage), compensation (in the form of those basic goods that a living wage would provide) is warranted to those harmed by exploitive economic structures that allow income disparities so great as to exclude some portion of the population (some community members) from the benefits that would constitute making a living. Such basic goods as food, shelter, and medical care, education for the youth, and retirement insurance for the elderly should be guaranteed (although not necessarily provided) by the state, for greater material security was one of the two basic grounds for justifying the legitimacy of moving from a communal state of nature to an authoritative state.

The justification for making the state the guarantor of the material security of its members in a free market economy is the liberal idea of checks and balances. Just as one branch of government must be used to check the abuses of another, so economic regulation and compensation to victims by government must be used to check the abuses of amassed economic power in corporations and other economic structures. In the interest of freedom, if private voluntary action can supply public goods and fair participation, this situation is ideal from a liberal point of view. (That was the dream of Adam Smith and John Stuart Mill, or so it seems to me.) But if private enterprise does not provide the public goods or enable all community members to make a living, then the option of state action on behalf of those disadvantaged by free economic social structures must be viewed as a balancing force necessary to check the abuses of private enterprise in a free market.

Moderate liberals have long recognized these points (although perhaps not in the form here presented) in their support of collective solutions to common problems, and they are right to do so.[12] These obligations cannot be met individually; they can only be met collectively by acknowledging common membership and instituting fair public policies. To do so is in no way incompatible with individualism, however, since it reflects a commitment to the significance of every individual, and recognizes that public policy and social institutions must embody that commitment. Thus, liberal individualism is and should be cooperative, not atomistic. An important part of what that means is the recognition of the cooperative economic community. As argued in chapter 8, political obligation cannot be justified without including some principle of economic equity.

I will now turn to a consideration of what the idea of a cooperative community means as applied to the sociomoral goods discussed in chapter 8.

2. Moral Integrity and Cooperative Individualism: Fragmented Values and the Moral Community

It is often charged, for a remarkable variety of reasons, that the liberal state is not compatible with the preservation of moral communities. Liberalism erodes morality, some say. From the perspective of a state of nature theory as I just constructed it, the preliminary question is whether the institution of the formal state, as such, necessarily undermines the moral community. There is no logical or conceptual reason to suppose that it must do so (states and communities are not logically contradictory); and empirically, informal communities have existed within formal states ever since the institution of formal states. So the short answer to the preliminary question must be no. Formal states may or may not foster morality, but they do not intrinsically impair the existence of informal communities that do foster morality. Thus, the moral community is not eliminated by the formal state as such.[13]

Yet in contemporary discussion much concern is expressed about the effect of particular policies and ideologies on the morality of the people who are subject to them. So, it is not the institution of the formal state as such that may undermine morality, but the institution of some particular state; the state with which we must be concerned, of course, is the liberal state. Is there any reason to suppose that the particular policies and commitments of the liberal state undermine the moral community? That is precisely the claim made by many contemporary conservatives, as well as some communitarians and socialists, although not on the same grounds or with the same conclusions. I will focus primarily on the conservative critique here, while the communitarian criticism will lead us to the next section. Again, the criticisms are very serious, since the liberal state cannot be justified if it undermines the communal environment necessary for moral life.

Briefly, the conservative offers two different sorts of criticisms: ideological and economic. In general, it is argued that permissive liberal ideology, value neutrality, and the indiscriminate protection of individual freedom and diversity undermine moral traditions and erode the moral community, leading to general moral decay and resulting in violence, promiscuity, irresponsibility, laziness, dishonesty, and the loss of integrity, faith, and respect for authority. Evidence for these claims is offered by referring to rising rates of crime, divorce and broken homes, illegitimate births, drug use, sexually transmitted diseases, and abortions, as well as the prevalence of sex and violence in the media, declining educational achievement, and dwindling religious observance. In addition, and more specifically, it is argued that the liberal "big government tax and spend" approach to social programs, and especially welfare policies, undermines the family, the virtue of self-reliance, faith in free enterprise, and the communal spirit of charity and volunteerism.[14]

The communitarian (or the socialist) critiques virtually turn the conservative position on its head. It is argued that individualism (particularly as manifested in capitalist economies) promotes selfishness, alienation, egoism, and cutthroat adversarial competition; erodes trust and cooperation; retards identification with the community or the common good; and fosters a narrow sense of justice (as noninterference alone) and a thin notion of (contractual) responsibility.[15]

All these critiques have something to be said for them. Many point to inadequacies and defects in liberal theory analogous to points that I have argued in earlier chapters of this book. But as refutations of liberalism in general they fail, in that either they refer to particular political experiments or programs that may have been initiated by liberals but are not essential to liberalism, or they refer to atomistic individualism, which I have argued need not and should not be the ideological basis of liberalism. Yet the objections raised are cause for concern, so I will consider several of the general positions here.

The economic conservative criticism can be quickly answered, since it is a clear instance of a particular complaint rather than a general critique. Particular governmental welfare programs may (or may not) have impaired family relations and fostered dependency among the poor, as conservatives complain. Suppose, for the sake of argument, they are right. If such programs have had unintended harmful effects, then the clear liberal response should be to reform or replace them, presumably with some other, hopefully better liberal programs. Liberalism has always been a reform movement dedicated to making life better, that is, more free and more secure, for all members of society. Nothing essential to liberalism necessitates some particular governmental program, as is demonstrated by recent shifts in some liberal positions on some particular welfare programs. Thus, a complaint against a specific program, even if correct, is no real objection to liberalism as such.

Having said that, let me point out (the obvious) that while a liberal view does not dictate particular policies and programs, it does set some parameters to the kinds of responses that could be made to complaints such as those of the economic conservative. For example, as is suggested by the previous chapter, it would not be a defensible liberal position to end welfare programs without meeting our communal obligation to combat poverty due to economic exclusion in some other, more effective way, say, by job creation. The interesting feature of the conservative economic critique is that it actually criticizes liberal social programs for being too collective or "socialistic," which is to say, not atomistic enough. The atomistic view often adopted by economic conservatives was addressed specifically in the first section and was discussed to a considerable extent in the previous chapter. Here it is sufficient to observe that the supposed moral criticism based on this view cannot be defended in any case, since that criticism relies on empirical claims tied to specific governmental policies (AFDC undermines the family, for example) that are not intrinsic to liberal commitments.

The conservative ideological criticism, on the other hand, strikes at the heart of liberalism and raises some troubling issues. If liberalism stands for anything, it stands for personal freedom—especially freedom of thought and expression, and freedom of tastes and pursuits. It is, according to liberals, up to individuals how they should live their private lives, provided only that they do not harm others. It should be noted, then, that liberalism has never tolerated violence, fraud, and dishonesty, or breach of responsibility, because it has always opposed harm to others. Any claim that liberals or liberalism condone such harmful conduct would be quite unfair, so the only plausible claim must be more indirect. It is, in fact, often suggested that liberal permissiveness and tolerance of plurality undermines the moral community itself. This in turn leads to the harmful conduct that is deplored by all.[16]

Liberalism does urge tolerance and oppose state interference in personal matters. "Liberalized" divorce law, abortion law, access to birth control, tolerance of diverse lifestyles—including cohabitation and homosexuality—are all instances of liberal opposition to state interference in personal life. Commercial promoters of violence and sex in the media, and the promoters of pornography, it must be admitted, often use liberal arguments for free speech to protect their enterprise. Indeed, to be consistent, it can be argued that liberals should oppose laws against adult drug use, prostitution, gambling, and other victimless crimes as paternalistic interferences with freedom. All these points grossly oversimplify the position and the issues, but they do represent the general idea of liberal permissiveness of which conservatives complain. Indeed, as just mentioned, it is precisely the rising rates of divorce, illegitimacy, drug use, abortion, and so forth that conservatives use as evidence of moral decay.

For the moment, supposing for the sake of argument that the conservative position on all these matters were simply conceded, what should be done about these problems? Is the argument that they should be controlled by law? Should abortion and divorce be made illegal again? Should access to birth control be limited and regulated by the state? Should women be barred from the work force if they are pregnant or have preschool children, as they once were? Legal restrictions such as these liberals would indeed oppose. But if the suggestion is to find (nonlegal) ways to bolster the moral community, to use moral persuasion to reinforce social standards, to raise our children according to these standards, to encourage people to take their commitments seriously, be responsible, and respect the integrity of others—why would liberals be opposed to any of that?

Is morality somehow incompatible with a liberal commitment to freedom as such? I believe that the conservative view can only be construed ultimately in those terms. How would such an argument go? In the same way that some liberals argue that economic life cannot be adequately represented as a series of discrete and un-related individual transactions but instead must be viewed as part of communal in-teraction, the conservative argues that individual morality is fostered by a moral en-vironment that is communal. The problems of violence, dishonesty, and disrespect for others arise from a general moral breakdown that follows from the erosion of communal institutions, especially those of family and faith, that once provided the source and standards of moral restraint, commitment, self-discipline, and respect for authority that are crucial to the moral health of any society.[17] One might say that the essence of morality is self-discipline or restraint, and that restraint is, after all, the antithesis of freedom.

In response to this argument, it must be recognized that liberty has never meant license in moral theory, not even for liberals. It may be that certain popular trends that might be construed as liberal have been misguided. The so-called sexual liberation movement is certainly one of the most confusing that comes readily to mind. Even liberals must consider it a mixed accomplishment. While some of the nastier forms of historical discrimination and intolerance have been at least weak-ened, promiscuity has been glorified. Women have become overt sex symbols in fashion, entertainment, and advertising. And mainstream media are often now diffi-cult to distinguish from pornography. This development has had an enormous im-pact on young people—many children are growing up too fast, like plants overex-posed to radiation. The problem seems to manifest itself, at least in the United States, in early and irresponsible sexual activity, sexually transmitted diseases, and teenage pregnancy, with all the tragic consequences that accompany such circum-stances. On the other hand, it certainly was not the case that women in the past were not considered sex symbols. Liberalism did not create that attitude, even if lib-eral reforms helped to break down the restriction of women that may have veiled such attitudes in the past. Still, if sexual liberation manifests itself as sexual irre-sponsibility that creates harmful effects, then it is a problem that must be dealt with. But it is not a special problem for liberals, since liberals do not defend any right to cause harm irresponsibly.

Another misguided popular trend has been the increased availability and use of drugs among young people, with similar tragic results for our children. School tru-ancy and the loss of motivation, education, and future prospects, as well as vio-lence, crime, and disease, have been common effects of this unfortunate activity among our youth.

These are serious social problems, and they may have been initiated or exacer-bated by some popular ideas that could be associated with the liberal ideology of freedom, although such an evaluation alone would be very simplistic and mislead-ing. Adequate explanation of such trends is likely to be fairly complex and highly speculative at best. But be that as it may, let us suppose that liberal ideas about free-dom contributed to these social problems. Is there some essential element of liberal ideology that would commit us to maintaining the conditions in which such prob-lems persist? There is no liberal commitment to promiscuous sex or drug use as such, so the relevant commitment can only be to freedom itself. But the liberal commitment to freedom has never been absolute. The commitment to freedom has never included the freedom to be irresponsible, much less harmful to others.

This point is particularly salient as applied to children, since the liberal position regarding children is that beyond the prohibition of abuse and neglect, and the universal availability of education, there should be no single centralized policy as to how children should be raised. Children are the responsibility of their parents. Liberalism defers to parental judgment and prefers the moral instruction of families to that of the state. But state prevention of harm to children is clearly appropriate. Nothing about liberalism would deny the legitimacy of criminalizing the sale of drugs to children, for example.

The same is true of attitudes about sexuality, as well as child development. It is not a liberal position to deny parental control over the sexual behavior, or even the fashion and entertainment, of their children. Quite the contrary. Yet it is argued that liberal sex education in the public schools undermines the ability of many parents to control the moral education of their children. These are very specific educational programs, however, intended to address particular social problems. Again, I make no attempt to support or oppose them here, but only point out that criticism of a particular program does not constiiute a criticism of liberalism.

Similarly, it is often claimed that liberals are "soft on crime," and this may be true of particular individual people. I make no pretense to defend or deny the particular position here. I only point out once again that there is nothing about liberalism that necessitates a particular position on crime control (other than respect for individuals). In fact, policies that have been the targets of recent criticism seem to have more to do with current theories of psychology or criminology, such as those of Karl Menninger, for example, than with liberalism as such.[18] Indeed, liberals hold a wide range of positions on crime and punishment, so there may well be as much debate on this issue within liberalism as outside it.

All these examples represent criticisms based on specific policies or programs that may (or may not) have been introduced or promoted by particular liberal individuals, but that have no intrinsic connection to liberalism as such. A liberal position on such matters might be any of a wide range of possibilities. If particular programs have been ineffective, then it is perfectly compatible with liberalism to revise or eliminate them in favor of better ones. Particular practical policies should not be confused with basic liberal commitments.

Not all criticisms are so easily answered, however. The general liberal commitment to personal freedom is basically what worries conservatives. I do not mean to dismiss this worry. Suppose that one considers it in terms of the problems associated with the liberal commitment to freedom of speech. It is often complained that the prevalence of sex and violence in the media, for example, make it nearly impossible for parents to maintain a reasonable environment in which to raise their children. And it is quickly noted that the liberal commitment to the freedom of expression protects this form of expression as well as any other. Unlike the previous complaints, this criticism raises an issue that is central to a basic liberal commitment. Nevertheless, the liberal protection of freedom, even freedom of expression, is not and never has been absolute. Libel, slander, and invasion of privacy have long placed restrictions on freedom of speech. Obscenity is restricted by community standards. Protection against nuisance and other competing interests allow for the regulation of the time, place, and manner in which the freedom of expression is exercised. Such matters require a balancing of interests, just as freedom of the press may be limited by the right to a fair trial or concern for national security.[19]

It is true that liberals are highly suspicious of censorship, and they should be. How many times in our history have great works of art been barred from public access by well-meaning city fathers? How many times have local school boards pulled classics from the libraries of our school children? Liberals are right to be cautious about censorship, since there will always be those who are overzealous in its application. The protection of the freedom of expression is a powerful commitment and a central tenet of liberalism. I do not want to suggest that the liberal commitment to personal freedom can be whittled away by competing considerations.

Yet it does not follow that the freedom of expression is or should be absolute. It never has been, even among liberals, and there is no reason to construe it so now. In particular, the regulation of the time, place, and manner of expression is perfectly compatible with liberal principles.[20] In such matters extremism is the enemy and cooperation the cure. Liberalism is not absolutist, nor opposed to a careful consideration of competing interests. The protection of children in the interest of the community is certainly one of those interests.[21]

Although the preceding is far from an exhaustive treatment of the topic, it should be sufficient to show that it is not obvious that a claim can be supported that the liberal commitment to freedom in itself is antithetical to the moral community. Since it is a very strong claim, perhaps the burden of proof should rest with the accuser.

Yet it is argued that liberal neutrality undermines the moral resources of family and faith. Does liberalism erode religious faith? It does insist that faith is a private matter that should not, and indeed, cannot effectively be controlled by the state. Hardly a more eloquent statement of that position could be found than John Locke's *Letter Concerning Toleration*, which was made for the very purpose of defending the free exercise of religion. Does it undermine religious faith to insist on toleration of diverse beliefs? Obviously, Locke didn't think so; nor did John Milton or Thomas Jefferson. The world's great religions have withstood the scrutiny of one another for some centuries without any of them disappearing. While there have been many religious wars and much cruelty from lack of toleration, religious faith was never eliminated, even by bloodshed. Why should it be eliminated by coexistence? If religious faith is fading in modern times, it is not because of liberalism, which only stands for tolerance.

Having said that, however, I would suggest again that extremism is the enemy in these matters as in the former ones, and cooperation the cure. Teaching a particular religion in the public schools of a diverse society is inappropriate; banning all discussion of religion in public schools is just as inappropriate. And prohibiting the use of public school facilities after hours for religious meetings, if those facilities are used for other meetings, is discriminatory and wrong. This is extremism. It is deplorable, but nothing about it is liberal, even if misguided zealots in the name of liberalism may have perpetrated the wrong in some particular cases.

There is, of course, no magic formula, but compromise is quite obviously the only answer where fundamentally competing views are involved. Promoting an attitude that acknowledges the significance of both the individual and the community could be a step in the direction of unity, or at least peaceful coexistence. Approaching such issues in the guise of cooperative individualism might help to keep both sides in focus and place a premium on negotiation and compromise, rather than adversarial extremism. What should be clear in all this is that peaceful coexistence of diverse religious practice is not antagonistic to liberalism. On the contrary, it illustrates the need for liberal tolerance to preserve a climate of religious freedom. But this is to respect religious practice, not to undermine it.

Does liberal ideology weaken the family? Conservatives cite high divorce rates and the increase of single-parent families, arguing that these trends are attributable to liberal attitudes about personal relations.[22] But such claims are impossible to substantiate. Certainly no causal connection can be shown, and many other plausible explanations for recent social trends are available. Furthermore, the very claim that the family is "declining" is questionable. On the one hand, the critics just mentioned note that two-parent families are still the norm, and divorce rates have leveled or declined since their peak in the 1970s. On the other hand, even if single-parent families are on the rise, single-parent families are families. It is the case that diverse family arrangements are now more acceptable, or at least less condemned, than they once were. Insofar as that reflects a tolerance for diverse lifestyles, it is not only compatible with liberal commitments; it is mandated by them. But does this tolerance undermine the family? It merely broadens the notion of what counts as a family. That is (or should be) fine with liberals, but not conservatives, perhaps.

It looks like the real complaint is that a very narrowly defined concept of the *traditional* family is possibly being eroded by liberal tolerance for diverse lifestyles.[23] But this is no argument against liberals at all, since liberals do not believe that the traditional family alone should be preserved in its entirety in any case. For example, liberals cannot consistently believe that patriarchal hierarchies should be supported, even though that is a central feature of the traditional family. Liberals should believe that couples should decide for themselves how to structure their personal relations (as long as they are not harmful), but a standard division of labor in the form of a male breadwinner and a female caretaker is central to the traditional middle-class family. In other words, given basic liberal principles of respect for individual freedom, liberals should reject some practices that turn out to be features of the traditional family, as narrowly defined by some conservatives. So, to complain that the *traditional* family is being undermined by liberal ideas is simply to concede that liberal ideas about family relations are being increasingly accepted, not to present an argument against them.

The curious point in all this is why liberalism should be perceived as undermining the family, when in fact the family has always been the bulwark of liberal society and a positive beneficiary of liberal governmental policies. I have suggested that the undue focus on individual autonomy and contractual relations in the form of atomistic individualism provides an inadequate foundation for a liberal theory of personal responsibility and creates the misimpression that liberalism is more extreme than in fact it is. The significance and centrality of family relations and obligations to liberal society have never been denied in liberal theory, but they have certainly been ignored. Contractual obligation has always been the centerpiece of liberal theory, and it has always been construed as more individual and overtly consensual than it typically is. Even political obligation has been forced into the contractual mold of aggregate individual consent, instead of being based on an acknowledgment of our cooperative requirements as community members. This atomistic focus never adequately accounted for liberal commitments—not family commitments, not professional commitments—and cannot begin to accommodate the moral foundations of cooperative communities, whether informal or formal.

This failing in turn leads to both conservative and communitarian suggestions that the liberal ideology of freedom and individualism encourages people to be irresponsible, to fail to take their commitments seriously. I think this charge is insupportable, since responsibility is not eliminated by but follows from moral autonomy, according to liberals. But the liberal focus on individual freedom (a crucially important focus) provides slim support for understanding the foundations of ongoing personal responsibility adequately, and even less for an account of community standards of reinforcement and compliance. If the communitarian claim is that liberal ideology erodes community standards that (would otherwise) reinforce individual morality, thus leading to greater noncompliance with the moral standards that individuals actually hold, how is the liberal to answer? If the claim is that (most) human beings need communal reinforcement to meet and maintain their own moral commitments, but individualism undermines that needed communal reinforcement, how is the liberal to answer? An atomistic individualist can have no answer. Liberals can have an answer, but we need to attend to this conservative point.

Conservatives and communitarians are right to observe that we live in a moral community. In the same way that economic transactions cannot be viewed in isolation, moral attitudes are not developed in isolation from the moral environment. Human beings are not perfectible. We will always have problems, weaknesses, vices, and failures. Yet, it does not follow that human beings are not improvable. The whole moral enterprise is based on the assumption that we can improve ourselves. My main point here is that we must improve ourselves together, and liberalism must be able to acknowledge and accommodate that point. Although moral responsibility is individual, we can only improve (or more conservatively speaking, maintain) the moral conditions of our lives as a group.

Suppose I live in a very bad neighborhood, but I myself oppose violence, and wish to raise my son to be nonviolent as well. The worse the neighborhood, and the fewer my resources to shield him from it, the lower my chances of success will be, since everything I try to teach him will be directly and personally tested and contradicted by the world in which he must live and interact every day. Yet success is not totally impossible. A few people do manage to prevail even under such adverse conditions. So let us suppose that I am one of those few, and my son comes to oppose violence as I do. My success (and his) will not make my neighborhood nonviolent, and it will not improve the conditions of my son's life. In fact, it is likely to make his life harder, for he will be faced with the dilemmas of a nonviolent person living in a violent world. Particular individuals are capable of maintaining high standards of morality even in the face of extreme adversity. But that is not the point of morality. The point of morality is to improve the ability of human beings to get along with one another, to enhance our prospects for living together.[24] To use G. J. Warnock's perspicuous description: the object of morality is to ameliorate the human tendency to make things worse. That objective cannot be accomplished by an individual alone, but only by a moral community. My neighborhood will not become nonviolent unless everyone in it is nonviolent—or at least nonviolence must be the norm. It must be a reasonable expectation of the community. Only as a general standard can morality improve human life and enhance (or maintain) our ability to live together.

This, I believe, is the basic conservative point. At the level of the clear case I just constructed, it surely must be correct. And at the level of the clear case, I don't suppose that any liberal would deny it. Of course, the further we move from the clear case, the harder it is to trace influences. If we are bombarded every day by sex and violence in the media, crass billboards, and crude advertising, shouldn't we expect such pervasive exposure to have some effect on our culture and our children? It seems like a reasonable assumption to me. On the other hand, most European countries have the same media exposure without any noticeable rise in their rates of violent crime, teenage pregnancy, abortion, or sexually transmitted disease. It is often argued that the availability of guns increases the level of violence in the United States. In Switzerland nearly every household has a gun, since almost every adult male is a member of the militia, but the Swiss have no violence problem to speak of at all. It is often argued that the prevalence of pornography erodes the common morality, but Denmark legalized pornography long ago, with no measurable effect on the moral behavior of its people whatsoever. It is far from clear what particular influences on morality might be, but despite these reservations, the clear case of the bad neighborhood illustrates that moral standards in general are communally reinforced or communally undermined.[25]

Unlike some responsibilities, however, moral standards cannot be legislated or allocated by government. The liberal commitment to individual freedom underscores this point, maintaining a longstanding opposition to state interference in personal and moral matters. Does the inclusion of duties of membership countermand this longstanding liberal commitment? I don't see why it would, since moral standards must be maintained by informal communities of belief, by community expectations. Yet the moral community is a cooperative endeavor, and the responsibility for maintaining it is a collective responsibility—not a state responsibility, but still a collective one.

Atomistic individualism cannot accommodate this point, but that does not constitute a refutation of liberalism. Instead, it provides an agenda for research and development within the liberal framework. What is needed is a more accurate articulation of the traditional liberal position of political neutrality toward differing ideals of the good life. This position is often described as value neutrality, but it is not that. It is the manifestation of a commitment to the value of tolerance. Yet we need to understand better the nature and limits of the doctrine of political neutrality or, for that matter, the nature and limits of tolerance. Perhaps an illustration would be helpful here.

A commitment to freedom does not imply tolerance of total freedom or anarchy. The freedom to be violent is not condoned by liberals, and is generally thought appropriate for legal restriction in almost any case. Opposing violence is clearly a liberal value. The freedom to be dishonest is also not condoned by liberals, although it is more often thought to fall in the domain of moral rather than legal enforcement. Perhaps we need some clearer understanding of what that means, or why it should be so. Yet, the opposition to dishonesty is a liberal value. Allowing violence and dishonesty, then, are not part of what it means to be politically neutral regarding competing visions of the good life, despite the fact that it may not be entirely clear what that amounts to in all cases of dishonesty. Irresponsibility is also not condoned by liberals, although the liberal position with regard to it is even more vague than the liberal position about dishonesty. Still, I believe that opposing irresponsibility is a liberal value, and once again I would presume that allowing irresponsibility is not part of what it means to be politically neutral. Being politically neutral is a manifestation of being tolerant. It is not relativism. But we need to understand better what it means and what falls outside of it.[26]

This is a need increasingly recognized, and a focus of research for a number of contemporary liberals.[27] Formulating an account of liberal values should help to provide an understanding of how our moral communities should function and what the limits of state interference should be. How political neutrality should be understood, and whether it should be construed as value neutrality, or even as neutrality at all, is the subject of considerable recent discussion and debate.[28] But this is a debate *within* liberalism, not a refutation of it. The conservative critic has not shown that liberalism is incompatible with a moral community, even though conservative and communitarian critiques may have pointed liberals in the direction of formulating a better account of what a liberal moral community should be.

Certain conservative criticisms are in some ways remarkably reversed by longstanding socialist or more recent communitarian critiques of liberal individualism. Very roughly speaking, it is argued that individualism promotes selfishness, apathy, or egoism, as well as destructive adversarial competition; erodes trust and cooperation; retards identification with the community or the common good; and fosters a narrow sense of justice and a thin notion of responsibility. Without evaluating this critique, or even trying to represent it more accurately here, just suppose it were all true.

Insofar as it is a critique of liberalism—rather than an indictment of modern society, as such, whatever its ideological foundations—what form of liberalism does it critique? Atomistic individualism. The version of individualism that I have been defending here would not, I believe, be susceptible to these criticisms. However, these criticisms reinforce the point that representations or constructions of liberalism *must* be cooperative, not atomistic. That is, I am suggesting that only cooperative individualism is supportive of informal moral communities, whereas atomistic individualism does indeed tend to undermine them. The position is as follows.

Liberalism stands for tolerance and individual freedom. Since these are values, it follows that liberalism is not value neutral, and it was a mistake ever to describe it as such. The mistake is a natural one, given the meaning of tolerance and freedom, which imply that the state should not interfere with the moral beliefs and practices of individuals so long as they are not causing harm to others. The question is, then, Does the institution of a state committed to protecting tolerance for diversity and individual freedom erode identification with informal communities necessary for moral instruction, socialization, and the reinforcement of moral life?

My view is that if the commitment to freedom and tolerance are construed as supporting the idea of individual self-sufficiency without acknowledgment of social connection and interdependence (i.e., as atomistic individualism), such a view does tend to promote egoism and selfishness, retard identification with community, and narrow the perceived scope of justice and responsibility. At least that seems to be a natural implication of an ideology of self-sufficiency. If such an attitude were widespread, it would seem to undermine commitment to community of any kind and so to informal communities (e.g., family, faith, or neighborhood) that would otherwise develop, inculcate, and reinforce moral standards.

This is not a matter of logic in the sense that the disappearance of informal moral communities necessarily follows from a prevalent social presumption of atomistic individualism. It is instead a matter of ideology, and thus of social tendency. If the prevailing attitude is that I am responsible for myself, and you are responsible for yourself, then I am not responsible for you. If you are poor, or sick, or suddenly incapacitated, that is your problem. You are on your own—unless there is something more to the story. My argument in the previous section was that atomistic individualism does not tell the whole story, whereas cooperative individualism can.

Furthermore, if you are on your own, and I am on my own, then no one is entitled to tell us what to do or think. I decide for myself what to do or think. I am an autonomous person. But part of what morality means is telling people (or at least persuading people of) what to do and think. That is what it means to be authoritative. So if moral autonomy is not qualified, where does that leave the moral community? Pretty seriously eroded. That is the communitarian/conservative point. If that point is correct, the liberal state cannot be justified on an atomistic construction, since it would undermine the conditions of moral agency provided by communal living in the first place. It violates the conditions of morality provided in the state of nature.

But that does not show that a liberal individualist state cannot be justified on a cooperative model. Indeed, the liberal answer to the moral communitarian/conservative criticism must be complex. Moral autonomy should not be denied, but it should be acknowledged as interactive or relational.[29] It is not that morality should be construed as *simply* telling people what to do. That would be an intolerably authoritarian view of morality. But if moral standards are authoritative, there is a sense in which they tell people what to do and think. So authority and autonomy must be coordinated, and to do that we need a theory that incorporates a cooperative social environment. That vision is presupposed by cooperative individualism, which enables it to handle potential deficiencies in a liberal account of both the economic and moral domains, and shows that the two are not as distinct as they are often presented. Both distributive justice and moral unity rely on a cooperative vision that acknowledges the significance of individuals interacting within communities.[30]

Thus, it needs to be made clear that while liberalism is individualistic, it is not atomistic; while it takes the individual as fundamentally significant, it does not suppose that the individual is fundamentally isolated from others; while it stands for tolerance and freedom, it does not reduce to egoism or subjective relativism. The idea of cooperative individualism would better represent this position. Yet it needs to be made clear what the position amounts to. I have argued here that it does not entail state interference in personal matters, although it must presume and thus encourage an attitude of cooperation that allows informal moral communities to flourish. This is a matter of ideology, not law. So, what would the ideology of the cooperative individualist look like, and how does it relate to a liberal understanding of affirmative obligation? I have suggested that economic and moral standards are not as distinct as often presented. What does such a claim mean? I will turn to these issues now.

3. Liberalism, Affirmative Obligation and Moral Unity: A New Image for the Twenty-first Century

Special positive duties are obligations owed to some particular individual or group because of explicit agreement or identification with that individual or group. Such identification is necessary for social cooperation—all societies rely on it, including liberal democracies. But individualism, if atomistic, tends to limit group identification, and since liberal individualism has never been well defined, it can be construed as atomistic as well as cooperative. Consequently, liberal accounts of social obligation are diverse and conflicting. We all function as neighbors and citizens for better or worse, and that could be described as a matter of consent, or social contract. After all, we don't have to participate (much) if we don't want to. We don't have to vote, or engage in civic organizations or causes. We do have to obey the law; that is not consensual, but it consists mainly of negative duties. And we do have to contribute our share economically. We have to work. We have to provide some service or product by which we make our living and also contribute to the common wealth. We like to think of those as contractual duties, but they are only consensual (at best) in terms of the kind of work we do, and not in terms of whether we will work at all. We have to pay our taxes to produce a common fund by which we address common problems or needs (schools, highways, police protection, national defense, etc.) collectively. Those are positive duties, and they are very controversial, especially for liberals.

I have suggested that this controversy is partly due to a narrow or ambiguous interpretation of the meaning of individualism and the responsibilities or affirmative obligations associated with it. The narrow scope of interpretation is reflected in the omission of family obligation from liberal theory. The ambiguity of interpretation is reflected in debates over the nature of contractual obligation, and even more in disputes over the scope and foundation of social responsibility or political obligation. This in turn can make it unclear what liberal commitments are. Is the tradition best represented by the cooperative social contract views of John Rawls or the classical libertarian views of Robert Nozick? Both are individualistic, but the sort of affirmative obligations they lead to are very different.

I think it needs to be made clear that liberal individualism is not reducible to egoism or atomism. These views cannot account for liberal institutions and practices. Not even family obligations or contractual obligations are adequately handled by them, and political obligation as well as more informal notions of social responsibility are skewed by the atomistic perspective. Articulating a cooperative individualism might help to clarify and refocus what individualism means or should mean to liberals. This would be a project of reconstruction, which construes the ideal of individualism in terms of the cooperative affirmative obligations that liberals have long defended. Approaches to it may be initially startling, but that is only because we have been so long immersed in the language and images of atomistic individualism.

An initial step in the direction of a cooperative individualist reconstruction would be to enable ourselves to think as parts of a larger entity—a player on a team, a musician in an orchestra, a plant in an ecosystem. This is not to suggest that any of us should ignore our individual identities. Quite the contrary, it is simply to recognize that there is always more than one way to describe anything. On one description, you are a unique and discrete individual. On another, you are a part of something larger than yourself alone. Both are true descriptions, generally recognized at some level by almost everyone. But we are not very good at thinking of ourselves as truly a part of something bigger, because three hundred years of atomistic individualism has focused our thinking in the other direction. And that has been useful and beneficial, to a point. But now, for many reasons, we need to manage to readjust our focus to include a cooperative communal vision as well as an individual one. We need to be able to look beyond ourselves alone, even to identify with a group larger than our own nuclear family. That means (to put it in jolting terms) that you need to be able to think of yourself as the finger or toe of a larger body, as a cell or corpuscle in a larger organism. Most of us, however, are not very good at doing that. No wonder we cannot construct full-bodied collective images. But this is exactly what we need to be able to do, as I will explain shortly.[31]

If we were to think of ourselves as collective persons—you and I, the cells of western civilization, or assuming that is too hard, as the cells of our national organism—what sort of person do you suppose we would be? What sort of characteristics would we have to acknowledge (proudly or shamefully) if we are to be truthful about our collective national identities? Each nation would have a slightly (or greatly) different list of characteristics, but there would surely be some similarities as well. Most highly developed nations of Western civilization, on the proud side, I think, could claim that we are talented and creative, highly accomplished, quite ingenious, and generally industrious. On the other hand, I think that most of the best of us would have to acknowledge that as collective personalities we are virtually all neurotic. The United States may provide the most extreme case—that is, we Americans may be the most neurotic as a collective being, but the problem is exemplified in other nations as well, especially diverse ones. That is, few nations, if any, today could truthfully describe themselves as well integrated and harmonious. What this situation reflects might be labeled the problem of disconnected or competitive pluralism. The authors of the *Federalist Papers* described it as the problem of factions. If diverse factions within a society are not integrated within some conception of a unified whole, then they disintegrate into unrelated, competing interests. Where this level of disintegration is high, it immobilizes the nation as a whole, because each part refuses to deal effectively with (or even acknowledge at all) the needs and requirements of the other parts. In the United States this problem at a national level is colloquially referred to as congressional gridlock. We have made it into an art

form and taken it to the logical absurdity of shutting down the government altogether. But this problem is not exclusive to American culture. Most European
democracies have similar problems, which come to a head from time to time, ne-
cessitating parliamentary capitulation or coalition. The most extreme case resolved
in recent years has to be the refusal of the president and parliament of the fledgling
Russian government to recognize the basic legitimacy of one another. The tragedy
is that the worst cases are not resolved, resulting in civil disintegration and bloodshed.

If one compares this problem of collective identity (that is, the lack of it) to a
personality disorder, it is like that of a neurotic person who refuses to accept responsibility for fixing what is wrong with his or her own life, willfully ignoring a debilitating condition. It is, for example, like a diabetic who will not face the restrictions
necessary for a healthy life that are imposed by that special condition; or an alco-
holic who will not acknowledge her problem and take the steps necessary to correct
it. It could even be compared to a clinically neurotic condition such as a person
with a phobia or compulsion who refuses to face the real problem in a way that will
fix it, that is, to take responsibility for it; and who thereby in effect refuses to develop
an integrated personality and remains instead fragmented and immobilized.

Collectively we are fragmented and immobilized in just this way. Collectively
we are living in Dante's Purgatory right now. The only reason we do not know it is
that we do not recognize ourselves as a single being. Like a Siamese twin who beats
his left side with his right, or a schizophrenic whose latent personality tries to anni-
hilate her primary personality, we refuse to acknowledge our common problems as
our own, because they seem to belong only to part of us, and that part seems to be
someone else.

Not long ago in an interesting book called *The Underclass*, Ken Auletta described a program that was designed to help people who could be thought of as
dysfunctional—former drug addicts and alcoholics, persistent petty criminals, and
long-term welfare recipients—to learn how to become productive members of
mainstream society. The very first step that was apparently necessary in this process
was the development of the person's ability to take responsibility for the problem,
no matter what caused it.[32] Until the person was able to take responsibility for her
problem personally, she was not able to solve it, even if someone else were actually
to blame. I wonder if we, as societies, could manage to see things that way.

Clear examples of this kind of problem at a societal level are the problems of
poverty and homelessness in the United States. The initial stumbling block with
such problems is that people disagree about how (or perhaps whether) they should
be addressed. Many people in the United States think that such problems should
not be (or cannot effectively be) addressed by government, that is to say, collectively
(at least, not any more than they already are). Thus, we don't see this as *our* problem. It is the poor people who have a problem. If we feel charitable, we can help
them out with *their* problem, but it is not *our* problem, not our responsibility.

So the preliminary issue is to determine what should be considered a "common" problem—a problem to be addressed by the collectivity as a whole. This
raises initial questions about taking collective responsibility for certain problems at
all. First, is this *our* problem? Is this a *public* problem, or should it be handled by

random individuals, by private initiative and voluntary association? Second, if it is a public problem, which public should handle it, which collectivity? For example, is this a national problem or a city problem? Or, as it is frequently put in the United States (and I am sure in any other highly bureaucratized society), "Whose department is this in?" Is this problem in *our* department? There are legitimate reasons for asking this question, but unfortunately it is often asked in order to shift responsibility—to remove the problem from direct view, that is, to get it out of your office and into someone else's, or at least to get it off your desk and onto someone else's. Of course, when we as human beings are on the other side of that process, we describe it as an unresponsive bureaucracy. It leads to cynicism and alienation, distrust and detachment. But as individuals there is very little we can do about large-scale social problems, no matter which side of the desk we happen to be on. So the problems linger on, and we become cynical and frustrated; we blame someone else, often the victim, or we practice denial. So there will always be controversy over what counts as a common problem, but large-scale social problems—homelessness, unemployment, poverty, crime—must be acknowledged as common problems (no matter what causes them), or they cannot be addressed at all. We cannot address them individually. And no problem can be addressed collectively (as well as individually) until it is acknowledged.[33]

To address these problems, we need a moral vision of collective responsibility that faces our common problems as *common*, that acknowledges and deals with them, that stops practicing avoidance and denial, that stops shifting blame and responsibility, that stops pitting one side against another to the immobility of all. We need to patch together our fragmented, tattered, collective soul, to provide the integrated and harmonious environment that we all long for and require in order to build functional and moral lives as social individuals.

But how? The old organic image obviously will not work. That is an ancient vision with enormous drawbacks that is not viable today. The new image must be compatible with the values of autonomy, freedom, and self-reliance established by the heritage of Western individualism. But it cannot remain there. Since the emerging image of the 1990s is the overloaded worker, the harried householder stretched to the limit with inadequate time to meet current personal obligations of work and family, it certainly cannot realistically be suggested that somehow we should redouble our efforts as individuals to meet social responsibilities or political obligations to our society as a whole. That limited perspective is precisely the problem.

Several philosophers have recognized this point in some recent work.[34] Thomas Nagel, for example, has argued that we need a moral division of labor between what he calls the partial and impartial (or personal and impersonal) moral requirements. The psychological makeup of all human beings, he argues, includes an impartial side, which universalizes the most fundamental requirements of justice, and which must somehow be harmonized or at least balanced against the personal side, which has special demands and needs, special projects and connections, that require time and resources to meet and that are not universalizable. Any adequate political theory, he suggests, must be able to accommodate both sides of human nature, and to do that we must be able to "externalize" the positive demands of universal or impartial morality by creating moral institutions within which individuals may pursue their personal lives and projects.[35] Nagel's view is reflected in and reinforces my earlier arguments that affirmative obligations cannot be universalized individually. If we acknowledge them on a large scale, they must be made collective.[36]

This point can be recognized at any level: local, national, global. The problem of world hunger discussed in chapter 3 is a prime example. It represents the effects of global maldistribution, which hangs over the heads of morally sensitive people who worry that they are participating in institutions that allow murderous conditions to persist that could be prevented, but who are nevertheless powerless to solve the problem on an individual level. Our impartial side says that nothing can justify this level of inequality. Those who are starving are human beings whose lives, impartially speaking, are worth as much as anyone else's. Our partial side, however, reminds us that we personally have families to think about, our own children, professional obligations, our own neighborhood, personal commitments, and people who are relying on us. We cannot disregard our personal obligations, destroy our lives and our loved ones, to dedicate ourselves individually to world problems that in any case we cannot solve on our own. So what can we do but practice denial? World hunger is not my responsibility. How could it be, since I cannot prevent it? Moral obligations must be possible to meet.

The same analysis applies to national problems or local ones, such as poverty and homelessness, as I mentioned before. Considered from an impartial perspective, there must be something wrong with a society that allows some of its members to languish in abject poverty, while a large percentage enjoy relative or extreme luxury. What could justify such a huge disparity in social benefits? The easy way out is to blame the victim; but from an impartial point of view I must admit that I am a privileged member of an unjust society, participating in—no, more accurately, benefiting from—unjust institutions every day. But is it my individual responsibility to correct poverty and homelessness? How can it be? As individuals, none of us can correct such problems. I know the situation is wrong, but I also know that I personally can't fix it. I can help someone, but for every one I help there will be two more left waiting. Affirmative obligations cannot be individually universalized.

To avoid oppressive positive moral requirements imposed by universal moral principles that individuals in any case could not meet, large-scale affirmative obligations (or social responsibilities) must be collectivized or institutionalized. A moral division of labor must be effected that reflects the two basic standpoints—the personal and the impartial—that are central to human psychology, as well as the requirements of justice and morality. We need to be able to specialize—to externalize our affirmative obligations, at least the large-scale ones.[37] In effect, we need to be able to hire professionals to take care of our social and political problems in the same way that we hire doctors, lawyers, teachers, and engineers. That is, affirmative social obligations need to be turned into economic obligations, so that they can be distributed across the community and allocated to specialists. To put it bluntly, we need to be able to buy out of personal involvement. By replacing time with money, we can buy our freedom without selling our morality.

Can that be true? Is such delegation consistent with the requirements of morality? There is no reason to suppose that it is not, as long as the obligations are impartial, and thus impersonal. By definition, it does not matter who meets these requirements, as long as we all contribute our share. It is personal obligations that cannot necessarily be delegated. There is nothing wrong with delegating impersonal obligations as such. Suppose I promise to provide transportation for some organization, say, the Girl Scouts, for one year. It does not follow that I must drive the bus myself, but only that I must see to it that someone does so reliably and safely. If I hire someone to drive the bus for a year, it does not follow that I have thereby shirked my responsibility; I have met it. Impersonal obligations can be delegated. Indeed, the only way to universalize affirmative obligations is to make them collective and economic, and thereby subject to allocation and specialization.

Is such collective problem-solving compatible with individualism? It is if my arguments in this book (or for that matter, Rawls's arguments for distributive justice, or utilitarian arguments for the common good) are correct, and this approach could lend itself to the formation of a new, more positive and liberating image that could replace the vision of the atomistic individualist that hasn't been relevant to human life since the days of the pioneers. It is the image of the valuable contributor, the team player, the specialist who cooperates in a common cause, who plays a crucial part in an ongoing effort organized to accomplish a worthy goal. The cooperative individualist is a community member, a human being with connections and commitments, as well as individual thoughts, judgments, and aspirations. The liberal individual is not an "unencumbered self" but a cooperative and committed one, a member of a family, a profession, a neighborhood, or a state. The image of the cooperative individualist is an ideal that extols the uniqueness of individuals, while acknowledging our communal connections to one another through bonds of morality, civility, and economic cooperation.

Readjusting our image in this way would require modifying or replacing the more extreme visions of atomistic individualism, trading in old heroes for new. The self-sufficient loner who rides into town, single-handedly wipes out evil, and then rides off alone into the sunset needs to be replaced by the winning team, or the dedicated community that fights the good fight, or builds something worth preserving. The isolated Rambo, who stands alone against a completely corrupt system, is understandable as a personification of our frustration and helplessness in the face of impassive bureaucracy, corruption, and crime, but we need to remember that all Rambo manages to do alone is destroy absolutely everything. Couldn't we focus instead on the people who manage to put things together rather than tearing them apart? Perhaps we could learn to appreciate the political leader who negotiates peace rather than engaging in war, or the business tycoon who finds a way to put people to work rather than making it big by laying them off. These should be our heroes. Finally, the myth of the self-made man would have to be revised to acknowledge that he does, after all, live and flourish within a community, without which he could not succeed, and to which he should be indebted.

Indeed, the very idea of self-reliance needs to be rearticulated to acknowledge that the self-reliant person is not self-sufficient (for no one in modern civilization is sufficient unto himself). Rather, self-reliance means that you earn what you get by providing a valuable contribution to the community, and that what you earn is at least as much as you need to live. Self-reliance simply means that you are able to earn as much as you need. It does not mean that you do not need the cooperation of anyone else, or even that you need not depend on any one else. All participants in what we call modern civilized society are completely dependent on one another for the most basic necessities of life: food, water, fuel, transportation, shelter. We do not provide these things for ourselves. We buy them from someone else, some specialist who provides them to us for a price. We can pay that price because we too are specialists who provide some valuable service or commodity for a price. And we are, all of us, entirely dependent for our very existence on the continued cooperation of and our own participation in this economic community and the more extensive moral and social community that undergirds and facilitates it. That is what self-reliance means, and what political obligation should facilitate.

This crucially cooperative element of life is not captured adequately or accurately by our current individualistic language, images, or heroes. Yet, it is completely compatible with models that abound in the individualistic history of the United States and other countries. Benjamin Franklin is frequently cited as a paradigm of the spirit of self-reliance at its best. But there is no question that his individualism included a powerful component of civic responsibility and communal cooperation. Could Franklin be described as disconnected or alienated? Never. Was he a self-reliant individual and an autonomous thinker? He certainly was, but he was also a cooperative community member, a contributor to and a beneficiary of the common good. He saw himself not only as an entrepreneur, but as a citizen; not only as an individual, but as an American and a Philadelphian who was dedicated to his city and his country. Did that impinge on his individualism? Not at all; on the contrary, it substantiated it.

This is the form of individualism I have in mind to be represented by the phrase "cooperative individualist." This is the individualism of Thomas Jefferson and John Stuart Mill, of Frederick Douglass and Susan B. Anthony. It entails a recognition of cooperative endeavor, of the value of social organization and institutional membership. Consequently, it acknowledges social obligation and civic responsibility. Cooperative individualists see themselves as part of a social unit, indeed as part of multiple overlapping social units, such as family, community, and country. As should be evident by my appeal to history, there is nothing new about cooperative individualism. Mine is simply an appeal to acknowledge that liberal individualism is indeed cooperative rather than atomistic. Accurately represented, it always has been so.

What may be a new twist, however, is the realization that addressing our collective obligations in a way that preserves individual freedom requires that they be allocated to cooperative specialists, and that doing this is a matter of collective responsibility. Failing to do it, collective irresponsibility, leaves moral burdens unmet on the shoulders of overburdened individuals who cannot meet them alone. Collective irresponsibility results in individual moral overload.

Thus, we need to share economic burdens so that we can delegate the burdens of time. We need to acknowledge our cooperative social life so that we can see the unity of values that underlie our diversity and make our moral life possible. Far from being incompatible with liberalism, this is the epitome of cooperative individualism as I have just described it.

Epilogue

Motivating Cooperative Individualism, or Why a
Liberal Individualist Should Accept Collective
Solutions to Large-scale Affirmative Obligations

The twentieth century has been dominated by two powerful images, one pre-dominantly European, the other predominantly American. Neither is exclusive of the other, however, as each has a counterpart within the other culture, and both exemplify what I will call collective irresponsibility.

The European image is that of an alienated, lost, and lonely individual living within a highly organized, unresponsive, and impersonal society. Modernity itself is frequently characterized as comprising disaffected, alienated individuals living fragmented, unanchored lives within frustrating, impassive institutions. Indeed, 'bureaucratic' is the word picked out as the single term most expressive of modern life. The significance of bureaucracy has been stressed by philosophers as divergent as Max Weber and Alistair MacIntyre. It is illustrated most trenchantly and frighteningly by Franz Kafka, but is also described by authors as diverse as Jean-Paul Sartre and Ernest Hemingway, Albert Camus and F. Scott Fitzgerald, Samuel Beckett and Arthur Miller. The American version of this image was laid out explicitly by David Riesman in a book called *The Lonely Crowd* in 1950. The modern malaise, according to this view, is to feel oneself to be an insignificant drop in an ocean, or worse, perhaps, an insignificant number in a data bank over which one has no control.

Indeed, number is precisely the problem on some accounts. Size alone makes modern society untenable—an inhospitable environment for human development, it is often claimed. There are so many of us now that our institutions are necessarily too large for humane interaction. A government today is a leviathan. No more a city-state, it stretches over vast territories, enclosing potentially billions of people. Just what do you suppose your chances are of getting an error on a government check corrected? If your income tax return somehow got misfiled, what are the chances that it will ever be found, much less during your lifetime? How likely is your voice to be heard in the legislature? Can we really convince people that it is important to vote if they know that each vote is one billionth of the total? How about one millionth? Does that help?

Similarly, a corporation today may be a colossus, larger than any state, spreading worldwide to the outer reaches of civilization and encompassing more people than some nations. Not long ago my husband and I went hiking in a fairly remote area in the Alps in the general region of the Matterhorn. Feeling temporarily alone in the world and refreshed, when we reached our icy destination we found . . . a Coca-Cola sign. Is there a city so remote that it will not display the golden arches of McDonald's? All countries may not have roads, but they probably all have Toyota dealerships. Human life is now highly organized. We are all ruled by diverse, overlapping, impersonal groups.

Even our most intimate needs have been bureaucratized. Before giving birth, completing a heart attack, and possibly even bleeding to death, one really should fill out the proper insurance forms at the front desk of all large hospitals. (Does there exist today a small hospital?) Furthermore, it may hold up the process considerably if you have not previously enrolled in an HMO or some other appropriate health protection collective. Your body may be your own, but your health is a massive group project.

Education is no better. Public schools get progressively larger and more centralized. Universities are the size of small cities. Ohio State University for example, has over seventy thousand students on one campus. Is it really an optimal learning experience for first-year students to spend their time in classes that number in the hundreds? If not quality of education, what is the motivating principle behind such institutional organization? Necessity? In 1986 I taught a special small seminar for first-year students at Harvard that was part of a special program apparently instituted in response to student complaints that their classes were so large that they were unable to identify their professors without a pair of binoculars. Harvard is often considered the best educational institution in America. Is that the best we can do with the numbers we have? The list of complaints could go on and on. Cities are sprawling and crowded. Highways are congested and stressful. Every move we make requires paperwork. These arc the complaints of modernity. Numbers require organization, organization is impersonal, and impersonal organization is unresponsive and alienating.

But others argue that it is not the size of current institutions that causes modern alienation, but the fragmentation of values, the lack of common commitments, the destruction of objective standards. We can always generate more questions than we can answer. We can always critique more than we can construct, and we appear to have destroyed any possibility of a foundation for objective values. Modern intellectual life is adrift on a deconstructed sea of relativism and subjectivity. The problem is not that there are too many of us, but that we are all disconnected. The legacy of the nineteenth-century unencumbered liberal will is the twentieth-century nihilist. Thus, the European image of the alienated individual.

The American image derives from the common ancestor of the nineteenth-century atomistic individualist, and it has both a positive and a negative construction. The positive version is actually a leftover nineteenth-century image that stressed individual strength, autonomy, and self-reliance, and that resonated with the proud pioneer spirit that survived long after the frontier was gone. Its modern manifestation is the illusion of the self-made man. The self-made man was supposed to have been a deprived child who grew up without any benefits from society, and who made himself through sheer determination, willpower, and hard work into a personal success, most generally economic, and certainly worthy of admiration and emulation. Such were the heroes of Horatio Alger's popular tales of rags to riches.

The problems with this image in a social setting rather than a wilderness are twofold. First, like the alienated European, the egoistic American is estranged from the society that surrounds him. He supposedly owes no debts; he has no necessary connections and therefore no particular commitments to other people who otherwise might be characterized as his fellow citizens. He is not a civilized participant in social life. He is a barbarian; he is an egoist. Second, unlike his frustrated and victimized European counterpart, this man is a conqueror. He seeks power. His associates are competitors, not companions. If there is no wilderness to dominate, then he will conquer other frontiers, even if that means nothing more than the domination of other people. Since in contemporary society the main road to power is economic, he becomes the economic egoist developed in the novels of Ayn Rand, and personified in its extreme form by Gordon Gecko, who conquered Wall Street, in the recent film of the same name, by using whatever technique functioned most effectively to achieve his own personal ends, while declaring, "Greed is good; greed works."

This ideal, for it is an ideal, despite our verbal disavowals of it, holds an ambiguous fascination in the recent public imagination and overshadows the older image of the alienated loser, personified for Americans by Willy Loman in Arthur Miller's *Death of a Salesman.* Gordon Gecko is grudgingly or secretly admired. He may be hated by some, but he is not despised, because he is a winner. He beats the system. Even if, like Michael Milkin, he goes to jail, he will be exceedingly well paid for the time he spends there. Laws against white-collar crime are notoriously mild, no doubt because of the power of those who tend to commit it. Anyway, the lawbreaker merely represents the extreme case of the economic egoist. The ideal is more commonly pursued within legal boundaries. In fact, part of the game, most frequently, is to find the loopholes and borders that keep one technically within the bounds of law while gaining every possible advantage in pursuit of egoistic goals. The typical economic egoist is not a lawbreaker (and should not have to be, given the control of the powerful over the law). The typical economic egoist is a freerider. He is a person who contrives to get more and contribute less than others must do.

This attitude manifested itself most strikingly in the recent social phenomenon of the Yuppie, the "me generation" of the 1980s, the decade of greed that carried the image of the economic egoist to its logical conclusion (although it is certainly too optimistic to construe conclusion as demise).

In any case, I believe these are the two images that have dominated public life and social attitudes in the twentieth century, each emerging and receding as it takes its turn capturing the public imagination or representing the tone of the times. We have the economic egoist and the alienated loser. Gordon Gecko and Willy Loman. The predator and the victim. The unconcerned and the overwhelmed. One beats the system; the other is beaten by it. But neither is part of it in one crucial respect. Both images are radically disconnected from the sources of social value and communal integration. They are moral outsiders, by choice or by default. They are socially and morally disconnected individuals.

This idea contrasts starkly with the highly organized institutions of which we are all, on one description, a part. From a certain perspective, the problem is not that we are disconnected, but that we are all too connected. We are connected in all sorts of ways with all sorts of groups, institutions, and other individuals. Disconnectedness is an image that we project on our daily interactions, a representation, as Emile Durkheim would put it, a way of describing these interactions, a way of feeling about them. We are in fact always engaged in constructing images, pictures, representations of life, interpretations that evaluate and make some kind of sense out of what we are doing, that situate and explain and motivate it.

These images are not strictly individual constructions. They are collective products. It is interesting that collectively we have produced a contemporary image of disconnectedness. Collectively we have determined that the problem of modernity is alienation. Even more surprisingly, in the nineteenth century, collectively we invented the atomistic individualist—the unencumbered self. It is, as they say, amazing what the human mind can do.

In fact, innumerable images of life, society, and individuality are potentially possible, and rarely will any one be all-encompassing, although certain ones, such as atomistic egoism or alienated frustration, will dominate the public imagination and set a certain tone or ambiance during certain periods of time, such as the egoistic '80s or the retroactive '50s. That is, the images that predominate in our thinking affect our world. You might say, what we think is what we are—or what we become. It is an interactive process.

Most recently, the Yuppie image has definitely faded from prominence. I believe that it is being replaced by a new image, a transitional one that will soon shift popular attitude back to the vision of the alienated individual (that is, unless something new happens to address recent problems and thus break the pattern). The emerging image is that of the scrambling worker or the harried householder—rushed, pushed, overcommitted, and underassisted, overburdened and underaided—with too many obligations and too few resources, juggling a job and a personal life without enough time for either. Recent public opinion polls in the United States and several European countries all indicate without exception that the greatest single complaint of the average middle-class person (male or female) was a lack of time. Life is becoming palpably fragmented, disharmonious, and accelerated in its pace. People feel stretched like rubber bands in opposite directions, by competing claims that are in no way humanely or efficiently coordinated with one another.

It is not hard to see that this is just an updated version of alienated individualism. This is just a new way to get run around by an irrational system, a new way to be a rat in a maze. And it is another alternation of the same two old tired images that have kept us running in circles without moral progress of an alleviating sort during the entire twentieth century.

I believe that both these images are manifestations of our collective irresponsibility, and until we can manage to take collective responsibility for our common problems and communal life—that is, for the social environment that constrains and structures our individual lives—we will continue to run in circles. Unless we take collective responsibility for the reconstruction of the maze, we are doomed to remain helpless, as individual rats within it.

This project is not incompatible with liberal individualism, although it is incompatible with atomistic individualism. An atomistic individualist cannot acknowledge that there is any maze. A liberal reformer, a cooperative individualist, should bring to bear on the problem of reconstruction certain principles and commitments of freedom and justice, of the significance of individual human worth, and of the quality of life that manifests itself in the form of the common good. These principles will sometimes provide constraints and sometimes building blocks for precisely such a reconstruction. A significant part of this project is the formulation of a contemporary liberal theory of responsibility, especially in terms of affirmative obligation, personal, professional, and political. This book is meant to be a small step in the direction of that goal.

Notes

1. Positive and Negative Duty in the Liberal Tradition

1. Hobbes, [1651], 1982.

2. This is not to deny the lag time or general discrepancies between principle (or rhetoric) and practice within the liberal or any other tradition. In practice all human beings have not been and still are not treated as equals. Yet I would argue that steady (if slow) progress has been made in the direction of equal treatment. Some of this progress is due to the leverage afforded dissenters and reformers by reference to liberal commitments to equality before the law. To be able to point to a discrepancy between principle and practice is a powerful tool for reform.

3. This statement is subject to the qualification of note 2. For example, despite considerable progress, in practice few societies offer women equal freedom in all aspects of social and political life as yet. Still, liberal principles have long been articulated in universal terms that provide a strong bargaining chip for reformers.

4. The traditional doctrine of positive and negative duty is laid out in many places. See in general, e.g., Donagan, 1977, Murphy, 1979, or Narveson, 1979. The distinction is also often described as that between duties to aid versus duties not to interfere.

5. There is considerable debate over the moral relevance of this distinction. See, e.g., Bennett, 1966, Morillo, 1977, Narveson, 1979, Foot, 1978, Mack, 1980, and Steinbock, 1980, among others.

6. On the nature and foundations of negative duty, see, e.g., Murphy, 1979, especially the first two essays; or Feinberg, 1973, chap. 4.

7. On the priority of negative duty, see, e.g., Murphy, 1979, or Donagan, 1977. For a clear exposition of Kant's view on the priority of duties of justice as noninterference, see Murphy, 1979.

8. See Feinberg, 1973, or Murphy, 1979.

9. See Kant [1785], 1956. For Kant the contrast is between duties of justice as noninterference and duties of benevolence in the form of assistance. See Murphy, 1973, 1979.

10. See, e.g., Donagan, 1977; Foot, 1967, 1978; or Murphy, 1973, 1979.

11. See Kant [1785], 1956, Donagan, 1977, Murphy, 1979.

12. E.g., Narveson, 1979, or Mack, 1980.

13. E.g., Murphy, 1979, or Donagan, 1977.

14. E.g., Nozick, 1974, or Finnis, 1980.

15. Although the distinction (between perfect and imperfect duty) can be found in Mill, various forms of it have been disputed by some recent utilitarians. See, e.g., Bennett, 1966, Singer, 1972, Unger, 1996.

16. See, e.g., Bennett, 1966, Singer, 1972, or Fishkin, 1982.

17. For discussion of the moral relevance or the act/omission distinction, see, e.g., Frankfurt, 1969, 1994; Harris, 1982; Clarke, 1994; or Smith, forthcoming.

18. See, e.g., Hayek, 1976, Narveson, 1988, or Nozick, 1974. Nozick argues that there is no such thing as distributive justice, and that the only legitimate obligations are those that are voluntarily incurred.

19. This is the rationale of social contract theories. See, e.g., Locke [1690], 1980, Rawls, 1971.

20. See, e.g., Singer, 1972, or Unger, 1996; for discussion, see Fishkin, 1982, or Nagel, 1991.

21. This is a point often noted by feminists, such as Held, 1993, and Meyers, 1994, or communitarians, such as May, 1992, 1996; or Taylor, 1989.

22. For work on this issue, see, e.g., Gutmann, 1980, Kymlicka, 1989, Held, 1993, or Meyers, 1989, 1994.

23. Justice as reciprocity is reflected in the ancient standard of *Lex Talionis* or the law of retaliation (see *Black's Law Dictionary*), most famously expressed in the Mosaic formula, "An eye for an eye, a tooth for a tooth." Early ideas analogous to *Lex Talionis* are found in most ancient societies. See Singer, 1981, or Maine, 1954.

24. See Singer, 1981.

25. See Aristotle, 1985.

26. See Plato, 1968, or Aristotle, 1985; for general discussion of reciprocity, see Gould, 1988; on reciprocity as a virtue see Becker, 1986.

27. See, e.g., Kant [1785], 1956, or Donagan, 1977.

28. Rawls, 1971.

29. Even utilitarians tend to construe justice in this narrow way, contrasting it with utility as the foundation of morality. Yet this is mostly a matter of emphasis. Given the focus on justice as noninterference, other conceptions simply fade into the background. They are not usually rejected outright.

30. A number of contemporary liberals have undertaken projects directly or indirectly related to this goal. See, e.g., Martin, 1993, Wellman, 1995, Dworkin, 1978, 1986, or Kymlicka, 1989.

31. E.g., Galston, 1991, Macedo, 1990, or Larmore, 1987.

32. Smith [1759], 1976.

33. Smith [1776], 1982.

34. For discussion, see Werhane, 1991.

35. See Smith, [1776], 1982.

36. See, e.g., Galston, 1991, or Macedo, 1990.

37. For discussion and defense, see Trammel, 1975, or Smith, 1991. It can be argued (although it is not generally held) that negative duties also impose costs or require resources. The argument may take several forms: (a) Prohibitions restrict my freedom and opportunity, thereby imposing costs on me. Answer: this is true, but the costs do not imply resources required to meet the duty. If I cannot commit fraud, for example, which costs me money I could have had by commiting fraud, it still requires no resources for me to meet the duty. (b) Although negative duties may not require resources, negative rights are relatively useless without enforcement, and enforcement requires resources, e.g. for police protection. (See Shue, 1980.) Answer: this is also true (at least sometimes), but it is a practical point

that in fact concedes the original moral and conceptual claim. See chapter 3 for further discussion.

38. Fishkin, 1982.

39. *Ibid.*, p. 9.

40. This is not to suggest that negative duties are not difficult to justify theoretically. Providing the justification for any moral duties is a colossal task that no one has yet satisfactorily accomplished. But at the same time, core negative duties have been generally recognized as morally binding since before the Ten Commandments were handed to Moses. And they are recognized almost universally in both law and moral custom without respect to culture. At a level of world practice, these are uncontroversial duties, and no plausible moral theory denies that they are. These duties are common knowledge, if anything is. Thus my claim that such duties are not hard to figure out.

41. See Held, 1984, or May 1987, 1992.

42. See Nagel, 1991, French, 1992, Gould, 1988, or Meyers, 1994.

43. I have dealt with these issues at length elsewhere. See the references in chapters 2 and 3 of this volume. See also my *Omission, Responsibility, and the Law*, forthcoming.

44. For overviews, see Kleinig, 1986, or Simester, 1995.

45. For elaboration, see chapter 2.

46. See, e.g., Murphy, 1973, 1979; or Narveson, 1979.

47. For discussion, see Kleinig, 1986, or Malm, 1990.

48. E.g., Singer, 1972, Rachels, 1975, Harris, 1982, or Unger, 1996.

49. But see Shue, 1980, who does argue for such positive rights.

50. These relations are laid out in Feinberg, 1973, or Becker, 1993, as well as in many other places.

51. See, e.g., Feinberg, 1973, or Becker, 1993.

2. *Special Circumstances and the Good Samaritan Exception*

1. In law, see, e.g.: Benditt, 1982, D'Amato, 1975, Frankel, 1965, Glazebrook, 1960, Hughes, 1958, Ratcliffe, 1966, Smith, 1984, Weinrib, 1980. In philosophy, see, e.g.: Feinberg, 1984, Green, 1980, Kleinig, 1986, Mack, 1980, Malm, 1990, 1991, Simester, 1995, Smith, 1990, 1991, Woozley, 1983.

2. This unease is evident in Anglo-American legal systems and scholarship, particularly in the U.S., where resistance is strong to good Samaritan statutes. In continental Europe and South America such statutes are typical, indeed, nearly universal, and not viewed as particularly problematic, much less inconsistent with liberal democratic institutions.

3. See, e.g., Narveson, 1979, 1988, or Epstein, 1973.

4. See, e.g. Rachels, 1975, 1979, or Singer, 1972; both are addressed in chapter 3, where this issue is the primary focus.

5. Joel Feinberg is one philosopher who has long construed the doctrine in this way. See Feinberg, 1973, 1984.

6. E.g., Murphy, 1973, 1979; Narveson, 1979; Epstein, 1973; Mack, 1980.

7. He does not have a duty to risk his life, of course, so assume that he has no reason to suppose that he would be in danger.

8. Murphy, 1980, p. 168.

9. Feinberg, 1984, chap. 4.

10. I will deal with unclear cases that have indeterminate parties in chapter 3, where I focus on how to define the duty.

11. See *Buch v Amory* (1897), p. 810.

12. Feinberg, 1984, chap. 4.

13. For discussion, see, e.g., Whelan, 1991, or Smith, 1991.

14. See Feinberg, 1984, or Smith, 1991.

15. Ames, 1908.

16. *Buch v Amory* (1897); and see Epstein, 1973, Murphy, 1979, or Mack, 1980.

17. See, e.g., Rachels, 1979; Singer, 1972; Harris, 1980, 1982; or Unger, 1996.

18. Feinberg, 1984, chap. 4.

19. See Husak, 1989.

20. Such cases are found in Husak, 1989; see also Hart and Honore, 1985, or Katz, 1987.

21. For discussion, see Smith, forthcoming.

22. See, e.g., Malm, 1990, 1991; or Narveson, 1979.

23. See, e.g., Malm, 1990, 1991; or Murphy, 1980.

3. *The Duty of Charity and the Equivalence Thesis*

1. See Singer, 1972, p. 4.

2. See Foot, 1967, 1978.

3. See Rachels, 1979.

4. I think that it is not a good argument against the good Samaritan obligation, but it clearly is a possible argument, a relevant argument, and one that has been often used.

5. See Bentham [1789], 1956. Bentham argued that if one passed a drunk lying face down in a puddle, it would be immoral not to reach down and turn his head to prevent him from drowning.

6. See the discussion in chapter 2.

7. See Thomson, 1971, p. 32.

8. For discussion, see Malm, 1990, or Whelan, 1991.

9. See Feinberg, 1984, for a comprehensive treatment of the nature of harm that eliminates the need to treat the topic here. Chapter 4 is especially relevant to the present discussion.

10. See Whelan, 1991.

11. See Smith, 1991, for further discussion.

12. It might still be a good thing to help out, of course. Duties of charity often apply when the perfect duty does not. I am only defining the narrow limits of the perfect duty here.

13. Being in control is sometimes analyzed as having the ability and opportunity to prevent or bring about some event or state of affairs. See Smith, 1984, or forthcoming. And see Husak, 1989.

14. Many psychological tests have shown that the bystanders who do not help are often anxious and undecided about what they should do. See, e.g., Darley and Latane, 1968, 1970.

15. See Smith, 1989, or forthcoming, for futher elaboration of this argument.

16. See Darley and Latane, 1968, 1970.

17. See, e.g., Murphy, 1980.

18. See Feinberg, 1984, chap. 4.

19. This case is discussed in chapter 2 of this volume. See also Murphy, 1980, or Feinberg, 1984.

20. Supervenience has been widely discussed. See, e.g., Feinberg, 1984, chap. 4, Bennett, 1995, chap. 1, or Mele, 1992, chaps. 1, 2, and 3.

21. This is not to say that it is not (ever) an emergency at all. The point is that Juan's case is the paradigm of a chronic or continuing condition. There is nothing you can do to stop it alone, although you can contribute to its solution.

22. Whether Singer's conclusions follow from that assumption is another matter. Some consequentialists would (and do) argue otherwise. See, e.g., Hardin, 1974.

23. Similarly, Peter Unger, 1996, explores what he calls Our Values, assuming something very like Singer's initial premise. However, he goes on to provide a number of arguments regarding consistent thinking on moral matters that are somewhat similar to those of Rachels. See also Kagan, 1989.

24. See also Unger, 1996, for extensive discussion of this issue. For a more moderate position, see Glover, 1977, or Shue, 1980. For rebuttal, see Kamm, 1993.

25. This is a very rough-and-ready formulation of the position. It is possible to make a stronger claim: not contributing to famine relief is equivalent to (second degree) murder, because we knowingly let the starving people die. It is not an accident, even if we don't intend or desire that result. Rachels makes this claim. In any case, the fine points of formulation will not be my concern here. The equivalence thesis is that there is no difference between blameworthiness for consequences we cause and those we allow to happen.

26. Rachels, 1979, p. 6. Unger, 1996, also provides a selection of arguments based on this formula.

27. Some find this claim counterintuitive. Ann Cudd (forthcoming), for example, suggested that fulfilling the obligations of promise or contract may require resources, but making a false promise violates a negative duty. This is true, but making a false promise violates a negative duty because it is lying. It requires no resources to tell the truth, although it may cost you dearly to do it. You may lose an opportunity, a friend, a lucrative contract. Still, it requires no resources to do it. On the other hand, if you make a promise intending to keep it, but later do not, you are violating a positive duty (indeed, a paradigm special positive duty), not a negative duty. Keeping a special positive duty *does* require resources, and you may violate the promise precisely because you find you haven't the resources to meet it. So it still seems to me that my claim is warranted. Perhaps *never* is too strong (although I don't think so). It seems to me true by definition, but even if I am wrong, it is certainly the case that negative duties almost never require resources, and positive duties almost always do.

28. For example, you cannot give even one penny to everyone in need. Of course, positive duties may be formulated in very abstract ways so as to universalize them in that form. Two examples are the duty to rescue and the duty to exercise due care. But both these examples show that universalization of positive duties requires qualification and limitation that hybridizes the duty, making it some combination of negative and special positive duty. Otherwise the duty becomes incoherent and impossible to meet.

29. See Trammel, 1975.

30. I take no position on this issue here. But see my *Omission, Responsibility and the Law*, forthcoming, where the issue is discussed at length.

4. Family Obligations and the Implications of Membership

1. The classical liberal philosophers (e.g., Hobbes, Locke, Kant) although briefly, deal more explicitly with family relations and the distinction between public and private spheres of life and obligation than do recent accounts (e.g., Rawls, Nozick, Dworkin). Feminist critiques have shown that the classical treatment of family obligations are indefensible, while recent treatments are inadequate. See, e.g., Elshtain, 1981, Pateman, 1988, 1989, Okin, 1979, 1989, Lloyd, 1984, O'Brien, 1989. My own view in general follows Okin on this issue.

2. See Filmer [1680], 1969. For discussion, see Pateman, 1988, or Cook, 1969.

3. Even Mill and many of the early feminists were reluctant to challenge the gendered structure and sexual division of labor within the family, although they challenged legal inequality. See Mill [1869], 1977, or Wollstonecraft [1792], 1967. For discussion, see, e.g., Elshtain, 1981, or Okin, 1979.

4. See the references listed in note 1.

5. See Locke [1690], 1980, bk. 2, chap. 6. For critiques, see, e.g., Pateman, 1988, Okin, 1979, or Elshtain, 1981.

6. See Pateman, 1988, chap. 4.

7. See Kant, [1785], 1956.

8. See Kant, [1797], 1887.

9. *Ibid.*, pp. 111–12.

10. For discussion, see Pateman, 1988.

11. See Bentham [1769], 1952; for discussion, see Elshtain, 1981.

12. See Mill [1869], 1977.

13. See Rhode, 1989.

14. See Okin, 1989.

15. Friedan, 1963, Millett, 1970, Firestone, 1970, are among the most famous.

16. See Okin, 1989, p. 111 (and more generally, all of chap. 6).

17. *Ibid.*, chap. 7.

18. E.g., Sandel, 1982, or Pateman, 1985, 1988.

19. See Okin, 1989, or Pateman, 1988.

20. The phrase 'duties of membership' is used (more or less in the way I use it) in Feinberg, "Duties, Rights, and Claims," reprinted in Feinberg, 1970. See also Held, 1989, or May, 1992, among others, for related views and usage.

21. See, e.g., Galston, 1980, Macedo, 1990, or Meyers, 1994.

22. E.g., Held, 1989, 1993; or Kymlicka, 1989.

23. For discussion see Gilbert, 1990 or Cudd, forthcoming. Cudd reviews intentionalist (e.g., Gilbert, Weber) and structuralist (e.g. Durkheim, Foucault) accounts of social group membership, retaining some features of each to formulate a more adequate theory of non-voluntary groups. Similarly, my examination here is concerned with understanding obligations that flow from relationships that seem to fall somewhere between consensual and non-consensual ones.

24. Explicating the idea of identification is, of course, a complex task. One may identify minimally or strongly with any group of which one is formally a member. In addition, it is possible to distinguish between identification with and having one's identity formed (or influenced) by some group or institution. Identification implies some level of consciousness or intentionality; identity formation does not. Both concepts have been the subject of extensive philosophical and psychological examination. For further discussion relevant to the present topic see, e.g., Cudd, forthcoming, May, 1987, Taylor, 1989, or Meyers, 1994.

25. This idea is reflected, for example, in the standard of negligence in tort law, which is judged by the "reasonable expectations of the community" or by evaluations of the intent of the parties in contract law in terms of "standard business practice." See, e.g., Dobbs, 1985, or Kessler and Gilmore, 1970.

26. This interesting idea has been worked out in the context of international relations, and particularly with regard to treaty obligations. See Fain, 1987. It is suggested that a better account of political obligation can be obtained by abandoning the traditional contract model of analysis for a model that focuses instead on the idea of commitment to communal tasks. The idea of commitment, like identification, can be weak or strong. For example, I may be proud to be an American without considering what that commits me to, or I may be specifically involved in causes that I identify as American. I am indebted to Ann Cudd for pointing this out. See also Gilbert, 1990, or Cudd, forthcoming.

27. The psychological literature on the concept and function of roles is enormous. For recent philosophical discussion see, e.g., Held, 1989, or May, 1992, 1996.

28. I hope to avoid the methodological dispute between structuralists and intentionalists, since it leads away from the topic. The psychological points made here are innocuous,

centrist, common-sense views. I make no claims about ultimate explanations of personal identity. See, e.g., Taylor, 1989, for a communitarian view, or Crittenden, 1992, for a liberal one.

29. See Meyers, 1994, or May, 1996.

30. This should be kept in mind when considering criticisms of liberal theories as presupposing or requiring a so-called atomistic vision of an unencumbered self. See, e.g., Sandel, 1982.

31. Traditionally, of course, this obligation has been sharply divided by gender. The male obligation was to provide economic support and physical defense and the female obligation was to provide nurturing care.

32. To provide for oneself for most of history has meant to participate in an economic system by producing what one needs directly or by providing an economically valuable service or product that could be traded for what one needed.

33. These three claims are not uncontroversial, of course. I have already mentioned that ideas about being self-sufficient are highly cultural and gender-specific, but in general it means first that every person must have something (usually a skill or service) to contribute to the group that is valuable enough to provide a living. Second, whether it is in a person's (and thus a child's) interest to be moral is one of philosophy's Big Questions. I don't expect to solve it here, but I will address it further in chapter 9. (I don't claim to solve it there either, but I do take a position on it.) It clearly is in the interest of society for all its members to be moral. Third, the obligation to make one's child socially well-adjusted is actually a tricky issue for a liberal individualist. I discuss this further in this section.

34. To put the point in this way as applied to women displays a contemporary bias (mine). Traditionally, of course, girls were not taught to be or to believe they could be self-sufficient. They were, nevertheless, taught to provide valuable services, even if this left them economically dependent. I am willing to claim that all children should be taught self-sufficiency in the sense I have outlined, whether male or female.

35. See Okin, 1989, or Mill [1869], 1977.

36. Larry May refers to this process of developing individuality out of a myriad of social influences over time as bootstrapping. See May, 1996.

37. I will address later the problems (and advantages) arising from communities that are not cohesive. See especially chapter 9.

38. See Sandel, 1982.

39. Indeed, the very existence of individuals may be questionable in the views of some critics.

40. See Rawls, 1985.

41. See, e.g., Kymlicka, 1989; Buchanan, 1991; or Nichol, 1990, 1994.

42. See Hart, 1961, or Rawls, 1971.

43. See, e.g., Nozick, 1974, or Narveson, 1988.

44. See, e.g., Daniels, 1988, pp. 29–33.

45. For discussion of duties of charity or beneficence, see chapters 1–3.

46. See Daniels, 1988, for a good summary of proposed justifications and objections. Daniels concludes that there is no clear moral justification, at least none that is appropriate as a basis for a coercive social policy requiring children to support their parents.

47. I take no position on this issue one way or the other. That is, I think some family obligations could be compatible with the requirements of justice and freedom, but other social arrangements might be compatible as well (such as tribal or communal living, perhaps). Issues of natural human need (e.g., do humans need to live in families) are empirical, not moral, issues.

48. E.g., Daniels, 1988, or Callahan, 1987.

49. Polls discussed, e.g., in Googins, 1991.

50. There is, of course, much controversy over just how such collective mechanisms should be structured and funded. Should they be state-operated or privately managed? My point is that either way they are collective devices for pooling resources, and thus social (not individual) solutions to the problem of elder care.

51. I am not the first to criticize marriage viewed as a contract. See, e.g., Okin, 1989, or Pateman, 1988. Pateman points out that in addition to the public exchange of vows, marriage requires consummation by sexual intercourse, refusal of which annuls the marriage. This condition is not negotiable by individual parties, although it could be mutually ignored.

52. Although public marital vows have always been general, historically they constituted a public declaration of the change of status of the parties involved, and included a vow of obedience on the part of the wife that was far from idle talk. See, e.g., Rhode, 1989.

53. This point also implicates the socialization process discussed in section 2. Men and women are socialized to understand that their obligations as husbands and wives or as fathers and mothers will normally be more or less what they grew up with, unless they consciously reject or rethink those assumptions. Similarly, parental socialization is liable to mirror community expectations unless they are consciously assessed and counteracted. But given the complexity of life, most such assumptions (what cognitive scientists call default assumptions) cannot be consciously assessed. There simply isn't enough time to do it. See Hofstadter, 1986.

54. This quality, by the way, makes them quite analogous to some mainstream contractual obligations, which are often specified by terms like 'standard business practice' or 'common professional standards,' etc. See, e.g., Summers and Hillman, 1987.

55. It should be noted that this standard of divided roles, while indeed prevalent, ignores the conditions of the poor, under which women worked (primarily as field hands and domestic servants) throughout history. See, e.g., Rosenberg, 1992, or Kessler-Harris, 1982.

56. There is nothing unique about this feature, by the way. Many contracts are voluntary in entry only, as noted by Max Radin and others. See Radin, 1943.

57. That is, if economic standards in marriage were truly settled (as they were, not long ago) various individual arrangements would not be allowed. Thus, the fact that such individual agreements are at least sometimes considered valid is evidence of community dissent or confusion.

58. In comparison, no one would dream of suggesting that a man whose wife could support him works "because he wants to." This disparity reflects community standards that work is essential for men (or even for manhood) which in turn is reflected in prejudice against women as not serious about their jobs (since work is not essential for them).

59. Recent, that is, within the middle class. Lower-class women, as noted earlier, have always worked outside the home, but they never seem to count in the formulation of what is normal. See, e.g., Googins, 1991, or Kessler-Harris, 1982.

60. See, e.g., Rosenberg, 1992, pp. 4, 93–98; or Googins, 1991, chap. 3.

61. See Googins, 1991, chap. 3; or Rosenberg, 1992, pp. 4, 96–98, 101–3, 131–36, 147–55.

62. There are interesting sociological studies that document various devices and attitudes used by both men and women of diverse cultures to cover up the earnings of women, that is, to make them invisible so as to maintain the male breadwinner standard even in the face of incompatible facts. See, e.g., essays by Stichter, Salaff, or Scott, in Stichter and Parpart, 1990.

63. Brownlee and Miller, 1997, discuss this common concern and the conflicting attitudes about women working.

64. See Brownlee and Miller, 1997, pp. 58–63, citing a Yankelovich Monitor Survey.

65. This point is reflected in social criticism on behalf of minority men who cannot get

work due to discrimination. The claim is that unemployment is emasculating. See Pateman, 1988, for discussion.

66. See, e.g., Googins, 1991, or Brownlee and Miller, 1997.

67. Statistics from the U.S. Census indicate that in 1960 the labor force participation of women over age sixteen stood at 35 percent. By 1994 it rose to 68 percent, including by 1986 more than 50 percent of women with children under age six. For discussion, see Okin, 1989, chap. 8; Rosenberg, 1992; Kessler-Harris, 1982; Googins, 1991; or Brownlee and Miller, 1997.

68. See, e.g., Brownlee and Miller, 1997, Kessler-Harris, 1982, Okin, 1989.

69. On conflicting standards and expectations for women, see Okin, 1989, Gerson, 1985, Bianchi and Spain, 1986.

70. On changing female aspirations, see, e.g., Okin, 1989, Gerson, 1985, Fuchs, 1988, Bianchi and Spain, 1986.

71. See, e.g., Fineman, 1995, or Weitzman, 1985.

5. Family Membership and Reciprocity

1. Many other examples could be given. I do not intend a restrictive notion of what constitutes a family. History and geography generally play a role in setting norms for the composition of families. In most (but not all) times and places, biological connection has been central, but alternatives have also been advocated (and adopted) that replace the genetic family with other social units that serve the same functions. It has been suggested that any small group that thinks it is a family is one. That idea may be adequate for what I am calling household but is not for family in the abstract. My purpose here is to distinguish these two in order to examine differences between them, not to claim one is family and the other is not.

2. For discussion, see Pateman, 1988. On marital status and the legal fiction of genetic connection, see Maine, [1864], 1954.

3. I am not suggesting that these ideas are rational or justified, but only that they are widely held. On the other hand, they are not universally held. Many people have no particular identification with a family name or a family tradition, that is, with family in the abstract, at all.

4. See Dworkin, 1978.

5. See Mill [1861], 1905.

6. See Maine, [1864], 1954.

7. There are further questions about consent beyond the construction of voluntariness, or at least subtleties about the nature of voluntariness that cannot be adequately pursued here. For example, voluntariness is commonly construed as an all-or-nothing trigger concept. Conduct is voluntary or not. But freedom and coercion are clearly matters of degree, and so voluntariness must also be a matter of degree. Thus, distinguishing between voluntary and involuntary conduct at the poles of the continuum is easy. But drawing a line in the middle of the range is a very tricky proposition, as is illustrated by the problems confronted here and in chapters 6 and 7.

8. That is, the twentieth century (as opposed to the nineteenth) is notable for the institution of many collective mechanisms for pooling resources outside of families, both by state and by private organization. Private life insurance, medical insurance, and pension plans are widely available. State plans for supplying retirement and medical needs (such as Social Security, Medicare, or Medicaid) are all programs that substitute state for family reliance. The availability of retirement and nursing homes has skyrocketed, another substitution of social for family care. This is not to say that universal care is available; that is certainly not true. Still, the trend to socialization is clear.

9. See, e.g., Daniels, 1988.

10. See Googins, 1991.

11. I am not suggesting that positive duties can never conflict with negative duties. My general position is that conflicts of negative with positive duties are uncommon and usually unnecessary. Where they do conflict, it indicates a need for institutional reform and creates a true dilemma that must be considered as an individual case. I discuss this problem at some length in chapter 7.

12. See Rawls, 1971.

13. See, for example, Gould, 1988, who argues that a just society requires protection of positive as well as negative freedom (or equal access to conditions of development as well as noninterference); Rawls, 1971, who argues that justice requires fair distribution of burdens and benefits, as well as noninterference; Okin, 1989, who argues that liberal justice must be applied to family relations that go beyond noninterference.

14. I am speaking again here of family as household. Family in the abstract cannot be justified by the idea of cooperative membership, since it is basically an abstract idea embodied in the family name or blood line. Just as family in the abstract cannot be an intentional actor (as noted in the case of debt) it cannot be a cooperative participant either. Family as household, in contrast, can be and is often a paradigm of cooperative participation of its members jointly and severally.

15. For discussion of reliance in contract law, see chapters 6 and 7.

16. See Held, 1989, on duties of trust.

17. See, e.g., Singer, 1981.

18. See, e.g., Murphy, 1979, on retribution. The significance of reciprocity as a moral concept has been discussed by some contemporary philosophers. See, e.g., Becker, 1986, Gould, 1988, or Rawls, 1971.

19. Aristotle, 1985, p. 436.

20. See Becker, 1986.

21. See Gould, 1988, or Rawls, 1971, for analysis of reciprocity.

22. Aristotle, 1985.

23. Libertarians to the contrary notwithstanding. As I will argue later, the contemporary libertarian concept of atomistic individual consent cannot be derived from earlier liberal views (e.g., Locke) and cannot account for liberal social practices. (Nor are all libertarian views alike on this point.)

24. See Hart, 1961.

25. Notice once again, by the way, that family as household is clearly supported by this rationale, but family in the abstract is not. There is no reason to suppose that human beings, as a matter of natural necessity, require dynastic family organization, since many human beings live perfectly well without it. But the idea that human beings innately need some form of intimate, long-term social association is not an implausible hypothesis.

26. This is a very controversial point that has been examined extensively by feminists. The distinction between public and private domains has been challenged and even denied by some. It has been usefully observed that relations within the family are political (as noted at the beginning of chapter 4), that family organization is structured and maintained by law, that family power structures are deeply influenced by broader social influences, opportunities, and assumptions, and that governmental decisions not to act or intercede in any given matter are no more neutral than decisions to act or intercede. I agree with all these points and do not believe anything I have said here contradicts them. Nevertheless, despite those points, I believe it is a useful political venture to set out "zones of privacy" that are considered exempt from governmental intrusion. This does not mean that such areas of life will be untouched by government, or even unregulated by government. But it should be harder to intrude. It should require greater justification. The preservation of privacy becomes ever

more important as our technological capacity to eliminate it increases. This does not mean that state power should not be exercised to prevent or address abuse or injustice within the family. The requirements of reciprocity extend the scope of justice; they do not contract it.

6. The Complexity of Consent in Legal Theory and Practice

1. See Maine, 1864.
2. See, e.g., Rawls, 1971, or Gautier, 1986.
3. See, e.g., Summers and Hillman, 1987, chap. 2.
4. See, e.g., Tigar and Levy, 1977, especially chap. 17; or Horwitz, 1977, chap. 6.
5. I am not suggesting that small town or preindustrial society was idyllic, or that all close associations are trustworthy, fair, or even amicable, but only that strangers have even less motivation for trustworthiness and fairness than nonstrangers.
6. See, e.g., Hart, 1961.
7. For the promise principle, see Fried, 1981. For historical overview of the will theory see, e.g., Horwitz, 1977, or Friedman, 1985.
8. Interesting historical accounts of the development of this position are provided by Horwitz, 1977, and Friedman, 1965. These explain the doctrine of consideration as a "remnant" of an earlier "equitable" theory of contract that did oversee the value exchanged.
9. See, e.g., Gilmore, 1974; Friedman, 1965; or Atiyah, 1979, 1981, 1986.
10. Summers and Hillman, 1987.
11. Gilmore, 1974, pp. 87–88.
12. See, e.g., Radin, 1943, or Kessler, 1943.
13. Radin, 1943.
14. *Ibid.*
15. See, e.g., Horwitz, 1977, Kessler, 1943, Friedman, 1965, Atiyah, 1981.
16. Of course, the idea of laissez faire also has staunch defenders, especially if it is construed as free market. See, e.g., Posner, 1977.
17. Kessler, 1943, p. 633.
18. *Adkins v Children's Hospital*, 1923, p. 531.
19. *Coppage v Kansas*, 1915, p. 4.
20. *Nebbia v New York*, 1934, p. 505.
21. *West Coast Hotel v Parrish*, 1937, p. 384.
22. The response of the court, however, was directed to conflicts within the middle class. Not only were court responses not designed to equalize classes, they were designed not to; they were designed to promote business at the expense of the laborer and the consumer (or anything else that might get in the way of developing enterprise). Law encouraged a probusiness environment in terms of individual profit. That is what laissez faire and freedom of contract stood for (but neutrally, of course).
23. Sandel, 1982.
24. Atiyah, 1986, p. 4.
25. *Ibid.*, p. 241.
26. Fried, 1981.
27. *Ibid.*
28. *Ibid.*
29. See Atiyah, 1986, especially chap. 6.
30. Fuller and Purdue, 1936.
31. Friedman, 1965, p. 20.
32. It could also be claimed (more cynically) that it is a collection of legal doctrines designed to protect the power of the powerful and the wealth of the wealthy. The point for pres-

ent purposes is that even if this description is accepted, it cannot be accommodated by an atomistic consent theory.

7. Consent and Role in Professional Obligation

1. I use the term 'professional' as synonymous with 'occupational' here.

2. As Joan Callahan pointed out to me, even this position has limits, both legally and personally. You may be legally liable for long-range consequences of your professional actions, even if you have retired from the business. And personally, relationships (e.g., of colleagues and mentors) may be formed that do not end even if the original professional connection is not applicable.

3. Even so, professional positions are generally much more open to negotiation than "nonprofessional" jobs. If you apply for a job at UPS, say, you don't get to negotiate your duties. The job is defined by specific duties; you can accept it or not. Professional positions may have more latitude for negotiation because the duties may be more vaguely defined, or because the potential employee has more power to negotiate. The latitude to negotiate is generally a sign of privilege, although there are exceptions. The higher the level of privilege, the more individual the negotiations and the more control an individual may have over the contents of the package.

4. I am not suggesting that we make excuses for ourselves, but the power of social conditioning should not be underestimated. We can consider as two separate questions: (1) Is this a legitimate excuse for certain conduct? and (2) Is this an accurate description of social life? As noted in chapter 4, unemployment is widely acknowledged as demoralizing and debilitating. For discussion, see, e.g., Pateman, 1988, or Googins, 1991.

5. Of course, I'm pointing out that we don't really have an option to refuse to work. But from the perspective of the unemployed, those who cannot get a job have no options at all.

6. The amount of choice depends on the population considered. If one is considering world population, the level of choice in occupation may not be very high. More highly developed nations offer more choices in general, but this condition is also dependent on the level of unemployment. The higher the level of unemployment, the fewer choices are available for workers.

7. Larry May discusses and analyzes obligations of profession as obligations of individuals within groups in a way that is sensitive to the complexities I am discussing here. See May, 1992.

8. The two concepts are overlapping and clearly not coextensive, since some memberships are not contractual, and some reliance is not reciprocal. In law, for example, the idea of detrimental reliance does not imply reciprocal reliance. In cases of family dependency, reliance may not be reciprocal. Infants, in particular, rely on parents who do not reciprocally rely on them.

9. This idea is not identical to the notion of reflexive identity that I applied to community membership. A community is constituted by its members, just as members are identified with the community. This clearly is not (necessarily) true of business enterprises, which are externally or hierarchically defined. See Gould, 1988 for interesting arguments for rights of workers participation that would make such relationships more reciprocal.

10. See, e.g., Wasserstrom, 1988.

11. A common complaint today is that employers are not loyal to their employees. Job security is tenuous; downsizing is common; layoffs may have nothing to do with job performance. In such a climate an obligation of worker loyalty would be hard to justify.

12. The use of the term 'ordinary morality' to focus on universal negative duties can be

disputed. I have no commitment to the terminology; nor do I intend do be making a particular statement by means of it. I am merely following common usage.

13. See, e.g., Callahan, 1988, Beauchamp and Bowie, 1988, or Freeman, 1991.

14. See Freedman, 1988.

15. Perhaps it should be noted that this controversy is about not whether the lawyer can lie, but only whether she can create a false impression. And it is not asked whether the lawyer can do wrong, so to speak, but whether she can allow her client to do wrong without withdrawing from the case. On conflicts of interest and conflicts of obligation in legal practice, see, e.g., Kipnis, 1986.

16. See Wasserstrom, 1988, p. 64.

17. There are also common conflicts of allegiance. The confidentiality required of fiduciary relations compels the refusal to reveal information to authorities that an ordinary citizen would be legally obliged to report, but this is a conflict of two positive duties, which is a separate problem, and a much more common one, since positive duties conflict quite often. On conflicts of professional duty see, e.g., Kipnis, 1986, or Goldman, 1980.

18. As with the consent element, the reciprocity of the benefit may be minimal, that is, very unequal, perhaps even unfair. Yet there will always be some mutual benefit for both parties. For discussion, see, e.g., Radin, 1943.

19. This distinction is not captured necessarily by any single interpretation of the terms I selected. We can only use them by stipulation to represent the distinction.

20. Fried, 1981.

21. See Held, 1984.

8. Justifying the Obligations of Neighbors and Citizens

1. There are exceptions, depending on how broadly liberalism is defined. The liberal tradition, broadly defined, includes a very diverse group. For example, Rousseau is a liberal in many respects (although his work may also be classified as conservative in some respects.) Rousseau, as a liberal, did not view society as an aggregate of individuals. The few exceptions, however, do not undermine the generalization.

2. See Smith [1776], 1982. For discussion, see Werhane, 1991.

3. This is not to say that it is not still attempted, of course. Many contemporary utilitarians argue for both freedom and justice on utilitarian grounds. The highly optimistic presumptions of the nineteenth-century thinkers (such as the invisible hand) made such arguments much easier to formulate.

4. See Rawls, 1971; but see qualifications in Rawls, 1993.

5. For discussion, see chapter 6.

6. See, e.g., Nozick, 1974.

7. See Mill [1863], 1979.

8. See Hart, 1955.

9. *Ibid.*, p. 182.

10. Rawls, 1971, p. 112.

11. Rawls, 1971, p. 114.

12. That is, it is the moderate liberal (as opposed to the libertarian) who tries to explain and justify *social* responsibility in general and affirmative obligations (such as a political obligation to help the poor or educate the young of one's society) in particular.

13. See, e.g., Held, 1993.

14. The examples of Hobbes and Rousseau counter this assumption as attached to social contract theory itself, however.

15. This approach, it has been noted, itself assumes certain values. Supposing that it does not is what I earlier called the morality of neutrality—confusing tolerance with relativism.

16. See MacIntyre, 1981.

17. That is, showing hypothetical consent may or may not justify obligations in the absence of actual consent, as the liberatarians argue. But if other grounds for obligation are accepted, such as cooperative communal membership, showing that people would not agree to certain obligations under fair bargaining conditions may be a good way to show that such obligations would be unfair to individuals and consequently to demonstrate the limits of communal obligation.

18. Note that this conclusion recapitulates the one drawn regarding family obligations that are not explicitly consensual, such as filial duty, namely, that their justification depends on the fairness and necessity of the institutions within which they function.

19. This is also true of the idea of democracy as the "consent of the governed," because, first, majority rule is not equal to individual consent (49 percent may not consent at all), and second, democracy does not necessarily guarantee fairness, which can still be assessed on other grounds, and is still relevant to evaluating social arrangements even if they were consented to by majority vote. This is not to argue against democracy, but only to point out that the basis of obligation in a democracy is cooperative participation, not consent as such.

20. See Rawls, 1993.

21. Hobbes [1651], 1960.

22. See Locke [1690], 1980.

23. Rousseau [1762], 1950.

24. Nozick, 1974.

25. In fact, Locke and Nozick both assume the communal cooperation of individuals without addressing its significance or preconditions. Hobbes seems to assume a cooperative community that degenerates into a state of nature as war. But all assume the accomplishments of communal living without accounting for those accomplishments. See Okin, 1979.

26. I will discuss this distinction as one between informal and formal associations, which is no new idea. Toennies [1887], 1963, explains it as gemeinschaft and gesellschaft. Hobhouse, 1911, also provides an interesting historical discussion that relates to this distinction.

27. This does not mean that it would necessarily meet the requirements of rational justification in terms of any particular moral theory, but only that it would be perceived and acted on as a moral requirement, and had the power of guiding behavior that is the function of moral duty.

28. See French, 1984.

29. See, e.g., Kymlicka, 1989.

30. This cooperation is both a communal and an individual good. The individual is provided with employment and economic reward; the community is provided with necessary material goods.

31. Of course, most (maybe all) societies do not meet these moral requirements of structural justice or substantive fairness, but that does not make them necessarily inefficient. It makes them unjust, a separate issue to be addressed shortly.

32. This is not to suggest that states are in fact organized to insure fair participation or eliminate conflicting duties. They are not, but they could be. The point is, they should be to be justified.

33. For discussion see Shue, 1980, or Sterba, 1988.

9. *Articulating the Scope of Political Obligation*

1. See George [1879], 1982, pp. 190, 196.

2. See Frank and Cook, 1995. Two years later unemployment dropped and the mood of the country improved, but in fact the income disparity has increased.

3. *Ibid.*, p. 5 and chapter 4.

4. Phillips, 1990, chap. 1 and pp. 239–45.

5. See, e.g., Friedman, 1985.

6. See George [1879], 1982; see also Sadler Committee Hearings, 1831, or Ashley Commission Hearings, 1842.

7. See Boroughs, January 1996, pp. 47–54.

8. Unemployment figures have fluctuated constantly during this century. Current reports place unemployment in the United States in 1997 at 5 percent, the lowest figure in twenty years, but percentages for certain populations (e.g., young black males) run much higher than the average.

9. See Boroughs, January 1996, pp. 47–54.

10. See, e.g., Hobhouse, 1964, for an articulation of this basic position specifically as principles of liberal philosophy. There are, of course, limits to justified regulation. In fact, from a liberal perspective, regulation should be as minimal as possible, since restriction is a presumptive evil that can only be justified to prevent some greater evil.

11. That is, provided that the community as a whole is not too poor to address the needs of its population. To evaluate that, the economic structures must be evaluated to determine where the wealth of the nation is going. Henry Shue makes similar arguments about basic rights. See Shue, 1980.

12. This does not mean that particular policies or programs are necessarily correct or successful, merely because they are liberal, of course. Many liberal policies have not been effective in fact. Determining whether any given initiative is a good one is a practical matter of evaluating its success in accomplishing intended goals at reasonable cost.

13. This point is important, because it is one way of posing the issue raised in chapter 8. If the formal state necessarily undermines the informal community that provides a social environment within which moral agency can develop, then the state could never be justified.

14. See, e.g., Bennett, 1995, Kristol, 1995, Gilder, 1986, or Murray, 1984.

15. See, e.g., Marcuse, 1964, or Barry, 1973.

16. See Bennett, 1995, or Kristol, 1995.

17. See, e.g., Bennett, 1995, or Kristol, 1995.

18. See Menninger, 1968.

19. See, e.g., Feinberg, 1985, or Schauer, 1982.

20. See, e.g., Feinberg, 1985, or Schauer, 1982.

21. I am not suggesting, however, that the reading or viewing materials of adults can or should be restricted to what is suitable for children.

22. See, e.g., Gilder, 1986, or Falwell, 1992.

23. Again, no causal connection to liberalism can be shown here, and influences are likely to be complex. Liberals can take neither blame nor credit for changing lifestyles or family structures. Such fundamental changes may be due to any number or combination of social forces.

24. See, e.g., Warnock, 1971, or Kilby, 1993.

25. See May, 1992.

26. In fact, some liberals now suggest that the phrase 'political neutrality' is an unfortunate choice of terminology. The basic concept needs to be rearticulated and renamed.

27. See, e.g., Galston, 1991, Macedo, 1990, Kymlicka, 1989.

28. See, e.g., Rawls, 1993, Larmore, 1987, Ackerman, 1980.

29. See, e.g., Meyers, 1997, or Mackenzie and Stoljar, 1998, on new developments in autonomy theory and relational autonomy in particular.

30. For similar views on individuals interacting within communities, see, e.g., Gould, 1988, or May, 1992.

31. As I hope will become apparent, I am not advocating this literally organic vision myself. I use it here for shock value only, to try to capture the radical adjustment or expansion of perspective that is needed to address our social problems.

32. See Auletta, 1982.

33. I am not suggesting that these problems cannot or should not be addressed by individuals at all, of course. It is a good and charitable thing to do. But while no individual can solve these problems, they could be solved as social problems if we took collective responsibility for solving them.

34. See, e.g., French, 1992, Held, 1984, Fishkin, 1982.

35. See Nagel, 1991.

36. See Fishkin, 1982.

37. See Fishkin, 1982.

Bibliography

Ackerman, Bruce. *Social Justice and the Liberal State*. Yale University Press: New Haven, 1980.

———. "What is Neutral about Neutrality?" *Ethics* 93 (January 1983).

Adkins v Children's Hospital, 261 US 525 (1923).

Alexander, L., and M. Schwarzschild. "Liberalism, Neutrality, and Equality of Welfare vs. Equality of Resources." *Philosophy and Public Affairs* 16 (1987).

Ames, James Barr. "Law and Morals." *Harvard Law Review* 22 (1908).

Andre, Judith. "Role Morality as a Complex Instance of Ordinary Morality." *American Philosophical Quarterly* (January 1991).

Ardal, Paul. "Promises and Reliance." *Dialogue* 15 (1976).

Aristotle. *Politics*. Edited by W. D. Ross. Oxford University Press: Oxford, 1962.

———. *Nicomachean Ethics*. Translated by T. Irwin. Hackett: Indianapolis, 1985.

Ashley Commission Hearings. 1842. Reprinted in *Poverty and Wealth*. Edited by K. E. Alrutz et al. University Press of America: Washington, D.C., 1982.

Atiyah, P. S. *The Rise and Fall of Contract*. Oxford University Press: Oxford, 1979.

———. *Promises, Morals, and Law*. Oxford University Press: Oxford, 1981.

———. *Essays on Contract*. Oxford University Press: Oxford, 1986.

Auletta, Ken. *The Underclass*. Random House: New York, 1982.

Barry, Brian. *The Liberal Theory of Justice*. Clarendon Press: Oxford, 1973.

Beauchamp, T., and N. Bowie, eds. *Ethical Theory and Business*. 3rd ed. Prentice-Hall: Englewood Cliffs, N.J., 1988.

Becker, Lawrence. *Reciprocity*. Routledge and Kegan Paul: New York, 1986.

———. "Rights." Reprinted in *The Nature and Process of Law*, edited by Patricia Smith. Oxford University Press: Oxford, 1993.

Bellah, Robert, et al. *Habits of the Heart: Individualism and Commitment in American Life*. Harper and Row: New York, 1986.

Benditt, T., "Liability For Failing To Rescue." *Law and Philosophy* (1982).

Bennett, Jonathan, "Whatever the Consequences." *Analysis* 26 (1966).

———. *The Act Itself*. Oxford University Press: New York, 1995.

Bennett, William. "Getting Used to Decadence: The Spirit of Democracy in Modern America." *Heritage Lectures* no. 477. 1993. Reprinted in *American Values*, edited by Charles Cozic. Greenhaven Press: San Diego, 1995.

Bentham, Jeremy. *Principles of Morals and Legislation*. 1769. Hackett: New York, 1952.

Berger, Peter, and Jack Neuhaus. *To Empower People: The Role of Mediating Structures in Public Policy*. American Enterprise Institute: Washington, D.C., 1977.

Bianchi, S., and D. Spain. *American Women in Transition*. Russell Sage: New York, 1986.

Bleustein, Jeffrey. *Parents and Children: The Ethics of the Family*. Oxford University Press: New York, 1982.

———. *Care and Commitment*. Oxford University Press: New York, 1991.

Boroughs, Don. "Winter of Discontent." *U.S. News and World Report*. January 22, 1996.

Bradley, F. H. *Ethical Studies*. 1876. Clarendon Press: Oxford, 1927.

Brandt, Richard. "The Concepts of Obligation and Duty." *Mind* 73 (1964).

Brownlee, S., and M. Miller. "Lies Parents Tell Themselves About Why They Work." *U.S. News and World Report* (May 12, 1997).

Buch v Amory Manufacturing Co., 69 NH 257 (1897).

Buchanan, Allan. *Marx and Social Justice: The Radical Critique of Liberalism*. Methuen: London, 1982.

———. "Assessing the Communitarian Critique of Liberalism." *Ethics* 99 (July 1989).

———. *Secession*. Westview: Boulder, 1991.

Burke, Edmund. *Burke's Politics: Selected Writings and Speeches*. Edited by R. Hoffman and P. Levack. Knopf: New York, 1949.

Callahan, Daniel. *Setting Limits: Medical Goals in an Aging Society*. Simon and Schuster: New York, 1987.

Callahan, Joan, ed., *Ethical Issues in Professional Life*. Oxford University Press: New York, 1988.

Capriotti, Emile. *The Grounds and Limits of Political Obligation*. Lang: New York, 1992.

Carey, Toni. "Institutional versus Moral Obligations." *Journal of Philosophy* 74 (1977).

Clarke, Randolf. "Ability and Responsibility for Omissions." *Philosophical Studies* 73 (1994).

Cook, Thomas, ed. Introduction to *John Locke: Two Treatises of Government*. Hafner: New York, 1969.

Coppage v Kansas, 236 US 1 (1919).

Crittenden, J. *Beyond Individualism*. Oxford University Press: New York, 1992.

Cudd, A. "Non-Voluntary Social Groups." Forthcoming in *Groups and Group Rights*. L. May, L. Francis, C. Sistare, eds. Kansas University Press: Lawrence, Kansas.

Daniels, Norman. *Am I My Parents' Keeper?* Oxford University Press: New York, 1988.

D'Amato, A. "The 'Bad Samaritan' Paradigm." *Northwestern University Law Review* 78 (1975).

Darley, J., and B. Latane. "When Will People Help in a Crisis?" *Psychology Today* (December 1968).

———. *The Unresponsive Bystander: Why Doesn't He Help?* Basic Books: New York, 1970.

Davis, Nancy. "The Doctrine of Double Effect: Problems of Interpretation." *Philosophical Quarterly* 65 (1984).

Dewey, John. *Human Nature and Conduct*. Henry Holt: New York, 1922.

———. *Reconstruction in Philosophy*. 1920. Beacon Press: Boston, 1957.

Dinan, Stephen. "The Moral Nature of Political Obligation." *Dialogue* 13 (1971).

Dobbs, D. *Torts and Compensation*. West: St. Paul, 1985.

Donagan, Alan. *The Theory of Morality*, Chicago University Press: Chicago, 1977.

Dunn, John. *Political Obligation in its Historical Context*. Cambridge University Press: Cambridge, 1980.

Dworkin, Ronald. "Liberalism." In *Public and Private Morality*, edited by Stuart Hampshire. Princeton University Press: Princeton, 1978a.

———. *Taking Rights Seriously*. Harvard University Press: Cambridge, 1978b.

Ebisch, Glen. "Nationality and Moral Obligations." *Journal of Social Philosophy* 9 (1978).

Elshtain, Jean. *Public Man, Private Woman*. Princeton University Press: Princeton, 1981.

English, Jane. "Justice Between Generations." *Philosophical Studies* 31 (1977).

———. "What Do Grown Children Owe Their Parents?" In *Having Children*, edited by Onora O'Neill. Oxford University Press: New York, 1979.

Epstein, Richard. "A Theory of Strict Liability." *Journal of Legal Studies* 2 (1973).

Fain, Haskel. *Normative Politics and the Community of Nations*. Temple University Press: Philadelphia, 1987.

Falwell, Jerry. *The New American Family*. Word: Dallas, 1992.

Feinberg, Joel. *Doing and Deserving*. Princeton University Press: Princeton, 1970.

———. *Social Philosophy*. Prentice-Hall: Englewood Cliffs, N.J., 1973.

———. *Harm To Others: The Moral Limits of the Criminal Law*. Vol. 1. Oxford University Press: New York, 1984.

———. *Offense To Others: The Moral Limits of the Criminal Law*. Vol. 2. Oxford University Press: New York, 1985.

Filmer, Robert. *Partriarcha*. 1680. Reprinted in *John Locke: Two Treatises of Government*, edited by Thomas Cook. Hafner: New York, 1969.

Fineman, Martha. *The Neutered Mother, The Sexual Family, and Other Twentieth Century Tragedies*. Routledge: New York, 1995.

Finnis, John. *Natural Law and Natural Rights*. Oxford University Press: Oxford, 1980.

Firestone, S. *The Dialectic of Sex*. Bantam: New York, 1970.

Fishkin, James. *The Limits of Obligation*. Yale University Press: New Haven, 1982.

———. *Justice, Equal Opportunity and the Family*. Yale University Press: New Haven, 1983.

———. "Towards a New Social Contract." *Nous* 24 (1990).

Flanagan, Owen. *Varieties of Moral Personality*. Harvard University Press: Cambridge, 1991.

Flathman, Richard. *Political Obligation*. Atheneum: New York, 1972.

Foot, Phillipa. "The Problem of Abortion and the Doctrine of the Double Effect." *Oxford Review* 5 (1967).

———. *Virtues and Vices*. University of California Press: Berkeley, 1978.

Frank, R., and P. Cook. *The Winner Take All Society*. Free Press: New York, 1995.

Frankel, J. "Criminal Omissions: A Legal Microcosm." *Wayne Law Review* 11 (1965).

Freedman, M. *Lawyers' Ethics in an Adversary System*. Bobbs-Merrill: Indianapolis, 1975.

———. "Professional Responsibility of the Criminal Defense Lawyer: The Three Hardest Questions" in *Ethical Issues in Professional Life* edited by Joan Callahan. Oxford University Press: New York, 1988, chapter 3.

Freeman, R. E., ed. *Business Ethics: The State of the Art*. Oxford University Press: New York, 1991.

French, Peter. *Collective and Corporate Responsibility*. Columbia University Press: New York, 1984.

———. *Responsibility Matters*. University of Kansas Press: Lawrence, Kansas., 1992.

Fried, Charles. *Right and Wrong*. Harvard University Press: Cambridge, 1978.

——— *Contract as Promise: A Theory of Contractual Obligation*. Harvard University Press: Cambridge, 1981.

Friedan, B. *The Feminine Mystique*. Random House: New York, 1963.

Friedman, Lawrence. *Contract Law in America, a Social and Economic Case Study*. University of Wisconisn Press: Madison, 1965.

———. *A History of American Law*. Simon and Schuster: New York, 1985.

———. *Republic of Choice*. Harvard University Press: Cambridge, 1990.

Fuchs, Victor. *Women's Quest for Economic Equality*. Harvard University Press: Cambridge, 1988, chapters 1 and 2.

Fuller, L., and J. Purdue. "The Reliance Interest in Contract Damages." 46 *Yale Law Journal*, 52 (1936).

Galston, William. *Justice and the Human Good*. University of Chicago Press: Chicago, 1980.

———. "Defending Liberalism." *American Political Science Review* 76 (1982).

———. *Liberal Purposes*. Cambridge University Press: Cambridge, 1991.

Gautier, David. *Morals by Agreement*. Oxford University Press: New York, 1986.

George, Henry. *Progress and Poverty*. 1879. Reprinted in *Poverty and Wealth*, edited by K. E. Alrutz et al. University Press of America: Washington, D.C., 1982.

Gerson, Kathleen. *Hard Choices: How Women Decide about Work, Career, and Motherhood*. University of California Press: Berkeley, 1985.

Gilbert, Margaret. *On Social Facts*. Oxford University Press, 1990.

———. "Group Membership and Political Obligation." *Monist* 76 (1993).

———. *Living Together: Rationality, Sociality and Obligation*. Rowman and Littlefield: Lanham, Md., 1996.

Gilder, George. *Men and Marriage*. Pelican Press: Gretna, La., 1986.

Gilmore, Grant. *The Death of Contract*. Ohio State University Press: Columbia, 1974.

Glazebrook, P. "Criminal Omissions." *Law Quarterly Review* 76 (1960).

Glover, Jonathan. *Causing Death and Saving Lives*. Penguin: Harmondsworth, 1977.

Goldman, A., *The Moral Foundations of Professional Ethics*. Rowman and Littlefield: Lanham, Md, 1980.

Googins, B. *Work/Family Conflicts*. Auburn House: New York, 1991.

Gould, Carol, *Marx's Social Ontology*. MIT Press: Cambridge, 1978.

———. *Rethinking Democracy: Freedom and Social Cooperation in Politics, Economy, and Society*. Cambridge University: Cambridge, 1988.

Graham, Keith. "Morality and Abstract Individualism." *Proceedings of the Aristotelian Society* 87 (1986–87).

Gray, J. *Liberalism*. University of Minnesota Press: Minneapolis, 1986.

Green, O. H. "Killing and Letting Die," *American Philosophical Quarterly*, July (1980).

Green, T. H. *Lectures on the Principles of Political Obligation*. Longman's, Green: London, 1941.

Greenspan, Patricia. *Moral Dilemmas, Emotions, and Social Norms*. Oxford University Press: New York, 1995.

Gutmann, Amy. *Liberal Equality*. Cambridge University Press: Cambridge, 1980.

———. "Communitarian Critics of Liberalism." *Philosophy and Public Affairs* 14 (1985).

———, and Dennis Thompson. *Democracy and Disagreement*. Harvard University Press: Cambridge, 1996.

Hampshire, Stuart. *Morality and Conflict*. Harvard University Press: Cambridge, 1983.

———. ed. *Public and Private Morality*. Princeton University Press: Princeton, 1978.

Hardin, Garrett. "Lifeboat Ethics: The Case against Helping the Poor." *Psychology Today* 8 (September 1974).

Harris, John, *Violence and Responsibility*. Oxford University Press: Oxford, 1980.

———. "Bad Samaritans Cause Harm." *Philosophical Quarterly* 32 (1982).

Hart, H. L. A., "Are There Any Natural Rights?" *Philosophical Review* 64 (April 1955).

———. *The Concept of Law*. Oxford University Press: London, 1961.

Hart, H., and T. Honore. *Causation in the Law*. Oxford University Press: Oxford, 1985.

Hayek, Friedrich. *Law, Legislation, and Liberty*. 3 vols. University of Chicago Press: Chicago, 1973.

———. *The Constitution of Liberty*. London, 1976.

Held, Virginia. *Rights and Goods: Justifying Social Action*. Free Press: New York, 1984.

————. *Feminist Morality: Transforming Culture, Society, and Politics.* University of Chicago Press: Chicago, 1993.

Hirschmann, Nancy. *Rethinking Obligation.* Cornell University Press: Ithaca, 1992.

Hobbes, Thomas. *Leviathan.* 1651. Ch. 35, in *Classical Selections on Great Issues*, edited by K. E. Alrutz et al. Vol. 3. University Press of America: Washington, D.C., 1982. p. 45.

Hobhouse, L. T. *Liberalism.* Oxford University Press: Oxford, 1964.

Hofstadter, Douglas. *Metamagical Themas.* Basic Books: New York, 1986.

Horwitz, Morton. *The Transformation of American Law 1780–1869.* Harvard University Press: Cambridge, 1977.

Hughes, G. "Criminal Omissions." *Yale Law Journal* 67 (1958).

Hume, David. *An Enquiry Concerning the Principles Morals.* In *Hume's Enquiries*, edited by L. A. Selby-Bigge. Oxford University Press: Oxford, 1965.

Husak, Douglas. "Omissions, Causation and Liability." *Philosophical Quarterly* 30 (1980).

————. *The Philosophy of the Criminal Law.* Rowman and Littlefield: Englewood Cliffs, N.J., 1989.

Jecker, Nancy. "Are Filial Duties Unfounded?" *American Philosophical Quarterly* 26 (1989).

Kagan, Shelly. *The Limits of Morality.* Oxford University Press: New York, 1989.

Kamm, F. M. *Morality/Mortality.* Vol. 1. Oxford University Press: New York, 1993.

Kant, Immanuel. *The Philosophy of Law.* 1797. Translated by W. Hastie. Edinburgh and Clark: London, 1887.

————. *Groundwork of the Metaphysics of Morals.* 1785. Translated by L. W. Beck. Bobbs-Merrill: Indianapolis, 1956.

————. *The Metaphysics of Morals.* 1797. (The Philosophy of Law.) In *Political Writings*, edited by H. Reiss, Cambridge University Press: Cambridge, 1970.

————. "Observations on the Feeling of the Beautiful and Sublime." In *Women in Western Thought*, edited by M. L. Osborne. Random House: New York, 1979.

Katz, L. *Bad Acts and Guilty Minds.* University of Chicago Press: Chicago, 1987.

Kessler, Friederich. "Contracts of Adhesion—Some Thoughts about Freedom of Contract." 43 *Columbia Law Review* 629 (1943).

Kessler, F., and G. Gilmore. *Contracts.* 2nd ed. Little, Brown, and Co.: Boston, 1970.

Kessler-Harris, Alice. *Out To Work: A History of Wage-earning Women in America.* Oxford University Press: New York, 1982.

Kilby, Richard. *The Study of Human Values.* University Press of America: Lanham, Md., 1993.

Kipnis, Kenneth. *Legal Ethics.* Prentice-Hall: Englewood Cliffs, NJ, 1986.

Kleinig, John. "Criminal Liability for Failures to Act." *Law and Contemporary Problems* 49 (Summer 1986).

Klosko, George. "Political Obligation and Natural Duties of Justice." *Philosophy and Public Affaris* 23 (Summer 1994).

Kristol, Irving. *Neo-conservatism: The Autobiography of an Idea.* Free Press: New York, 1995.

Kymlicka, Will. *Liberalism, Community and Culture.* Clarendon Press: Oxford, 1989.

Larmore, Charles. *Patterns of Moral Complexity.* Cambridge University Press: Cambridge, 1987.

Lloyd, G. *The Man of Reason: "Male" and "Female" in Western Philosophy.* University of Minnesota Press: Minneapolis, 1984.

Locke, John. *Two Treatises of Government.* 1690. Hackett: Indianapolis, 1980.

MacCormick, Neil. "Law, Obligation and Consent." *Archives Fur Rechts- und Sozialphilosophie* 65 (1979).

Macedo, Steven. *Liberal Virtues.* Clarendon Press: Oxford, 1990.

MacIntyre, Alistair. *After Virtue*. Notre Dame University Press: Notre Dame, 1981.

Mack, Eric. "Bad Samaritanism and the Causation of Harm." *Philosophy and Public Affairs* 31 (1980).

Mackenzie, Catriona, and Natalie Stoljar. *Relational Autonomy: Feminist Perspectives on Autonomy, Agency and the Social Self*. Oxford University Press: New York, forthcoming, 1998.

MacPherson, C. B. *The Political Theory of Possessive Individualism: Hobbes to Locke*. Oxford University Press: New York, 1962.

————. *The Life and Times of Liberal Democracy*. Oxford University Press: Oxford, 1977.

Maine, Sir Henry. *Ancient Law*. 1864. Dutton: New York, 1954.

Malm, Heidi. "Directions of Justification in the Negative-Positive Duty Debate." *American Philosophical Quarterly* (October 1990).

————. "Between the Horns of the Negative-Positive Duty Debate." *Philosophical Studies* (March 1991).

Marcuse, Herbert. *One Dimensional Man*. Beacon Press: Boston,1964.

Martin, Rex. *A System of Rights*. Clarendon Press: Oxford, 1993.

May, Larry. *The Morality of Groups*. Notre Dame University Press: Notre Dame, 1987.

————. *Sharing Responsibility*. Chicago University Press: Chicago, 1992.

————. *The Socially Responsive Self*. University of Chicago Press: Chicago, 1996.

Mele, Alfred. *Springs of Action*. Oxford University Press: New York, 1992.

Menninger, Karl. *The Crime of Punishment*. Viking Press: New York, 1968.

Meyer, Michael. "Rights between Friends." *Journal of Philosophy* 89 (1992).

Meyers, Diana. *Inalienable Rights: A Defense*. Columbia University Press: New York, 1987.

————. *Self, Society, and Personal Choice*. Columbia University Press: New York, 1989.

————. *Subjection and Subjectivity*. Routledge: New York, 1994.

————, ed. *Feminists Reconsider the Self*, Westview Press: Boulder, 1997.

Mill, J. S. *Considerations on Representative Government*. 1861. Routledge: London, 1905.

————. *The Subjection of Women*, 1869, reprinted (5th ed.) MIT Press:Cambridge, 1977.

————. *On Liberty*. 1849. Hackett: Indianapolis, 1978.

————. *Utilitarianism*. 1863. Hackett: Indianapolis, 1979.

Minow, Martha. *Making All the Difference*. Cornell University Press: New York, 1990.

Moon, J. Donald. *Constructing Community: Moral Pluralism and Tragic Conflict*. Princeton University Press: Princeton, 1993.

Morillo, Carolyn. "Doing, Refraining and the Strenuousness of Morality." *American Philosophical Quarterly* 14 (1977).

Murdoch, Iris. *The Sovereignty of the Good*. Oxford University Press: Oxford, 1969.

Murray, Charles. *Losing Ground: American Social Policy 1950–1980*. Basic Books: New York, 1984.

Murphy, Jeffrie. *Kant, The Philosophy of Right*, Macmillan: London, 1970.

————. Is Killing the Innocent Absolutely Prohibited?" *Monist* 57 (1973).

————. *Justice, Retribution and Therapy*, Reidel: Dordrecht, 1979.

————. "Blackmail: A Preliminary Inquiry." *Monist* 63 (1980).

Nagel, Thomas. *Equality and Partiality*. Oxford University Press: New York, 1991.

Nakhnakian, George. "The Principle of Reciprocal Obligations." *Philosophical Studies* 55 (1989).

Narveson, Jan. "Positive/Negative: Why Bother?" *Tulane Studies in Philosophy* 28 (1979).

————. *The Libertarian Idea*. Temple University Press: Philadelphia, 1988.

Nebbia v New York, 291 US 501 (1934).

Nelson, William. "Special Rights, General Rights and Social Justice." *Philosophy and Public Affairs* 3 (1974).

Nickel, James. "Rawls on the Political Community and Principles of Justice." *Law and Philosophy* 9 (1990).
———. "The Value of Cultural Belonging: Expanding Kymlicka's Theory." *Dialogue* 33 (1994).
Nielsen, Kai. *Equality and Liberty: A defense of Radical Egalitarianism*. Rowman and Allenheld: Totowa, NJ, 1985.
Nozick, Robert. *Anarchy, State and Utopia*. Basic Books: New York, 1974.
O'Brien, M. *Reproducing the World*. Westview: Boulder, 1989.
Okin, Susan. *Women in Western Political Thought*. Princeton University Press: Princeton, 1979.
———. *Justice, Gender and the Family*. Basic Books: New York, 1989.
Olsen, Francis. "The Family and the Market." *Harvard Law Review* 96 (1983).
O'Neil, Richard. "Schoeman's Alternative to the Liberal View of the Family." *Philosophical Research Archives* 13 (1987–88).
Parsons, Talcott. *The Evolution of Societies*. Prentice-Hall: Englewood Cliffs, N.J., 1977.
Pateman, Carole, *The Problem of Political Obligation*. Polity Press: Cambridge, 1985.
———. *The Sexual Contract*. Stanford University Press: Stanford, 1988.
———. *The Disorder of Women*. Stanford University Press: Stanford, 1989.
Phillips, Kevin. *The Politics of Rich and Poor*. Random House: New York, 1990.
Plato. *Republic*. Translated by A. Bloom. Hackett: New York, 1968.
Posner, Richard. *The Economic Analysis of Law*. Little, Brown: Boston, 1973, 2nd ed. 1977.
Post, Stephen. "Justice, Redistribution and the Family." *Journal of Social Philosophy* (Fall/Winter 1990).
Postow, Betsy. "A Possible Ground of Political Obligation." *Southern Journal of Philosophy* 18 (1980).
Rachels, James. "Active and Passive Euthanasia." *New England Journal of Medicine* 292, (January 1975).
———. "Killing and Starving to Death." *Philosophy* 54 (April 1979).
Radin, Max. "Contractual Obligation and the Human Will." *Columbia Law Review* 43 (1943).
Ratcliffe, J., ed. *The Good Samaritan and the Law*. Doubleday: New York, 1966.
Rawls, John. *A Theory of Justice*. Harvard University Press: Cambridge, 1971.
———. "Justice as Fairness: Political not Metaphysical." *Philosophy and Public Affairs* 14 (1985).
———. *Political Liberalism*. Columbia University Press: New York, 1993.
Raz, Joseph. "Liberalism, Autonomy and the Politics of Neutral Concern." *Midwest Studies in Philosophy* 7 (1982).
———. *The Morality of Freedom*. Oxford University Press: Oxford, 1986.
Rhode, Deborah. *Justice and Gender*. Harvard University Press: Cambridge, 1989.
Richards, David. "The Individual, the Family, and the Constitution: A Jurisprudential Perspective." *New York University Law Review* 55 (1980).
Riesman, David. *The Lonely Crowd*. Yale University Press: New Haven, 1950.
Roosevelt, Franklin. *Looking Forward*. 1933; In *Poverty and Wealth*, edited by K. E. Alrutz, et al. University Press of America: Washington, D.C., 1982.
Rosenberg, Rosalind. *Divided Lives: American Women in the Twentieth Century*. Noonday Press: New York, 1992.
Ross, Jacob. *The Virtues of the Family*. Free Press: New York, 1994.
Rousseau, Jean. *The Social Contract*. 1762. Translated by G. D. H. Cole. Dutton: New York, 1950.

Sadler Committee Hearings. In *Poverty and Wealth*, edited by K. E. Alrutz et al. University Press of America: Washington, D.C., 1982.

Sandel, Michael. *Liberalism and the Limits of Justice*. Cambridge University Press: Cambridge, 1982.

Schauer, Frederick. *Free Speech: A Philosophical Essay*. Oxford University Press: New York, 1982.

Schmidtz, David. *The Limits of Government: An Essay on the Public Goods Argument*. Westview: Boulder, 1981.

Scruton, Roger. *The Meaning of Conservatism*. Penguin: Harmondsworth, 1980.

Shue, Henry. *Basic Rights: Subsistence, Affluence and U.S. Foreign Policy*. Princeton University Press: Princeton, 1980.

Simester, A. P. "Why Omissions Are Special." *Legal Theory* 1 (September 1995).

Singer, Peter. "Famine, Affluence, and Morality." *Philosophy and Public Affairs* 1 (1972).

———. *The Expanding Circle: Ethics and Sociobiology*. Farrar, Straus, and Giroux: New York, 1981.

Sistare, Christine. *Responsibility and Criminal Liability*. Klewer: Dordrecht, 1989.

Shklar, Judith. *Ordinary Vices*. Harvard University Press: Cambridge, 1984.

Smith, Adam. *Theory of the Moral Sentiments*. 1759. Liberty Classics: Indianapolis, 1976.

———. *Wealth of Nations*. 1776. In *Poverty and Wealth*, edited by K. E. Alrutz et al. University Press of America: Washington, D.C., 1982.

Smith, Patricia. "The Concept of Allowing." *Southern Journal of Philosophy* 22 (Summer 1984).

———. "Recklessness, Omission and Responsibility: Some Reflections on the Moral Relevance of Causation." *Southern Journal of Philosophy* (Fall/Winter 1989).

———. "The Duty to Rescue and the Slippery Slope Problem." *Social Theory and Practice* 12 (1990).

———. "The Duty to Rescue and Wilful Disregard." *Social Theory and Practice* 17 (1991).

———. *Omission, Responsibility and the Law*. Forthcoming.

Sommers, C. H. "Filial Morality." *Journal of Philosophy* 83 (1986).

Steinbock, B., ed., *Killing and Letting Die*. Prentice Hall: Englewood Cliffs, N.J., 1980.

Sterba, James. *Demands of Justice*. Notre Dame Press: Notre Dame, 1980.

———. *How To Make People Just: A Practical Reconciliation of Alternative Perspectives*. Rowman and Littlefield: Totowa, N.J., 1988.

Stichter, S., and J. Parpart. *Women, Employment and the Family in the International Division of Labor*. Macmillan: London, 1990.

Stocker, Michael. *Plural and Conflicting Values*. Clarendon Press: Oxford, 1990.

Summers, R., and R. Hillman. *Contract and Related Obligations*. West: St. Paul, 1987.

Taylor, Charles. *Philosophical Papers*. Vol 2. Cambridge University Press: Cambridge, 1985.

———. *Sources of the Self*. Harvard University Press: Cambridge, 1989.

Thomas, Lawrence. *Living Morally: A Psychology of Moral Character*. Temple University Press: Philadelphia, 1989.

Thomson, J., "A Defense of Abortion." *Philosophy and Public Affairs* 1 (1971).

Tigar, L., and M. Levy. *Law and the Rise of Capitalism*, Monthly Review Press: New York, 1977.

Toennies, Friedrich. *Gemeinschaft und Gesellschaft*. 1887. [*Community and Society*.] Translated by Charles Loomis. Harper and Row: New York, 1963.

Trammell, Richard. "Saving Life and Taking Life," *Journal of Philosophy* 62 (1975).

Unger, Peter. *Living High and Letting Die*. Oxford University Press: New York, 1996.

Unger, Roberto. *Knowledge and Politics*. Macmillan: New York, 1984.

van Wyck, Robert. "Perspectives on World Hunger and the Extent of Our Positive Duties," *Public Affairs Quarterly* 2 (April 1988).

Veblen, Thorstein. *The Theory of the Leisure Class*. In *Poverty and Wealth*, edited by K. E. Alrutz et al. University Press of America: Washington, D.C., 1982, pp. 234–82.

von Leyden, W. *Hobbes and Locke: The Politics of Freedom and Obligation*. St. Martin's Press: New York, 1982.

Waldron, Jeremy. "Theoretical Foundations of Liberalism." *Philosophical Quarterly* 37 (1987).

———. "Family Justice and Social Justice." *Pacific Philosophical Quarterly* 75 (1994).

Walzer, Michael. *Obligations: Essays on Disobedience, War and Citizenship*, Harvard University Press: Cambridge, 1970.

———. *Spheres of Justice*. Basic Books: New York, 1983.

Warnock, G. J., *The Object of Morality*. Methuen: London, 1971.

Wasserstrom, Richard. 1975. "Lawyers As Professionals: Some Moral Issues." In *Ethical Issues in Professional Life*, edited by Joan Callahan. Oxford University Press: New York, 1988.

Weitzman, L. *The Divorce Revolution*. Free Press: New York, 1985.

Wellman, C. *Real Rights*. OUP: New York, 1995.

Werhane, Patricia. *Adam Smith and His Legacy for Modern Capitalism*. Oxford University Press: New York, 1991.

West Coast Hotel v Parrish, 300 US 379 (1937).

Whelan, John. "Charity and the Duty to Rescue." *Social Theory and Practice* 17 (1991).

Williams, Bernard. *Moral Luck*. Cambridge University Press: Cambridge, 1981.

Wolf, Susan. "Moral Saints." *Journal of Philosophy* 79 (1982).

———. *Freedom within Reason*. Oxford University Press: New York, 1990.

Wolff, Jonathan. "What is the Problem of Political Obligation?" *Proceedings of the Aristotelian Society* 91 (1991).

Wollstonecraft, Mary. *A Vindication of the Rights of Women*. 1792. Edited by C. Hagelman. Norton: New York, 1967.

Woozley, A. "A Duty to Rescue: Some Thoughts on Criminal Liability," *Virginia Law Review* 69 (1983).

Zimmerman, Michael. *An Essay on Moral Responsibility*. Rowman and Littlefield: Totowa, N.J., 1988.

Index